T0313729

Dark Matter Credit

THE PRINCETON ECONOMIC HISTORY OF THE WESTERN WORLD

Joel Mokyr, Series Editor

A list of titles
in this series
appears at the back
of the book

Dark Matter Credit

THE DEVELOPMENT OF PEER-TO-PEER LENDING AND BANKING IN FRANCE

Philip T. Hoffman
Gilles Postel-Vinay
Jean-Laurent Rosenthal

PRINCETON UNIVERSITY PRESS
PRINCETON AND OXFORD

Published by Princeton University Press

41 William Street, Princeton, New Jersey 08540

6 Oxford Street, Woodstock, Oxfordshire OX20 1TR
press.princeton.edu

Library of Congress Control Number 2018953892

ISBN 978-0-691-18217-9
British Library Cataloging-in-Publication Data is available

Editorial: Joe Jackson & Samantha Nader

Production Editorial: Ali Parrington

Text and Jacket/Cover Design: Leslie Flis

Production: Erin Suydam

Publicity: Tayler Lord
This book has been composed in Sabon

Printed on acid-free paper. ∞

Printed in the United States of America

1 3 5 7 9 10 8 6 4 2

Contents

Acknowledgments

The Russell Sage Foundation generously supported this project in its early stages, and the California Institute of Technology, the Paris School of Economics, and UCLA helped bring it to fruition. We would also like to thank the Center of European and Eurasian Studies and the Collins Fund at UCLA for financial support, and the École des Hautes Études en Sciences Sociales and the Paris School of Economics for hosting Hoffman and Rosenthal in Paris.

We have benefited enormously from the comments and suggestions made by many colleagues: Jérôme Bourdieu, Tracy Dennison, Dave Grether, Steve Haber, Lionel Kesztenbaum, Naomi Lamoreaux, Annie Lunel, Thierry Magnac, Eric Monnet, Larry Neal, Oscar Gelderblom, Timothy Guinnane, Joost Jonker, Steve Quinn, Paula Scott, William Sewell, Akiko Suwa-Eisenmann, Peter Temin, Francesca Trivellato, Joachim Voth, Jan de Vries, Kirstin Wandschneider; the referees at *Explorations in Economic History* and *Social Science History*, where two related articles were published; Karen S. Cook, Margaret Levi, and Russell Hardin, who edited a volume in which another related article appeared; participants at seminars at Berkeley, Harvard, the Paris School of Economics, the Russel Sage Foundation, Yale, and USC; members of the audience in talks at meetings of the All-UC Economic History group, the Economic History Association, and the Social Science History Association; two readers at Princeton University Press, who gave us valuable criticisms and advice about improving our manuscript; our editor at Princeton, Joe Jackson, who nudged us along with guidance and encouragement; and, last but not least, Joel Mokyr, who has helped us and so many other economic historians to write better economic history. This book would never have been finished without the unstinting efforts of Laura Betancour, Maria Chichtchenkova, Alena Lapatniovna, and Asli Sumer, who helped photograph and code much of the data. We deeply appreciate their expert assistance. Two economic historians inspired us, long ago, to work on debt: the late Lance Davis and Maurice Lévy-Leboyer. They deserve our thanks.

Dark Matter Credit

Introduction

Anemic financial markets mire countries in poverty. There are other reasons why countries remain poor, but a feeble financial system blocks economic growth; or so both modern econometric evidence and historical studies seem to show. Banks and credit markets are particularly important—even essential.[1] Without banks, incomes languish, but when they open their doors, lending surges, and economic growth takes off.

This argument has become a commonplace. Yet it is hard to reconcile with an inconvenient fact: that somehow much of Europe managed to grow rich long before banks became widespread in the nineteenth century.[2] If the usual argument is correct, the wealthy parts of Europe should have been penniless too, for, without banks, they—like the rest of Europe—ought to have been condemned to poverty. But they were prosperous by the standards of the day, not poor.

Could it be that credit abounded in Europe even before banks spread across the continent? That was the question we set out to answer, using data for France. Since France (unlike Italy, England, or the Low Countries) has long been considered a laggard in developing banks, it was an ideal test case, because as early as the eighteenth century, much of the country was clearly well off by world standards.[3] How, then, could it have grown wealthy in the eighteenth century, and even richer in the nineteenth, without having a large number of banks? Could the French tap other, hidden sources of credit and do so on a large scale? If so, then borrowers in other leading countries could likely do the same.

As this book shows, there were ways to borrow in France before banks opened their doors, and the mountain of debt this shadow credit system raised was big, even by modern standards. As early as 1740, the system allowed nearly a third of French families to borrow; if measured relative to GDP, then by 1840 it was mobilizing as much credit for mortgages as the United States' banking system did in the 1950s.[4] Moreover, much of this capital was raised for agriculture and urban real estate, sectors critical in a developing economy that banks often shun because of the risks of farming and the long loan maturities of real estate lending.

Until now, virtually no one has noticed this big debt, despite its size. In a way, it is like the dark matter that makes up some eighty-five percent of the universe but cannot be directly observed. And while astronomers and physicists can infer the existence of dark matter from its effects, economists, historians, and other social scientists are not that lucky. Worse yet, they have simply assumed that what cannot easily be observed—private credit in the past or in poor countries today—was insignificant or simply not there at all.[5]

That assumption is mistaken, as is the argument that banks are an essential first step toward mobilizing large amounts of financial capital and building a thriving debt market for private borrowers. And that is not all that is wrong either. France, we found out, eventually got more banks than anyone imagined. If these banks were a more efficient source of credit, as the claim about their importance supposes, then their proliferation should have made the shadow lending disappear. But it did not vanish. Indeed, it persisted in France, and elsewhere too, up to World War I, and was only killed off by government intervention that tipped the scales in favor of banks. The reason was that banking and the shadow lending system were not competing sources of credit. Rather, they complemented one another, so that both thrived together.

We know all this because we actually measured the dark matter of private credit before 1900, rather than just supposing it was trivial (see table 1). We also counted the number of banks using new historical evidence. Private credit, we learned, was big and pervasive, and not at all challenged by the diffusion of banks in the nineteenth century. If anything, our measurements are likely underestimates, because they omit lending that we did not count even though it might be substantial.[6]

We reached these conclusions for France thanks to unique fiscal records that survive for the period 1740–1931. These records let us gather the necessary data at relatively low cost. We thought it would be worth exploiting them because of the large amount of lending we had already uncovered in Paris using a different source of evidence.[7] It was not at all clear, however, that the example of Paris would generalize, for two reasons. First, Paris had an unusually large number of wealthy investors who could fund loans. Furthermore, the city's lenders, borrowers, and potential financial intermediaries dwelled near one another and might interact repeatedly, which would make it easier to arrange loans. Conditions would not be the same elsewhere, particularly where credit markets were thin and where lenders, borrowers, and intermediaries lived too far apart even to find one another. The question was whether Paris was atypical, and the fiscal records gave us the answer.

Those records are peculiar to France, but the evidence they yield can be compared with data from Germany, Great Britain, and the United States. The comparison shows that France is not at all unusual. The shadow credit system flourished in the past in these other wealthy countries too, and it may loom large in many developing economies as well, if researchers take the time to measure it.

Our discovery of all the debt financed by the shadow credit system not only overturns the standard argument about banks and economic growth;

Table 1. Estimates of notarized lending in France

	Year					
	1740	1780	1807	1840	1865	1899
Number of loans in year (thousands)	437	368	362	556	395	265
Number of outstanding loans (thousands)	1,696	1,477	856	1,419	1,328	1,645
Value of loans (million livres/francs)	161	336	329	772	914	1180
Stock of outstanding debt (million livres/francs)	1426	2398	1120	3650	4150	7690
Maturity (years, unweighted)	5.8	4.3	2.4	2.6	3.4	6.2
Maturity (years weighted by loan value)	8.9	7.1	3.4	4.7	4.5	6.5
Per capita stock of debt (livres/francs)	58.0	86.9	37.7	104.6	109.0	191.5
Stock of debt to GDP (percent)	15.8	22.8	9.6	27.2	19.9	23.6

Source: Estimates from our sample. For details, see chapter 1.
Note: For GDP estimates for France after 1800, we relied on Toutain (1987). Because there are no GDP estimates for France before 1800, we simply assumed total income was growing at 0.4 percent per year from 1740 to 1780, and again from 1780 to 1807. Netting out population growth leads per capita income to grow at 0.1 percent per year before 1780, and 0.125 percent from 1780 to 1807. Monetary amounts in 1740 and 1780 are in livres, the money of account before the French Revolution; for 1807–99, they are in francs, the currency created during the French Revolution. For the years of our cross sections, they both had the same value in silver.

it raises other important questions. To begin with, how was credit allocated before banks? The big debt, it turns out, consisted of thousands of bilateral loans, loans that matched up a borrower and a lender, as in modern peer-to-peer lending. These loans were sizable, had maturities that were frequently two years or more (see table 1), and often involved people who did not know each other. For such loans, lenders cannot simply assume borrowers will repay, and charging a higher interest rate to offset the risk may attract nothing but deadbeats who have no intention of paying off their debts. Securing the loans with collateral may not solve the problem, either. How does a lender tell what a pledged property is worth and how that value will evolve, particularly in an economic downturn like that which struck the US mortgage market after 2006? Borrowers usually have a good sense both of their creditworthiness and of the value of their collateral, but lenders' information is typically much skimpier. In the language of economics, lenders' and borrowers' information is asymmetric.

Unlike some peer-to-peer lending on the web today, the bilateral loans in the past were arranged by a network of brokers. The brokers not only brought the borrowers and the lenders together, but overcame the problems of asymmetric information, which afflict all credit markets. That was true not just in Paris, where the brokers interacted with one another repeatedly in a way that could easily spread information about creditworthiness; it was also true in small towns, where their dealings would be much rarer. Even there our brokers certified borrowers and their collateral, and gave lenders better information. That proved essential to building a large stock of debt to GDP.

The brokers, both in Paris and the rest of France, were notaries, government sanctioned keepers of legal records in countries influenced by Roman law, who combined the preservation of records with the roles of lawyer, financial adviser, and real estate broker. Their network arose because the records they kept revealed what collateral was worth and who was a good credit risk. The information they could cull from their records allowed the notaries to match up lenders with creditworthy borrowers and so solve debt markets' vexing informational problems.

The solution therefore grew out of a peculiar feature of Roman law. That itself is a surprise, for Roman law, and its modern offspring—the civil law that holds sway in continental Europe and Latin America—are thought to hobble financial development.[8] Yet in France, as we shall see, this infrastructure of Roman law nurtured a thriving financial structure. The structure did evolve in a different direction from its British counterpart, which may in fact have been biased toward banks. Both financial systems, however, did fund economic growth, and by 1900, Paris was, like London, an international financial center. The two financial systems had started apart and followed dissimilar paths as they developed, but by 1913 they both had large thriving equity and debt markets. [9]

That is not all we uncovered. We also analyze how lending in the shadow credit system was shaped by geography and the growth of cities. Since cities had more savers with large sums to lend, borrowing in a city might be appealing, but the cost of travel ruled out long trips to find a loan. We work out how the network of notaries dealt with travel costs and urban savings, and we chart how their dealings changed over time.

Finally, beyond simply assessing how the shadow credit system was affected by the diffusion of banks, we also determine whether any obstacles slowed bank entry—an important topic since France has been held up as a poster child for the economic damage caused by barriers to the development of a banking system. Economic historians have long believed that a delayed spread of banks in France retarded the country's industrialization and slowed economic growth. Economists have pushed the argument further, blaming the French legal system for hindering financial development, not just in France itself, but in all the countries around the world that inherited its particular brand of civil law. Those two claims turn out to be wrong too. Nothing blocked bank entry in France, and that is why we found that the country in fact had far more banks than economic historians thought. French civil law did not hamper financial innovation either. More generally, while France may not have been the leading economy in Europe, its performance was good enough to provide resources for three centuries of military competition, first with the vast and rich Hapsburg empires and later with England.

Our discoveries have significant implications for the world today. To begin with, they cast doubt on the evidence backing the claim that anemic conventional financial markets have impeded economic growth in poor countries. The claim is supported by cross-country regressions, but the regressions assume that private lending outside of banks and other modern financial intermediaries is measured accurately. If this sort of private lending is not measured accurately, then the true relationship between financial development and economic growth—so our French evidence suggests—may well be far weaker than everyone assumes.[10]

Successfully measuring private credit has other significant implications. In particular, it corrects the standard story of how credit markets develop. That story begins in a world of no lending and then traces a small set of innovations (such as stock and bond exchanges or big universal banks with branches and a variety of services). It focuses on these innovations because they spread internationally, as people learned how to imitate the financial innovators and how to copy their institutions and organizations.[11] Yet change in credit markets has never followed this sort of unique path, and neither has financial development more generally, either in the past or in poor countries today. Financial development, it turns out, can take many different routes to abundant credit and easy mobilization of financial capital, and the road selected depends on politics, on inequality, on economic shocks and legal institutions, and on the spatial development of cities and the economy. No one has analyzed this long-run process of change until now. We do in this book, which reaches back over two centuries and continues through industrialization and across enormous political and social upheavals, ranging from the French Revolution and the Napoleonic Empire to the rise of democracy and World War I.

Along the way, we learn how private credit markets in France functioned in the past and how they changed as the economy grew, partly as a result of shifts in demand, and partly as a result of shifts in supply, driven by institutional innovations and political and legal innovations. We see how borrowers and lenders devised new loan contracts, created ingenious ways of securing loans, and made the transition from ancient ways of lending (annuities and medium-term loans with a balloon payment) to the modern mortgage. We also find out how financial capital was mobilized across space in the era before railroads, when transportation was rudimentary. And, above all else, we discover how our brokers solved the daunting problems of asymmetric information in credit markets, and did so on a large scale, long before the arrival of modern banks and stock exchanges and the creation of government lien registries and private credit ratings. Our conclusions are derived from the French data, but they are likely to apply to credit in other economies as well, because in most parts of Western Europe borrowers and lenders could avail themselves of very similar sets of contracts and information systems.

Figuring out how these credit markets worked required more than measurement alone. We also had to model how borrowers, lenders, and brokers acted. The economic models, which are explained in plain language for readers unfamiliar with economics, proved essential. They made our arguments precise, let us test our claims, and revealed what was happening when the historical sources fell silent. Without them, we would still be trying to make sense of all the dark matter of private credit.

The story we tell about the evolution of private credit will interest not just readers in economics, but in history, law, and in all the social sciences. Historians, for instance, will gain a new perspective on the social and economic history of lending. The large historiography devoted to the subject of credit has invoked debt to explain both peasant immiseration and the expansion of markets, and assumes personal ties between debtors and creditors to characterize a noncapitalist economy. Much of this literature, though, is limited to a particular locality, using local account books, family papers, or loan contracts that have survived in one particular place. Much of it is confined to traditional periods of historical study as well—in France, the Old Regime, or the French Revolution and the Napoleonic Empire, or the century from 1815 to 1914. In this book we broke free of these restrictions, because we want to chart the evolution of credit across nearly two centuries of massive legal and organizational change, including the coming of banks. And we wanted to measure lending for the whole economy, not one particular locality, and see how it changed over time and how different credit markets were related.

By using our evidence as a benchmark, historians who undertake new local studies of credit can now ask how lending in their locality was connected with other markets. Historians will also be able to assess, for the first time, the lasting impact that the French Revolution had on private borrowing—an impact that was negative in the short run but overwhelmingly positive over the long run.[12] These enduring economic consequences of the French Revolution have long been neglected, particularly the long-run positive ones, which had echoes outside of France.

Outside of history, sociologists will benefit from the questions we raise about the common method of analyzing networks that are limited to similar individuals. So will economists who work on networks. Similarly, legal scholars and political scientists will profit from the doubt we cast on the widespread argument that civil law condemns an economy to economic stagnation. The same goes for political scientists who believe that political institutions shape economic development.

To make all these discoveries, we had to proceed differently from economists or historians who study credit markets. Unlike economists who have focused heavily on the recent experience of developing countries, we reach back and study credit in a diverse set of localities over nearly two centuries. And, unlike historians, we have not done a local study. Instead, we gathered extensive quantitative data and estimated medium and long-term private indebtedness for the economy as a whole. We needed all this data to analyze the network of brokers and to gauge the impact of banks as more and more of them opened their doors. The data had to extend back in time well before the Industrial Revolution and stretch forward through the nineteenth century as banks proliferated and the economy developed. And it had to continue into the twentieth century to see what finally killed off the shadow credit system.

We begin our book by describing the data that revealed how much private credit there was and how loans were arranged. The bulk of this evidence concerns 239,269 individual loans and the variables that affected lending in a sample of ninety-nine French credit markets. The markets ranged from Paris to small villages, and for each market, we gathered the data for six years (1740, 1780, 1807, 1840, 1865, and 1899). For a subset of these years, we also gathered evidence from seventy-three additional markets. Beyond these two large samples, we collected much smaller samples in 1912, 1927, and 1931 to chart the demise of peer-to-peer lending.

So that readers can understand how we measured private debt, we explain the construction of our samples and the legal and political institutions that governed the credit market. We then estimate the size of the market in 1740 and explore who was involved in it (chapter 1). The next issue is determining what boosted the volume of private lending between 1740 and 1780 (chapter 2). Prominent among the explanations were innovative loan contracts and better ways of protecting lenders against default. The background in these first two chapters is essential for another reason as well: it lays out the problems private credit markets faced and how these peer-to-peer lending systems operated.

Grasping how private credit markets function also requires assessing the impact the French Revolution had on lending institutions. The private credit market was laid low by hyperinflation during the French Revolution, but in the long run it benefited from the revolution's institutional reforms, such as the creation of lien registries, which helped protect lenders. Although these reforms took decades to diffuse, they helped the credit market recover completely from the damage done by the revolutionary inflation. After assessing the effect of the inflation (in chapter 3), we explore these new institutions and then analyze how notaries matched up lenders with creditworthy borrowers. When a notary could not find a match among his own clients, he referred the prospective borrower or lender to other nearby notaries, whom he cooperated with in what would become a local lending network. The resulting networks linked markets throughout France and overcame local imbalances of supply and demand.

How all this happened only became clear when we built our economic models in chapters 3 and 4. In the process, we analyzed how the notaries made referrals and what that implied for the spatial distribution of borrower-lender matches. It was impossible to test the models against evidence from the notaries' business records, which do not survive. But we could test them against data from the fiscal records. Remarkably, the fiscal data support our models and reject a very different interpretation of the notaries' behavior.

We also investigated how the notaries interacted with other financial intermediaries, such as banks—the subject of chapters 5 through 7. The notaries were innovative, and in the nineteenth century they devised a new type of loan contract that involved dealing with bankers and merchants, as we show in chapter 5. This new contract and earlier innovations by notaries both run counter to the claim that countries such as France would be slow to develop financially, because they were governed by the supposedly rigid Napoleonic civil law. In reality, civil law was far more flexible than many scholars believe, and it certainly did not keep notaries from discovering new ways of doing things.

To measure the interaction between banks and notarial credit, we gathered new data on the number of banks in France in the nineteenth and early twentieth centuries. Chapter 6 analyzes the spread of banks in France and compares their diffusion with similar data for the United Kingdom. France had more banks than anyone imagined, and it erected no barriers to bank entry. If France did end up with proportionally fewer banks than England, it was because of demand and—surprisingly—because of the relative weakness of the British peer-to-peer credit system.

Chapter 7 then asks whether banks were so much more efficient that they drove notaries out of the business of arranging peer-to-peer loans as they spread across France. As we discovered, nothing was further from the truth. A notary, it turns out, had nothing to fear from bankers, who dared not compete with the notary in his own specialty of mortgage lending (unless, of course, they had government backing and a government monopoly, like the Crédit Foncier). The bankers and notaries in fact focused on different corners of the credit market, and their businesses were complementary: they reinforced one another.

Surprisingly, the huge number of loans that we discovered in the dark matter credit market were almost all made at one interest rate: one price. This outcome—a priceless equilibrium in the language of economics—derived from usury legislation and from the incentives created by the asymmetric information in the private credit markets. Prices only began to matter again (they had played a role in French private credit markets in the seventeenth century) in the late nineteenth and early twentieth century, when the government began to intervene in the market on a large scale. As we show in chapter 8, the government first provided financial backing to a large mortgage loan bank, the Crédit Foncier, and gave it a monopoly on the issuance of mortgage-backed securities. Then the government started subsidizing loans to private borrowers.

This first history of dark matter credit markets carries important lessons for financial markets and governments today, as we suggest in the conclusion (chapter 9). One lesson is that there is no single path to financial development. Another is that existing traditional financial institutions may be far more important than anyone supposes. Replacing them may therefore be a mistake and may leave new market entrants (such as modern banks) vulnerable to problems of adverse selection when they get stuck with all the bad credit risks. Finally, a third lesson is that banks are not likely to enter mortgage markets unless they have government backing. Otherwise, even the largest banks run the risk of falling victim to defaulting borrowers, as happened in the 2008 financial crisis. All three lessons should not be forgotten.

CHAPTER 1

1740 and the Rules of the Game

The big debt we discovered consisted of peer-to-peer loans, long before that term emerged on the web. In France there were millions of them, even centuries ago. What were they like? Here is one example: in 1740 Jean Pajot traveled eleven kilometers from his home to the town of Bellac in central France (see figure 1.1) to borrow forty *livres* (about two or three months pay for a rural laborer) from Guillaume Reymond.[1] Pajot was not alone, even in Bellac. Other borrowers from the town and its environs had local notaries draw up over one hundred loan contracts that year, totaling twenty thousand *livres*.

Since Bellac and the nearby villages in this remote part of France counted only some 8,500 inhabitants in 1740, it might seem, at least at first glance, that relatively few people were taking out peer-to-peer loans. But if we consider households rather than individuals, the participation rate was far from trivial. If each household averaged four persons, then seven percent of local households took out loans in 1740. And since loans typically had to be paid back in two years, some fourteen percent of households would owe money in this market at any time. The number of lenders would be smaller, because many lenders made multiple loans, but it still seems likely that at least twenty percent of the households in Bellac were involved in notarial credit in 1740, either as borrowers or lenders. That is a significant fraction.

And Bellac is only one example, for borrowers were taking out similar numbers of loans across France. If we take all of the ninety-nine markets in our sample together and extrapolate to France as a whole, then at least 430,000 loans were made in 1740, for a total of 160 million livres, and some 1.7 million debt contracts were outstanding, worth 1.4 billion livres (table I.1).

These numbers are large. The stock of notarial debt, even though it excluded nearly all commercial and consumer credit, amounted to sixteen percent of GDP in 1740 (table 1). Although that may at first glance seem paltry, especially when compared to the level of mortgage debt accumulated in some economies on the eve of the 2008 crisis, it is more than what mortgage markets achieve in many developing economies today. And while it totaled somewhat less than what the government owed its creditors (some two billion livres in 1740), it was still huge. The volume of lending coursing through the notarial credit market every year in fact dwarfed one

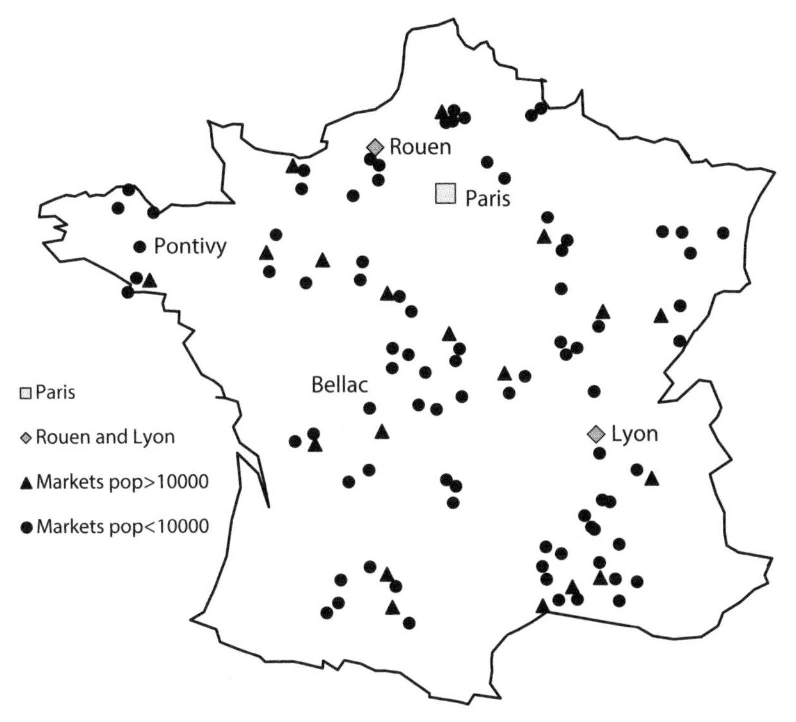

Figure 1.1. The sample.
Source: See text.

of the major components of the national debt—the government's General Farm (*Ferme Générale*), which was only half the size.[2] When averaged over the whole population, outstanding notarial debt came to almost sixty livres per person in 1740, or two months of per capita income. Even more surprising, the 1.7 million loans outstanding suggest that notarial lending allowed nearly one third of France's six million households to borrow, even more than what we found for Bellac.

This mountain of private, nongovernmental debt raises some serious questions. First of all, how can we reconstruct past lending in a society, particularly for credit markets that have long been shrouded from view? How do we know what happened, and how reliable is our knowledge?

Second, even if we can accurately count these loans, add up their values, or average their maturities, how can we speak of credit markets back in 1740? After all, this is a half century before the French Revolution, in what historians call Old Regime France, and it is not exactly the obvious place to look for capital markets. Like most of Western Europe back then, it was an absolutist monarchy, with an economy as yet unsullied by industrialization.

Table 1.1. Notarized loans in France (1740)

	Population bin					
	Paris	1	2	3	4	Total
	France					
Number of chef-lieux	1	5	59	134	2,498	2,697
Population (thousands)	576	421	1,920	2,205	19,480	24,602
	Sample					
Number of chef-lieux	1	2	17	18	61	99
Population (thousands)	576	181	369	119	153	1,397
Weight	1.00	2.13	3.36	8.39	39.66	11.72
	Sample					
Number of loans in year	6155	2645	8870	4539	8413	30623
Value of loans (million livres)	44.10	4.11	6.47	1.55	1.78	58.01
Number of outstanding loans	68,221	14,068	49,627	16,659	31,371	179,947
Stock of outstanding debt (million livres)	522.0	34.8	71.2	12.0	11.6	651.6

Average maturity (years unweighted)	11.08	4.88	5.58	4.38	3.45	5.83
Weighted average maturity (years weighted by loan value)	11.84	8.47	11.01	7.75	6.50	11.23
	France					
Number of loans in year	6,155	5,644	30,680	45,172	349,501	437,153
Value of loans (million livres)	44.1	8.75	21.7	15.7	70.8	161.05
Number of outstanding loans	68,221	29,965	166,745	186,440	1,244,185	1,695,557
Stock of outstanding debt (million livres)	522	74	239	133	458	1,426
Average maturity (years unweighted)	11.08	4.88	5.58	4.38	3.45	5.83
Weighted average maturity (years weighted by loan value)	11.84	8.45	11.01	8.47	6.47	8.85

Note: Population bins are based on the population of the chef-lieu of the canton where the bureau was located. The bin with column heading 1 included cities other than Paris with populations over 60,000; the bin with heading 2, cities between 10,000 and 60,000 people; bin 3, towns with populations between 5,000 to 10,000 people; and bin 4, chef-lieux with fewer than 5,000 inhabitants. The stock of loans is the sum of the loan maturities; the stock of debt is the sum of the loan values times the loan maturities; the unweighted average maturity is the stock of loans divided by the number of loans; and weighted average maturity is the stock of debt divided by the total value of the loans.
Source: See text.

Some sixty percent of the population were peasants toiling full time in agriculture, land was the predominant source of wealth, and much of it was held by nobles, government officials, and the Church, as elsewhere in Europe. One would look in vain for the usual actors and visible symbols of modern credit markets. There were no credit rating agencies, no escrow companies, and very few banks, and the stock exchange, the *Bourse*, had been moribund after an abortive experiment with paper money and an accompanying financial panic in 1720.[3] And, as in much of Western Europe, most debts did not even state interest rates, while others did not set a repayment date. Instead, private borrowers and lenders simply met in a notary's office to draw up loan contracts. Furthermore, although lenders could sue defaulting borrowers in the various royal or seigneurial courts that covered the country, the loan contracts did not systematize the process of repayment by regular amortization over the term of the loan.

Fortunately, we can reconstruct past lending, for it left a trace in the archives. The archival records that permit this were created by legal and fiscal institutions, so understanding them is essential to seeing how we can accurately estimate the magnitude of private lending. We also have to explain how we extracted the evidence from the archives: in particular, how we chose our core sample of ninety-nine French markets; how we settled on observing them in the years 1740, 1780, 1807, 1840, 1865, and 1899; and how we translated the archival data into volumes of lending and outstanding debt for each of these six annual observations. As is standard, we will call these annual samples across all ninety-nine markets our six cross sections.

The archival evidence also makes it abundantly clear that private peer-to-peer credit markets did in fact exist in 1740.[4] But to see how they functioned, we also have to understand the problems borrowers and lenders faced. Their biggest problem (both in 1740 and other years) was obstacles to arranging loans that economists call transaction costs. Some of these obstacles have to do with the need for information. Others involve transportation costs.

To begin with, lenders had to decide whom to lend to, and thus acquire some notion of the ability of potential borrowers to repay.[5] How, for instance, did our Guillaume Reymond know that Jean Pajot would repay the forty livres he borrowed? If collateral was posted, lenders had to figure out its value and their ability to repossess it. Failure to get adequate information about these matters would allow particularly awful borrowers to undermine credit markets—what economists call adverse selection. Second, once a loan was made, the odds of repayment and the value of the collateral could both be affected by the borrower's actions. The borrower, for instance, might plant riskier crops than the lender would like, or, if the borrower fell behind on his loan, he might fail to maintain the value of the property. Behavior of this sort after the loan was made would reduce the lender's return—what economists call moral hazard. Lenders were not alone in confronting such problems: borrowers did too. In particular, because many loans involved repaying the entire principal by making a balloon payment at maturity, most borrowers would want to know whether the lender would roll over the loan or wait for repayment to accommodate a borrower who was temporarily short of cash. A good lender would be accommodating, while a bad one might use his power to foreclose strategically. A borrower who could not discern which kind of lender he or she faced might well shy away from credit.

Such troubles were not peculiar to 1740. They have in fact long plagued credit markets and afflicted them once again in the post-2008 implosion of the US mortgage market. But there was another, far more severe problem in 1740 and on up, into the early nineteenth century: the payment mechanism was rudimentary, a severe hindrance for anyone lending at a distance, because it meant that lenders might have to personally visit their debtors to get paid.

All these obstacles were real and they were serious enough that lending might easily have been confined to people who already had reasons to trust one other. Yet lending, as we shall show, was not limited to borrowers and lenders who knew one another that well—far from it. In fact, in 1740, borrowers and lenders often had only limited information about each other. Someone else must have matched them up and helped to bridge the information gap. As we shall see, someone did: notaries.

Explaining all this involves some issues that crop up not just in 1740 but in the other cross-sections as well. That is true for our description of the legal and fiscal institutions, our account of how we sampled the evidence and assembled our data, and our analysis of the peer-to-peer markets and of collateral and the notaries' role in arranging loans. We will take up these general issues first and then turn to matters that concern primarily 1740: who the notaries' clients were in 1740, and how lending in 1740 was shaped by France's distinctive urban structure, which differed from that of other Western European countries.

Notaries and the Fisc

That we can reconstruct credit markets from 1899 all the way back to the Old Regime is only possible because of two seemingly obscure sets of scriveners in the French legal and fiscal systems: first, the notaries; and, second, the receivers of the Contrôle des actes, an even less visible group of officials, who recorded summaries of private transactions while collecting taxes.

Let us start with the notaries. In the Middle Ages, notaries had been appointed by courts to record what had previously been oral contracts and agreements. They arose throughout Western Europe, save in Britain.[6] While clients would be given copies of their contracts, another record (the *minute*) was often deposited in the court's archives. Because the notary was court appointed, the contracts and any legal document he drew up were presumed valid if challenged, and he faced severe penalties for fraud.

From the Middle Ages to the eighteenth century, the rules under which notaries operated diverged across Europe; what follows only applies to France (Limon 1992; Gaston 1991; Descimon 2004; Arnoux and Guyotjeannin 2011). By the eighteenth century, a notary in France purchased his office, which was attached to a locality. Someone who wanted to become a notary had to go through some legal training, serve an apprenticeship as a notary's clerk, and then buy a notarial office from an incumbent. Once installed in his office, a notary, like an attorney in Britain, drew up private contracts and legal documents for his clients. But, unlike attorneys, notaries were required to keep a copy of most contracts they drew up; these copies were the minutes preserved in the notaries' archives. The only exception was for certain less formal contracts (so-called contracts *en brevet*, or *brevets* for short) for which the notaries kept no copy (Massé 1828 Vol. 1:73–77). By the eighteenth century, the minutes went to the new owner when a notarial office changed hands. And, beginning in the nineteenth century, most of the notaries deposited their old records in the archives of the local department. (France is divided into approximately one hundred departments, which are about twice the size of an average US county.)

Absent destruction by war or fires, the entire set of minutes ever signed is available to researchers, as long as the records are over seventy-five years old.[7] This hoard includes credit contracts, and much more as well, making it the Mount Everest of archival record sets. The reason is that notaries, as we have said, had to preserve virtually everything they drafted—not just loans, but marriage contracts, wills and estate divisions, powers of attorney, real estate sales, and leases. A single notary's contracts could pile up to six feet high every year, often with no index except for a chronological one, filling shelf after shelf. The archives measure the number of notarized contracts they store in kilometers of linear shelf space; the *minutier central* of Paris, where Parisian notaries' archives are stored, boasts that its holdings take up twenty-one kilometers of shelf space, and the notarial minutes stretch for kilometers in other departmental archives as well, particularly when the department had a sizable city.[8]

For many scholars, the solution to this surfeit of evidence has been to focus on a specific region or town (Servais 1982; Brennan 2006; Poisson 1990), much as we did for Paris in our earlier work (Hoffman et al. 2000). Yet while such an approach is extremely valuable, it unfortunately cannot help us measure the dark matter of private credit. For that, we need data from a variety of locations, and the only practical way to get it is to sample. Sampling is also the only way to understand the impact that institutions have on credit markets and on their growth, for what we observe in one market could simply reflect random variations in the local demand and supply for loans, not the effect of institutions.

If we want to sample more than a trivial number of locations, though, then we cannot recover anything like the two centuries of monthly loan totals that we gathered for Paris, where we worked with the original notarial records. It would simply take too much time to sample the requisite number of notaries, particularly for that many years and months.

Fortunately, Louis XIV's appetite for tax revenue provided us with a shortcut that was much faster than working with the notarial records directly. In 1693 he established a tax known as the *Contrôle des actes* that was levied on all new documents notaries drew up, whether they were brevets or preserved as minutes (Massaloux 1989; Etienne and Limon-Bonnet 2013). All contracts drafted by private parties without the help of a notary (so-called *actes sous seing privé*) had to pay the tax too before they could be introduced as evidence in a judicial proceedings, and there is also evidence that some private debt contracts, written up by private parties, were registered even if no formal complaint was ever filed with a court.[9]

To collect this tax, the crown set up bureaus all over the country, except in Paris and a few provinces such as Alsace in the east and Artois in the north that had recently been added to the French kingdom. As in any major administrative effort, the distribution of bureaus was initially unstable, and the preservation of records spotty. Over time, however, the system came into its own and by the 1740s the registers of the Contrôle des actes were being maintained well enough that they survive to the present day for most bureaus. The records were ordered chronologically, as notaries came in to register the acts they had drawn up, with urban notaries usually stopping by the Contrôle office every other day and rural ones coming by once a week. (In no case could registration occur later than two weeks after an act was signed by all the concerned parties.)

The Contrôle des actes records have the advantage over the notarial archives in that they are complete: they enumerate all the transactions signed in front of local notaries, whether or not the individual notaries' records survive. By contrast, individual notarial records have sometimes been lost, and—worse yet—because there is no census of notaries for the Old Regime, we cannot even tell which notarial records have been preserved and which ones have been lost in any specific region. In addition, the Contrôle des actes includes actes en brevet, which the notaries often did not keep even if their minutes have survived, and contracts drawn up without the help of a notary.

The Contrôle, however, has one drawback: its summaries reveal much less than the notarial contracts themselves, for the simple reason that the recording clerks did not copy the whole of the notarized contract. At first, the information recorded included only names, type of contract, and value. The record of the forty livres loan that Guillaume Reymond made to Jean Pajot, for example, mentions their names, the last name and residence of the notary—Crouzaud from Bellac—the amount of the loan, and, as an unusual detail, where Pajot lived, but nothing more.[10] By the middle of the eighteenth century, though, the registers of the Contrôle began recording more such information, including in many cases the addresses and occupations of the borrowers and lenders. By the nineteenth century the records (now of the revolutionary successor to the Contrôle, the *Enregistrement des actes civils publics,* or Enregistrement for short) tell us even more.

Yet even with the added detail in the nineteenth century, the summaries, in most cases, still take up less than half a page. They are therefore compact, both for the Old-Regime Contrôle and for the nineteenth-century Enregistrement. In a small market like Bellac, the Contrôle des actes for 1740 comes to a total of only 160 pages in two volumes. Even in 1899, the Enregistrement records for all of Paris runs only to a hundred volumes or so. These fiscal registers can be photographed in their entirety, without having to sift out the noncredit transactions. Moreover, the photos have the enormous advantage of picking up the dealings registered by all the notaries in the vicinity.

We started sampling the Contrôle in 1740, one of the earliest years for which the records exist in most of France. It is not a representative year, and it is certainly not the dawn of the capitalist era or the beginning of credit markets in France. Because 1740 was a bad harvest year, it may well be that credit was either abnormally low or high (depending on whether or not the increased demand for insurance credit trumps the reduced supply of loans). Yet if we are interested in how the markets worked at that time, this is not essential. What is more important is a conclusion the 1740 sample makes obvious: notarized credit contracts were ubiquitous then. The same turns out to be true for every other year we sampled up into the twentieth century.

What Lending Did We Count?

Notaries and the Contrôle gave us our data. But what did we count? In other words, what qualifies as credit? At one extreme, any intertemporal contract could be counted since it involves someone getting something today in return for a promise of payments in the future. Clearly that definition would be too extreme; it would also be impractical, since it is often difficult to infer just how much credit a transaction involves. Another approach—one that would be broad but not quite so inclusive—would start with contracts that involved debt alone and then add dealings in which credit was extended as a part of a larger transaction—for example, a sale of real estate financed by a loan from the seller (Baehrel 1962, 1: 600; Garnier 1982).

We chose a more restrictive definition and considered only contracts that were exclusively credit. In other words, we limited ourselves to contracts that were clearly loans and that were not part of a document concerning a broader transaction. The reason is that if we sought to estimate the size of the credit market, we did not want to artificially inflate our figures by counting loans that were included in land sales or other so-called tied contracts that linked a debt to some other noncredit agreement. Our figures are therefore lower bounds, and actual lending may have been higher than our figures suggest.[11]

There is another reason we chose the narrower definition—namely, because the tied contracts could be interpreted as evidence that the credit market did not function very well. After all, why would the seller of an asset, who presumably wanted to raise cash from the sale, extend credit to someone? Was the only way to arrange the sale to have the seller finance it and accept the asset being sold as collateral, since, as the former owner, he would know its value? If so, the implication would be that other lenders would have no way to assess the value of collateral or the creditworthiness of borrowers.

If we want to determine whether a credit market performed well, or at least how much of it functioned well, we should therefore look at contracts that involved credit alone and no other transactions. That is what we did, and it let us see whether the market managed to match lenders and borrowers who did not have other reasons to interact, such as the sale of property in a tied transaction. Our narrow definition still leaves us with plenty of contracts to count.

There was a second limit to the data we gathered, at least for our 1740 and 1780 cross sections, a limit imposed by French law in effect during the Old Regime and also by canon law. The laws, which applied to nearly all of France until they were repealed during the French Revolution, made it illegal to write a loan contract that specified both the interest rate and the term of the loan. Doing so amounted to usury. That meant it was impossible to gather information on the interest rate and the loan duration from any single loan contract.

Within the confines of the usury legislation, there were two well-established ways to make loans: annuities and obligations. Annuities specified a set of payments, but no repayment date. In perpetual annuities (*rentes constituées*), the borrower made an annual interest payment and could reimburse the capital whenever convenient. Of the 108 contracts in Bellac in 1740, for instance, there were five of these perpetual annuities. In the other type of annuity, life annuities, payments stopped when a person named in the contract (the "life," who was often the lender) died; Bellac had only three of those. In either case, the lender had surrendered control of his capital, which allowed him to earn a return without running afoul of laws against usury. What interest could be charged was limited by royal edict. In the eighteenth century, the cap for perpetual annuities was five percent. Life annuities most often involved payments of ten percent of capital per year but when older individuals were named, payments could rise to fourteen percent or more.

If a lender was not willing to enter into such a contract, he or she could still accept an obligation, a type of loan in which the borrower promised to return a certain sum of money at some specified time in the future. Except in a few regions or a few instances (such as loans by Jews, or loans financing international trade), these obligations could not and did not specify interest rates.[12] But interest was paid, in one of two ways. First, the sum to be repaid could include both the capital lent and the interest due. The loan in that case was effectively discounted. This stratagem worked well when debts were medium or short term. A second stratagem was for the borrower to pay interest on the side, and if it was not paid, the lender would request payment of the capital. Over time, obligations became more popular but it was not until the French Revolution allowed interest rates to be specified in all contracts that they came to dominate.

Annuities and obligations were not distributed uniformly. Annuities were more common in the north of France than in the south. The reason may be that southerners had gotten an early start on a shift toward greater use of the obligation that would eventually reach all of France. Annuities were also more popular in urban areas than in the countryside, perhaps because urban households had more liquid wealth that could be lent out via annuities to provide family members and descendants with a flow of income.

Collateral in Annuities and Obligations and the Role Notaries Played

Many annuities and obligations were in fact mortgages, in the sense that they were collateralized by real estate. (They were still not modern mortgages, which amortize the debt over a fixed repayment term.) Broadly speaking, there were three ways to deal with collateral. The first involved the borrower securing the loan (as nowadays) with a specific asset, most often a piece of real estate. In the second, the borrower pledged all his goods movable and real, present and future—in effect taking a general mortgage on all his property.[13] With the third, the borrower could provide weaker security by collateralizing movables, shifting repayments to the near future, offering a vague claim on his goods, or allowing the lender to have him arrested in case of nonperformance. Still, there might be no collateral at all. In 1740, annuities were more likely than obligations to take the first route and be collateralized by specific real property.

These three methods of securing a loan provided different levels of protection when a borrower defaulted. The third method offered the least security. With it, the lender had little recourse if the borrower failed to pay, for in 1740, as today, the third method usually left the lender holding nothing more than an unsecured loan, and that did not entitle him to grab the borrower's assets. He had a claim, but it would almost always be a junior one, meaning he would be near the end of the line when the borrower's debts were paid off.

If, however, the borrower had pledged some stronger collateral, as with the first or second route, then the lender stood a better chance of being repaid. How much better would depend on the nature and value of the collateral and on the lender's seniority as a creditor.

Real property usually provided greater security, but seniority (essentially how close to the front of the line the lender was) mattered too. For most secured debt, seniority was determined by the date of the loan. That was true both for loans with a general pledge of assets (the second method of securing a loan) and for loans pledging a specific asset (the first method). Secured lenders who had picked one of these first two ways of backing up the loan would then be reimbursed by selling the real property that had been pledged as collateral, with the oldest loans being paid off first. The pledged property would include all the borrower's real estate with the second method. If the real assets pledged as collateral proved insufficient to retire all the secured loans, then any remaining lenders with unpaid secured debt would join the unsecured creditors and divide up the borrower's movable property.

A lender could enjoy greater security by asking for real property as collateral and selecting one of the first two ways of securing the loan. Here one might wonder whether the first method (pledging specific assets) offered any advantages over the second one (the general pledge of assets). As far as the seniority of the lender's claim is concerned, it did not; perhaps for that reason, loans that took this first option almost always combined it with the second option of the general pledge. But why then did lenders and borrowers even bother to pledge a specific asset if it gave no greater seniority, particularly since it would require more of the notary's time and therefore cost more?

There were two reasons why this first option of a specific pledge was attractive. First of all, it provided the lender with information about specific real assets the borrower possessed.[14] That information would be particularly useful for a long-term loan such as a perpetual annuity, where interest payments could continue for years, even after the lender died. With the first option, the lender's heirs would have a much easier time tracking down and seizing the specific assets if the borrower defaulted on any interest payments. Second, and even more important, the first option gave the lender added protection if the borrower sold the specific real property securing the loan. The borrower had to tell the buyer that the property was mortgaged; the buyer would then take over the loan payments or require that the loan be paid off before the property was sold. If the borrower did not reveal the mortgage, then the buyer could sue him, and so could the lender, who could also seize the property from the buyer. Lenders who entered into annuities would therefore gain additional security by adding a pledge of a specific asset to the loan; so would the lenders' heirs even years later, because the obligation to reveal mortgages on specific assets applied to any owner of the pledged assets, even the borrower's own inheritors.[15]

The value of collateral clearly depended on the borrower's earlier debts. If a borrower was deeply indebted, a lien on the collateral could be nearly worthless. Hence, lenders would want reliable information not just about the value of the collateral itself, but about whether it had been pledged before, and about the borrower's whole credit history. That lenders wanted this information is obvious, but so did borrowers, for it improved their access to credit. Unfortunately, at the time there were no credit rating agencies, credit scoring firms, or lien registries. There were, however, notaries, and they, as we shall see, could help solve the problem.

Notaries greased the wheels of credit in other ways as well. They drew up most of the loan contracts, even though there was no legal requirement that they do so. At least in theory, private individuals could have drafted their own loan documents, and some of them did. The fiscal records (the Contrôle des actes) in fact contain many private debt contracts that had never been notarized; in Bellac, for instance, there were thirty-five of them in 1740.

But borrowers and lenders who considered writing up their own loan documents did face a problem: collateral pledges in the loan usually had to be authenticated by a notary. Some provinces were exceptions to this requirement, such as Normandy, where borrowers and lenders drafted their own annuity contracts without the help of a notary and then registered them several years later. In most cases, though, drawing up contracts without a notary imposed a big risk on lenders, at least if they wanted loans to be backed with the most secure form of collateral: real property. For a mortgage on real property to be legally binding, the borrower and lender had to have the notary draw up the original contract itself or have him recognize the contract that they themselves had drafted. Waiting to have him recognize the loan would add to the risk, because the later recognition would reduce the loan's seniority.[16] Reducing the risks here would, once again, benefit lenders, and borrowers too since it would give them greater access to credit. That is why most medium and long-term loans (those intended to last at least a year) were drawn up by notaries. And it is why mortgages were rarely signed without a notary. So there was a good reason to have notaries involved in nearly all medium and long-term credit, particularly if the debt was secured by a mortgage.

People used notaries for many reasons. Those who were illiterate—a substantial fraction of the population, particularly in rural areas, at least before the middle of the nineteenth century—would have wanted a notary's help in drawing up a contract. That was the original function of the notaries in the Middle Ages, and it had not fully disappeared. There were clearly cases too where the notary's legal expertise mattered—for instance, when loans involved minors or incompetents. But most often people turned to notaries because they wanted information. Because people used notaries for real estate transactions, to arrange marriage contracts, and to deal with inheritances, notaries had information about people's indebtedness and the value of their assets. And as long as people used notaries for credit, notaries knew their credit histories. As we shall see, the notaries' ability to manage that information was critical in the credit market.

Building a Data Set

Our goal in constructing this data set was to estimate how big credit markets were in France at different times, but we also wanted to capture regional differences in lending. One thing was clear: we could not hope to recover all of the loans in France for any year, even 1740. That task would exhaust anyone's resources, no matter how well funded, so, as we said, we had to sample. The sampling strategy and the methods used in 1740 were repeated for each of the five other cross sections (1780, 1807, 1840, 1865, 1899) in our core data set. How then did we construct the sample? How did we select the ninety-nine markets that form the core data set and why did we measure lending in each of them in those six years? And what sort of loan contracts did we sample? The choices we made have to be explained, because they are important.

The easiest to explain is our choice of the years for our cross sections: we wanted them to be roughly a generation apart. As we said, we started with 1740, because that was when our fiscal records first became useable throughout France. We ended in 1899, because when we embarked on this project, that was the latest year when we could get access to the fiscal records. As for the years in between, we wanted one date just before the French Revolution (1780) and one date after (1807). We picked 1807 because it came after the revolutionary turmoil and inflation were over and at a time when the emperor Napoleon had just put into place a five-percent interest rate ceiling for private debts. We then selected 1840 because by then France had recovered from the revolution but industrialization was in its infancy; and 1865, because industrialization was now well under way, but universal banks had not yet begun to spread branch banking throughout the country.

It is also easy to explain what contracts we sampled. We limited our samples to credit contracts that were notarized, because they were all recorded in the registers of the Contrôle des actes in 1740 and so could be counted. We omitted loans that were not notarized, because not all of them left a trace in the Contrôle. We adopted the same policy for all the other cross sections, with the only difference being that from 1807 on, the Enregistrement took the place of its Old-Regime predecessor, the Contrôle. What then did we not count? Letters of exchange and other commercial transactions, because they were rarely notarized, and private IOUs. They could be numerous, but the private IOUs involved only small sums of money, and the commercial contracts were not used for medium- and long-term loans. So for medium- and long-term credit, our counts are close to totals.

Why, then, did we choose to follow ninety-nine markets across two centuries? One could certainly imagine an alternative strategy of sampling not markets, but contracts, randomly across all of France. But that strategy would have required knowing roughly the size of the population of contracts and their locations throughout the entire country, which was one of the things we hoped to establish. It would also have been extremely inefficient because we would have had to access the records of a very large number of notaries in a very large number of different locations. Conceivably, one could sample individual notaries, but there again just the task of establishing how many notaries' records have survived in each department would have required visiting each departmental archive, at an enormous cost in time. Instead, we chose an efficient shortcut and decided to sample bureaus of the Contrôle des actes in 1740, which had the added advantage of allowing us to recover all the notarized credit for a given geographical area. We did the same for all of the later cross sections, using the similar records of the Enregistrement from 1807 on.

With a little patience we were able to draw up a list of all the bureaus in 1740 (see figure 1.2).[17] Doing so led us to find nearly 2,300 bureaus, or about one for each of the cantons of the early nineteenth century. (Cantons were the second smallest administrative district in France; on average, each one included a dozen villages or towns.[18]) The bureaus were, however, not evenly distributed. There is an area in northern France, ranging from the Oise through the Côte d'Or and the Moselle, that was abundantly endowed with bureaus, while the rest of the country was more sparsely populated with fiscal offices (see figure 1.2). Nine departments (Alpes-Maritimes, Nord, Pas-de-Calais, Bas-Rhin, Haut-Rhin, Paris, Savoie, Haute-Savoie, and Vaucluse) had virtually no bureaus in 1740. For most, it was either because they were not yet part of France, or had been recently acquired and were thus exempted from this tax. [19] For Paris, however, it was because the notaries of the capital had bought the tax back when it was first instituted (Hoffman et al. 2001). In any case, it is safe to say that there were more than two thousand bureaus in France. How might we sample among them?

One approach that might seem appealing, at least at first glance, would be to sample randomly among the candidate bureaus. In this case, French totals would equal the sample totals divided by the sampling rate. That method, however, would have required heavy sampling, for the frequency of borrowing and the size of loans varied systematically with the population of the biggest town or city in each credit market, and the same was true of size and duration of loans. Borrowing was more frequent when the major settlement in a market was small, but the loans were tiny too. When the settlement was large, borrowing was less common, but loans were bigger—so much bigger that per capita lending rose dramatically with the population of a market's biggest town or city. In our 1740 sample, for instance, only one percent of Parisians borrowed, while twice that many did in most rural areas. The average loan size in Paris, however, was 7,200 livres, versus just 170 livres in the rural areas. Although a 170-livre rural loan was sizable (more than six month's wages), it was dwarfed by the average Parisian loan. As a result, the ratio of the value of loans to the population was seventy-six to one in Paris, versus only four to one in rural areas. Loan durations also rose with the population of a market's

Figure 1.2. Bureaus of the Contrôle des actes about 1740.
Source: Departmental archive inventories.
Note: In Paris, in the extreme north, in the east, and in the Vaucluse, there were simply no bureaus before the revolution. In the Manche and the Pyrénées Atlantiques, the records were destroyed, and we were unable to access the inventory for the Alpes de Haute Provence.

major settlement, making the stock of loans larger. In 1740, Paris had a stock of debt that was thirty-six times larger than average stock of debt in the most rural markets.

The systematic relationship here—what we will call the urban hierarchy—held for all of our cross sections; it was not peculiar to 1740. As the population of the major settlement in a market rose, the frequency of borrowing fell, but loan sizes and durations rose dramatically, enough to increase both per capita lending and the stock of oustanding debt.

This relationship argued against simply choosing bureaus randomly. In 1740, for example, there were about 123 cities in France with populations over ten thousand inhabitants. Each had its own bureau. There were also 237 towns with populations of five to ten thousand. Nearly all of them also had their own bureaus. That left about 2,300 bureaus where the population fell below five thousand. If we collected a random one percent sample of the bureaus (or twice as many as we actually collected), we would have data from only one or two cities, two or three towns, and two hundred or more of the smaller bureaus. But because borrowing was concentrated in cities, our one percent random sample would yield highly uncertain estimates of outstanding debt, and tell us little about regional variations in lending.

Clearly, we had to oversample the urban bureaus. We therefore collected a stratified sample, where the stratification depended on urban population. Obviously, Paris had to be in the sample. Then we chose two other big cities in different regions that were commercial centers throughout the entire period we studied (Lyon in southeastern France and Rouen in northwestern France), some medium-sized cities with populations above ten thousand that were scattered across the country, and a reasonable sample of the rest of the distribution. This argued for a simple strategy of collecting data for the main city in each department (for instance, the city of Troyes in the department of the Aube, which is roughly one hundred miles east of Paris) and for one medium town (Arcis-sur-Aube) and one or two smaller markets (Bar-sur-Seine, and Vendeuvre) in the same department. Since the records we used (the Contrôle and Enregistrement) are stored in one location for each department, this strategy gave us the necessary stratification and at the same time cut down on the number of archives we had to visit.

Gathering data for all the cross sections and for three or four bureaus in each of the departments we selected required the cooperation of the departmental archives.[20] Some were more helpful than others, so we actually collected data from 109 locations in thirty-five departments (see figure 1.1).[21] Because ten of these were missing at least a year among our six cross sections, we ended up relying on our core data set of ninety-nine markets. With each bureau, we tried to read the registers of the Contrôle des actes (and later the Enregistrement) for the entire year for each of our cross sections.[22]

Then all that was left to do was to go through the photographs and enter data for each loan in a spread sheet.

From Counting Loans to French Totals

To estimate the total number of loans for France as a whole involves a number of steps. Since most of these steps are repeated for each cross section, we will describe them in detail here. Readers less interested in how we did this can simply skip to the next section.

The first step was to correct our data. For a small number of markets we had information on less than the full year of tax records. In correcting for these lacunae, we assumed that any missing data was random. That involved only a small number of markets and mattered little for the outcomes, save in Paris (where we have only one loan in five), and in the cities of Blois and Angoulême (where we have only a six-month sample). In 1740, this procedure leads us to 30,633 debt contracts (of which 20,515 are obligations, 9,148 are perpetual annuities, and 960 are life annuities). Similar corrections were applied to the other cross sections.

To extend our stratified sample to France as a whole, we allocated our localities to population bins. For a given bin—say cities other than Paris with population 60,000 or larger—the inflation coefficient is simply the French population living in that category of cities divided by the population of those cities that appear in our sample. In 1740, French cities in that category included Bordeaux, Lille, Lyon, Marseille, and Rouen, and their total population was 420,000. Lyon and Rouen were in our sample, with a total population of 197,000. Our procedure implies an inflation coefficient of 420,000/197,000 = 2.13 for the loans we counted in the bureaus in Lyon and Rouen.

We followed a similar procedure with smaller cities and towns, but we had to make allowances for the way these less populous municipalities overlapped with the bureaus and with the location of notaries' offices. In large cities, bureaus tended to be restricted to the cities themselves, so assigning the loans recorded in these bureaus to the cities where they were situated made sense. In smaller markets, though, the problem was a bit more complex. If there had been notaries in every municipality, we could have simply used municipal populations. (For 1740 and 1780, we would have had to employ the population of the Old-Regime equivalent, the parish, for small municipalities, and aggregate parish populations for multiparish municipalities.) But on average notaries had offices in only one of every eight or so municipalities, because they tended to congregate in large villages, towns, and cities. And although the Contrôle bureaus nominally had authority over a well-defined geographic area, it is rarely possible to determine precisely which parishes belonged to each bureau.[23]

Clearly, we need a geographic unit greater than the parish or municipality, one that would always include both notaries and bureaus. To keep things simple, we chose to use 1806 cantons, the level of political administration in France just above the municipality. Doing so allowed us to match two well-defined values: the population of the canton, and the set of contracts drawn up by notaries with offices in the canton. For 1806, we got population totals by aggregating the population of the villages in the canton including its chef-lieu (the administrative center, and typically most important municipality in the canton), all taken from a census conducted that year. Then we restricted our data set to include only notaries whose offices lay in the canton where the bureau was headquartered. For example, the Contrôle des actes registers from the bureau in the small town of Pontivy in western France contain the acts of notaries in Pontivy itself, and in Noyal-Pontivy and Moustoir, both localities within the canton of Pontivy in 1806. But the registers also included acts recorded by notaries from the communities of Neuillac and Cléguérec, which belong to a different canton. The contracts from Neuillac and Cléguérec had to be removed to allow us to match notaries to cantons. Now it is possible (though unlikely) that some notaries in an 1806 canton with a bureau reported to a bureau outside of it. If so, we may be undercounting credit, but our procedure at least insures that we are not overestimating it.[24]

We will use these 1806 cantons throughout this chapter and the next (on the 1780 cross section) even though they were not created until the French Revolution.[25] Their clear boundaries outweigh the anachronism of discussing cantons in 1740 or 1780. And we will continue to use these cantons to define our markets for all of our other cross sections in order to keep the geographic boundaries fixed.

Having estimated lending totals for well-defined geographical units (the 1806 cantons), we had to calculate corresponding population totals as well. We had selected five population bins based on the populations of the administrative centers of the cantons (the chef-lieux): Paris; other cities with more than 60,000 inhabitants; cities with 10 to 60 thousand people; towns with 5 to 10 thousand people; and, finally, rural cantons, with chef-lieu populations under than 5,000 inhabitants. For each of our cross sections, from 1807 on, there is a population census within 4 years of each of our survey years (the 1806 census for the 1807 cross section, the 1841 census for 1840, etc.). Before 1807, we relied on data developed by urban and demographic historians.[26] In 1740, for example, the total urban population (in municipalities with a population above 5,000) comes out to just above 3 million. Since the population of France as a whole was 24.6 million in 1740 and 29.5 million in 1806, by subtraction the population of all communities with fewer than 5,000 people was 21.6 million in 1740; a similar calculation gives us a figure of 25.23 million for this rural population in 1806. Comparing these two levels implies that the 1740 rural population was 85 percent of its 1806 value. For chef-lieux (the seats of the cantons) below the 10,000 inhabitant threshold in 1740, we assign them 73 percent of their 1806 population if they were larger than 5,000 in 1806, and 85 percent of their 1806 population if they had a population less than 5,000 in 1806.[27] Everywhere, the population not living in the chef-lieu is estimated at 85 percent of its 1806 level. That is the procedure for 1740. It is similar for 1780, and thereafter we use populations from the nearest census year.

We apply this method, which is both simple and reasonable, to estimate population levels for our cantons and for the different parts of the distribution of French city sizes. We can then produce inflation coefficients, which equal the ratio of the French population living in a size category of cantons divided by the population of those in cantons of our sample. In 1740 (and in all the other cross sections) we assign cantons to a size category based on the population of its chef-lieu. Not surprisingly, the inflation coefficient declines with size of this municipality: in 1740, it is 1 for Paris, between 2 and 4 for cities above 10,000, then jumps up to 8.4 for cantons with chef-lieux between 5,000 and 10,000 inhabitants and 39.6 for those with less than 5,000 inhabitants. We repeat the same steps (using different weights) for each cross section after 1740.

Table 1.1 displays the results of applying these coefficients to our sample in 1740, and is the source for the totals given at the beginning of the chapter. We have tried a variety of different techniques to estimate total lending based on our sample; although the other techniques produce somewhat different estimates, the French totals are very likely to be within an interval of plus or minus ten percent of the estimates reported in table 1.1, and, if anything, our totals are likely to underestimate lending slightly, rather than overestimate it.[28]

One thing is evident: the number of notarized credit transactions in 1740 was very large and the sums involved were significant. At two hundred livres, the average loan in rural areas represented several months' income, and in Paris the average loan size was, at seven thousand livres, many times per capita income. These loans clearly represented an important flow of resources across the early modern French economy, even in 1740. Furthermore, they were dispersed throughout the kingdom and not concentrated (like commercial letters of exchange) in the largest cities, or in the hands of a small number of bankers.

The second thing that emerges from the totals for 1740 (a point which we will return to in the last section of the chapter) is that they clearly display our urban hierarchy. We estimate that the value of loans made in the sixty-five cantons whose chef-lieux had over ten thousand people exceeds all the lending in the 2,500 cantons where the chef-lieux had populations under five thousand. And that was so even though the cantons with the larger chef-lieux held about ten percent of the French population, while the smaller ones contained more than eighty percent of the population.

From Loans to Credit Markets

For many economists, a capital market is an exchange mechanism that features anonymous transactions in a homogeneous good that all clear at the same price in the same location. Roughly speaking, that means that the market is trading goods that are all the same (for instance, shares of one company's stock), and all that matters to the buyer is the price, not the seller. One might further require that demand and supply be well behaved and that the trades be anonymous: a buyer can get more of the good or service by paying more, a seller can place more of his goods or services by making them cheaper, and the buyer and seller do not have to know one another. That description is in fact how modern stock markets seem to work.

If capital markets have to meet these narrow conditions, then notarized loans were not market transactions. They simply fail on all counts, both in 1740 and in all of our other cross sections. None of the transactions were anonymous; to the contrary, the bilateral contracts made it essential that the lender and borrower come to know each other. And the identity of the borrower (in effect, the seller of the debt) certainly mattered. The size of the loan depended on it, and so did other loan terms, in all our cross sections—a fact that remains true of mortgage lending even today. Furthermore, it is impossible to establish that transactions all cleared at the same price, since we do not observe interest rates in the vast majority of transactions. And there is yet another difference that distinguishes our peer-to-peer credit markets from a modern stock market: the transactions were dispersed throughout France, and not consolidated in some central marketplace, like the *Bourse* (the equity market in Paris) or the London Stock Exchange. In 1740, for example, lenders made loans in more than five thousand different locations in France, and even in Paris, debts were arranged in each of the offices of each of the city's 113 notaries. Our other cross sections were similar. Clearly, the peer-to-peer lending market was not in any way a central marketplace.

And yet each of these places where peer-to-peer loans were arranged constituted a credit market, both in 1740 and our other cross sections. They were simply not centralized. And if prices were not mentioned in the loan contracts, it just meant that that credit in each of the markets was rationed. There was an interest rate, and an individual borrower with a particular credit history and income, and a specific asset to use as collateral, could borrow up to some amount (usually the minimum of some multiple of his or her income or some fraction of the collateral value). But the borrowers could not get a larger loan by offering to pay a higher interest rate. That was the rationing: paying more would not get the borrower more debt.

The reason there was rationing is that lenders worry about adverse selection: the kind of borrower most willing to make such an offer is the one who is least likely to repay.[29] Deviating from this pattern of behavior can wreak havoc, as the recent subprime mortgage crisis shows. (In the subprime crisis, lenders started making outsized loans to borrowers with lower incomes and less home equity.) In effect, markets of this sort allocate goods in a way that is different from most "normal" markets, where goods are sold to the highest bidder, information about the seller is irrelevant, and the only thing that matters is the price. In mortgage markets, that sort of price competition is suppressed; there are no bids. Instead, would-be borrowers compete on information. To increase the likelihood of getting a loan, borrowers offer more collateral, and other kinds of information about themselves. And with a fixed interest rate, lenders are most attracted to the safest borrowers.

We shall also not read too much into the fact that these markets did not aggregate demand and supply through the kind of financial organizations we might call banks. Though 1740 was not the dawn of credit in France, it was a period in time when there were very few banks (and none in small localities), and those that did exist were not involved in the long-term credit market. Their business revolved around offering short-term commercial loans and payment services to merchants, typically via letters of exchange; some of them also made short-term loans to the government. Bankers had to know borrowers well before they would grant them a loan, which barred many customers from getting access to short-term credit or payment services, particularly if they were not successful merchants. Some commercial credit was also provided through tied contracts—for instance, when wine brokers offered credit to wine buyers. But, again, the parties had to know one another, and the tied contracts are a sign that short-term credit was severely limited in 1740, and would likely remain so until later in the nineteenth century.[30]

Why did our medium and long-term credit markets remain local and bilateral and not pass through banks, as is the case with mortgage lending today? The reason was that a smooth flow of information and continuity of contract (see Neal 2010) were more important to these transactions than whatever efficiency increases might have been attained by entrusting mortgage lending to a bank, as is done today.

To see why, consider how a mortgage bank might have operated in 1740. To start with, it could act as a limited partnership (where investors hold shares in the bank, but these are not tradable). Its assets would be a portfolio of mortgages, and its liabilities the investors' equity. The investors might well have preferred the reduced risk of getting the average return on the portfolio of mortgages to the more variable return from holding a specific mortgage. That, after all, is one reason behind the creation of mortgage-backed securities. But if information is good (if default rates on individual mortgages are low and recovery rates high), then the gain in risk reduction from creating the bank will be small. The bank could perhaps provide another benefit, liquidity, by allowing investors to sell their shares. That would make our mortgage bank essentially a mutual fund. The supply of credit might well increase, because now lenders could recover their funds if they need to. There might be a further advantage: investors could allow loans of longer maturity if their investments are tradable. But as long as the mortgage portfolios are local, the market for the equity in the mutual fund is going to be very thin, and the liquidity it provides may well be expensive.

A third possibility is that the bank issues debt to fund the mortgages, in effect offering investors a choice between a higher-risk (and higher-return) equity investment in the bank or a safer (and thus lower-return) investment in its bonds. This organization would combine the three key functions of a bank: risk diversification, liquidity, and financial transformation. Yet these benefits would likely be small unless the bank could operate beyond the local geographic scale, which in our case means the canton. An individual investor might well spurn the average return on a portfolio of mortgages offered by the bank and instead invest in a mortgage whose return is negatively correlated with his or her own income: a wine grower, for instance, might lend to an artisan or to someone who raises cattle or grows wheat. If local information brokers are good at their job, such transactions will occur without banks (see Snowden 1995).

The true advantages of a mortgage bank, however, do not lie in risk diversification, transformation, or liquidity, but with a different form of diversification: namely, being able to match up a regional rather than a local source of supply and demand. If loans are restricted to the locality, local supply has to equal local demand. In boom times, local demand for loans is likely to outstrip local supply, while in bad times local demand is likely to drop more than local supply. In the same way that merchant banks smoothed the working of the European commercial system (by making payments across regions and arranging short-term credit across regions), mortgage banks could smooth out the local peaks and troughs of mortgage markets by moving resources through space. A bank could draw on resources from localities with net savings and place them in localities where loan demand exceeded local supply.

Doing that, however, required that information travel over space, for potential investors might well hesitate to put their money in the bank out of fear that it would face adverse selection that better informed local lenders (such as notaries) could avoid. Instead, the investors might well prefer to place their funds with specific borrowers whose characteristics they understood well. These fears are not idle speculation. Indeed, there are plenty of historical examples where the entry of sophisticated financial institutions has been defeated by informational problems, and not just in France.[31]

All the problems inherent in our mortgage markets imply that they did not work in the same way as an anonymous market where price is the only thing that matters. First of all, they featured exchange in two dimensions:

money and information. That both dimensions mattered implied that the mortgage market could not be anonymous, because the lender had to know something about the borrower, both before the loan was made and while it was in progress. (That is, in fact, also true of mortgage markets today: home mortgages, for instance, may prohibit leasing out the home because tenants may be more likely to damage the collateral.) Second, constraints on the flow of information likely shaped the structure of our markets: for example, how far they extended spatially, how long the loans were contracted for, and which borrowers were matched up with which lenders. These two characteristics of mortgage markets in 1740 and all the other cross sections should leave clear traces in our samples. It turns out that they do, and the samples reveal other features of mortgage markets that confirm our analysis of how the markets functioned.

The Notaries' Clients

Markets exchange goods and services; ideally they match potential buyers with high demand with suppliers who can meet their needs. In a mortgage market, one expects funds to flow between people who are different—between borrowers and lenders. Such a market is also expected to allow individuals who either cannot participate directly in business enterprises, or who choose not to do so, to invest money by making loans.

A good market should also break down boundaries to exchange (Rosenthal 1993). By "boundaries" we mean that lending only occurs among members of a restricted group—an ethnic or professional community, for instance, such as all contractors and building tradesmen. In these cases, trust is limited to members of the group, either because some historical event has destroyed intergroup trust, or because it is difficult to acquire information about outsiders, who are socially or physically distant (Greif 1989, 1993). The criteria here are general; they can be applied to judge any credit market. What do they say about our notarial credit markets?

The answer is clear, at least if we judge from the evidence in 1740. In that year, there were no such boundaries among the notaries' clients and the borrower-lender pairs they served. Lending, as we shall see, was not limited to small professional groups, such as the contractors and building craftsmen, and loans passed between borrowers and lenders in completely unrelated professions, as well as between men and women, and between individuals who lived in different communities and who were unlikely to have known one another personally.

The Contrôle des actes was our source of information about lending in 1740, and while relying on it sped the collection of data, it also meant sacrificing details about the loans and the borrowers and lenders. The same was true to a certain extent in other years, but the sacrifices were particularly large in our first sample year, 1740. At that time, the fiscal officials charged with registering the loans often did not bother to write down more than the names of the borrower and lender, the type of contract, the principal of the loan, and the name of the notary. From the names, we can at least infer the sex of the borrowers and lenders with reasonable accuracy (in particular because widows and married women are noted as such). But occupation and residence were rarer in 1740 than in the other cross sections, so our conclusions here will have to be more tentative.

The Contrôle des actes seldom mentioned the purpose of the loans. Neither did the much more detailed loan contracts that we read in notarial archives. Often, for obligations, descriptions of the purpose of the loans were limited to the vague phrase "*emprunté pour employer à ses affaires*," or, in other words, "borrowed to use for his or her purposes." There were some exceptions, most notably when the loan was designed to improve the value of the collateral—for instance, if the mortgage concerned property where the borrower wanted to build a house. There were other cases where we could infer the purpose of the loan, because its value was close to that of some capital equipment. In the city of Troyes, east of Paris, for example, handloom weavers tended to borrow amounts close to the cost of buying a loom. The reason the purpose was omitted from loans was simple: once the loan was made, the lender had no control over the use of the money. So long as no clause governing the service of the loan was violated, the borrower could decide to invest his loan or spend it all in a tavern; the lender could do little about it.

One might think that the borrower's occupation or business would serve as rough proxy for the purpose of a loan. In some cases, it may do so, as in the nineteenth century, when one of the biggest iron-making companies in France helped finance new technology via notarial loans (Hoffman et al. 2001, 214). But occupations are hardly a reliable proxy. In 1899, a lawyer borrowed heavily in the notarial credit market in Lyon, not to create a law firm, but a large electrical utility.[32]

An even bigger obstacle to determining the purpose of loans is the lack of any distinction between a household's accounts and the finances of the business that sustains it. Consider, for instance, an individual who mortgages a plot of land to plant vines. One might imagine that if he had not gotten the loan, he would not have planted the vines: the loan is for investment. It is equally possible, however, that without the loan he would have planted the vines anyway and then given a smaller dowry to his child, or simply reduced his consumption for a few years. Is the money therefore borrowed to sustain consumption, to marry off a child, or to plant vines? Should the lender care? Then and now, the answer is often simply no.

From table 1.1, we already know that a substantial proportion of households were engaged in credit markets in 1740. With 430,000 new loans annually, at least ten percent of France's six million or so households were involved.[33] Very little of the lending passed money among family members. Of the 14,012 loans in 1740 for which we have data, only 587, or about four percent, see a family member lend to a relative. This number is perhaps an underestimate, because we may overlook borrowers and lenders related by marriage, but, as we shall see for later cross sections (when relationships of marriage are noted in detail), family loans are always negligible. Individuals turned to a notary for a variety of family affairs (marriages, bequests, apprenticeships) but rarely to draw up a loan contract among family members.

Table 1.2 displays what we know about the sex of the lenders and borrowers.[34] The numbers of loans are large enough that we can both evaluate the gender patterns for different kinds of markets and for France as a whole. One fact is clear: most loans (eighty percent or more) involved credit from men to men. This staggering figure reflects a combination of different factors. In some parts of France before the French Revolution (and throughout the country after it), married women had the right to maintain their property separately from their husbands. In 1740, however, it was extremely common for a husband to have discretion over his wife's assets. Thus, when a husband acted as a lender, he had no need for his wife to appear in the contract if he was using household resources. Yet a wife whose dowry was folded into the household assets retained a senior claim to it, if the assets of the household were threatened by creditors. As a result, when a husband appeared as borrower, lenders frequently insisted the wife cosign loan contracts, and loan contracts themselves made this requirement explicit.

The Contrôle officers, however, did not bother with such niceties, because they had no effect on the tax they would collect. (But if a third party acted as a surety, an additional tax was due.)[35] In the table, therefore, the category "Men" actually stands for men acting as heads of households. The category "Women" includes women acting as heads of household (widows and unmarried women) and women acting on their own even though they were married. Women to women loans were rare in 1740, accounting for one in a hundred or less of all the loans. But about fourteen percent of loans involved flows between men and women; even in the most rural areas, women were involved in eleven percent. As we move up the city size distribution, the proportion rises to nineteen percent in cities with at least ten thousand inhabitants, twenty-two percent in Lyon, and thirty-five percent in Paris. For a society as dominated by men as mid-eighteenth-century France, these numbers are not consistent with women being excluded from credit.

Table 1.2. Sex distribution of borrowers and lenders in 1740 (percent)

		Canton chef-lieu population < 5K		Canton chef-lieu between 5k and 10K		Canton chef-lieu between 10k and 60K	
		Lenders		Lenders		Lenders	
		Women	Men	Women	Men	Women	Men
Borrowers	Women	1.1	4.5	1.2	5.1	3.5	8.0
	Men	7.5	86.9	8.7	85.0	13.9	74.6
		N=5351		N=3025		N=5255	

		Over 60k except Paris		Paris	
Borrowers	Women	2.7	8.3	4.8	11.4
	Men	15.0	74.0	23.7	60.1
		N=699		N=1185	

		Sample		Sample weighted by population	
Borrowers	Women	1.7	5.4	1.0	4.1
	Men	9.2	81.4	7.0	85.6
		N=15515			

Note: Couples are counted as men, because the number of bureaus where this information is recorded accurately is small. N is the number of cases in each category where we observe sex for both parties.

Our information on social characteristics, when they are mentioned in the Contrôle des actes, is extremely detailed. (In 1740, unfortunately, they were often omitted.) Occupations and social status, when noted, are described with great precision. We can distinguish roofers who use straw from those who use slate, wine growers from ploughmen, lace makers and weavers by the kind of thread they use. Nobles and royal officials always sport a plethora of titles and job descriptions (*écuyer*, *secrétaire du roi*, *notaire au Châtelet*; or *comte*, *baron*, *maréchal de camp*). For our purpose here, that was too much detail, so we reduced social status and all occupations to ten categories: agriculture, clergy, communication and transport, construction, manufactures and crafts, nobles, public administration, services, trade and commerce, and "unknown" for the large number of borrowers and lenders with no listed occupation or status.[36]

As table 1.3 shows, in the smallest markets, for instance, we only have data for about one thousand occupations for borrowers and lenders and only 420 contracts where we have occupations for both sides of the transaction. Aggregating them into a national total would be meaningless. Instead, we report a simple set of measures that captures what is happening in different sized markets. The first of these measures is the proportion of loans where borrower and lender share the same occupation. If we produce a matrix of occupation pairs, then these loans are on the diagonal of the matrix.

This number is largest at both ends of the distribution of settlement size. At one end of the distribution, in the most rural areas, loans between people of the same occupation are concentrated in agriculture, which is no surprise, since it was by far the dominant activity. At the other end, in Paris, the high number of on-the-diagonal loans comes from services and trade, the two largest activities in the data. Even in the capital, however, only thirty percent of loans come from people in the same aggregated occupational category (see table 1.3). Had we used a finer grid that distinguished judges from military officers and butchers from bakers, the shared-occupation proportion of loans would have been much smaller. Clearly, then, most loans occur between people who are from different occupations.

Occupations, of course, are not equally represented among lenders and borrowers, and one might want to correct for that inequality, because it could limit lending within occupational groups. One way to make this correction would be to compare the number of borrowers and lenders in each occupational group and use the smaller of the two numbers to estimate an upper bound for the number of loans that would be possible if all lending were confined to borrowers and lenders having the same occupation. For instance, in the smallest markets there are 356 borrowers from agriculture and 126 lenders, so our hypothetical calculation would restrict lending within the agricultural occupational group to a maximum of 126 loans in the smallest markets. If we repeat this calculation of an upper bound on the number of loans for all other markets and occupations, it turns out that the maximum number of loans possible within occupational groups is always at least sixty-five percent of the total number of loans made. Meanwhile, the actual number of loans within occupational groups never exceeds thirty-two percent of this total. By this standard, notaries were drawing up far more loans between people who were different from each other than loans between people who were alike, as the right hand column of the bottom panel of table 1.3 shows.

Table 1.3. Occupations in 1740 by market size (canton chef-lieu population)

		Loans with reported occupations					
	Total	Borrower	Lender	Both	Same occupation	Max possible same occupation	Same occupation as percent of max
					Percent		
1 <5k	8,744	5.7	7.5	3.3	32.3	61.1	52.9
2 5–10k	4,620	16.0	17.3	11.8	25.8	57.0	45.2
3 10–60K	8,185	20.1	15.3	9.1	27.9	62.2	44.8
4 60K+	1,833	7.7	8.0	5.4	14.1	60.3	23.4
5 Paris	1,231	95.8	86.4	82.9	23.0	69.8	32.9

	Agriculture		Noble	
	Borrower	Lender	Borrower	Lender
4 <5k	50.4	13.9	5.2	14.7
3 5–10k	43.8	12.2	10.7	6.3
2 10–60K	34.7	6.2	15.1	11.6
1 60K+	2.8	0.0	17.7	10.9
Paris	3.2	1.5	15.7	6.5

Note: The maximum possible share of loans occurring within an occupational group is constrained by the minimum of the number of lenders and borrowers in a group. For instance, if agriculture has 136 borrowers and 66 lenders, then the most loans that can be made within agriculture is 66. To get the maximum possible share of loans within occupation, we sum these minima over our 11 occupational categories and divide by the total number of loans with identified occupations.
Source: See text.

One reason for all the lending across occupations is the way occupations vary as we move across the city size distribution. In rural areas, agriculture is the dominant economic activity and the most frequent occupation of borrowers: nearly three times as many debtors come from agriculture than from trade, the next most common occupation among those seeking loans. Agriculture still dominates in the cantons where the chef-lieu is a town with five to ten thousand inhabitants, but thereafter its importance falls as markets grow in size. In cities, the nobles dominate as borrowers, but not as lenders. And in the largest cities, it is trade and services that provide most lenders, while public officials and nobles are the most important borrowers.

The evidence here argues against notarial lending being driven by nonmarket social relationships. In fact, the pattern of lending is just what we would expect if credit was passing through a market where the allocation of credit depended not on price as the equilibrating mechanism, but on the quality of the borrower. Simple risk considerations would make a lender prefer borrowers who were not in the same line of work as the lender, because the borrowers would then be less likely to default at a bad time for the lender. Similarly, one might also guess that demand for credit is correlated within occupation, which would make borrowing within an occupation difficult. If one weaver wants to borrow to expand production, then other weavers are likely to want to do so as well, so other weavers would be less likely to want to make the loan. Overall, then, we would expect lending to cross-occupational lines wherever possible. The evidence is from 1740 alone, but the same argument about the virtues of lending across occupations will apply to our other cross sections as well.

France in the Mirror of Its Neighbors

The population of cities clearly explains a great deal of what was going on in the credit markets in 1740, from the popularity of annuities to participation rates of women and the odds of cross-occupational lending. In particular, although borrowing grows less frequent in larger cities, the value of lending per capita and the stock of outstanding debt per capita both rise in larger cities. The urban hierarchy therefore had a big effect both on the amount of debt and on the sort of borrowers and lenders who were engaged in the credit market. How big, though, was this effect for the French credit market as a whole?

To find out, we compared France with countries that had very different urban structures. In table 1.1, we broke France down into five settlement sizes and in the process produced estimates of credit per person for each of these categories. We then asked two questions. First, what might notarial credit have looked like if France had had the urban structure of one of its neighbors: England and Wales, the Low Countries (Belgium and the Netherlands), Germany, Italy, and Iberia? Second, how large would these credit markets in these neighboring countries have been if their inhabitants had the same propensity to borrow or lend as in France?

The data assembled by Jan de Vries (1984) allows us to recreate the city size distribution above ten thousand for each of France's neighbors; we then distribute the rest of the population (between cantons with a chef-lieu above ten thousand inhabitants and below that threshold) in the same proportion as in France. Those data appear in the top panel of table 1.4. We should note that for the cities with a population greater than ten thousand, our totals are larger than those of de Vries, because in building bureaus we have added in their hypothetical rural inhabitants. We then compute (but do not report) population shares by city size for each country. In the next panel, we calculate how many loans would have been signed in each sized market if the share of the population of France living in given city size had been similar to that of the other countries.

The most striking finding is that frequency of borrowing is insensitive to urban structure: in the simulations where we vary the urban structure in France, the number of loans per capita is always between seventeen and eighteen per thousand (table 1.4). The reason is that, nearly everywhere, eighty percent of the population lived in and around market towns with a population less than ten thousand, where participation was high. The relatively lower participation of the more urbanized parts of the population ends up having a small effect on the total participation rate. The reason for the lower participation rate in cities is simple: since landownership in cities was quite concentrated (the share of urban dwellers who were renters was increasing with city size), most of the population had no collateral.

On the other hand, in cities like London or Paris, those residents who did have collateral in fact had lots of it. As a result, an urban structure with very large cities would boost the amount of lending and also the stock of outstanding debt. We can see what that would do in France if we assign France the high rates of urbanization in England and Wales. Because London contained nearly 12 percent of the population of England and Wales, an equivalent urban structure in France would require a counterfactual Paris of 2.7 million inhabitants rather than the actual 1740 figure of 575,000. This enormous Parisian population mechanically produces a volume of credit nearly five times larger than what we actually observed in Paris in 1740, and doubles the stock of debt per person for France as a whole, if it had England's urban structure. The magnitude of the effect is yet another mark of London's importance, as Tony Wrigley (1967) emphasized decades ago.

Table 1.4. Notaries and the urban hierarchy in 1740

	France	England and Wales	Low Countries	Germany	Italy	Iberia
Populations	"cantonal population in thousands"					
Cities>300K	576	675	0	0	305	0
More than 60K	421	0	358	184	854	491
10k to 60K	1,920	537	1,015	1,311	1,658	845
Less than 10K	21,685	4,889	2,729	15,502	12,484	9,660
Total	24,602	6,100	4,102	16,997	15,301	10,996
	Counterfactual 1 Values if we give France the candidate country's urban structure (pop. in all cases 24.6 million)					
	Number of loans					
Cities>300K	6,155	29,088	0	0	5,240	0
More than 60K	5,644	0	28,837	3,571	18,431	14,745
10k to 60K	30,680	34,569	97,313	30,312	42,592	30,173
Less than 10K	394,673	358,957	298,301	408,221	365,423	393,134
France	437,153	422,614	424,451	442,105	431,687	438,051
	Value of loans (millions of livres)					
Cities>300K	44.1	208.3	0	0	37.5	0
More than 60K	8.8	0	44.7	5.5	28.6	22.9
10k to 60K	21.7	24.6	69.1	21.5	30.3	21.4
Less than 10K	86.5	79.0	66.0	90.0	81.0	87.0
France	161.5	312.0	180.0	117.0	177.0	131.0
	Stock of outstanding debt (millions of livres)					
France	1,426	3,275	1,587	894	1,566	1,017
	Value per capita					
Loans	0.018	0.017	0.017	0.018	0.018	0.018
Value of loans	6.56	12.69	7.27	4.75	7.19	5.32
Stock of debt	57.96	133.14	64.52	36.32	63.67	41.34

Table 1.4. (*continued*)

	Counterfactual 2 Value if we give each country the French propensity for credit given town size					
Loans	437, 153	104,795	70,742	305,519	268,488	195,912
Value of loans (millions)	161.5	77	30	81	110	59
Stock of debt (millions)	1,426	812	265	618	974	455

Taking London as the capital of only England and Wales is an extreme assumption, for the English monarch also ruled Ireland and Scotland. If we take the United Kingdom (Great Britain and Ireland) as London's hinterland, then London's share in population falls by almost half, which reduces the counterfactual Paris from 2.7 million (if it had had 12 percent of the French population) to 1.5 million, which is still much larger than the 575,000 inhabitants in Paris in 1740. If France had that urban structure, then total lending the country in 1740 would be 9.3 livres per person, which is still considerably larger than the 6.6 livres per person that we observed.

The Low Countries, Germany, and Iberia did not have a city above 300,000 inhabitants, so imposing their urban structure on the French data does not make the volume of lending jump. Italy did have a big city (Naples), but it was smaller than Paris, so Italy's urban structure raised the total volume of loans in France by only seven percent (177 million livres rather than 161.5). The same is true when we give France the urban structure of the Low Countries. Iberia and Germany's urban structure are thin enough that our counterfactual France would have credit totals that are twenty to twenty-eight percent lower than what we found in reality. The stock of outstanding debt figures produces a similar ranking, but the correlation between city size and contracted maturity pushes down the German and Iberian counterfactual because these distributions are the least urban, and pushes both the Anglo-Welsh and Brito-Irish counterfactuals up.

One can also imagine what credit totals would have been like if lending in the medium- and long-term market were the same (conditional on city size) for all of France's neighbors. This counterfactual scenario (see the bottom of table 1.4) would yield 812 million livres of outstanding debt in England and Wales, or some thirty-two million pounds (there being twenty-five livres to the pound), about the size of the British public debt.[37]

The debt would amount to about thirty-six percent of British GDP in the mid-eighteenth century. While it is possible that these levels were that high, it is important to note that nearly all of the very high stock that our counterfactual produces in England comes from the "London" effect. The Italian market is roughly the same size, or about two thirds of the French totals. Germany, Iberia, and the Low Countries have smaller totals because of smaller populations and/or low urbanization. The implication is that we must pay close attention to the urban structure and its interactions with evolution of the mortgage market. This is particularly important because the urban structure of France (and of other European countries) evolved dramatically between 1740 and 1899. In France, the share of the population living in cantons with a chef-lieu smaller than five thousand inhabitants fell from nearly eighty to sixty-five percent over those years, while the share of the population that lived in cities with population larger than sixty thousand rose from four to 10.4 percent. Urbanization, as we shall see, had profound effects on participation in the mortgage markets and on the sums of money that traded hands.

The Road Ahead

So far, we have considered each of our markets as an isolated entity. Even large cities had little impact outside the city walls, since population was only used to measure different propensities to borrow. Our method therefore resembled the urban history literature (Béaur 1994 and Lepetit 1988 for France; de Vries 1984) that seeks to explain the interaction between the population of a locality and the activities that arise there. The logic behind such an approach is partly Smithian: if specialization is limited by the size of the market, larger cities will witness more specialization and may thus attract consumers with more discriminating tastes.

But the logic is also partly Ricardian, in two senses. First, a large city implies large locational rents with the consequent reorganization of the real estate and financial sectors. Second, the higher costs from the rents imply that the comparative advantage of large cities will be different from smaller ones. The new urban economics has combined these different effects and added to them the notion that many economic processes benefit from local externalities: the more an industry is concentrated in one location, the lower are its costs. Armed with these ideas, scholars have investigated how the urban system evolves. In the end, however, the urban system remains a structure of islands: conceptually an activity occurs in different locations, with some having more and some less, but connections between locations are limited.

When we come to credit markets, one can use the same notions to think about the supply and demand for credit across localities. One might well guess that asymmetric information would be worse, at least initially, in larger cities than in smaller ones. Yet one might also suppose that the size of the potential market might facilitate the rise of intermediaries specialized in overcoming the challenges of asymmetric information. Further, the demand for credit should be stronger in larger cities because real estate prices should be higher and because big cities will harbor the more capital-intensive activities.

One might also suppose that mortgages signed in a given location would involve only lenders and borrowers who reside in that location. In fact, there are sound economic grounds to hypothesize that these markets would be isolated one from another. Most models in the economics of information assume that information circuits are somehow closed; otherwise lenders in one locality face adverse selection when extending loans to borrowers from the outside. That suggests that each borrower and lender selects (or is selected by) a market and must interact with counterparties there (notaries, lenders, borrowers). The simplest version of this would be that each market is restricted to those individuals who dwell in the given canton. There is also a more extreme version of this island credit, where individuals only interact with neighbors—those people who live in their municipality.

The credit data give little credence to the existence of sharp geographical boundaries. Only fifty-one percent of the contracts in the 1740 sample that provide residence have the borrower and lender coming from the same municipality, and a full thirty percent come from different cantons (see table 1.5). What is more, these numbers vary systematically with the urban structure. In small markets (cantons where the chef-lieu has fewer than five thousand inhabitants) less than half the contracts involve people who live in the same village, and a full third have borrowers and lenders from different cantons. Of course, in these rural areas, traveling beyond the arrondissement to borrow or lend was exceptional. The share of the contracts where borrowers and lenders come from the same municipality does rise as the markets become more urban and reaches seventy-eight percent in Paris, but the share from the same *département* is actually smaller in the big markets than in the less populous ones.

The implication is clear. As early as 1740, these different notarial credit locations did not function as closed units: borrowers and lenders could and did "move" from one to another. This fact raises some important and troubling questions. Why would a lender from one canton accept a borrower from another canton? Why did that lender not infer that the borrower had been denied a loan at home? What kept these credit migrants

Table 1.5. Shared residence in 1740

	With identified residence	Share of borrowers and lenders from same unit (percent)				Number of obs
		Same municipality	Same canton	Same arrondissement	Same department	
Paris	99.0	78.3	78.3	78.3	78.3	1231
More than 60,000	5.9	75.9	75.9	88.0	89.8	1833
10000 to 60,000	28.6	63.5	73.2	88.4	95.0	8185
5000 to 10,000	39.0	55.8	71.4	87.2	92.6	4620
Less than 5000	42.0	48.9	70.0	84.9	93.9	8744
France	37.1	51.5	71.1	85.3	93.2	24613

Note: For the cities other than Paris with populations over 60,000, we did not collect residence data for Rouen, and very few of the summaries in the Contrôle in Lyon mention residence.

from becoming the bad apples of the system? How, in short, did these borrowers and lenders—particularly those who lived far apart—end up finding one another and ensuring that they had made a good match? These questions lead to the heart of our explanation for how our credit markets worked, both in 1740 and thereafter. We will begin to answer them in the next chapter.

CHAPTER 2

Spatial Variety versus Centralization

CHANGE IN EIGHTEENTH-CENTURY CREDIT MARKETS

Jumping from 1740 to 1780 reveals a much bigger credit market in France. But the lending market was not the only thing that had changed; French society as a whole was showing signs of an impending metamorphosis. The French Revolution would not erupt until 1789, but brilliant writers—Enlightenment philosophes such as Voltaire, Diderot, or Rousseau—had been invoking reason to attack political institutions and existing social norms. After they targeted organized religion, one of the bulwarks of the existing social order, its hold on the population began to slip away. Even when banned, their works became bestsellers, with references to philosophes in books skyrocketing between 1740 and 1780. The writings that fueled the French Revolution were thus all in place, even though revolution itself was nine years away.[1]

Iconoclastic ideas, though, were not the only revolutionary tinder that was piling up in the decades before 1780. The government deficit swelled during the American Revolution, and pushed public debt to such heights that the king was forced to make concessions in an effort to get a permanent tax increase. By 1789 his financial desperation and his own political missteps had forced him to call for a meeting of an ancient representative body, the Estates General, which had not assembled in nearly two hundred years. The combination of new ideas, a fiscal crisis, and a national assembly proved explosive, because the assembly gave reformers eager to put the ideas into practice a powerful means of extracting constitutional reforms.[2] The process was not simple, because it was compounded by a bad harvest in 1788, subsequent food riots, and widespread rumors of marauding brigands and of an impending noble reaction. The result, though, was the French Revolution.

Since 1740, in the long buildup to the 1780s, the economy had been growing, along with the population, literacy rates, and inequality. At the same time, the volume of private lending had soared, particularly in cities, and more so in Paris than anywhere else. But lending in 1780 was not simply a city affair, for loans were made throughout France. In fact, in 1780, eighty percent of borrowers still got their loans in communities of fewer than five thousand inhabitants.[3]

So the volume of new debt was centralized in cities, even though loans themselves were still dispersed across small towns and villages. The credit market, in short, was diverse, and it was changing, in ways that affected the types of loan contracts that lenders and borrowers chose and the services that notaries provided. Our goal in this chapter will be to measure all this diversity and then to explain it, and finally to account for the change and the growth. To do so, we must accept that heterogeneity is inherent in our credit markets. We also have to keep in mind the legal, political, and social context in which the loans were made. This kind of historical knowledge is necessary to understanding how our data sets were produced and thus how they can be compared across time and space. To grasp what all of the lending meant requires the approach of both a historian and an economist.

The task before us, it should be stressed, touches upon major questions in the history of financial development. The standard history yokes together sophistication, intermediation, and the centralization of credit markets, but it pays little or no attention to peer-to-peer lending (Gerschenkron 1962; Ferguson 2001; Sylla 2002; Rousseau and Sylla 2003). At least implicit in the story is the assumption that peer-to-peer transactions are either insignificant or that they have to give way to intermediated credit that passes through financial centers. Savers must deposit their money with banks headquartered in a financial center, and these banks must in turn distribute loans throughout the economy. Similarly, illiquid equity in partnerships must yield to publicly traded corporations, with shares floated by financial center banks and traded on a central exchange. Without these changes, financial development will halt, and economic growth will falter. In this story, France serves as the poster child for the harm done by failing to centralize, particularly when it is compared with England. At the heart of the comparison is the contrast between Paris and London. By the second half of the eighteenth century, London could boast of a thriving stock and bond market, while its Parisian analogue was at best moribund. It had a large bank (the Bank of England) that came to dominate the issue of bank notes, while Paris had to wait until the nineteenth century for something equivalent. There was also a growing network of banks that linked London, other cities in Britain, and financial centers abroad (Neal and Quinn 2003; Quinn 2004). In France, by contrast, although there were banks in Paris, they by and large did not diffuse into the rest of the country (or so it has been argued) until the middle of the nineteenth century, and their tardy arrival is supposed to have slowed French economic growth.[4]

Here we will not contest the claims about the lack of banks in France; that will be the job of chapter 6. Instead, we present French evidence that financial deepening does not require intermediation by banks and centralization. French credit markets grew rapidly during the half century before the French Revolution, even though banks were not arranging the loans. Lending did tend to concentrate in cities, but the centralization was incomplete, and large numbers of loans were still being made in small markets. The rapid growth shows that banks are not prerequisites for financial development; peer-to-peer lending can do the trick. And it should caution against the hasty conclusion that complete centralization is necessary. That sets the stage for later chapters where we ask just how long one must wait for the standard story to finally take hold.

Markets Big and Small Under the Old Regime

To illustrate the wide variety of lending, consider Paris in 1780. For credit, the year was exceptional for one simple reason: the lease of the General Farm was renewed. The General Farm was a large syndicate of tax farmers charged with collecting indirect taxes throughout much of France. In return for this contract, they advanced a year's worth of indirect tax receipts to the crown, or about half of the crown's revenue. Going back to the seventeenth century, the advance had been made by a group known as the general farmers. They were each extremely rich—at least at the end of their careers—and deeply connected to the world of banking and government finance because they had to centralize revenue collected throughout France (Durand 1971). In 1780, each general farmer was required to raise a million and a half livres, at a time when per capita income was only 380 livres per year.[5]

One might expect the general farmers to have turned to their banking allies to borrow the part of their advance that they did not want to fund from their own savings. But as one particularly famous general farmer observed (the scientist Lavoisier, the father of modern chemistry), they did not rely on bankers, even though there were at least seventy-one of them in Paris in 1780. Instead, they used notaries: "[The general farmers] must deduct the interest on the 1,560,000 livres loan of at least 6 percent, if one considers that several of them borrow at this rate and that they all pay notary fees that can be put at 1.5 percent for the first year."[6] In a later essay, he noted that the general farmers were not alone in seeking funds from notaries: "The government financiers and their accountants are nearly all in the same situation; few of them own the totality of the sums they advance to the government: these funds have been provided by lenders from whom they have taken out obligation loans that come due at the end of the lease."[7] The same was true of the individuals who by royal grace were given small equity interest in a position (the croupiers): "Most those who have received an equity interest, being unable to furnish the required funds, must get loans from notaries or other private parties."[8] One might ask why the general farmers did not raise money by simply issuing *billets de caisse*, the short-term commercial bills they often employed. But that source of funds would have been a risky way to finance a farmer's advance since the bills (which might last several months but no more than a year) would have to be renewed repeatedly for the entire seven years of the lease. Mortgages made more sense, particularly if lenders accepted the government's receipt as primary collateral.

Parisian notarial archives confirm Lavoisier's statements. We sampled every fifth box of the Parisian notaries' records for 1780 and found nearly two thousand credit contracts. Among them were eighty-four loans taken out by general farmers to fund their advance. Overall, twenty-six of the company's forty farmers borrowed a total of 5.5 million livres in this way. Since our sample is random, we can just multiply its values by five to estimate total borrowing by the general farmers. The implication is that they raised about 27.5 million livres from notaries in 1780, or just a bit less than half of the total they needed.[9] Almost all the loans were nonnegotiable obligations with a seven-year term—the exact length of the lease.

General farmers who financed offices or funded performance bonds were not the only borrowers who turned to notaries in Paris. As we demonstrated in earlier work, the market also attracted a wide variety of other borrowers, and of lenders too: aristocrats, merchants, entrepreneurs, and even prosperous peasants who either had money to lend or wanted to make an investment (Hoffman et al. 2001). What is striking, however, is the size of the loans taken out by the general farmers. An individual general farmer could raise a quarter million livres in a single loan, and on average they borrowed 64,000 livres per loan, almost four times the mean for Paris as a whole. The difference between the general farmers' median and the median for all Paris borrowers is even larger: 33,000 livres versus only 6,000. Even the smallest loan one of them took out—4,000 livres—amounted to 10.5 times per capita income in 1780 (380 livres).

Now let us move 700 kilometers south, to the town of Mirande. The eight notaries in there and in the surrounding canton recorded 83 loans in 1780, for a total value of 36,818 livres.[10] Over half of the borrowers worked in agriculture; they received 36 percent of the funds. Another 31 percent went to borrowers in trades and services; 8 percent went to construction and crafts; the last quarter or so of credit involved debtors who did not report an occupation (half of them were widows). (See table 2.1.) Mirande, in fact, seems to be the poster child for the lessons that small markets discourage transactions. Its population was about 1,500, and if we assume that another 6,000 people lived in its hinterland, then the entire market had a population of 7,500, or about one-eightieth of the Parisian population. If Paris had had the same number and value of loans per inhabitant as Mirande, then only some 6,680 loans would have been arranged in Paris for a total value of only 2.9 million livres. The actual totals in Paris were larger, particularly for the value of loans, which was astronomically

Table 2.1. Credit in Mirande in 1780

Borrower occupation	Fraction of all loans (percent)	Fraction of total amount borrowed (percent)
Agriculture	57	36
Clergy	1	3
Construction and crafts	12	8
Services and trade	13	31
Unknown	17	22

Note: There were 81 loans in Mirande in 1780, with a total value of 36,079 livres.
Source: Our sample of loans for Mirande.

higher. We estimate that the capital's notaries drew up about 9,000 loans with an aggregate value of 152 million livres—50 times what we would expect if we simply extrapolated from the credit market in Mirande.

Big cities, it seems, had disproportionately large markets. The contrast was not so much the participation rate (the ratio of population to loans), which in Paris was only one-third larger than Mirande. It was that the Parisian loans were huge: thirty-five times larger on average than in Mirande (470 livres). At a mere 4,500 livres, even the largest loan in Mirande does not come close to the median loan in Paris (6,000 livres).

Variations Across Space and Over Time

The contrast between Paris and Mirande raises the question whether notaries offered different services in large markets like Paris and small ones like Mirande. Some of the notaries' services, it is true, were the same everywhere: the notaries all drew up and stored private contracts. But the data from Mirande and Paris should make one wonder whether and how the services notaries provided might have changed across space and over time as well.

As we saw in chapter 1, notaries had started by recording oral contracts. The problem was that court enforcement of oral contracts required producing witnesses, and that might not be easy if the contract lasted for a substantial time, as it easily could with a property sale or a loan. With high mortality rates, witnesses might die. They might also just move away. The alternative was written contracts, but they posed legal problems in societies where few could read or write. Someone who was illiterate could not verify the content of a contract and thus could not be obliged to observe it, and someone who could not sign could hardly be bound by a mark on a purely private document.

Notaries solved these problems because they were able to produce legally binding written records of agreements between private parties. In effect, the notarized document substituted for witnesses. By the eighteenth century, long after courts had accepted privately drafted documents as valid contracts, notaries remained important in these societies with low literacy rates. As sworn agents of the court, they could jump into the breach, read the contract to the illiterate parties, and, with witnesses, have them affirm that they had agreed to be bound by it.

Now, illiteracy, as measured by ability to sign (the usual measure historians use), did vary considerably over space. In particular, more people in cities could read. Notaries might thus have been busier as literacy intermediaries in Mirande and other rural locations than in Paris, where people could usually read and write. They might also have been busier early in the eighteenth century than later on, because literacy rates rose over time. But growing literacy has an important implication: if the notaries' sole function was to bind the illiterate to their contracts, then they would have been doomed by the diffusion of primary schools in the nineteenth century, and credit contracts would have disappeared from their archives. That, as we show, was simply not the case.

The reason was that their status as private agents of the courts gave them a second function: they certified the legality of the contracts individuals entered into. By law, notaries could only draw up a contract if it was enforceable. They were also required to verify the identities of the parties. As a result, anyone contesting a contract drawn by a notary had to bear the burden of proof. Here again a tension emerges when we consider the demand for such expertise across space. On the one hand, most people in Mirande had limited familiarity with the law (at least relative to sophisticated Parisians). That alone should have made them more dependent on notaries' know-how. But at the same time they used a more limited menu of contracts and may therefore have had less need for notaries' arcane knowledge. It is thus not clear—so far at least—whether their demand for the notaries' expertise would be higher or lower.

But there was more to lending than drawing up a contract that could be enforced and that the parties understood. In the case of mortgages (and most other contracts as well) additional information was required, which could increase demand for the notaries' advice. Consider, for example, how a lender can ensure that a loan will be repaid. One way he can do that is to scrutinize the borrower's net worth. Perhaps he interacts with the borrower regularly and so knows precisely what the borrower's assets and liabilities are. As we saw in chapter 1, however, that is unlikely.

A second possibility was to have the borrower secure the loan with collateral, such as a piece of property. But then the lender had to determine what the property was worth, whether it had already been mortgaged, and whether the borrower actually owned it. One way to do so would be to have borrower swear that he was the owner and that the property had not previously been mortgaged. If the borrower was lying, he was guilty of *stellionat*, an offense that could be punished by imprisonment.

Most parties, however, would prefer to ascertain the validity of claims more directly, instead of relying on an oath and the vagaries of criminal prosecution. (That was particularly true under the Old Regime, because the police force was minimal and most criminal complaints were simply a first step in negotiating some sort of private settlement.[11]) In practical terms, a lender would like to answer two questions: first, whether the borrower owned the property that was to serve as collateral; and second, how much debt was already outstanding on it. Answering the two questions would involve access to asset registries or to someone who had private information about the ownership of property and claims on it. As we have argued elsewhere, notaries possessed that sort of private information (Hoffman et al. 2001). In Mirande, borrowers and lenders might know one another well enough to tell whether a borrower owned a piece of land or had previously mortgaged it. However, Parisian lenders would be much less likely to have that sort of knowledge about potential borrowers. If so, a lender in Paris might have more demand for a notary's services than an identical lender in Mirande.

After a loan contract was signed, notaries could (and did) offer other services to facilitate its execution. They could provide escrow accounts, payment services, and assistance in litigation should one of the two parties fail to deliver on his or her promises. All of these forms of help would be more valuable in places and times where there were few alternatives. For instance, before the establishment of the Caisse des Dépôts et Consignations in 1816, notaries had to handle escrow. Similarly, before banks spread throughout France in the 1800s, notaries served as the agents of distant landlords. In the 1780s, for example, the head of the noble Saulx-Tavanes family in Paris hired local notaries to help administer their properties in Burgundy and Normandy.[12] And even after banks opened throughout the country, individuals still maintained accounts with notaries who lent out money or leased land for them, and collected interest payments and rent.[13] That kind of activity is easy to spot, for the contracts specify that the borrower will make his or her payments in the notary's office.

Finally, notaries provided one other important service as well: they were matchmakers. In a world where asset markets were thin, they were unspecialized brokers whose activities ranged from arranging loans to putting together real estate sales and leases. There was no legal requirement that any of these transactions be drawn up by a notary. As a result, when we count notarized debt we are totaling all those loans in which borrowers and lenders had chosen to use a notary. When notarial debt grows, it can therefore either be because the size of the debt market has grown or because the demand for notarial services has grown. What is clear, however, is that we cannot assume that the notaries' services remained the same across time or across space.

Do Literacy and Collateral Affect Loan Size?

Tracking fluctuations in notaries' services over time is easier than analyzing their variations over space. Indeed one of the most dramatic shifts in notarial credit involves changes in the size distribution of loans that notaries drew up. If we consider the median loan for each of our markets, its size doubled on average between 1740 and 1780.[14] (The loan sizes in 1740 and 1780 are in livres, but, as we explained in chapter 1, this nominal money of account had the same value in terms of silver in 1740 and 1780, and its silver value was essentially the same as that of the nineteenth-century French franc.) A closer look at the distributions shows a very regular pattern, with the loan values at the bottom ten, twenty-five, seventy-five, or ninety percent of the distribution, all rising about seventy percent between 1740 and 1780. The vast majority of our markets witnessed this sort of increase, and in over forty percent of the cantons each of these critical values jumped by more than fifty percent. In other words, in most markets, the distribution of loan sizes was shifting to the right—toward larger loans.

The shift is evident if we reconstruct the distribution of loan sizes for France as a whole by weighting each market by population.[15] The result is displayed in figure 2.1, which shows the cumulative distribution of loan sizes for 1740, 1780, and 1807. The distribution of loan sizes is moving inexorably to the right. To grasp the magnitude of the increase in loan size, let us compare it to per capita GDP.[16] In 1740, a full eighty-three percent of all contracts were for an amount less than GDP per capita (365 livres).[17] By 1780, the share of contracts worth less than GDP per capita had fallen to seventy-three percent. The decline was particularly steep in the bottom part of the distribution, where the fraction of contracts worth less than half of GDP per capita fell from sixty-nine percent in 1740 to fifty-one percent in 1780. The shrinking number of contracts worth less than a quarter of GDP per capita explains most of the shift in the distribution: such loans dropped from forty-eight to twenty-nine percent of the contracts. The movement away from small loans and toward bigger ones

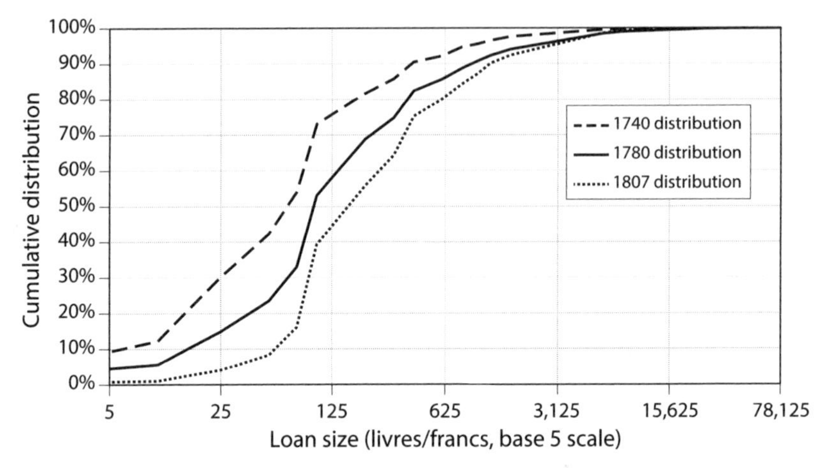

Figure 2.1. Cumulative distribution of loan size by cross section, 1740–1807. *Note:* Loan sizes are in livres in 1740 and 1780, and in francs in 1807; in terms of silver, both units of currency were essentially the same. In 1740 and 1780, the livre was worth 4.45 grams of silver; in 1807, the franc was worth 4.50 grams of silver.

continued unabated after the revolution. By 1807, the share of loans smaller than a quarter of GDP per capita had fallen to eleven percent, and the fraction worth twice GDP per capita or more had risen to nineteen percent (doubling its share since 1740).

The rightward shift of the loan size distribution could conceivably stem from higher incomes and urbanization. Loan sizes were always larger in bigger markets and income growth would raise the average loan size if loans were rationed to multiples of income. But neither rising income nor city growth is likely to account for much of the shift. Although urbanization did increase somewhat (cities above five thousand inhabitants were eleven percent of the population in 1740 versus 12.6 percent in 1780, and incomes did creep up a bit from 365 to 380 livres on average), neither effect is large enough to explain a leap in median loan size from about one hundred livres to just under two hundred. That big of a jump is not likely to be the result of more extreme inequality either.[18]

To explain the shift in the distribution of loan values we have to look elsewhere—to changes in the demand for and the supply of the different services notaries provided. In earlier work on Paris (Hoffman et al. 2001), we had emphasized supply. We reasoned that the capital's 113 notaries faced capacity constraints. Although, like busy lawyers today, they employed any number of clerks to draft contracts and make copies, each contract required a modicum of the notary's time. He, personally, had to read each contract to the parties, make the changes they required, and then have each change initialed by parties. There were therefore practical limits to how many contracts a particular notary could draw up, and he would, obviously, prefer ones that had higher value. While a notary could not legally refuse his services to anyone, there were many ways to discourage potential clients who demanded services that would be unprofitable—in particular, making them pay fees or wait.

If these constraints on the supply of the notaries' services grew more severe, they would lead notaries to avoid small loans, which required almost as much time as a larger contract. That might possibly account for a declining number of small loans in Paris, in other big cities, and in some western parts of France where notaries were relatively scarce and quite busy. Yet tightening supply constraints cannot explain what happened in places like Mirande, where small loans vanished, even though the notaries there could hardly be said to have been swamped with work. In fact, the distribution of loans moved to the right both in places where notaries were busy and where they would have welcomed additional business even if it was not very lucrative. And if their poorer clients had been put off by high fees for small loans, notaries still could have offered to draw up acts *en brevet* at a cut rate price.[19] But we would have seen them in the fiscal records, because the acts en brevet were registered with the Contrôle. So there must be something else besides changes in supply that was making the distribution of loan sizes shift to the right.

That something else was demand. To understand what was happening to demand for the notaries' services, let us examine the changes in lending more closely. While loan sizes were rising between 1740 and 1780, the number of loans was falling, from 437,000 in 1740 to 368,000 in 1780. This thirteen percent drop in the number of loans is startling, because the population was growing, as was the economy, albeit slowly by later standards. The decline in the number of loans was quite general, affecting two-thirds of our markets, but not cities, where loans totals did not budge. Lending was contracting in the countryside, or more precisely in cantons whose chef-lieux had fewer than ten thousand inhabitants. There the number of loans dropped nearly fifteen percent, and that decline accounts for all the decrease in the total number of loans between 1740 and 1780 in France as a whole.

Rural notaries were drafting fewer and fewer small loans. But it was not because they were swamped for business. Instead, it seems that demand for notarization of small loans was shriveling up in the countryside. What, then, was the source of demand for these small rural loans? We should keep in mind that there was no legal requirement that debt contracts (including mortgages) be notarized. And although notarization provided additional security of contract, it came at a cost: roughly one percent of the value of the debt. For the small rural loans, the reason the parties consulted a notary was probably not greater security; in all likelihood they did so because they were illiterate or unfamiliar with the language of written debt contracts. That source of demand, however, was drying up in the eighteenth century. According to Furet and Ozouf (1977), the fraction of French men who could sign their names jumped eighteen percent between 1690 and 1790. Presumably, fewer and fewer borrowers and lenders needed to have notaries read their contracts out loud and attest that they had agreed to the terms of the loan. The effect would be felt primarily on small loans, for at a time when schooling was neither mandatory nor free, literacy was positively correlated with income, as was loan size. The illiterates would therefore have lower average incomes and borrow and lend smaller amounts. And as their numbers shrank, so would small loans.

One way to test this hypothesis would be to see whether literacy predicts the distribution of loan sizes in our markets. The trouble is that we do not have literacy rates for our markets until the 1820s, when we can use the fraction of recruits who can neither read nor write at the canton level. This is eighty years after 1740, but if the relative ranking in literacy is stable, then it is an appropriate statistic for literacy in 1740, and the same can be said for urbanization. We ran (but do not report) a regression of the median loan value in each market on illiteracy in the 1820s and on the population of the main city in the canton (the chef-lieu) as a proxy for urbanization. We ran (and again do not report) similar regressions using the first decile or first quartile loan values in place of the median. We included urbanization in all the regressions to control for its effects on literacy and on loan size. The regressions all show that illiteracy was closely associated with small loan sizes—and the results hold whether or not we include the largest markets (municipal population greater than twenty thousand). To be sure, because illiteracy is often associated with poverty, which would also reduce loan sizes, the evidence is only suggestive. But it cannot be simply dismissed out of hand.

A more convincing test draws on direct evidence of literacy in debt contracts. If we are correct, then illiterate borrowers or lenders should appear most frequently in small loans. That, it turns out, is precisely what we observed in a subsample of our loans in Paris in 1740 and 1780. We see the same pattern in another subsample of loans drawn from three of our markets in the department of the Aube, to the east of Paris: the city of Troyes, which counted eighteen thousand inhabitants in 1740 and 35,000 in 1780, and the rural cantons of Arcis-sur-Aube and Bar-sur-Seine, where the population of each chef-lieux was under three thousand people. For each loan in these samples, we noted if at least one party was illiterate in the sense that he (or she) could not sign the contract. Whether parties could sign a contract was systematically recorded by notaries at the end of each contract.

When we breakdown the loans by quintiles according to loan size (table 2.2), each sample produced a strong negative relationship between loan

Table 2.2. Illiteracy and loan size in four markets, 1740–80

		Loan Size Quintile					
		1	2	3	4	5	All
Paris 1740	Average loan size	487	1,511	3,117	6,516	24,100	
(N=731)	One party illiterate (percent)	32.4	13.1	4.3	5.0	0.8	11.1
Paris 1780	Average loan size	792	2,716	5,852	13,039	59,711	
(N=269)	One party illiterate (percent)	18.1	5.5	0.0	0.0	0.0	4.7
Arcis/Bar 1740	Average loan size	68	130	262	528	1,710	
(N=78)	One party illiterate (percent)	80	80	69	47	18	57
Arcis/Bar 1780	Average loan size	74	187	324	616	1,992	
(N=101)	One party illiterate (percent)	90	55	50	45	23	53
Troyes 1740	Average loan size	76	288	475	970	2,932	
(N=98)	One party illiterate (percent)	95	60	68	53	19	59
Troyes 1780	Average loan size	41	158	416	947	3,295	
(N=117)	One party illiterate (percent)	72	64	32	20	24	45

Note: N is the number of observations in each sample. Quintile 1 concerns the smallest 20 percent of the loans in each market, and quintile 5 the largest 20 percent of loans in each market. Average loan size is in livres and is the mean size for each quintile. Percentages are row percentages. One party to the loan was considered illiterate if he or she was unable to sign the contract. Because of rounding error, the percent illiterate for the entire sample may not equal the average percent illiterate in each quintile.
Source: See text. The data comes from reading the notarial records for a sample of loans in Paris, the city of Troyes, and the rural cantons of Arcis-sur-Aube and Bar-sur-Seine.

Table 2.3. Percent of notarial contracts secured with collateral: Arcis-sur-Aube and Bar-sur-Seine, 1740–80

Type of claim	1740 (percent)	1780 (percent)
Claim on movables or implicit general claim	25.3	54.4
General claim on all the borrower's real property and movables	63.2	31.6
Claim on specific financial assets	0.0	1.0
Claim on specific real property	11.5	13.2
Contracts with cosigner	1.1	3.5
Number of contracts	87	114

Note: As we explained in chapter 1, loan contracts usually combined a specific claim (whether on financial assets or real property) with a general claim on all the borrower's real property and movables. In the table, the general claim is restricted to loans that made no mention of specific collateral. The implicit general claim concerns loans containing an abbreviation (*s'obligeant*) that amounted to an implicit general claim.
Source: See text.

size and the likelihood that someone could not sign, just as we expected. The relationship cropped up in all of the markets. In Paris, illiteracy was rare and dropped to under five percent of the contracts in 1780: the parties could sign over eighty percent of the loan documents even in the quintile of smallest loans. In the Aube markets, by contrast, the rate of illiteracy among the smallest loans never fell below seventy-two percent. In the rural cantons of Arcis-sur-Aube and Bar-sur-Seine, evidence from marriage records implies that there was a better than fifty percent chance that either a borrower or lender would be illiterate in 1780, making a notary obligatory if the loan contract was to be binding.[20]

If literacy was one important source of the demand for the notaries' services, help with evaluating collateral was potentially another. Greater demand for such assistance could, at least in theory, have caused the shift in the distribution of loan sizes in the eighteenth century. It could have done so if rural lenders grew leery of lending money unless the loan was secured by specific financial or real assets, which would reduce the risks lenders faced. That sort of collateral would give the lender added security beyond even a general claim on all of the borrower's assets, including both real property and movables. But because the lien on specific financial or real assets required additional effort from the notary (effort that would not be proportional to the size of the loan), it would be prohibitively expensive for small loans, and as a result small loans would fade away in the countryside.

Table 2.4. Percent of notarial contracts secured with collateral: Paris, 1740–80

Loan size (livres)	Claim on movables or implicit general claim (1)	General claim on all real property and movables (2)	Claim on specific real property (3)	Claim on specific financial assets (4)	Sum of columns (3) and (4)
			1740		
Under 1,000	17	51	24	8	32
1,000–4,999	4	51	34	11	45
5,000–9,999	2	34	49	15	64
10,000–29,999	2	27	46	26	71
30,000+	0	30	35	35	70
			1780		
Under 1,000	5	77	9	10	18
1,000–4,999	3	70	18	9	28
5,000–9,999	3	62	22	12	34
10,000–29,999	0	48	29	22	52
30,000+	0	30	22	47	70

Note: Claim on movables included loans secured by promises to provide labor, and the implicit general claim concerns loans with the abbreviation *s'obligeant*. The specific claims on real property or on financial assets always included a general claim, and the specific claim on financial assets sometimes also included a claim on specific real property as well. Columns may not add up because of rounding.
Source: Our sample.

Was that what was happening between 1740 and 1780? If so, requests for such collateral should crop up much more frequently in rural loans in 1780. But they did not, at least in our subsample of loans from Arcis-sur-Aube and Bar-sur-Seine in the Aube (table 2.3). The fraction of loans secured with specific collateral increased slightly (from 11.5 in 1740 to 14.2 percent in 1780, if we combine specific financial assets and real property), but that can explain only a small portion of the shift in the distribution of loan sizes.[21] In fact, most of the change in collateral involved a shift from the general mortgage to vaguer claims on movables.

Was there a growing call for this sort of specific collateral in the big city of Paris? There we have enough loans to break down types of collateral by loan size, and the requests for specific collateral were generally more frequent in large loans (table 2.4), just as we would expect if they imposed an additional fixed cost on borrowers. The trend is particularly clear if we combine liens on specific real property and specific financial assets. Stipulating specific collateral was especially common among the biggest loans whose growth in Paris was spectacular between 1740 and 1780.

The different patterns of lending in eighteenth-century Paris involved far more, though, than a shift toward larger loans with additional collateral. The type of contract the parties selected changed as well—and changed dramatically—as borrowers and lenders abandoned annuities in favor of obligations. As we shall see, this upheaval in lending in Paris had its own consequences for the sort of collateral creditors required, for with the obligation they grew more and more likely to demand specific collateral as security.

The Rise of the Obligation

Before the 1750s, Parisian notarial credit had long been dominated by perpetual annuities, an interest-only mortgage in which the borrower decided when to pay off the principal (hence the designation as perpetual). The main alternative, which would eventually triumph in the credit market, was the obligation. Under the Old Regime, the obligation specified the term of the loan but not the interest rate. Interest was paid, however, as is clear from Lavoisier's observation that the general farmers were paying six percent to borrow via obligations. In 1740, obligations already represented nearly thirty percent of the new loan contracts signed in Paris but only about two percent of the stock of loans, because the sums involved were small and the loan durations short (seventeen months on average) (figure 2.2). Many of these 1740 obligations likely formalized earlier debts that had not been repaid as expected. In that sense, many of the early obligations in Paris do not represent the kinds of transactions we seek to track—those in which two parties come together solely to arrange a loan.

By the 1780s, however, obligations in Paris had been transformed. They were now larger and lasted much longer. The average obligation in Paris was now nearly twice the size of the average annuity; back in 1740, obligations had, on average, been only two-thirds the size of annuities. Their duration had doubled since 1740, from seventeen months to nearly three years, while the duration of annuities remained stable at fifteen years on average. The obligations had become far more popular as well, jumping from twenty-nine percent of new loans in 1740 to fifty-three percent in 1780. And they were being used for a variety of purposes—for instance, by general farmers such as Lavoisier, who, as we have seen, turned to the obligations to raise money for investments in gigantic tax farms.

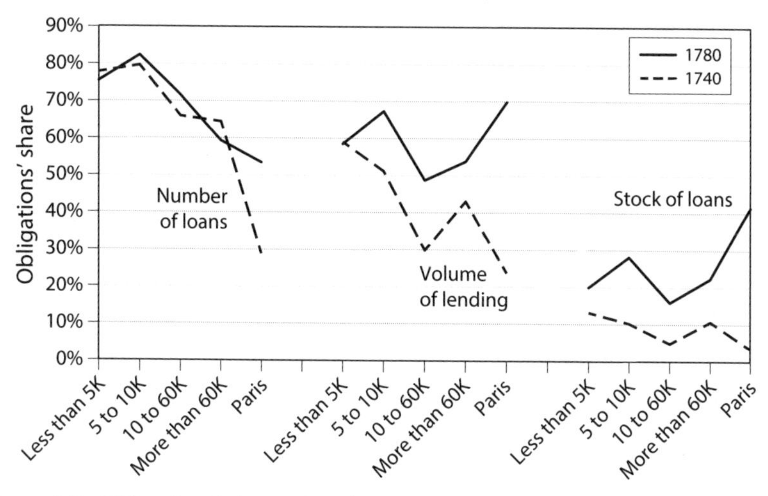

Figure 2.2. Obligations' share of credit, 1740–1780.
Note: We measure market size by the population of the canton's chef-lieu. The values shown are the share of obligations in the total number of loans, volume of lending, and stock of outstanding debts.
Source: Our sample of loans.

Beyond their greater size and their longer maturity, obligations in Paris in 1780 were also more likely to pledge specific collateral. In 1780, forty-five percent of all obligations mentioned specific pledges, up from twenty-seven percent in 1740. Within those specific pledges, financial assets cropped up more often as collateral (twenty-seven percent of the time as opposed to only eleven percent in 1740, according to table 2.5). The debt secured in this way included not just loans taken out by the general farmers but also obligations taken out by other officials, perhaps to buy one of the positions or public offices the government sold.[22] And there were other innovations too, including loans with repayment schedules instead of a balloon payment at the end. When in 1780 the Parisian army officer Octavien Saucher Dalvinard borrowed 22,000 livres from the Parisian nobleman Jean Ignace Lefaucheux, for instance, he promised to reimburse the loan in four equal annual payments spread out over the next four years.[23]

The obligation was not some legal or financial innovation. It had been used for centuries. But in Paris, as we shall see, it began to be employed in novel ways and was on its way to becoming the dominant credit instrument.

Outside of Paris, obligations also grew more important, but the trend was tempered because obligations had always been common in small

Table 2.5. Percent of notarial contracts that specify collateral: Paris, 1740–80

	1740		1780	
Type of loan	Obligations	Perpetual annuities	Obligations	Perpetual annuities
Claim on movables or implicit general claim (1)	17	1	4	0
General claim on all real and movable property (2)	56	35	52	57
Claim on specific real property (3)	15	47	18	31
Claim on specific financial assets (4)	11	17	27	12
Sum of rows (3) and (4)	27	64	45	43

Note: Rows may not add up because of rounding error.
Source: As in table 2.4.

markets. We can see as much in the left panel of figure 2.2, which displays the share of obligations in all contracts as a function of market size, measured by the population of the canton's chef-lieu. In 1740, that share is about eighty percent in the smallest markets (those whose chef-lieux had fewer than five thousand inhabitants), and it changed little by 1780. In larger markets (those with over ten thousand people), the obligation failed to reach that level of popularity but its importance did grow.

The size of the obligations also grew and helped them gain a bigger share of volume of lending in 1780, as the middle panel of figure 2.2 shows. But only in Paris did that share attain seventy percent. Outside Paris, notaries may have drawn up four obligations for every annuity, but the annuities were so much larger that they remained a sizable portion of the credit market.

When we turn to stocks of outstanding debt, which cumulate changes in numbers, size, and maturity, the advantage of annuities is even larger. The average annuity was paid off in a decade and a half; by contrast, obligations in the eighteenth century rarely lasted more than three years. Yet the stock of debt in obligations did grow in importance between 1740 and 1780. It did so because the maturity of obligations nearly doubled, while the duration of annuities did not increase.[24] One reason obligations were lasting longer was the growing practice of spreading repayment over the duration of the loan, as with Dalvinard's debt to Lefaucheux.

Such a repayment schedule was the first step toward what would eventually become the modern mortgage—a loan secured by property and with the debt amortized over a fixed payment period.

Two opposing trends were therefore roiling credit markets in the late eighteenth century. On the one hand, obligations were gaining in size and duration and becoming the most popular type of loan in the biggest markets; in Paris, they were supplanting annuities. On the other hand, an older type of obligation—one requiring a notary's help because the borrower or lender was illiterate—was fading away. This older obligation was usually a small loan and was more common in the rural markets. But it was disappearing as more people learned to read. In the long run, it would vanish altogether, and the obligation would become the modern mortgage.

Yet these two trends masked enormous variation among markets, even those of the same size. Obligations may have been lasting longer and getting bigger and more popular in most of the large cities, and tiny obligations may have been disappearing in small rural markets, but it varied greatly to what extent the two trends changed lending between 1740 and 1780 among markets of the same size. This heterogeneity is apparent in figure 2.3, which charts the share of obligations in the stock of debt in 1780 against their share in 1740 for each of the markets that we sampled. The dark line in the center is the forty-five-degree line. In markets

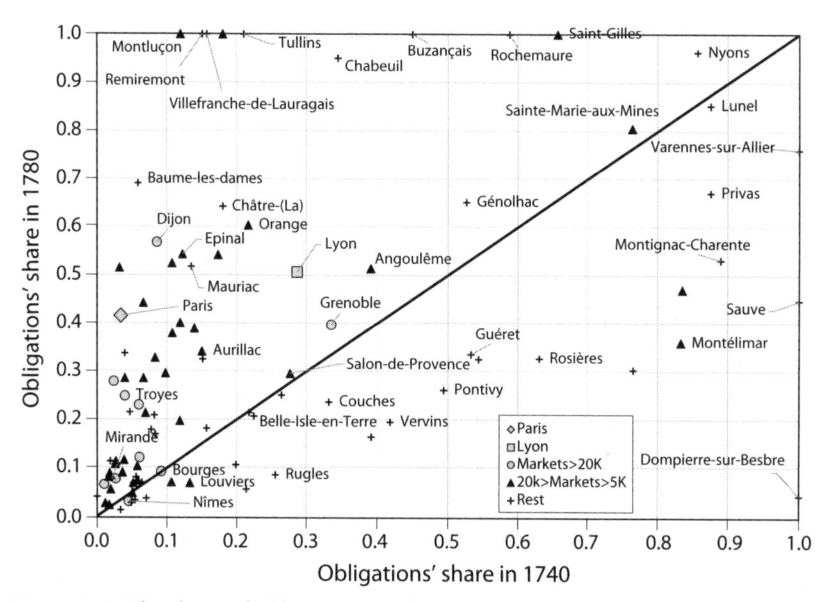

Figure 2.3. The share of obligations in the stock of debt, 1740–80. The shares are plotted for each of our markets.
Source: See text.

above the forty-five-degree line—three-quarters of the markets we sampled—obligations claimed a greater share of the stock of debt in 1780 than they had forty years before, as we would expect if they were lasting longer and getting bigger and more popular. Yet one thing stands out: there is tremendous variation from market to market. In our second largest market, the city of Lyon, obligations gained in importance in 1780, even though they had already captured a large share of the debt market in 1740. But the two other large markets—Rouen and Toulouse—continued to have a low share of obligations in 1780 (they are in the cloud of points near the origin of figure 2.3). As the figures reveal, there were many markets where obligations thrived, alongside others—even large ones—where they languished. Why these differences existed, we cannot say, but in all likelihood they depended on unknown local characteristics that really mattered in determining what kinds of credit contracts would prevail.

Can the Urban Hierarchy Explain Centralization?

While obligations gained ground in most of the big markets, lending was increasingly concentrated in cities, where it was booming. Although the centralization of the credit market in cities was incomplete, it was clearly a trend between 1740 and 1780. How then do we explain it? Was it the result of our urban hierarchy—in other words, of the greater demand for loans and greater supply of savings to lend in cities?

To answer those questions, we can start by analyzing the growth in lending between 1740 and 1780 and how it was related to market size. Table 2.6 gives totals for France as a whole for the two years, and the share of lending in markets by size category, using three different measures: the number of loans, the volume of lending, and the stock of outstanding debt.

The boom in lending between 1740 and 1780 stands out clearly in table 2.6: the volume of lending more than doubled. But Paris, with its bigger obligations, captured most of the growth. Large obligations caught on in other big cities too—Lyon was one example—but as we know, some big cities lagged behind (figure 2.3). As a result, the overall share of the volume of lending rose only from five to seven percent in the urban markets that were just below Paris (table 2.6). Change in the stock of debt tells the same story: lending was concentrating in Paris and several other big cities, but it persisted in smaller markets too—our incomplete centralization.

To understand this incomplete centralization in eighteenth-century France, we have to ask why there was more lending in Paris and in a select number of other big cities. Why, in other words, was there an urban hierarchy? It was not population alone that boosted lending in the biggest cit-

Table 2.6. Market size and lending, 1740–80

Market size (chef-lieux population)	Number of loans		Volume of lending		Stock of outstanding debt	
	1740	1780	1740	1780	1740	1780
	Share by market size (percent)					
Paris	1	3	27	45	37	46
Over 60 thousand	1	2	5	7	5	7
10 to 60 thousand	7	8	13	10	17	13
5 to 10 thousand	10	7	10	4	9	4
Under 5 thousand	80	81	44	34	32	30
	Totals for France as a whole					
	(thousands)		(millions of livres)		(millions of livres)	
Totals for France as a whole	437	368	161	337	1,426	2,406

Source: Our sample.

ies. The per capita volume of lending was higher too, because loans were larger than in smaller markets. In Paris, it was over ten times the average for France as a whole in 1780, and over three times the French average in the other cities with more than sixty thousand inhabitants. The per capita stock of debt was higher in big cities as well, and these gaps in the per capita stock of debt or volume of loans had widened since 1740.[25]

Understanding why that urban hierarchy arises is an important problem, and not just because it sheds light on the centralization of lending in France. To explain such a hierarchy, economic geography models (see, for instance, Fujita et al. 2001 and Glaeser and Resseger 2010) often highlight two extreme outcomes. At one end of the spectrum, the spatial distribution of economic activity is so hemmed in by transaction costs that it stays close to the population of consumers (as with barber shops). At the other, transaction costs are so small that all activity in the sector takes place in a single location (as with car manufacturing when Detroit was in its heyday). Our credit markets lie in between these two extremes. Unlike automobiles or stock exchanges, lending was never channeled into a small number of locations. Unlike barber shops, though, lending was not evenly dispersed where everyone lived. The variation in the way it spread around is our incomplete centralization—exactly what we want to understand.

Variations in lending must reflect difference in demand, supply, or transaction costs. It may follow the supply of savings from lenders, so that an influx of savers into, say, La Châtre (a small city in the middle of France) will attract borrowers and raise the outstanding level of debt. More savings per resident in La Châtre would yield the same outcome. Alternatively, lending could concentrate where there is more demand—in other words, where borrowers (presumably with suitable collateral) are gathered. A boom in demand in Falaise (a municipality in Normandy), for instance, would cause more lenders to bring their money to local notaries and lead to more loans being signed there.

As for transactions costs, a city such as Avignon in the southeast of France might conceivably witness more lending than the nearby city of Nîmes because the notaries and judicial system in Avignon are more efficient at matching borrowers and lenders, drawing up contracts, and resolving insolvencies. In this case, borrowers and lenders living in the vicinity would flock to Avignon to do their business there.[26]

Clearly, there is a coordination issue here: on the one hand, if borrowers decide to congregate in Nîmes, lenders have little choice but to follow. On the other hand, if some fraction of lenders refused to do business there, then borrowers might want to track them down in their home location—for instance, Avignon. Centralization and our urban hierarchy may therefore change, because credit follows movements of the population or changes in the economy. If nobles, for example, had all moved to Paris in the eighteenth century, then credit might well have followed them, for they had the collateral to secure borrowing on a large scale, and many of them had the savings to fund large-scale loans. The same thing could have happened if Parisian nobles had grown wealthier, for their savings could fund more loans in Paris, and their assets could have secured more debt.

Could such processes account for the rise of the Paris market and for our incomplete centralization? Although the evidence is scarce, it seems unlikely. Consider the aristocracy's choice of residence. Starting in the seventeenth century, more and more of the aristocracy moved to Paris from the provinces. Later, in the second half of Louis XIV's reign, many nobles followed the king to nearby Versailles. While the first movement might have increased lending in Paris, it occurred too early for us. The flight to Versailles would have reduced rather than increased lending in Paris and it also peaked long before 1740. So aristocrats do not seem to be the explanation for the surge of lending in Paris. Something else had to be at work.

To get a better sense of the issues, let us adopt the same approach we used in chapter 1. Let us estimate the counterfactual of how credit markets might have evolved if the per capita variables of 1740 had prevailed forever. The procedure is simple. We multiply the stock of outstanding per capita debt for cantons of a given size in 1740 by the population totals

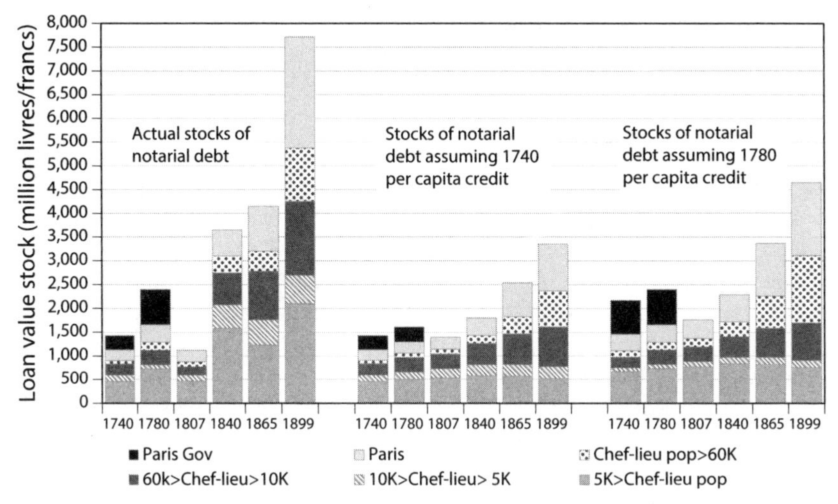

Figure 2.4. Counterfactual evolution of credit in France.
Note: "Paris Gov" are loans made to government officials like general farmers who themselves supplied credit to the crown.
Source: See text.

for markets of that size in 1780 and in the other years of our cross sections. The assumption is that the only forces changing lending are population growth and the movement of people.

We compare that result with actual stock of debt for each size category of market and for France as a whole, which is shown in the left panel of figure 2.4. The middle panel then shows the result of our simple exercise: what would happen if the per capita stock of debt remained constant after 1740 and lending only varied because of variation in the population. We extend the exercise further in the right panel, which shows the result of a similar exercise that uses not the 1740 per capita debt, but the 1780 per capita stock of debt. Both of these counterfactual calculations depict what we might expect if lending simply grew with population and people's movement across space.

Three things emerge from these counterfactual calculations. First, the actual stock of outstanding debt in 1780 was much larger than could have been foreseen by simply applying 1740 per capita debt to the 1780 populations. Notarial lending was funding a far bigger level of debt than population movements between 1740 and 1780 can explain, and it was doing so both in the smallest and the largest markets. Clearly, notarial credit was abundant in 1780, even though it was dispersed across the country and only incompletely centralized. That fact alone casts doubt on the argument that complete centralization is essential for financial development.

Second, the extrapolation based on 1780 per capita debt produces much higher totals than the one based on 1740 per capita debt. In a sense, the end of the Old Regime was thus an apex of notarial credit. But, even so, the extrapolation based on the 1780 numbers does not come close to matching the actual debt stock in the nineteenth century. Part of the reason was that government borrowing had changed. After the French Revolution, there were no longer general farmers or government officials taking out private notarial loans to fund the loans they made to the government. That sort of indirect government borrowing (chiefly in Paris) therefore disappeared from the nineteenth-century totals in figure 2.4. The change in government borrowing, though, was not the whole story. In the nineteenth century, notarial lending was also growing far more rapidly than the population, causing per capita levels to jump by 117 percent between 1780 and 1899. Clearly, the notarial credit market was dynamic, both during the Old Regime and in the nineteenth century, despite the entry of more modern intermediaries like investment and commercial banks. How notaries managed to thrive in this new environment will be a key question for the second half of the book.

The third conclusion from these comparisons is that the revolution was a massive setback for notarial credit. In 1807—a full decade after the end of the revolutionary inflation (and at a time when Napoleon's empire was at its peak)—lending stood at a mere sixty percent of the level implied by the 1780 counterfactual. Every city size category displays a decline, and the drop was sharpest in Paris. This shock and its consequences obviously deserve a chapter of their own—a subject taken up in the next chapter—but let us first consider the necessary infrastructure needed to sustain growth in lending.

The Economics of Information

Simply projecting forward per capita lending levels therefore leaves a great deal unexplained, even when it comes to elucidating the differences between 1780 and 1740. To gain more insight into what was happening in our credit markets, let us move from the demand and supply of loans to the demand and supply of financial services, the sort that our notaries provided. On the demand side for financial services we have borrowers and lenders; on the supply side we have financial intermediaries—namely, our notaries. The borrowers and lenders pay the financial intermediaries to reduce the transaction costs associated with a particular contract. These costs include what a notary or other agent might charge for arranging a loan (making a match between a borrower and a lender), for drawing up the contract, and for other fees that might improve the security of the transaction. They would also have to encompass potential harm done to the borrower or lender: the liquidity problems that the borrower might face if an intermediary's claims about the ease of rolling over a loan turn out to be wrong, and the losses the lender could suffer if the borrower defaulted. Take, for example, a lender who makes a one-year loan at five percent. She earns five percent if she gets her capital back with full interest at the end of a year. If, however, the borrower is delinquent, she will incur losses, and if he defaults and his collateral is worth less than anticipated, her losses will be bigger—if only because she may face delay in getting paid.

Delinquency and default can arise either because of exogenous events (the harvest was bad, the economy collapsed), or because the intermediary did a poor job of sifting between good and bad applicants for loans—in other words, the information he provided was poor. Similarly, a borrower could face losses if the intermediary gave him bad information about the ease with which he could renew his one-year loan. For our markets, notaries were the intermediaries; they provided what we might call the information technology. By considering how this technology works, we can come to understand one more reason why lending might vary across our credit markets—why, in other words, we end up getting an outcome that includes incomplete centralization in Paris and persistent lending in small markets.

The notaries' information technology certainly reflected local conditions. In particular, it had to reflect local custom and the varying influence of Roman law, for France, like the rest of continental Europe, did not have a unified legal system before the French Revolution. In the South of France, Roman law had enormous influence on legal practices, and it encouraged the use of notaries to draft and store legal documents. It had less influence in the north. Therefore, it stands to reason that notaries in southern France would have had a much greater store of information about property values and business transactions in their records. That information could easily be relevant for arranging loans. In contrast, northern notaries with fewer records would have had a harder time providing information.

The notaries' information technology would also have been affected by the distributions of wealth and income within their areas. The wealthy and the rich were more likely to be literate. They would also be more likely to have assets with which secure loans. Because they were literate, they would not need a notary to draw up a loan contract. But they might well be eager to consult him if he could reassure a lender about the value of the property they wanted to use as collateral for a loan.

Market size would have an impact on the notaries' information technology, as would physical distances in a world where transportation was slow. Information quality likely declined as the market population increased. It would get harder to evaluate the net wealth of individuals as the market grew because lenders and borrowers would have more opportunity to interact with more unknown third parties. Information quality also deteriorated with distance; it was simply harder to gather reliable information about faraway collateral than assets next door.

The factors that we have considered so far have all been local in the sense that they ignore connections linking different credit markets. But these credit markets were not isolated; they were not like islands in the Pacific, where outsiders rarely visit. Borrowers and lenders constantly traveled from one locality to another, and up and down our urban hierarchy. The flows of borrowers and lenders were a central feature of all of our credit markets. The implication is that although the information technology had to fit local peculiarities, it had to work across markets.

How such an information technology could develop is a central issue in the history of credit markets in general, especially when it comes to mortgages and other secured loans. The issue is discovering how seemingly different local lending practices allowed information about collateral to be transmitted over space, for in our eighteenth-century French markets, nobles and other elites could certainly borrow at a distance. Consider, for instance, Jacques Cottin de Joncy, who was a judge at the sovereign law court (*conseiller au parlement*) in Dijon, a city in the eastern French province of Burgundy. He turned to the notary Lièvre in Lyon, some two hundred kilometers south of Dijon, and used him as his agent to borrow 11,500 livres from two clients of a second Lyon notary named Baroud.[27] Cottin de Joncy's property in the Burgundian village of Joncy was a little closer to Lyon, but it was still 122 kilometers away. Or, to take another example of property owners in Burgundy, consider the the Bourrée de Corberon family. To manage their affairs, they ended up relying on notaries in Dijon, in the nearby town of Nuits-Saint-Georges, and in Paris, which lay three hundred kilometers from Dijon.[28]

For transactions to take place over such distances, lenders in large and distant cities such as Lyon or Paris had to believe that collateral pledges of Burgundian lands were valuable and plausible. That required information, and if intermediaries had not provided it, then the nobles in Burgundy could only have borrowed from other Burgundians, because each lender would have had to rely on his provincial connections to check on the collateral offered. A Parisian office holder or a Lyon merchant would not have known what the collateral was worth and so would have refused to grant the Burgundian noble a loan.

The implication is that our intermediaries—the notaries—furnished information services over a broad geographical area. That is what allowed peer-to-peer credit markets to grow even though they were not completely centralized and even though banks were not involved in the lending, as the standard story of financial development would require. Notaries did a better job of matching borrowers and lenders than other intermediaries, and certainly a better job than the borrowers and lenders could have done themselves if they had relied on their own limited personal connections. Notaries also did a better job than banks could do, at least in the case of the general farmers, who relied on them for funding rather than the numerous banks they could easily have turned to. Notaries had the advantage in that they knew what loans were safe and who had money to lend for the medium and long term. Providing that crucial information is precisely what notaries had in fact been doing for a long time. Explaining how they managed this accomplishment will be the task of chapters 3 and 4.

CHAPTER 3

The Revolution

COLLAPSE, REFORM, AND MODELING THE SPACE OF DEBT

Nine years after our 1780 cross section, the French Revolution erupted. It buried the absolute monarchy, raised up the country's first republic, and ended in the autocratic grip of the emperor Napoleon, but not before he remade the legal system and the administrative bureaucracy. Along the way, the revolutionaries battled opponents within France, both in the countryside (the Vendée, most famously) and in cities such as Lyon and Nantes. The revolutionaries and Napoleon also fought the rest of Europe, in wars that lasted until 1815. Initially, the conflict was financed by printing paper money—the *Assignats*. That triggered rapid inflation not brought under control until 1797.

Our next cross section—in 1807—leaps over most of this turmoil. We chose 1807 because in that year Napoleon reestablished the five-percent interest rate ceiling on private debts which had been lifted in 1791.[1] Although one might object to our skipping much of what happened between 1789 and 1807, our subject, it should be emphasized, is long-term change, not crises.

So instead of covering all the turbulence in detail, we will focus on the revolution's impact on credit markets and the long-term implications for lending. We begin with the revolution's fundamental institutional reforms, which shaped credit markets for the rest of the nineteenth century. We then analyze the effect of the reforms and the consequences of the revolutionary inflation. That entails looking at how borrowers and lenders reacted, both in the short and long run. It also involves examining shifts in their demand for notaries' services, whether to draw up contracts if clients were illiterate, or to secure loans with collateral.

Finally, we take up an enduring problem that came into even sharper focus after the revolution caused lending to collapse: the difficulty that borrowers and lenders had in our peer-to-peer matching markets where only a few loans were made each month. One intuitive solution is to extend the geographical reach of the pool of potential matches; in our findings, that is precisely what notaries did. To understand how peer-to-peer lending contends with this sort of spatial problem, we devise a queuing model that produces simple predictions about when borrowers and lenders would travel to nearby markets in search of a better match. The model's predictions turn out to match the data, and they suggest that if scholars want to understand lending in the past, then they should abandon the sort of local study of credit that has long prevailed in the historical literature.

Institutional Reforms

Leaving aside the revolution's gyrations does not deny its importance. For credit markets, the French Revolution was earth shattering; indeed, it was both the worst and the best of times. It was the worst of times for lenders who had handed off their capital in perpetual annuities. The *Assignat* inflation drove down the value of these annuities to next to nothing. Debtors could reimburse the annuities at any time they chose, and with the inflation, repayment in 1795 could cost them less than a hundredth of what it would have back in 1788. Understandably, most of the debtors chose to repay. Creditors suffered losses equal to debtors' gains. To make matters worse, the government consolidated the public debt in 1797, leaving government bondholders with about a third of what they had had in 1788. Among the losers were sophisticated Genevan bankers who assembled what seemed like low-risk investment pools to put money into French government debt. When the bankers began receiving debt payments in worthless paper money, they defaulted, because they owed the investors hard Genevan currency (Cramer 1946). But the losers were not just sophisticated bankers and wealthy foreign investors; they also included many women and older people who relied on government and private annuities for income. The losses were particularly severe for modest investors, who might be left penniless in old age.[2] In short, from 1789 to 1797, France was a bondholder's nightmare.

But it was also the best of times, at least for institutional reform. The revolution broke the political logjam created by the Old Regime's hodgepodge of overlapping courts, law codes, and political and fiscal authorities. They were replaced in a wave of reforms. The legal system was consolidated with civil, commercial, and criminal codes that applied to the whole of the country. The fiscal system was also unified under a common national tax regime in force everywhere. And in a move that affected credit markets, the revolutionaries abolished venality, the Old Regime practice whereby individuals who wanted a government office had to buy one. Office holders valued the positions because they provided a mix of status, tax exemptions, income from the crown, or fees paid by users of government services. Selling the offices provided the state with a convenient vehicle for borrowing in difficult times, especially in the seventeenth century. With the revolution's changes, public officials now drew salaries, and public offices ceased being a source of credit for the state.

Credit markets were affected by three other sets of reforms that we summarize here but have detailed in our previous work.[3] The first clarified the rights and obligations of real estate owners and their ability to mortgage their land. The new measures were multifaceted. Some may seem mere technicalities but they were actually important—for instance, the law of 1803 that created rules limiting the number of notaries per canton. Other measures were more spectacular, such as the complete survey of French real estate (the Cadastre) that was designed to equalize the tax burden across properties. Progress was slow, with the Cadastre not completed until the 1840s.

A whole new lien registry service, the Hypothèques, was also created, where liens and property transfers could be recorded for a fee. Although the service was available relatively quickly, it took even longer than for the Cadastre for it to become useful, for registration was still far from universal even at the end of the nineteenth century. The goal of the Hypothèques was to help publicize liens, which were now limited to specific pieces of real property. The service was voluntary, and a lender and borrower could reduce the cost of a loan by not using the lien registry, because doing so required more of the notary's time plus a registration fee that could be sizable, especially for a small loan. The virtue of registration was that it gave the lender a senior claim on the specific property that was mortgaged. (Seniority for liens on real property was determined by the date of registration, and registration would reveal earlier liens.) That could be advantageous in case of default, particularly if there were other creditors. Even so, registration might not be worth the cost. There might be no other creditors, and even if there were, registration would not help a lender seize the borrower's other assets. Furthermore, it revealed nothing about the borrower's net worth or about claims that took precedence over even a senior lien, such as court costs or the rights a borrower's wife had to her dowry. There, a lender would have to continue to rely on the notary's information, and the lender might simply be better off doing that than paying for registration. Well into the nineteenth century, as we shall see, many lenders therefore decided not to register the liens in their loans.[4]

A second set of reforms affected notaries and the Contrôle des actes. Although the revolutionaries had initially wanted to abolish all venal positions, including notaries, in the end that was impractical and politically unworkable. Under the empire, notaries were granted a status close to the one they had enjoyed under the Old Regime: they were regulated, fee-for-service enterprises. Regulation meant that the state dictated minimum competence and training, retained a veto over anyone it deemed unqualified to take a position, and controlled the number of positions and their geographic distribution.

Anyone who wanted to become a notary still had to buy a position from an incumbent. From the Napoleonic Empire forward, the necessary qualifications came to depend solely on the administrative importance of the locality where the notary's office was located. For a rural notary, a year's legal study and a couple of years of apprenticeship with a notary in a town was sufficient. Serving in a large city required both longer study and apprenticeship with a notary in a major legal center. As for the number of notaries overall, the revolution's rationalization of government finance meant that the state no longer needed to expand the corps of notaries for fiscal reasons. It instead pursued a policy of steadily shrinking their ranks, particularly in the South and east of France where the influence of Roman law had bolstered their numbers. As a result, by the 1820s every rural canton had between three and five notaries. In cities, rules based on population applied, but very few new positions were opened.

The reform of the Contrôle des actes revamped the registration system for contracts and legal documents and split it into two parts: *Enregistrement des actes civils publics* (acts drawn up by notaries or public officials), and *Enregistrement des actes sous seing privé* (acts drafted by private parties that were to be used in some legal or administrative process). While registration of notarized contracts when they were first drawn up was mandatory, it was not compulsory for private contracts drafted without a notary's help. For private contracts, one party decided whether to have them registered, and if they were registered, they would show up in the archives of the Enregistrement des actes sous seing privé. Clearly, only a selected fraction of all private contracts ended up being registered.

The third and final set of reforms did away with most of the usury legislation. Through the early modern period, nearly all of France had applied the rule that loan contracts with a fixed term could not mention payment of interest. For those contracts (annuities) with an uncertain or indeterminate term, interest rates were capped and the ceiling left at the discretion of the crown. During the revolution, the rate cap was removed, and although a five-percent cap was reimposed in 1807 (and would remain in force until 1914), obligations could now specify interest rates explicitly.

Overall, the positive reforms of the revolution should have made contracting easier in the nineteenth century than before. Yet, as we shall see, the impact of these reforms would depend heavily on how quickly intermediaries, borrowers, and lenders chose to take advantage of them.

The Impact of the Reforms and the Revolutionary Inflation

The deluge of change brought about by the revolution can be broken down into two distinct torrents of reform: one that harmed credit markets, and one that helped them. The harmful flood of change included both the rapid inflation and the end of venality (the market for government offices). Why inflation damaged credit markets is clear. It was such a negative shock to financial wealth that lenders simply shunned long-term debt contracts with fixed interest rates. As for venality, eliminating it cut the demand for loans and also removed an important source of collateral—the venal offices themselves, which could be mortgaged.[5] The disappearance of this collateral asset then reduced the size of the peer-to-peer lending market. Yet another reduction came from the decision made during the revolution to place all the government's long-term debt through bankers rather than to have it sold by notaries. Since markets of this sort often have scale economies, eliminating the notaries' role in public borrowing could harm their private loan brokerage. That certainly fits the continuing difficulties that the Paris credit market faced after 1789.

But alongside this harmful torrent, there was the second spate of beneficial changes—all the institutional reforms described above. These reforms should have reduced transactions costs in credit markets by freeing up contract choice and by making lien registration easier and thereby fostering their growth. The complication is that both harmful and beneficial changes swept over markets at the same time; the question is whether the net effect of these two contrary torrents was positive or negative. Additionally, when did the effects of the two opposing floods make themselves felt?

To answer those questions, we would ideally chart the chronology and magnitude of the collapse of credit from the late 1780s on, in *all* of our 108 markets and then do the same for the recovery of credit through the restoration of the Bourbon monarchy. The necessary research would be daunting and would have broken our research bank. But we have analyzed the relevant records for Paris (we did it for an earlier book), and we have found a unique archival document that allows us to count the annual number of credit contracts for notaries in the department of the Gard in southern France. The sources from Paris and the Gard both trace out a similar chronology, and along with the evidence from our sample, all point to a massive collapse of private credit markets during the revolution. In this generalized downturn, though, there were nonetheless important differences from market to market in how the collapse was felt, differences that data from our 1807 sample (and from the sources in Paris and the Gard) make clear.

We possess the document for the Gard because in 1807 the state's representative in the department, the prefect, required all the department's notaries to fill out a preprinted form that tabulated the types of contracts they had drawn up. All told, the form included thirty-five categories, including a hodgepodge residual category.[6] Most valuable for us are the four columns that total up contracts for perpetual annuities, life annuities, obligations, and *quittances* (debt repayments). The survey is not perfect, because it omits notaries' offices that closed during the revolution or during a later reduction in the number of rural notaries. The survey is also terse; it offers no information on the value of the contracts or their maturity. Yet for our purposes the survey provides ample evidence of how the revolution affected credit, and that conclusion does not depend on whether or how we reintroduce the missing notaries.[7]

As the Gard survey shows, the number of notarized credit contracts was declining after 1780, which is consistent with the long-term trend in the eighteenth century toward a smaller number of bigger debt contracts. From an average of about five thousand loans a year (of which less than two hundred were annuities), the number of contracts jumped temporarily in 1793 and then dropped to under two thousand contracts in 1796. Thereafter lending slowly recovered, and by the last year of the survey (1808) the number of loans had regained their level of the mid-1780s. But by then the market was dominated by obligations. The number of annuities had dropped to less than a third of its prerevolutionary value; they accounted for less than one percent of the loans (figure 3.1).

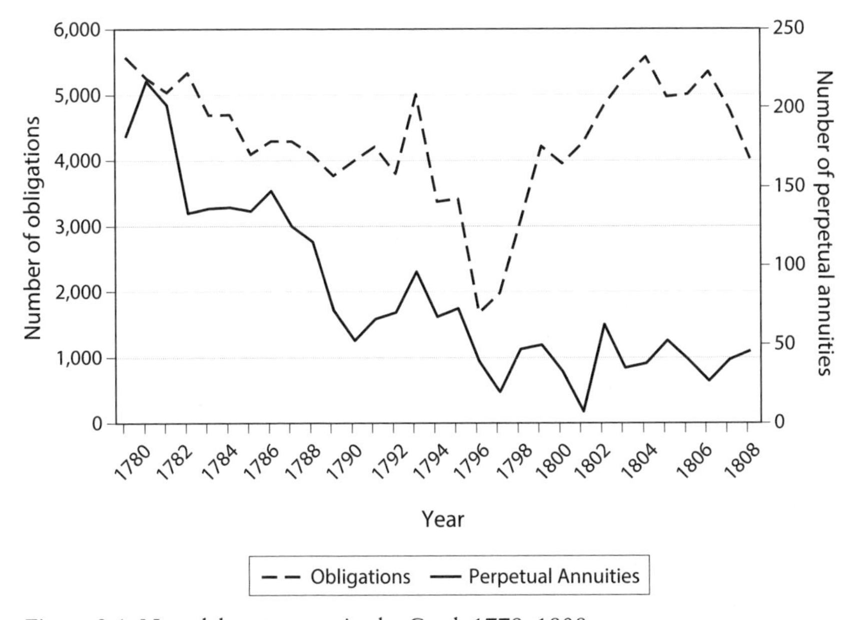

Figure 3.1. New debt contracts in the Gard, 1779–1808.
Note: When the Revolutionary Calendar was in effect, the years have been fitted to the Gregorian Calendar.
Source: AD Gard 6M 728–31.

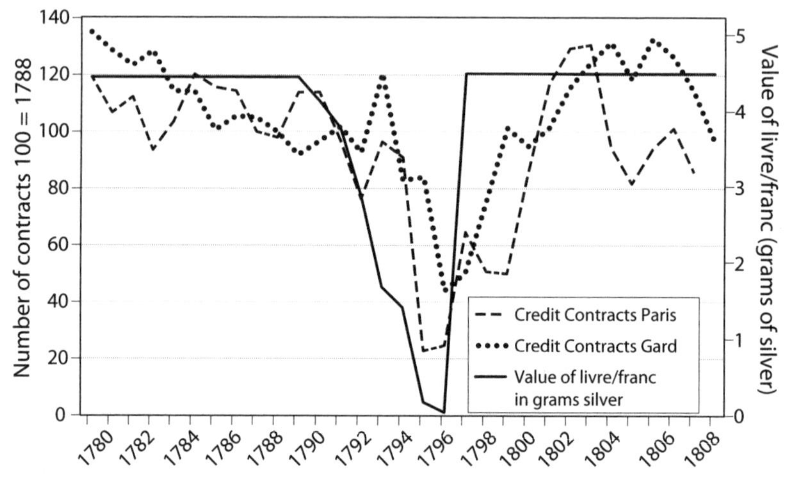

Figure 3.2. Obligations during the revolution. Credit contracts in the Gard and Paris, 1779–1803 (1788 = 100).
Source: See text.

The trend in total credit contracts we find in the Gard is nearly identical to what we see in Paris—a striking parallel (figure 3.2). This pattern, which in the Gard was common, from the city of Nîmes to the smallest villages, shows that for credit markets, as for so much else, the revolution was truly a national event. This should serve as a warning to anyone who mistakenly believes that rural villages were cut off from the financial and economic turmoil during that period. Although the villagers may have gotten news after a delay, they did act on it and did not behave as if their local social structures insulated them from the incentives created by rapid inflation.[8] Their markets, and indeed all markets in France, were devastated by the revolutionary inflation at more or less the same rate—the inflation was a true macroeconomic event.

Although the sources from Paris and the Gard trace out a similar chronology both for the collapse of credit during the revolution and for the subsequent recovery, the magnitude of the decline varies greatly from market to market. The same is true for the recovery. Both the collapse and the revival depended on the size of the market. This heterogeneity among the markets is clear if we compare the stock of outstanding debt in each of our markets in 1807 with the stock back in 1780, before the revolution (figure 3.3). The range of variation is huge, and just as big if instead we look at the per capita stock of debt.

At the bottom, experiencing the worst damage, are the markets of Nuits-Saint-Georges in the eastern French province of Burgundy and L'Isle-sur-Sorgues in in the southern region of Provence, where the total

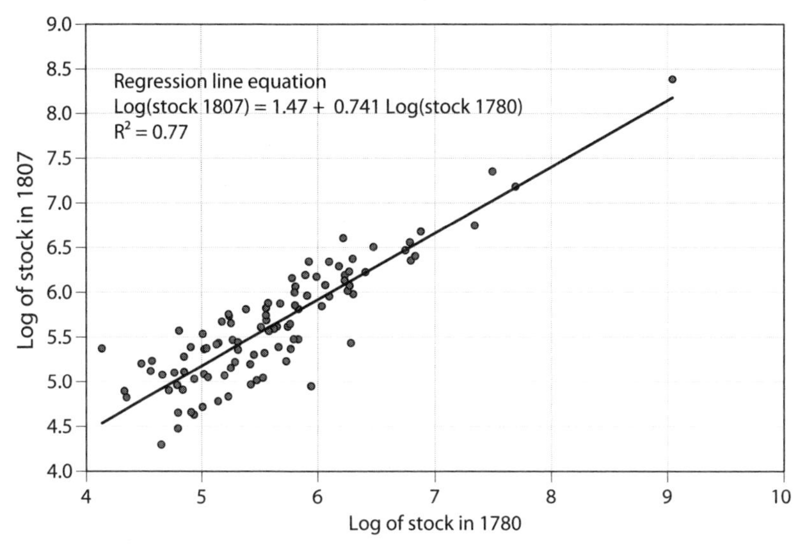

Figure 3.3. Total debt stock in our markets, 1780–1807.
Note: The markets are the cantons in our sample.
Source: Our sample.

debt stocks in 1807 shrank to only ten percent of what they had been in 1780. The destruction of Nuits-Saint Georges's market was probably the result of the complicated redistribution of land that occurred in that area, for it was a canton with major religious and aristocratic properties that were confiscated by the revolutionary governments and then sold to individuals. The demise of the market in L'Isle-sur-Sorgues likely reflected the end of the town's status as part of an enclave of papal rule. When the enclave was integrated into France in 1790, the town lost the advantages of having a more stable papal currency and more relaxed papal credit regulations than in nearby communities in Provence that had not been subject to papal rule. Thereafter, investors in these communities had little reason to place their funds in L'Isle-sur-Sorgues' credit market. At the other extreme from the moribund Nuits-Saint-Georges and L'Isle-sur-Sorgues, we have the booming credit market of Buzançais in the center of France, where the total stock of debt jumped by an astounding factor of seventeen between 1780 and 1807. There were a number of other markets as well where lending grew by a factor of two or three over the same interval.

To extrapolate from our markets and estimate lending for France as a whole in 1807, we have to combine the contrasting patterns of growth in some markets and decline in others. About half of our markets grew between 1780 and 1807. But the largest markets suffered declines, and that was true within each size class if we classify markets according to

Table 3.1. Market size and lending, 1780–1807

Market size (chef-lieux population)	Number of loans		Volume of lending		Stock of outstanding debt	
	1780	1807	1780	1807	1780	1807
Market size category	(thousands)		millions of livres/francs		millions of livres/francs	
Paris	9	7	152	71.2	1,110	242
Over 60 thousand population	6	6	20.9	25.4	168	107
10 to 60 thousand	28	34	33.6	49.6	304	179
5 to 10 thousand	25	50	14.4	34.9	87.7	125
Under 5 thousand	276	258	107	142	728	467
Totals for France as a whole	345	354	328	323	2,398	1,120

Source: Our sample.

population. As a result, the overall stock of debt dropped between 1780 and 1807 in all but one of our five size categories and in France as a whole as well (table 3.1).

As table 3.1 shows, notaries drafted nearly as many credit contracts in 1807 as in 1780 (354,000 versus 345,000, well within the error bounds of our procedures). The rough stability in the number of loans is true both in the countryside and for cities. The volume of lending also changed little (323 million francs versus 328 million in 1780). But the stable number of loans and volume of lending mask a dramatic collapse in the debt market's growth rate: from nearly a two-percent annual rate of increase in the volume of lending between 1740 and 1780 to essentially nothing between 1780 and 1807. They also hide a massive spatial redistribution of credit: the volume of lending grew in markets with populations below 60,000 people, stood still on average in larger cities other than Paris, and plummeted in the capital (table 3.1). Maturities also plunged, falling nearly fifty percent.[9] The stock of debt tumbled by more than half, from 2.4 billion francs in 1780 to only 1.1 in 1807. The revolution (and in particular, the assignat inflation) therefore set lending back in France, not because it delayed the arrival of credit markets but because it traumatized markets that had been thriving.

But the consequences for credit markets were not limited to damage. The revolution also hastened a striking transformation in the type of loan contracts borrowers and lenders chose. Between 1780 and 1807, the obli-

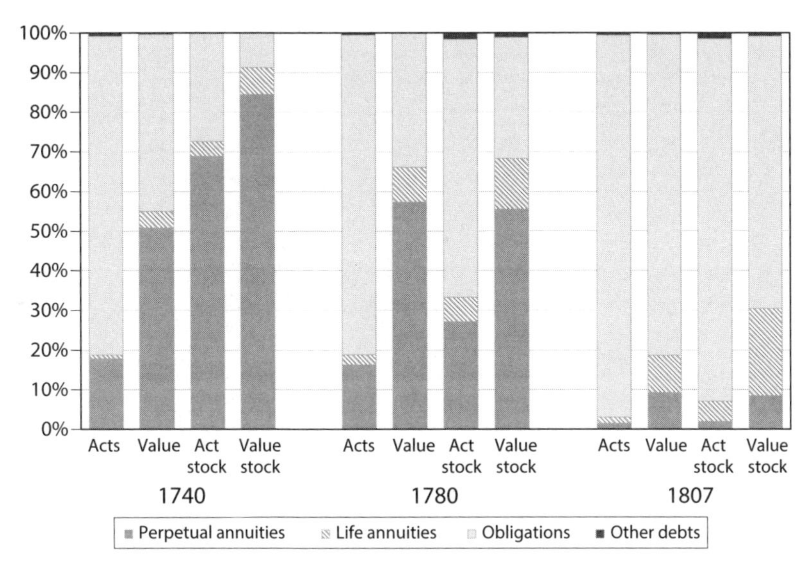

Figure 3.4. Debts by contract type.

gation pushed aside annuities and came to dominate credit markets. That was true whether for the number of loans, the volume of lending, or the stock of outstanding debt (figure 3.4). While the obligation gained significant market share over the eighteenth century (moving from ten to thirty percent of the debt stock), the revolution made it the overwhelming choice. By 1807, ninety-six percent of all new loans were obligations, which accounted for seventy percent of the outstanding debt. The disadvantage of both the perpetual and life annuities was that they kept lenders from having any control over repayment of principal; lenders therefore faced both the idiosyncratic risk of default and the aggregate risk of inflation. Obligations mitigated both those problems, leaving lenders little reason to accept annuity contracts.[10] Moreover, lenders kept obligation maturities short (a year or two) to limit their exposure to inflation. If inflation accelerated, they could simply refuse to roll over the loan.

This transformation was what drove the fifty percent drop in the average duration of loan contracts. Both life and perpetual annuities had an expected duration of about fifteen years. Obligations in 1807, by contrast, lasted only about a year and a half, and that number had not changed, so the shift to obligations cut the stock of loans drastically, particularly since annuities were also larger. To have kept the stock of debt at the same level (assuming that the size and duration of obligations remained the same) would have required ten times as many new obligations as in 1780—an increase that is unthinkable.

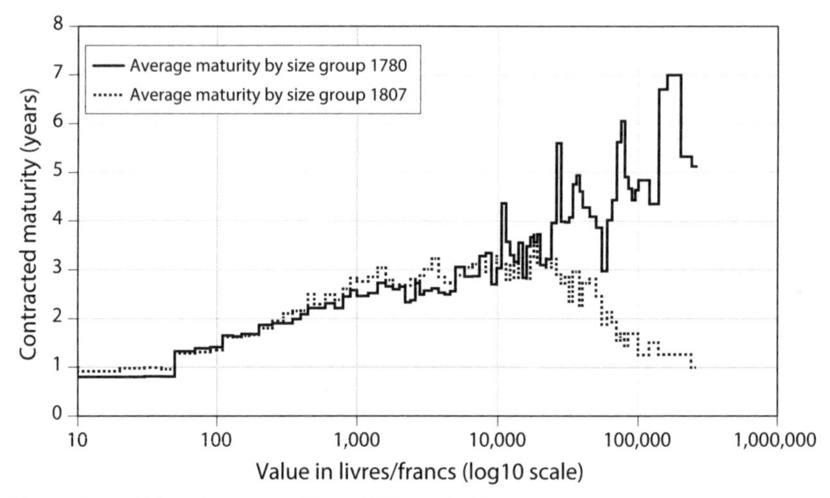

Figure 3.5. Obligation maturities, 1780 and 1807.

Although the average duration of obligations did not change between 1780 and 1807, there was a sharp difference in 1807 in the relationship between duration and loan size. The difference is a clear sign of lenders' continuing fears of inflation. Back in 1780, duration rose in lockstep with the size of the obligation. In 1807, by contrast, that relationship between size and expected maturity broke down for loans over ten thousand francs (figure 3.5). Those large loans were the ones that posed the greatest inflation risk for creditors. It is no wonder, then, that lenders refused to commit their money for such a long term. The revolution taught them to fear inflation, and they acted accordingly.

Overall, credit markets were harmed by the revolutionary inflation. The damage, as we have seen, was particularly severe in large cities. Lenders reacted everywhere, and not just in large cities, by abandoning annuities in favor of obligations and by avoiding long-term commitments of large sums. Borrowers shifted to obligations too, because the supply of funds for annuities had shriveled up. But these were not the only effects that the revolution had upon credit markets.

Literacy and Collateral

Beyond the assignat inflation and the institutional reforms, the revolution also affected demand for notaries' services. Notaries, as we know, could match lenders with creditworthy borrowers, draft contracts for the illiterate, and secure loans with pledges of specific collateral. Was demand for these services affected—for the two latter services in particular?

To find out, we returned to the city of Troyes and the rural cantons of Bar-sur-Seine and Arcis-sur-Aube in the department of the Aube, where we had already collected a subsample of loan contracts from the notarial records in 1740 and 1780 in order to analyze literacy rates and details about collateral pledges. We then collected two additional samples from the notarial records in these same markets in the Aube: one in 1807, and one in 1800. We gathered the earlier sample because we wanted to see how quickly individuals responded to the shock of the revolution. 1800 has the advantage that it was a mere three years after the financial gyrations of the revolution ended; it was also four years before the enactment of Napoleon's law codes, which gave France its first uniform national system of property and credit law and created French civil law.

Bar-sur-Seine and Arcis-sur-Aube were the sorts of markets that were devastated by the inflation. As one would expect, loans in 1800 were tiny: at 253 francs, the average loan size was only forty percent of what it had been in 1780. Some seventy percent of the loans involved someone who was illiterate, up from fifty-three percent in 1780 (table 3.2). In 1800, many of the loans seem to have been the culmination of transactions in which a promised payment turned out to be late. By 1807, the markets in Arcis and Bar had begun to recover. The average loan value was now twice as high as it had been in 1780, and with larger loans being made, the fraction involving illiterates had dropped to less than half.

Troyes was different. It recovered much faster from the revolution. By 1800, the average loan was already larger than in 1780. By 1807, the market had returned to an equilibrium that resembled what had prevailed before 1789: for loans under four hundred francs, most contracts involved someone who was illiterate; above that, more and more of the parties could sign their names.

The contrast between the locations suggests that the stress brought on by the revolutionary inflation reshaped the spatial organization of the debt market. Literate borrowers and lenders spurned notaries in small markets such as Bar and Arcis. The remaining lenders who were willing to invest flocked instead to the larger towns and cities like Troyes.

The use of collateral points in the same direction. Literate borrowers and lenders would be less likely to turn to notaries for help drafting a loan contract and more likely to seek their help with collateral and with other ways of protecting against default. They would be more likely to use the liens on specific real property that the revolutionary legislation emphasized. That is exactly what we see in the market they frequented—Troyes—where the fraction of loans with such liens soared from seven percent in 1780 to

Table 3.2. Signature rate and loan size in the Aube, 1780–1807

Sample year		Loan size quintile: Smallest 20 percent	2	3	4	5	All
		Arcis/Bar					
1780 (N=101)	Average loan size	74	187	325	616	1,992	639
	One party illiterate (percent)	90	55	50	45	23	53
1800 (N=42)	Average loan size	55	105	181	277	645	253
	One party illiterate (percent)	75	75	67	88	44	70
1807 (N=58)	Average loan size	131	318	600	1,075	5,169	1,496
	One party illiterate (percent)	82	50	27	67	17	48
		Troyes					
1780 (N=117)	Average loan size	41	158	427	975	3377	996
	One party illiterate (percent)	83	65	33	22	25	46
1800 (N=75)	Average loan size	171	390	769	1,504	6,018	1,770
	One party illiterate (percent)	57	27	47	40	13	37
1807 (N=330)	Average loan size	142	338	571	1045	5481	1496
	One party illiterate (percent)	55	56	50	39	12	48

Note: Average loan sizes are in livres (1780) and francs (1800 and 1807).
Source: See text.

eighty-three percent in 1800. In the smaller markets of Bar and Arcis, by contrast, only fifty-two percent of the loans in 1800 relied on specific liens.

More telling evidence for this sort of market reorganization comes from how far borrowers and lenders travelled to meet in Arcis, Bar, or Troyes in 1800. For Arcis and Bar the median distance for both borrowers and lenders stayed below three kilometers in 1780, in 1800, and again in 1807. The two markets were local and remained so both under the Old Regime and during the French Revolution, but because Arcis and Bar were also small, the lender and borrower in a loan tended to come from different villages or towns, even though they might both be from the same canton. Troyes, by contrast, was a city, and there borrowers and lenders would be more likely to find matches within Troyes itself. That is exactly what happened in 1780, when the median distance between borrowers and lenders was zero: both of them came from Troyes. But that distance jumped to three kilometers in 1800, a clear sign that borrowers and lenders (among them literate ones) were travelling to Troyes to find matches. It went on to grow further in 1807—to 4.5 kilometers, further evidence for a reshuffling of markets.

After the revolution, the Troyes market was becoming more open. In 1800, it was accommodating more borrowers and lenders from further away. The larger loan sizes in Troyes in 1800 (table 3.2) likely helped justify bearing the costs of the travel, which would have been prohibitive for smaller loans. Instead of limiting itself to borrowers and lenders from the city itself, by 1800 Troyes was serving almost the entire arrondissement, and by 1807 it was attracting even more outside lenders.

What was the cause behind this reorganization of markets? The cause was the revolution's disruption of credit markets. It had reduced lending in small local markets such as Arcis-sur-Aube or Bar-sur-Seine to the point where it was dangerously thin. There were simply very few loans arranged per unit of time, particularly when the amounts lent exceeded five hundred francs. As we have explained, prices did not clear these markets, and borrowers therefore had to wait until lenders arrived. With markets thinned out by the damage done during the revolution, the wait would grow too long. Borrowers would then travel to a larger market with more lenders, where the wait time would be less. In the Aube in 1800, that larger market was Troyes.

The logic for borrowers applies to lenders as well. And because the cost of traveling from, say, Bar-sur-Seine to Troyes was fixed and did not vary with the size of the loan, a borrower or lender who sought to arrange a larger transaction would benefit more from going to Troyes than someone who wanted to take care of a small debt. That is just what we observed in the Aube in 1800: small loans remained local, while larger loans concentrated in large towns and cities like Troyes. By 1807, local markets such as Bar and Arcis had reabsorbed more transactions because participants wanted to save on travel costs; travel to Troyes became less frequent. But because prices still did not clear credit markets, the general problem remained: How long then would borrowers and lenders wait in a small market, and how far would they travel? The problem of queuing for loans had existed under the Old Regime, just as it would later in the nineteenth century. The revolution had simply exacerbated the problem and made it stand out.

Keeping queuing costs under control, it turns out, lies at the heart of understanding how credit markets operated and the services notaries provided. To understand it, we need to build a model of the choices borrowers and lenders make about where to go to arrange loans when local credit markets are thin.

Modeling Thin Markets

Most of our credit markets had always been thin, with few transactions per unit of time. The revolution simply made them even skinnier, and they remained thin in 1807 despite a partial recovery from the havoc wreaked by the revolutionary inflation. In 1807, half of our markets saw fewer than four transactions per week, and in ninety percent of them fewer than ten loans a week. Given that the smaller markets in our sample account for about eighty percent of all of the markets in France, transactions were in fact infrequent.

The problem was compounded by heterogeneity in loan size demand and supply, so that for any given borrower or lender the actual frequency of potential matches was much smaller than the aggregate frequency of transactions. A borrower or lender would thus have to wait for a suitable partner to emerge in the local market. And because borrowers and lenders arrive randomly, queues were likely to form. In markets where too many borrowers had arrived relative to lenders, borrowers would have to queue, and where the reverse happened, lenders would.

These queues could be reduced (so we will argue below) if individual lenders and borrowers could travel to other markets to find matches. Yet traveling raised thorny problems of asymmetric information. How could a borrower who arrives in another market avoid being tagged as a bad risk? And how could a lender who travels secure information about good credit risks? In this chapter, we will put these problems aside for now and assume that borrowers who travel are identical to those who stay home and that lenders who travel have the same information about local borrowers as anyone else. In other words, we for the moment assume away the problem of asymmetric information to focus on the queuing problem. We take up the information problem in chapter 4.

In most markets, prices adjust so that supply equals demand and the market clears. But as we mentioned in chapter 1, prices in our credit markets neither rose nor fell in response to variations in supply or demand. Each local market was therefore almost sure to have too many borrowers or too many lenders—in other words, a queue, which is inefficient. What impact then did this inefficiency have on the development of markets? Was it more severe in the countryside or in cities? Did markets evolve to minimize the cost of these priceless interactions? One extreme hypothesis would be that the incomplete centralization of the credit markets that we observed in the eighteenth century was the result of the way lending was structured, with peer-to-peer loans arranged by small-scale local brokers. With that structure, in other words, lending would never be completely centralized, and the standard story of financial development dominated by big banks and major exchange would simply not apply.

To answer these questions, we have to model how queues developed and when borrowers and lenders decided to travel. To keep things simple, consider a situation where individuals come to the market to borrow or lend for personal reasons. In short, they arrive randomly. Consider someone who wants to borrow. He may face two situations. In the first situation, there are excess lenders, so he is matched to one of them immediately. In the other situation, there are already borrowers waiting to be matched. Our borrower must therefore decide whether or not to join the queue and wait his turn for a lender. In a market that is isolated, not joining the queue means going about his affairs with only his resources. Notice that delay here acts like a price: the longer the queue, the dearer the credit. If the market is not isolated, our borrower must consider whether to travel to a market that has a queue of lenders. In doing so, he shortens both the queue at home and the queue in the other market and thereby reduces the inefficiencies of long wait times. But travel is costly; that is the problem he faces.

In appendix B, we develop a formal model of this problem in two steps: first by analyzing the single isolated market and then by considering the more realistic case of two or more markets. Readers interested in seeing how the model works should jump to appendix B. Here we will simply sketch the model's key implications. We will test these implications later in this chapter using actual evidence of how far borrowers and lenders traveled.

The simplest version of the model—with just a single credit market—already has some interesting implications when travel is costly. Borrowers or lenders will almost always face queues, even when they have outside options. But the time they can expect to spend waiting in the queue will diminish as the market's population grows, because the interval between new arrivals will fall.

When there is more than one credit market, travel can reduce the length of the queues (and hence the market inefficiency) by letting individuals leave markets with long queues and go to ones with shorter wait times—in particular, larger markets. Whether or not to travel will depend on whether the borrower in our example prefers to pay the travel costs and be matched immediately or instead decides to bear the cost of waiting at home and thereby save on the travel costs. If we analyze the travel decisions and assume that lenders have no trouble determining whether borrowers are credit worthy, then our model has the following implications:

- Travel costs will limit the distance borrowers and lenders will go to find a match.
- If travel costs are high enough, travel will be rare.
- Traveling to find a match will be more likely for large loans.
- Borrowers and lenders will prefer traveling to larger markets than to smaller ones, because the wait times (for queues of the same length) will be shorter in the larger markets.

Evidence of Travel

There are several ways to test the implications derived from our model. The simplest one is to ask whether borrowers and lenders came from the same place. If not, then one of them must have traveled some distance.

If we take the most restrictive definition of being from the same place (namely, residing in the same municipality, which means the same village or city), then we can see that travel is common in 1807, particularly in small municipalities (table 3.3). For borrowers who lived in municipalities with less than five thousand individuals, at least half contracted with people who lived in another municipality, and the pattern of contracting with these "strangers," particularly in tiny markets, strengthens in our later cross sections.[11] The higher likelihood that borrower and lenders travel when they are from smaller markets certainly fits our model, for it implies that waiting times (for queues of the same length) will be shorter in big markets, making travel to them appealing.

The relationship does weaken for borrowers in Paris and, after 1840, in other large cities. That, however, may be the result of the greater frequency of large loans in the biggest cities, because larger loan sizes also encouraged travel. Travel from small municipalities to larger ones could also be the result of other causes besides shorter wait times, including lower transportation costs along routes leading into larger cities. The travel costs may have been lower because those roads had been improved earlier, or because the cities could be reached by water transportation (Lepetit 1984). Still, the evidence of travel out of small municipalities is what our model predicts.

There were also limits to the distance borrowers and lenders would travel, as our model would lead us to expect. In 1807, the fraction of borrowers who voyaged outside their department (which on average were about twice the size of the typical US county) in search of a loan was extremely small: it varied slightly depending on the size of the borrower's market, but never exceeded eleven percent. The same was true of lenders in 1807, except in the biggest markets, where the lenders' willingness

Table 3.3. Percent of loans with borrowers and lenders from the same municipality, 1807–99

	Population of borrower's municipality				Population of lender's municipality			
Municipality size	1807	1840	1865	1899	1807	1840	1865	1899
Paris	92	72	64	58	76	61	68	42
100,000–500,000	93	89	74	67	49	50	63	61
20,000–99999	86	77	75	66	49	43	50	58
5000–19999	71	67	58	52	46	37	44	42
2500–4999	51	49	47	39	45	43	44	35
1000–2499	43	35	34	21	53	46	39	28
500–999	31	24	24	17	47	40	33	23
Less than 500	24	17	21	20	39	29	27	27

Note: Percentages are calculated relative to the total number of loans with residences for both borrowers and lenders. Loans where the borrower's or lender's residence is unknown are omitted.
Source: Our sample.

to set out was likely the result, once again, of the large loans they wanted to make. But for the other lenders and for nearly all borrowers, travel rarely exceeded thirty kilometers.

The distance a borrower or lender would go for a loan rose with the size of the loan contract, as in our model. In 1807, that relationship held in markets both small and large, except for Paris and the biggest cities (figure 3.6). There, travel diminished for the largest loans, perhaps because the distribution of wealth in one of these big markets made it easier to find a single investor who could fund the entire loan in the city itself. That would mean that the loan would not have to be broken up into smaller transactions.

Logit regressions using data from all of our cross sections confirm our model's predictions. From the regressions, we can estimate the effect of market population and loan size on a borrower's and lender's decision to travel. Our measure of travel is, once again, simply whether the borrower and lender came from different markets. (Asking whether the borrower or lender traveled to the notary leads to similar results.) We estimate the effects separately for small, medium, and large markets in case the decision to travel was affected by the higher wealth in large markets and the availability of a notary in the smallest ones. For similar reasons, we included other covariates that might affect the estimation (table 3.4).

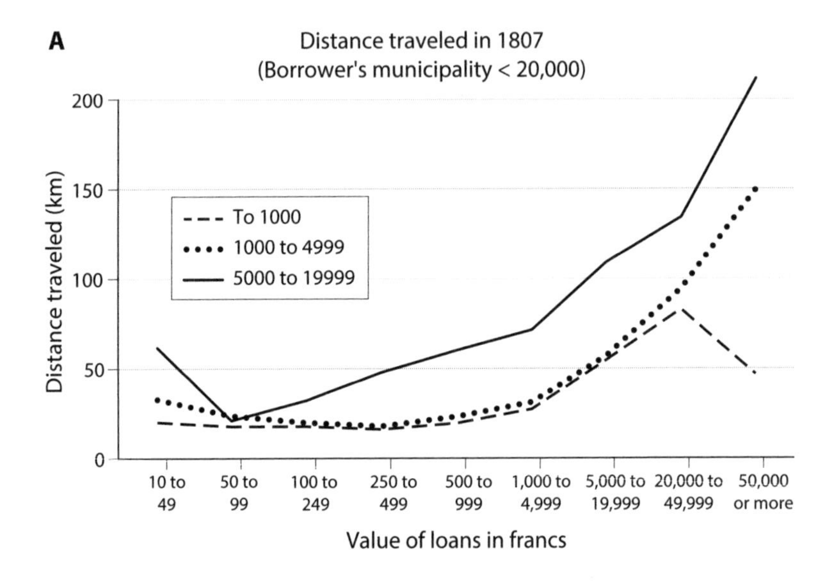

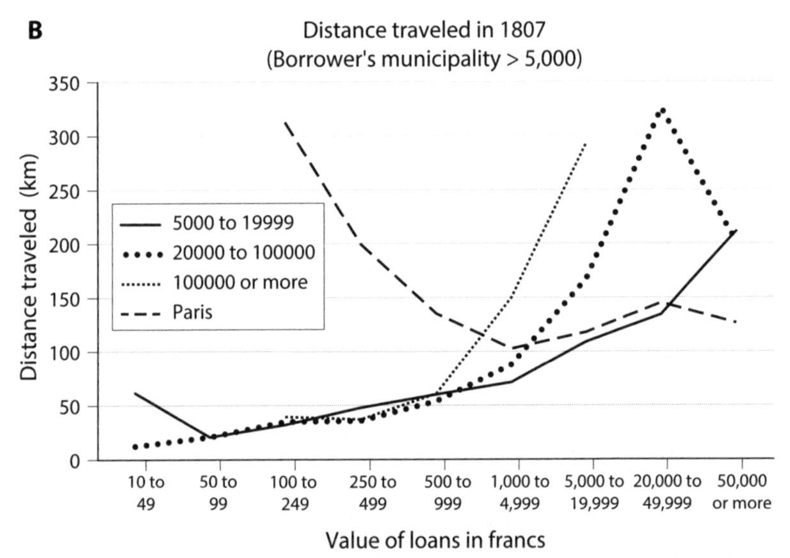

Figure 3.6. Distance traveled, loan size, and size of market, 1807.
Note: Distances in these figures are pulled up by outliers. Using medians or the 75th percentile produces similar results.

Table 3.4. Logit analysis of the probability that borrowers and lenders travel

	Marginal effect on the probability of traveling		
	Sample restrictions on markets		
Explanatory variable	Population < 5000	Population between 5,000 and 20,000	Population ≥ 20,000
Population of borrower's market (thousands)	–0.073***	–0.013***	0.00065
Loan size (millions of livres or francs)	30.9***	16.6***	0.0055
Loan size squared	–.28***	–.58***	–0.0047
N	67305	14413	30313

*** = $p < 0.001$; ** = $p < 0.01$; * = $p < 0.05$

Note: The marginal effects were estimated from logit regressions using all of our cross sections and averaged over all observations in each regression. The regressions included fixed effects for each year; for summer and fall seasons, to account for possible seasonality; and for markets in the north of France, where there were fewer notaries. The dependent variable equals 0 when borrowers and lenders resided in the same market. Otherwise, it is 1, meaning that either the borrower or the lender had to travel to complete the transaction. Market population was the population of the borrower's market.

Source: Our sample.

In the small and medium markets, greater market size discouraged travel. In other words, borrowers and lenders left small markets for larger ones, just as our model predicted. In large markets—those with over twenty thousand inhabitants—greater market population actually encouraged travel, but the effect was minuscule. In these large markets, there was thus little reason to travel.

As for greater loan size, it encouraged travel in the small and medium markets, as our model would lead us to expect, at least for loans that were not too large. But the effect disappears in the largest markets. That matches the nonlinear relationship between loan size and actual distance traveled that we see in figure 3.6.

Our model seems to work fairly well, then, for all of our samples. Borrowers and lenders did travel, particularly when they lived in small markets or sought out large-scale loans. The implication is that lending was not limited to one's neighbors or friends or to other local borrowers whom the lenders knew well, as much of the historical literature on credit markets assumes. To appreciate just how extensive the traveling was (and how far the notarial lending markets were from being closed), consider a canton with a chef-lieu population of less than five thousand, which would be typical for one of our rural bureaus. In 1807 in such a canton, fifty-nine percent of loans involved a borrower and lender who were not from the same municipality and a full third had a borrower and lender who were not even from the same canton. These numbers were even higher in later years. Our model of queues, which takes seriously the inefficiencies of local peer-to-peer lending, predicts that borrowers and lenders will cross geographical boundaries with increasing frequency as their home municipality gets smaller and as travel costs fall. That is just what we observe.

For those who believe that credit markets are part of an economy based on neighborhood, local hierarchies, and reputations among people who all know one another well, these nonlocal loans are difficult to explain. At best, they would be errors that local reputations would not predict. Yet these nonlocal loans are simply too common to dismiss as errors, and since we find them in all our cross sections, they must be integral to the local economy.

Conclusion

The peer-to-peer mortgage markets in France were thus both local and yet integrated with other markets. They were local because at least half of all transactions occurred between a borrower and a lender who lived less than ten miles apart. But they were integrated: in at least a quarter of the loans the borrowers and lenders came from different markets, and in fifteen percent of them they lived more than thirty miles apart. Because these loans where borrowers and lenders traveled were the large ones (just as our model would lead us to expect), the amount of capital involved was huge. This large-scale circulation of capital raises a new set of questions involving the circulation of information. When so much capital was at stake and borrowers and lenders were not neighbors who knew each other well, how did the borrower find the willing lender? And how did the lender decide that the borrower was creditworthy or that his collateral was valuable? We can reject here the ideas that all individual lenders could resolve problems of adverse selection and moral hazard. Too many borrowers lived far away, meaning that lenders could not know enough about them or monitor them closely. The only possibility is that there was an information system that solved the information problem and matched up borrowers and lenders. That is the topic of chapter 4.

CHAPTER 4

Networks of Knowledge

In the wake of the French Revolution's devastating inflation, local, peer-to-peer credit markets recuperated slowly. After such enormous losses, conditions for lending were hardly promising. Worse yet, one of the major revolutionary reforms that would eventually bolster credit markets—the Hypothèques registers created to record liens—took decades to take hold, particularly outside Paris. Furthermore, the modern financial institutions that arose during the revolution and under Napoleon (the Banque de France, established in 1800 and given a monopoly on the issue of bank notes in 1803; and the Paris Stock Exchange, or Bourse, which revived as the center for trading government debt after 1797) did little to promote lending in the French hinterland in the first half of the century.

Yet despite these obstacles, credit markets did grow outside Paris and they did so substantially. By 1840, the stock of debt outside Paris exceeded its Old Regime peak. As figure 4.1 shows, eighty-seven percent of our sample markets had a larger debt stock in 1840 than in 1780. (The markets with a larger debt stock in 1840 than in 1780 are the ones lying to the left of the 45 degree line in the figure). Nearly all of the markets exceeded their 1807 levels as well, for the triangles are above the black circles. Clearly, the three decades between 1807 and 1840 was a time when notarial credit revived and expanded.

Explaining this recovery is the chief goal of this chapter. The first step is to analyze the growth in lending; we then turn briefly to the reasons why the credit revival varied from place to place and, in particular, why Paris lagged behind. But the big question raised by our evidence is how peer-to-peer credit markets could thrive both before and after the revolution in the face of an enormous problem of asymmetric information.[1] The problem was that the lenders did not usually know whether borrowers were good credit risks or not. How could they find increasing numbers of creditworthy borrowers with solid collateral when they knew little about credit histories or the value of assets backing loans?

The difficulty here was especially severe when borrowers and lenders traveled, as we know they did. We will illustrate the problem with a telling example and with evidence from loan maturities, and we will explain why the Hypothèques registers were not yet of much help. The solution came from notaries who arranged loans and shared information by referring

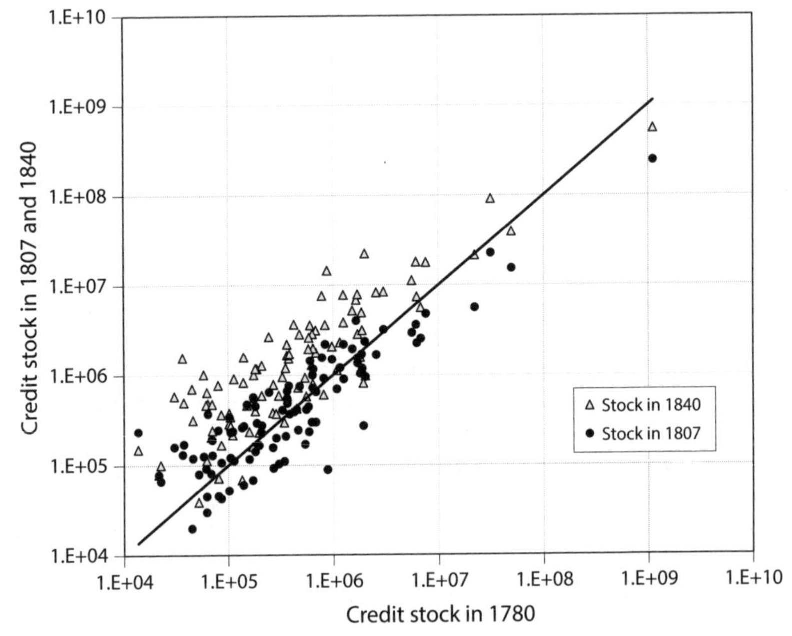

Figure 4.1. Credit stock in 1780, 1807, and 1840.
Note: Although credit stocks are nominal, a graph of real stocks would be identical, because the nominal currencies (livres in 1780 and francs in 1807 and 1840) all had the essentially the same value in silver.
Source: Our sample.

borrowers and lenders to one another. Along with heightened demand for long-term loans, this information sharing via referrals was what made the growth in lending possible. We therefore model how the sharing functioned and then use our data to confirm that the model works. The model offers the ultimate explanation for the recovery; it reveals how notarial credit markets grew well beyond simply being Lilliputian islands of lending, with long waits for loans and imbalances between demand and supply, and how they ended up allocating funds across space.

Recovery Almost Everywhere

In 1840, the stock of outstanding notarial debt in France came to about 3.7 billion francs, three times the total for 1807 and about sixty percent more than in 1780 (table 4.1). To put these numbers in perspective, the national debt in 1840 stood at 4.5 billion francs, and French national income amounted to eleven billion francs. The stock of notarial debt was

Table 4.1. Estimated notarial lending, 1807–40

	Number of loans (thousands)		Volume of lending (million francs)		Stock of debt (million francs)	
	1807	1840	1807	1840	1807	1840
Paris	7	6	71	129	242	547
Rest of France	355	550	258	643	878	3103
Total	362	556	329	772	1120	3650
Growth rate for France, 1807–40 (percent/year)	1.30		2.58		3.58	

Source: Our sample.

twenty-seven percent of national income, and it had expanded about 3.5 percent a year since 1807, much faster than the economy as a whole, which was progressing at less than a one-percent annual rate.[2]

For now, let us leave Paris aside, because the growth of lending in Paris (2.5 percent annually since 1807, from the figures in table 4.1) was much slower than in the rest of the country. There, in what we will call the provinces for short, the stock of debt had been climbing 3.8 percent per year since 1807, multiplying it nearly fourfold (table 4.1). The conclusion seems clear: outside Paris, the revolution was a transitory phenomenon for notarial credit markets. Despite all of its violence and destruction, its economic effects were erased over the course of a long generation, at least for the notarial credit market. To a development economist, this may seem like an extraordinarily slow recovery, but to a historian, the recovery from the revolution and its hyperinflation was quick.

To understand this process of growth, we can break down the stock of debt, which equals the number of loans times their average value times their duration. The stock changes when any one of these three values changes. The mix of contracts had of course changed during the revolution as well, as we explained in chapter 3. Obligations in 1840 accounted for eighty-five percent of the stock of debt; of the rest, nine percent were life annuities.

If we start with the number of loans outside Paris, it soared well above a half million credit contracts in 1840 (table 4.1). That exceeds, by a long shot, the counts in any of the other cross sections. The number of loans outside Paris in 1840 was more than fifty percent higher than in 1780 or 1807. If borrowers and lenders had had the same propensity to contract

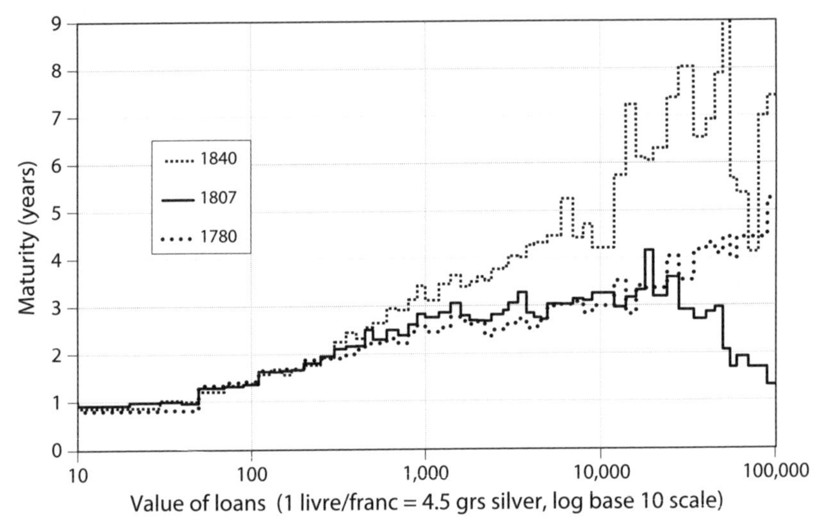

Figure 4.2. Contracted maturity as a function of loan size.
Source: Our sample.

in 1807, then the stock of provincial debt that year, instead of succumbing to the revolutionary turmoil, would have actually surpassed its prerevolutionary peak.

Loan maturities outside Paris also jumped in 1840 to 4.8 years, up from only 3.4 in 1807. That too added to the stock of debt. The figures are nearly identical for France as a whole. Under the Old Regime, notarial lending had been split between long-term annuities and medium-term obligations, whose maturities ranged from one to four years. In the provinces, obligations before the revolution were small, and maturities rarely exceeded two years. In 1807, as we saw in chapter 3, maturities matched those of 1780 up to about fifty thousand Francs (figure 4.2). Beyond that level, loans were overwhelmingly Parisian. By 1840, the duration of loans had changed again. For loans above two hundred francs (sixty percent of the number of loans and ninety-six percent of the value of the loans made), maturities exceeded those in the past and by an increasing amount for larger loans. For a three-thousand-franc loan, the maturity in 1840 was a year longer than it had been in 1780 (figure 4.2). If loans in 1807 had the same maturity as in 1840—and nothing else in 1807 had changed—then provincial credit would have already exceeded the level attained back in 1780.

The last driver of growth in 1840 was loan size, which surged sixty-one percent outside of Paris, more than either the number of loans or their maturity. By itself, that increase explains thirty-eight percent of the total

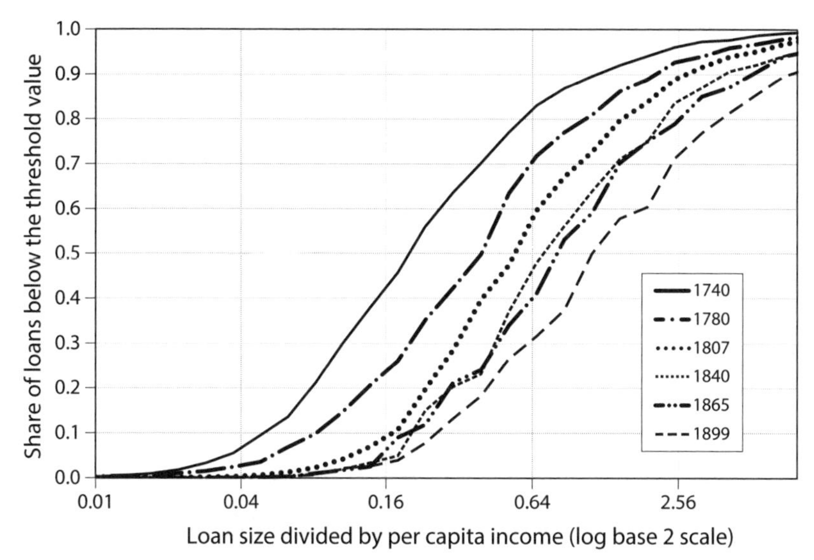

Figure 4.3. Cumulative distributions of loans (below 4 times per capita income).
Note: Loans from inside Paris excluded.
Source: Our sample.

growth in stocks outside Paris between 1807 and 1840, while the number of loans accounts for about thirty-five percent and longer maturities twenty-eight percent. Over the long run between 1740 and 1840, the median loan outside Paris had grown by a factor of four.

To see how loan sizes evolved, we divide loans by per capita GDP in the year of the cross section and graph the resulting distribution of loan sizes. We break the graph into two pieces. (As in the rest of this section, the calculations omit loans in Paris.) The first part of the graph (figure 4.3) gives the distribution up to four times per capita income. (The scale is in log base 2.) The progressive shift in the loan size distribution outside of Paris is striking. Despite significant growth in loan size under the Old Regime, the median loan did not reach half of GDP per capita before the revolution. By 1807 it had reached seventy-five percent of per capita income; as this trend continued, by 1840 the median loan was just about equal to per capita income. This same shift to the right works for other critical values of the distribution. The ninetieth percentile of the distribution is reached, for instance, before loans are twice GDP per person in 1740 and 1780. After 1807, by contrast, that threshold surpassed three times individual income.

Behind this change in the size of loans lay a shift in what the loans were accomplishing. Under the Old Regime, people had notaries draw up a

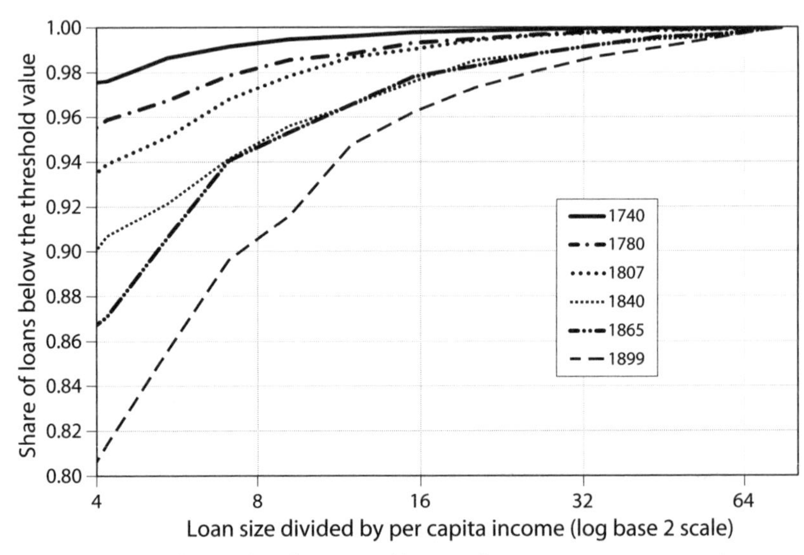

Figure 4.4. Cumulative distributions of loans (above 4 times per capita income).
Note: Loans from inside Paris excluded.
Source: Our sample.

variety of credit contracts for many different purposes and for debts large and small. In the nineteenth century, notarized loans were progressively becoming what we think of now as mortgages: loans secured by real estate and amortized over a long period. The increasing durations and loan sizes were signs of the shift.

Consider now the top range of the distribution, for loans above four times per capita GDP (figure 4.4). Once again, loans from inside Paris are excluded.[3] For these large loans, notarial credit took a different path. In 1807, the devastation caused by the French Revolution stands out clearly: outside Paris, there are essentially no loans more than twenty times per capita income. The distributions for 1840 and 1865 are then further to the right than 1780, and 1899 involved even larger loans, the result (as we shall see) of the rise of a specialized intermediary focused on delivering big loans.

Why care about these big loans—say those totaling more than four times per capita income? The reason is that they make up a huge fraction of the lending. In 1807, although only 8.8 percent of the loans made outside of Paris were that large, they still accounted for fifty-seven percent of the volume of lending. If we just focus on smaller markets with a chef-lieu of fewer than ten thousand inhabitants, loans exceeding four times per capita income still constituted forty-four percent of the value of new lending in 1807 and more than two-thirds of the value in 1899. There were thus two credit markets at work at the same time, one involving many smaller loans and another involving substantial sums.

Why Paris Lagged Behind

So far our account of the recovery has left out Paris. Its performance was strikingly different from the rest of the country. It was, in a word, dismal, with a growth rate of the stock of debt that lagged behind the rest of the country (table 4.1). Although we devoted an entire book—*Priceless Markets*—to the evolution of notarized credit in Paris, fifteen years' worth of further research makes it worthwhile to reconsider what happened there.

In that book, we emphasized how sensitive notarial credit was to political risk. The volume of new loans and the stock of outstanding debt plunged every time the fate of the political regime was in danger, as we could show with the annual data we collected in Paris. The series dropped when doubts arose about the fate of the Napoleonic Empire, and then again with the revolutions of 1830 and 1848. Mortgage lending did not actually recover until the establishment of the Crédit Foncier (a government-backed bank that issued bonds on the capital market and funded very large mortgages).

Our conclusion was that credit markets had been harmed by the political and financial transformation that the revolution had launched. But we reached that conclusion knowing little about credit markets outside Paris. The data from other markets that we have now collected makes it clear that we overstated the role of political uncertainty for France as whole.

The history of the city of Lyon, for instance, tells a story completely different from Paris, for despite dramatic uprisings by local silk workers and harsh repression during both the revolution and in the 1830s, notaries there saw an ever-increasing amount of business. The per capita stock of loans in Lyon was in fact 155 percent higher in 1840 than it had been in 1780; in Paris, it had dropped sixty-six percent. To explain this contrast by arguing that political risk weighed more on Paris than on Lyon is simply implausible. If anything, the risk should have exerted even more of a drag on Lyon, with its seething army of silk workers, and its merchants and manufacturers who had never forgotten the revolutionary era repression (Trenard 1992; Chassagne 2012). So, although fear of revolution might have slowed the growth of these markets, it did not make growth impossible.

Our new research reveals, though, that there was another reason for Paris to lag behind, besides political risk. That was the end of lending tied to government offices. The detailed sample of Parisian notarized contracts that we collected for 1780 showed that a substantial part of the growth of lending in late eighteenth-century Paris derived from the market for government offices, which was becoming centralized there.[4] In 1740, sixteen percent of the loans in Paris either funded the purchase of an office or were secured using an office as collateral, and loans of this sort totaled twenty-one percent of the stock of outstanding debt. By 1780, those numbers had jumped to nineteen percent and twenty-six percent. But the revolution eliminated the offices and with them all the lending that they generated. If we remove the twenty-six percent of loans that were tied to offices in 1780, then the stock of outstanding debt in Paris in that year would only be 821 million livres. Full recovery in Paris in 1840, without any office lending, would only involve bridging the gap between that figure and the actual 1840 stock of debt in Paris of 547 million francs. From this perspective, Paris's private lending in 1840 fell short of its Old Regime level by only 274 million francs.[5]

The missing 274 million francs are likely explained by two transformations. The first was that the revolution fundamentally altered the way the government borrowed money. Although the national debt in 1840 (4.5 billion francs) was somewhat larger than in 1780 (about four billion), it was now almost all publicly traded. Moreover, much more of it was likely held in Paris than in 1780, when over a billion francs was held by office holders scattered throughout the country.[6] The second transformation was the rise of equity markets. They now offered new assets for wealthy Parisians to invest in, with the authorized capital of registered companies in Paris reaching 213 million francs in 1840 (Lamoreaux and Rosenthal 2005). Since most partnerships were contracted for about three years and joint stock companies for even longer, the equity market was now of equivalent size to notarized credit. That had certainly not been the case in the 1780s. In sum, then, notaries were no longer so central to the investment opportunities of Parisians, and there were new forums for investment that drew away potential lenders. Those were the reasons—rather than politics—why notarial credit in Paris lagged behind.

The Problem of Asymmetric Information

Although we can understand why Paris lagged behind, we still have a big question to answer: How could the notarial credit markets outside Paris thrive in the face of enormous asymmetric information? How, in other words, could lenders find enough creditworthy borrowers to make all the new peer-to-peer loans? And how could they find sufficient solid collateral to back bigger and bigger debts? Whatever the local problem of asymmetic information, it was magnified when borrowers and lenders traveled, which we know they did. Yet somehow they overcame that problem, and they did so both before the French Revolution and after.

To see the problem with information and what conceivable solutions there might have been, let us look at a particular example. It does involve an extraordinary loan, but it will make the problem with information crystal clear, and also help us eliminate some of the possible solutions. The example comes from Nuits-Saint-Georges, a wine-making town in the southeastern region of Burgundy, where, on March 3, 1840, notary Machard drew up a loan contract that was certainly unusual.[7] It involved what turned out to be the second largest debt in our 1840 sample—a loan of 1.1 million francs for twelve years. The loan was distinctive in other respects too. The borrower was Victor Felix David, a prominent banker from the city of Dijon, thirty kilometers away. He had traveled to sign the loan contract, but the lenders lived even further away. There were an exceptionally large number of them—forty-three in all—and they hailed from Switzerland, chiefly Neuchâtel. The lenders clearly had worries about the enormous loan, because they required more than just David's signature on the contract. They in fact insisted that it be cosigned by Antoinette Coquet, the widow of Gérard Bouault, who had founded David's bank; by her three sons, Charles Antoine, Henri, and Alexis Eugène Bouault; and by her daughter, Marie Antoinette, who was David's wife. The lenders also demanded that it be secured by liens on David's and the Bouault's substantial property holdings in the arrondissements around Nuits and around Dijon, and they had the liens registered with the appropriate Hypothèques offices. What made the big loan feasible was a gigantic real estate portfolio assembled in the region by the Bouault family, a portfolio that included valuable vineyards in Burgundy.

The loan was not some attempt to fund an emerging enterprise; rather, it was the last gasp in a desperate attempt by David to stave off disaster after an economic downturn in 1839 (Jobert 1975, 1999). The bank had been reconstituted as a limited partnership (*commandite*) after Gérard Bouault's death in 1830. David, the managing partner, had invested heavily in two iron foundries and one textile mill, and when these businesses faltered in the downturn, the bank suffered heavy losses, obliging the Bouault family to come to the rescue via the huge loan. Until they cosigned it, the ownership structure of the bank (it was a limited partnership) shielded the family's landed wealth from the bank's troubles because the family members who cosigned were limited partners. Their liability for the bank's debts was limited to loss of their investment, and they themselves did not have to declare bankruptcy if the bank failed. But when they signed the big loan contract, they took on more liability because their real property now secured the loan. Unfortunately for the Bouaults, the rescue failed and by 1841 the bank was insolvent. After two years of trying to reach an agreement with the bank's creditors, David had to declare personal bankruptcy in 1843. The ultimate losses to the bank's unsecured creditors—its depositors and holders of its commercial paper—were severe: they managed to recuperate only ten percent of what they were owed. The Swiss investors, who funded the notarial loan, fared much better, however, because they were protected by their lien on the family's real estate: they were actually paid in full.

This example is striking for a number of reasons. One, obviously, is its size. Another is that it demonstrates how financial capital could flow from traditional intermediaries to the modern ones such as banks, and not the other way around.

Its importance for us, though, is what it says about the problem of asymmetric information. Our credit markets, we have learned, were thin, and borrowers and lenders traveled to arrange loans. Outside cities, the borrowers and lenders came from different municipalities in half or more of our loans (table 3.4). Travel was particularly likely, for reasons the model of chapter 3 makes clear, when the sums at stake were large, as with the gigantic Bouault loan. But how, when the borrowers and the lenders came from different places and did not know one another well, did the lenders determine that the borrowers were creditworthy and possessed solid collateral? How, in other words, did the lenders solve the problem of asymmetric information?

The issue was serious, because losses from a default could be punishing: witness what happened to the Bouault bank's unsecured creditors. The secured creditors who made the huge loan were spared such a debacle by the collateral. Its value must have been clear even in Switzerland, because the vineyards of Burgundy and their wines were prized throughout Europe. But Burgundy vineyards were exceptional; how did other lenders determine the value of collateral in a distant place if they or the borrowers traveled?[8]

There were other difficulties with lending (or borrowing) at a distance. How were the lenders in the Bouault bank loan—all forty-three of them—matched up with David? Personal connections might have linked them to him, and even given them a sense of his creditworthiness, but most borrowers and lenders would never have such ties if they traveled, or even if they lived in the same large city.[9] The lenders would never have encountered the borrowers before making the loan.

Simply registering enough collateral with the Hypothèques, as the Bouault lenders did, would not fully resolve the problem of asymmetric information, at least for most lenders, for they would still have to determine the value of the mortgaged property. Doing so, however, did not provide the lenders with any knowledge about the borrower's net worth or

Table 4.2. Family links and cosignature

	Percent contracts between family members			Percent contracts with cosigners		
	South	North	Paris	South	North	Paris
1740	2.3	1.1	8.2	0.1	0.02	1.9
1780	3.3	2.5	5.2	0.6	0.2	2.8
1807	3.4	2.6	2.4	2.1	0.5	1.7
1840	3.6	2.5	3.1	1.9	1.11	1.9
1865	2.5	1.0	1.6	0.4	0.5	2.0
1899	1.7	0.7	0.9	0.4	0.1	1.0

Note: North excludes Paris.
Source: All loans in the 99 markets.

about claims on his assets that took precedence over a registered lien. In theory, they could reconstruct part of the borrower's credit history—and so estimate his net worth—by asking the Hypothèques office for information about all the loans he had taken out. But that information would only shed light on his secured debt, and even then it would only be useful if the borrower had registered all of his loans that had been secured by collateral. Most borrowers and lenders, however, chose not to register loans with the Hypothèques, so credit histories from the Hypothèques office would not be trustworthy. In 1840, for example, we estimate that only about sixteen percent of notarial loans were registered with the Hypothèques (Hoffman et al. 2001, 229–56). Drawing reliable credit histories from the Hypothèques office would not be possible until most borrowers and lenders used it, and that, as we shall see, did not happen until much later in the nineteenth century.[10]

Another possible remedy for asymmetric information—having a large number of cosigners, as in the Bouault loan—is not the answer either. For one thing, it glossed over the difficulties of determining what the cosigners' net worth was. More important, it was not the remedy that borrowers and lenders actually adopted to guarantee repayment. Cosigners were in fact extremely rare in all of our cross sections, rarer even than lending between family members, potentially another solution to the problem of asymmetric information (table 4.2).

Other conceivable solution—social capital—is a dead end too. One might imagine that social capital would protect lenders, because the shame of default would ensure repayment and keep poor credit risks from taking out loans. But tests with an earlier version of our sample failed to detect any such social capital, and our full sample does not support it either.[11]

What then was the solution? We have a real enigma here, since our samples make it clear that difficulties with asymmetric information were, in fact, overcome. The evidence that they were surmounted is apparent not only in the growth of lending between 1807 and 1840 but also in the relationship between the duration of individual loans and the distance between borrowers' and lenders' residences. If the difficulties with asymmetric information had not been resolved, then lenders would have only lent to borrowers they knew well, such as their neighbors. In the extreme, borrowers and lenders would not have traveled at all. Or lenders would have adjusted the terms of the loan to fit the information available about the borrowers. If the borrower lived far away, for example, the lender could cut the duration of the loan, so as to give the borrower less time to engage in behavior that would endanger repayment. A borrower who lived nearby would not have to be kept on such a short leash, because his behavior could be more easily monitored.

So if the problem with asymmetric information had not been overcome, then we should observe loan durations falling with distance between the borrower's and the lender's residences. If, however, the problem had been surmounted, then that distance should have no effect on loan maturities.

Although there is too little data on maturities in our cross sections from 1807 and the eighteenth century to determine which prediction is true, we can test it in 1840. We do so by plotting loan maturities for three sets of borrower-lender pairs who live in different municipalities: loans in which they live less than ten kilometers apart; between ten and twenty kilometers apart; and over twenty kilometers apart. Each line is normalized by the maturity for loans of identical size where the borrower and lender come from the same municipality; figure 4.5 shows the results of this exercise. The graph also includes loan size, since we know that bigger loans encourage travel. As the graphs make strikingly clear, loan maturities conditional on loan size do not depend on distance between borrower and lender.[12]

A related way to test the relationship between loan maturity and the distance between the borrower's and the lender's residences is to see whether the maturity differs if the borrower came from a different canton than the lender. If the problem of asymmetric information has been overcome, then loan durations should not depend on whether or not the borrower came from the same canton as the lender. But if the problem has not been surmounted, lenders would presumably know less about a borrower who was not from the same canton and so would grant him a shorter loan. Here we also take into account the population of the market chef-lieu, because it would affect the delay a borrower would face in

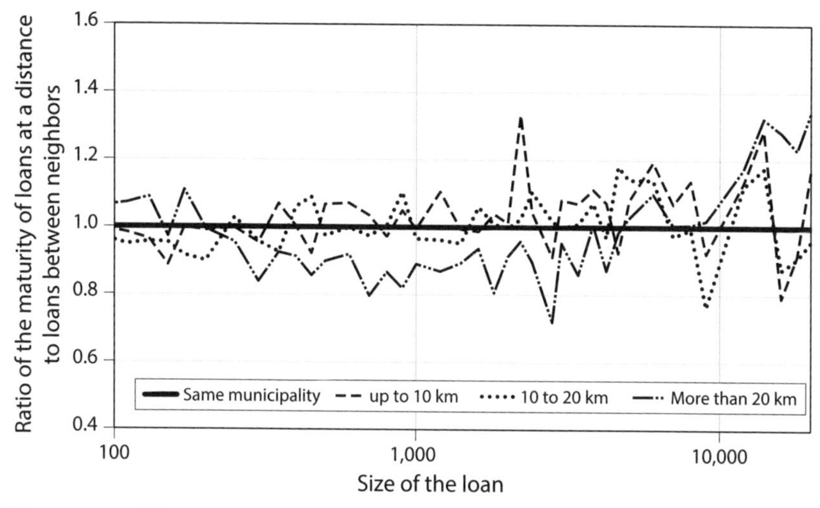

Figure 4.5. Obligation maturity by distance (relative to loans between neighbors).
Source: Our sample.

getting a loan and hence his decision to travel. For cantons with a small chef-lieu (a population under 2,500 inhabitants), lenders offered borrowers from the same canton loans of two years and three months; borrowers from a different canton received loans that were actually slightly longer—two years and four months. The difference is minuscule; the durations are essentially the same. Results are similar for larger cantons as well. In short, our data imply that individuals behaved as though the problem of asymmetric information had been overcome.

Modeling the Notaries' Information Network

But how, then, did the necessary information about borrowers circulate? It was not by lenders relying on family ties, cosigners, social capital, or the use of Hypothèques. Rather, lenders acquired reliable information about borrowers from a network of notaries. The question then becomes: Why were the notaries trusted? To the extent that they were, they could become the informational linchpin of the peer-to-peer lending system.

The mechanism that made them trustworthy is intuitive and similar to the logic that explained the pattern of lending we uncovered in Paris (Hoffman, Postel-Vinay, Rosenthal, 2000, 114–36). Because a notary's income depended on the number of contracts he drew up, he had a powerful incentive to match borrowers up with other notaries' lenders when he himself did not have an available match; that would make more matches possible than if he relied solely on his own clientele. The notary would therefore want to share his excess borrowers or lenders with other notaries who had the opposite problem. Sharing involved one notary referring a borrower or lender to another notary (a correspondent) in order to find a match. Correspondents would worry, though, that each notary faced at least a short-term incentive to pass on borrowers who were not so creditworthy or lenders who were difficult to deal with, thereby preserving the best part of his clientele for himself. Correspondents, in other words, would fear that they faced a lemons problem (Akerlof 1970). Yet at the same time, notaries did have a long-term incentive to send other notaries clients who were creditworthy: the value of future business if they maintained a reputation for being trustworthy with their correspondents and for making timely matches with their clients. If, as we argue below, this long-term incentive prevails over the short one, then the notary will take care to match up lenders dispatched by another notary with solid borrowers among his own clients. The referrals will therefore overcome the problem of asymmetric information.

This intuitive sketch of what was happening is, by and large, correct. One might be tempted to appeal to the theory of repeated games to support our argument, but the issue is not that simple, because the notaries were distributed across space. Since there were limits to how far clients would travel, a notary could only refer his clients to other notaries within a limited geographical neighborhood. But that causes complications, because a notary's own neighborhood for referrals differed from the neighborhoods used for referrals by his colleagues who received his referrals or sent him clients of their own. Thus, arguments based on a well-defined set of notaries in a locality who only deal with each other (as in a simple application of the theory of repeated games) will not work. We have to model how these different neighborhoods affected the notaries' referrals and follow through by testing the model, using our data. Only then can we really see how the obstacle of asymmetric information was surmounted. We sketch the model in the next few paragraph; appendix C contains the technical details.

Our model has to explain how notaries referred clients to one another and thereby shared information. It has to take into account the limits that geography imposed on the notaries' ability to communicate with one another, because communication would allow them to punish colleagues who misbehaved when making or receiving referrals. For our analysis, we focus on borrowers who are referred to other notaries (the case of referred lenders is identical). To simplify, we assume that there are only two types of borrowers: good ones with low probability of default, and bad ones with a higher probability of default. If information is good enough for lenders to discriminate between the two types, they will not fund the bad borrowers. But that may not be the case with borrowers who are referred by other notaries. After all, the other notaries have discretion when they make a referral. They can send either a good or a bad borrower, and the correspondent notary cannot distinguish between them. In such a situation, where information on a borrower's quality is not immediately verifiable, a one-period model yields an equilibrium where notaries refer every excess borrower, good or bad, to correspondents. If the share of bad borrowers is high enough, notaries accept no referrals for fear of falling victim to the lemons problem. In short, interlocal loans do not occur.

A more realistic model has to allow for repeated interaction, with each notary worrying that his colleagues will detect his bad referrals and then exclude him from similar deals in the future. He must also worry that if he cheats, his queue will lengthen, and his clients will desert him. Although we could have considered these repeated games as reciprocal interactions where two notaries refer clients to each other, the actual pattern of interaction among notaries suggests that something broader was at work: notaries referred clients to many fellow notaries, but their relationships with them were not symmetric, as they would be in a reciprocal interaction. If notaries had simple reciprocal relationships with one another, then we would expect the number of referred borrowers to be the same in each direction. But they are not, even if we take into account the probability that notaries would make more referrals to bigger markets, where finding a match would be easier (table 4.3). In villages with 1,000 to 2,500 inhabitants, for instance, notaries received half their borrowers from smaller markets, but a smaller number—only a third—of their lenders.

The asymmetric origins of borrowers and lenders makes a purely reciprocal relationship unlikely. And, as we shall see, there are other asymmetries in the relationships among notaries. So we have to allow notaries to interact in a more complex way than in a reciprocal relationship.

That these interactions take place in space has important consequences. Some simple geographies often used in economics (a line, a grid, or a circle) turn out to cause problems for information diffusion. To model these problems, we have to consider a more realistic geography, and to keep things manageable, we focus on the notaries' dealings with one another and set aside the question of whether notaries mistreat their own clients. We assume that reputational incentives suffice to keep notaries from ever knowingly matching up a bad borrower with a lender from their own clientele. What matters, then, is the reliability of referrals to other notaries. We have to develop a theory where that reliability derives from something besides reciprocal interactions among notaries.

The simplest geography that produces a realistic network puts each notary at the center of a hexagon of colleagues, as in figure 4.6. The notary at the center (let us call him "Home") can communicate with and refer borrowers to notaries around his hexagon. The notaries around this

Table 4.3. Origins of borrowers and lenders

Population of notary's residence	Percent of borrowers who come from			Percent of lenders who come from		
	Smaller markets	Markets of same size	Larger markets	Smaller markets	Markets of same size	Larger markets
<500	15.7	10.4	73.9	14.3	16.1	69.6
500–999	48.1	20.6	31.4	34.3	31.1	34.6
1,000–2,499	49.8	36.2	14.0	33.5	43.3	23.3
2,500–4,999	62.5	34.5	3.0	39.9	50.4	9.7
5,000–20,000	65.4	33.4	1.3	35.8	58.4	5.8
>20,000	45.9	53.1	1.0	21.4	77.4	1.2

Source: All loans in 1840 where location is identified for borrower, lender, and notary (N=46,364).

hexagon that is centered on Home we will call his neighbors. Home's neighbors, in turn, can refer borrowers not just to Home himself, but to other notaries around their own hexagons. They can also communicate with these notaries in their hexagons and tell them about Home's behavior. Their hexagons—their neighborhoods—are not the same as his. Finally, we assume a notary does not refer clients to colleagues beyond his neighborhood because of the costs of travel.

In the equilibrium of this model, Home will make reliable referrals (in other words, he will never send a bad borrower off to a colleague) if the gains from being reliable exceed the losses from being dishonest by telling the colleague that a bad borrower is good. If Home lies, then the colleague who has been cheated can tell the other notaries in his own hexagon—in other words, in his own neighborhood—that Home is unreliable. That is a penalty that Home must take into account.

If we take the incentives and the geography of strategic interactions into account, then we end up with important predictions about the pattern of referrals that we should observe. The key predictions are quite simple:

- Home will refer borrowers to only a fraction of his colleagues.
- Just because Home sends referrals to Correspondent A does not imply that Correspondent A will send referrals to Home.
- An additional correspondent can be either a complement to the existing set of correspondents or a substitute.

What we should therefore observe is that a notary should not send borrowers (or lenders, either, since the same argument applies to referrals

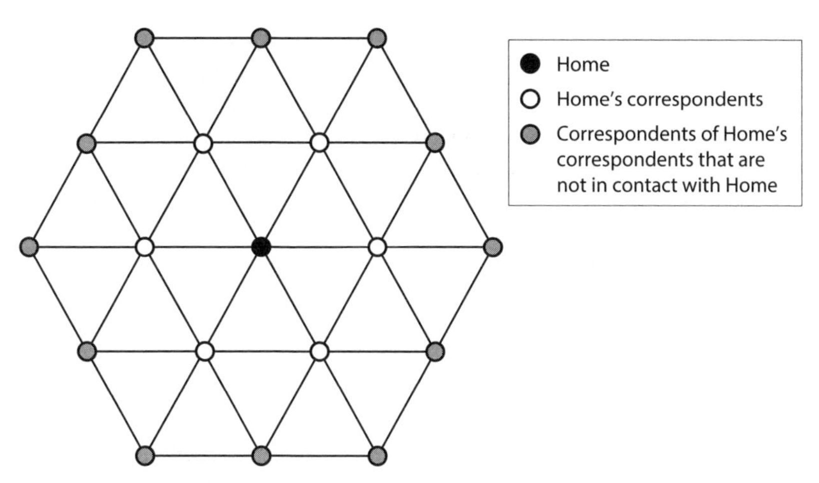

Figure 4.6. The hexagon.
Note: For the interpretation of this figure, see the text.

involving them) to all nearby notaries. Rather, he will limit his referrals to a subset of these neighbors. We will call the neighbors who receive his referrals his correspondents. They will make up only a fraction of the notaries in his neighborhood.

These predictions of the model can be compared with the predictions of two alternative models and tested with the empirical evidence of referrals. The first alternative model involves Panglossian full information, where any notary is willing to accept any other notary's referral—thus referrals are random. This model, as we shall see, predicts a high ratio of correspondents to neighbors, which is in stark contrast with the first implication of our model. The second model involves reciprocal relationships that sustain honest behavior and is in stark contrast with the second implication of our model. As we will discuss at the end of the chapter, the full information model would be the best outcome, but it is out of reach. In general, however, the hexagon model's equilibrium produces more connections than the reciprocal model, and more connections are more efficient, because they allow faster matches.

From Theory to Evidence

We can compare our model with the two other models of referrals that could also limit referrals to a subset of a notary's neighbors. In the first of these alternative models (which we will call the random referrals model), a notary's referrals are limited only by the cost of transportation; they are made randomly, without any strategic considerations. The notary should interact with more correspondents, as the number of referrals rises. If, however, referrals are rare, we might not be able to observe the full set of possible interactions, and we would just see referrals made to a subset of his neighbors. The second model, reciprocal relationships, assumes that notary pairs exchange favors. If notary A accepts referral from notary B, the reverse is also true. Further, as long as each notary has reciprocal relationships with a small number of his neighbors, that model would also yield referrals to only a subset of a notary's neighbors. We will show that the evidence is inconsistent with both the random referrals and the reciprocal relationships model. It supports, though, our hexagon model.

To test the models, we need data about referrals. For our purposes, the crucial information flows from the borrower's notary to the lender's notary. A lender will worry that the borrower may default, and he will want information from the borrower's notary about the borrower—in particular, his creditworthiness and the value of any collateral securing the loan. To get information about a borrower in one location to a lender in another requires a referral by the borrower's notary. This is true whether the borrower travels to the lender's notary or the lender comes to the borrower's notary. A borrower from the southeastern city of Avignon who goes to the nearby city of Nîmes, for example, will need a referral from a notary in Avignon. Similarly, a lender who leaves Nîmes to make a loan to a borrower in Avignon would still be accepting a referral from an Avignon notary.

Ideally, we would have evidence that the notaries were writing to one another and mentioning referrals. But notaries did not save their correspondence or any other records that mentioned referrals. The fiscal registers and original loan contracts make no mention of referrals either, nor do they speak of transactions between notaries. The one exceptional case where the accounting records of a notarial business were preserved does make it clear that the notary was in contact with other notaries and that he did carry out financial transactions for them, but that is simply one example.[13] An equally unusual list of a provincial notary's personal investments demonstrates that he relied on neighboring notaries to find reliable borrowers for his own portfolio.[14]

Although this fragmentary evidence does fit the model's predictions, there is no other direct evidence of referrals. We can, though, use information about the identity of the notary who completes a loan contract, and about the residences of the borrower and lender, to infer the patterns of referrals. To employ this indirect evidence, we needed a denser sample of markets that would include all of a notary's potential neighbors. So we took a subset of our markets and gathered additional data on lending in all the neighboring cantons in 1840 and 1865. This denser sample included 111 cantons: seventy-two in the south and thirty-eight in the north. [15] We needed the denser sample to make sure we observed all referrals (at least within the limits of transportation costs), and not just those limited to our core sample. Specifically, we consider the loan contracts in this denser sample where the borrower came from one of the 111 cantons and the lender from a different one of the 111 cantons.

One problem with these loans is that we can observe when a notary accepts a referral but we cannot tell which notary sent it to him. When, for example, a notary in Nîmes draws up a contract between a borrower from Avignon and a lender from Nîmes, we know that the notary has accepted a referral from Avignon, but we do not know which notary in Avignon has sent it. Similarly, when the notary in Nîmes draws up a contract between a lender from Avignon and a borrower from Nîmes, we know that a lender has been dispatched by a notary from Avignon but, again, we cannot tell which one. However, this lack of information about precisely which notary is referring borrowers or lenders is not a severe sacrifice. We end up having enough information to reject the two alternative models of referrals, even though our tests are biased in their favor and against our model. That we can still reject them despite the bias simply makes us all more confident that the other two models are wrong and that ours is correct.

We will first establish that referrals go only to a proper subset of neighboring notaries, which is consistent with our model, but also (under certain conditions that we explain below) with the other two. Let us define a notary's neighbors to be all the notaries in cantons within thirty-five kilometers of his own, where distance is measured between the chef-lieux of each. At that distance, a borrower sent off with a referral would spend about a day going to the other market on horseback or in a carriage, meeting with the lender and signing the contract, and then coming back home. Beyond that distance, the travel costs would increase, because the borrower would have to stay overnight. This definition, it should be stressed, groups all the notaries in a canton together and gives them all the same neighbors. Our tests will also aggregate all the data at the level of the canton. Aggregation of this sort will suffice to show that only a subset of neighbors received referrals. It will also be enough to rule out the alternative models.

If referrals went to all of a notary's neighbors and not to a proper subset of them, then the number of correspondents a notary had should equal the number of his neighbors. A regression of the number of correspondents on the number of neighbors should have a coefficient of one. Because we cannot observe precisely which notary in a canton makes the referral, we will group all the notaries in the canton together and actually regress the number of cantons where they have correspondents on the total number of cantons where they have neighbors—in other words, the cantons

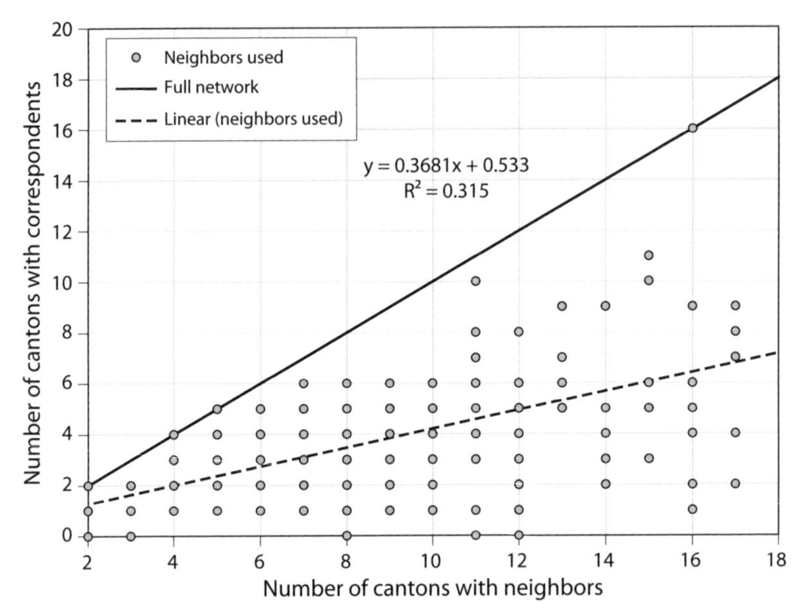

Figure 4.7. Neighbors who are correspondents.
Source: Our sample.

within thirty-five kilometers. The regression coefficient should still be one if referrals go to all of a notary's neighbors.

The dashed line in figure 4.7 shows the result of the regression. The dots are the cantons in our denser sample; the horizontal axis is the number of cantons with neighboring notaries; the vertical axis is the number of cantons with correspondents. The slope of regression line is the fraction of neighbors who receive referrals. It tells us that about thirty-seven percent of observed cantons do get referrals. That is well below the one hundred percent figure (shown by the solid black diagonal line in figure 4.7) that we would expect if all neighbors received referrals. The regression leaves little doubt that referrals went to only a fraction of a notary's neighbors.

If we redefine neighbors to be cantons within twenty-five instead of thirty-five kilometers, we lose a lot of cantons that receive referrals and ones that do not. Still, the pattern is the same: about a third of all cantons in that neighborhood do not receive referrals. And the aggregation by cantons biases both regressions in favor of finding that referrals go to all neighboring notaries. The reason is that if only some notaries in each neighboring canton receive referrals while the others do not, then the aggregation still classifies that outcome as a referral to all the neighbors, even though it would be a clear case of referrals going to only a fraction of them.

The regression does fit our hexagon model, but it is also consistent with the models of random referrals and of reciprocal relationships. Those two models, however, impose specific patterns on the data that we can check. Our tests are simple and by and large nonparametric, but, as we will see, they soundly reject both reciprocal relationships and random referrals.

Let us start with the model of reciprocal relationships, where notaries exchange favors with one another. When, for instance, a notary in Nîmes matches a borrower sent to him by a notary in Avignon, he expects that in the future he will dispatch one of his own borrowers in the reverse direction, to the notary in Avignon. In the long run, the number of borrowers from Avignon matched with lenders from Nîmes should be the same as the number of borrowers from Nîmes matched to lenders from Avignon. Over time, the relationship between the two notaries will become perfectly symmetric. That suggests two ways of testing for reciprocal relationships.

First of all, if all referral relationships between individual pairs of notaries are symmetric, then relationships between cantons must be symmetric too. Over time, the number of referrals N_{ij} from canton i to canton j should equal the number of referrals N_{ji} from canton j to canton i ($N_{ij}=N_{ji}$). A simple way to test whether that is true for the entire sample is to compute the statistic $\frac{\sum_{i\neq j}|N_{ij}-N_{ji}|}{\sum_{i\neq j}2N_{ij}}$. If the matrix is exactly symmetric ($N_{ij}=N_{ji}$), then this statistic is zero, its lowest possible value. Its highest value, one, occurs when $N_{ij}>0$ implies $N_{ji}=0$, or, in other words, that referrals from i to j are never matched by referrals from j to i. If we compute this statistic using our denser samples for 1840 and 1865, it is always well above the value of zero that we would see with exact symmetry. We have done the computation separately for cantons in the north and the south, because there were more notaries in the south. In the south, the statistic is 0.59 in 1840, and 0.48 in 1865. In the north, it is 0.57 in 1840 and 0.47 in 1865. We can also show that the failure of symmetry is not simply the result of the difference between urban markets, which accept a large number of referrals, and rural ones, which send many referrals. If we remove the largest markets, the statistic remains well above zero, although it falls a bit.

Our test does presume that a year is long enough to average away differences in referrals. Conceivably, an imbalance in credit could build up over the course of a year (for instance, a surge in demand for loans in Nîmes in 1840), and referrals in the reverse direction would take longer than a year to appear. If so, then our statistic will be biased against the reciprocal relationships. But there is another, weaker test that does not demand that referrals equalize over the course of a year. That weaker test is simply to require that a notary accept referrals only from a notary who takes referrals in the opposite direction. Mathematically, if $N_{ij} > 0$ then $N_{ji} > 0$; note that to pass the test, the two numbers need not be equal.

In asking whether our dense samples both in 1840 and 1865 have this property, we look once again at the north and south separately. In the south in 1840, 134 canton pairs have referrals going in both directions, but 170 canton pairs have referrals going in only one direction, which fails the test. For 1865, 189 canton pairs in the south have referrals in both directions, but 138 pairs fail the test. In the north, in both 1840 and 1865, 57 canton pairs have referrals in both directions, but 47 do not. The results continue to argue against reciprocal referrals, even with this less demanding test, and that conclusion is unchanged if we drop the largest markets to correct for the different pattern of referrals between big markets and small ones.

The data, in short, reject reciprocal relationships as a model of the notaries' referrals, even though our final test is biased in favor of accepting reciprocal referrals. The bias is not simply that the test relaxes the requirement that referrals in each direction equalize within a year; it also overlooks the possibility that the canton-to-canton relationships can be symmetric even if referrals between individual notaries are not. Suppose, for instance, notary Pons in Avignon accepts referrals from notary Bérard in Nîmes, but not vice versa, and notary Martin in Nîmes accepts referrals referred by notary Fortunet in Avignon, but not vice versa. The aggregate data from these two cantons, which is the sort of data we have, would not reject reciprocal relationships, because referrals from Avignon are accepted in Nîmes and those from Nîmes are accepted in Avigon. It would do so even though the dealings between pairs of notaries are not symmetric.

The other alternative to our model—random referrals—assumes that notaries refer clients to all of their neighbors and do so randomly, without any strategic considerations. Although in the long run, the referrals would eventually spread over all the neighboring notaries, in the short run, some neighbors would not receive referrals, because the credit markets were thin. That outcome is, in fact, inevitable if the number of referrals is less than the number of neighboring notaries.

To devise a test for random referrals, imagine that a notary (whom we will again call Home) has neighbors in M nearby cantons. If we assume that each of these M cantons is equally likely to get a referral from Home, then the probability that a particular canton receives a referral from Home is simply $\frac{1}{M}$. If the referrals are made randomly, then the probability that the canton does not get a referral from Home is $\frac{M-1}{M}$, and the probability that the canton has not been solicited after Home has sent out N referrals is $\left(\frac{M-1}{M}\right)^N$. Similarly, the likelihood that m cantons do not receive a referral from Home is $\frac{M-m}{M}$, and the probability that those m cantons are empty handed after N referrals from Home is $\left(\frac{M-m}{M}\right)^N$.

With those assumptions (random referrals and each canton with neighboring notaries having an equal likelihood of receiving a referral) and our definition of neighbors (notaries in cantons within thirty-five kilometers), we can carry out this calculation for any notary in France. We have done so for our denser samples from 1840 and 1865. Because our data is aggregated at the canton level, we only observe referrals by all the notaries in a canton, not by a single one such as Home. But these notaries in Home's cantons would all have the same neighboring notaries and the same probability of targeting any notary in a nearby canton. Because the random referrals would make the choice of all the destinations independent, the chances that a notary in a particular canton would skip m_s of the M_s nearby cantons with neighboring notaries when sending out referrals would be $\left(\frac{M_s-m_s}{M_s}\right)^{N_s}$, where N_s is the number of referrals the notaries in the canton send out. Here $\left(\frac{M_s-m_s}{M_s}\right)=1-\frac{m_s}{M_s}$ is the fraction of cantons with neighboring notaries that do receive referrals. If we calculate $\left(\frac{M_s-m_s}{M_s}\right)^{N_s}$ for each canton in our denser sample, we can isolate the observations that violate the assumption of random assignment. They are the ones for which $\left(\frac{M_s-m_s}{M_s}\right)^{N_s}$ is extremely low.

Figure 4.8 graphs the results of the calculation. Each canton in the denser sample appears as a dot (for 1840) or a triangle (for 1865), where the Y axis is the number of referrals N_s sent out by the canton, and the X axis is the share $\left(\frac{M_s-m_s}{M_s}\right)$ of cantons with neighboring notaries that receive referrals. The two curved lines show the lower boundary of the regions where the hypothesis of random assignment can be rejected with ninety-five- or ninety-nine-percent confidence. For a point above the solid ninety-five-percent line, the hypothesis of random assignment is rejected with more than ninety-five-percent confidence in that market; for a point above the dotted ninety-nine-percent confidence line, the hypothesis is

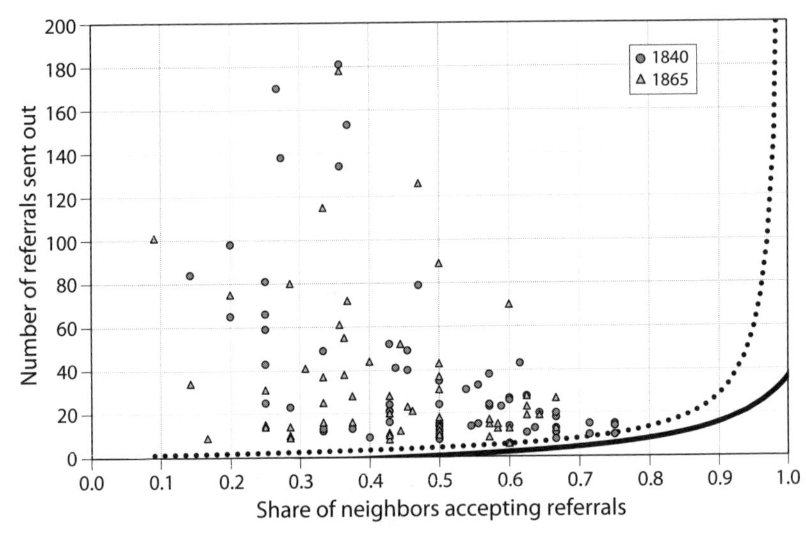

Figure 4.8. Testing for randomness.
Source: Our sample.

rejected with ninety-nine-percent confidence. As figure 4.8 shows, the hypothesis is rejected with ninety-nine-percent confidence for all but ten of 220 markets. The ten markets that are consistent with random referrals are the ones below and to the right of the dotted ninety-nine-percent line—in other words, with a large X coordinate for the number of referrals. The results are even clearer for the solid ninety-five-percent confidence line. Clearly, referrals were not allocated randomly.

Readers might well worry that the results here are sensitive to the definition of neighborhood, but increasing the size of the neighborhood boosts the number of cantons with neighboring notaries and makes it easier to reject randomness. If we reduce the maximum distance to a neighbor to twenty-five kilometers, about one-third of all cantons with neighboring notaries end up receiving no referrals, and we can again reject the hypothesis of randomness with ninety-five-percent confidence interval for fifty-six percent of the cantons. Of the forty-four percent where it is not rejected, half are markets with few (less than three) observed referrals. Thus, how we define the neighborhood has little effect on our results.

Once again, aggregating our data at the canton level biases this test in favor of the hypothesis we want to disprove. Suppose, for example, that the canton of Avignon has only two cantons with neighboring notaries—Nîmes and another nearby city, Carpentras. Suppose notary Pons in Avignon only makes five referrals to Carpentras and none to Nîmes, while his colleague Fortunet in Avignon makes five referrals to Nîmes and none to Carpentras. In this case, we can reject random referrals with ninety-seven-percent confidence for each notary and better than ninety-nine percent for the two of them. But we cannot reject randomness at the canton level because Avignon notaries make half their referrals to Nîmes and half to Carpentras.

There is one other potential worry, for our tests of random referrals assume neighboring notaries are equally likely to receive referrals, even though we know that borrowers are more likely to go from small cantons to large ones. That tendency would concentrate referrals in a small number of cantons. To see if the resulting urban bias would change our results, we took into account the likelihood of getting a referral by the receiving canton's population and then redid the calculations using the 1840 and 1865 denser samples. The results were hardly changed; once again, too many cantons lacked referrals for the notaries' behavior to be random.[16]

As the evidence from the denser samples shows, the network spun by the notaries' referrals has a clear structure. Notaries had correspondents, but not too many of them, and their referrals were neither random nor reciprocal. That is no surprise, because the notaries' correspondents are both complements (in the sense that they help a notary match borrowers and lenders) and substitutes (in the sense that if a notary cheats one correspondent, he can turn to another). The notary network seems to have balanced these two elements in the relationship between correspondents. That in turn points to a significant historical insight: mapping a network in the past requires us to think both about the whole potential network (here, the set of geographic neighbors) and their strategic interactions, which develop over time. When we consider both, a richer set of questions emerge that allow scholars to go beyond mapping the network with tools that suggest that more is better (as in more friends on Facebook). At first glance, this may be true only in some settings, but even then relationships have to be managed. A teenager's Facebook friends, for instance, may value her more if she has more friends overall, particularly if she is a good conduit to these other friends. But her Facebook friends may prefer that she have fewer friends so that she can pay more attention to each one of them.[17] This same logic explains why the referral network is far sparser than geography would allow.

Conclusion

This chapter and the preceding one have analyzed how notaries' peer-to-peer credit markets actually worked. We began the analysis, in chapter 3, by breaking with the tradition of treating local credit markets in the past as isolated from one another. That simple model lies behind the local histories of credit that many historians have undertaken. Such an approach has a number of advantages. After all, when borrowers and lenders never do business outside the confines of particular locality, then one can learn a great deal by studying that particular place. Treating these isolated markets as local economies also allows their individual characteristics to be correlated with the volume of lending.

Although such studies are extremely useful, our larger data set raises questions about the the premise behind them. Credit markets in different places—as our data shows—were clearly linked in 1840, and the scantier evidence from our earlier cross sections suggests that trade between markets was an essential component of lending even in 1740.

All this interlocal trade forced us to move our analysis beyond individual localities. In the process, we brought something new to the study of credit in the past: by recognizing that if notaries were the primary brokers of credit, then they had a powerful incentive to overcome the thinness of the local debt market. They could do so by giving borrowers and lenders a way to travel outside the local credit market in order to find good matches more quickly.

Borrowers and lenders, we know, did travel. But the question then became how they overcame the problem of asymmetric information that plagues credit markets. Here, again, our data set lets us do more than simply assume away the travel costs or the informational issues by appealing to reputational concerns for notaries. It in fact allows us to understand the structure of the information flows by confirming what our model was telling us and rejecting other competing patterns of behavior. As in our model, the typical notary helped reduce the length of queues by referring a creditworthy borrower to another notary or by matching up a lender who had been dispatched to him with a quality borrower. Each notary had a limited number of correspondents who trusted him to send good referrals. He could not abuse their trust, for they could stop doing business with him in the future should he misbehave. France was thus covered by a network of referrals, a network that had long existed. Each notary in the network both made and accepted referrals, and each notary had his personal set of correspondents to whom he could send referrals and a likely different set of correspondents from whom he accepted them.

We are confident in our analysis, even though we cannot observe the referrals directly, for the simple reason that our data support our claims. The referrals and the information that they passed along between notaries made more lending possible than would otherwise have been the case. It is therefore no surprise that notaries were the primary source of private capital in France throughout the first two-thirds of the nineteenth century. Being the primary source, though, does not mean that the notarial credit markets were necessarily efficient. Indeed, just as we described the incomplete centralization of credit markets in chapter 2, here we lay out an incomplete solution to the problem of information. The system is not efficient, because that would imply that referrals were randomly distributed among the notary's neighbors. The system was, however, efficacious. It was much better than what notaries could have accomplished by isolating their clienteles, and better too than structuring referrals in pairwise alliances and reciprocal relationships, because of the prevalence of local credit imbalances. This efficacy was likely a reason why notaries persisted as important credit intermediaries even though there were other networks of financial intermediaries spreading across France—networks that, as we shall see, were quite different.

CHAPTER 5

The Brief but Significant Life of an Institutional Innovation

The French Revolution, as we learned in chapter 3, reshaped the debt market and made the obligation (a standard balloon payment mortgage with a five-percent coupon) the dominant medium and long-term loan by 1807. That remained the case in the northern two-thirds of France up to World War I.

The South of France, however, took a different route. In the 1820s notaries started to draw up novel loan contracts for farmers and proprietors—notarized letters of exchange. To take a real example, in 1834, Jean Dumigron, a farmer who lived near Bordeaux, owed a certain Mister Penaud eight hundred francs for a property sale. Dumigron had a notary draw up a letter of exchange that told Jacques Duthil, a wholesale merchant (*négociant*) living in the nearby city of Libourne, to pay Penaud the eight hundred francs over time and with interest.[1] In effect, the merchant Duthil was instructed to lend to Dumigron by paying off his earlier debt to Penaud.

Notarized letters of exchange (henceforth NLE) like this one turn out to have been common in southern France throughout much of the nineteenth century. They were medium-term instruments (only ten percent were issued with a maturity of less than eight months, and less than seventeen percent had a maturity of more than two years), and since most were drawn up in the countryside, they were of smaller value than obligations. (In our samples, ninety-four percent of all NLE were less than six hundred francs, while only fifty-seven percent of obligations were that small.) They were based on the letter of exchange, the means of making payments and short-term borrowing that had been used in commerce since the Middle Ages, but that sort of credit had traditionally been limited to merchants, traders, and artisans. The notarized letter of exchange gave farmers and others who were not in commerce access to this sort of debt for the first time, and it is no surprise that it was popular. Yet despite the wide use of the NLE in the south, they virtually disappeared by the end of the century.

It might seem that the NLE were just some minor footnote in financial history. But they were not. Their half-century existence, in fact, points to serious problems in many areas of comparative social science, problems that are important enough to make the notarized letter of exchange worth exploring in detail.

To begin with, the NLE is a surprising contradiction, for two reasons. First of all, as a commercial contract, in principle, it should not have been notarized. Rather, it should have been drawn up privately. Second, as we have already noted, it did not involve the usual parties to commercial contracts, such as merchants, traders, and artisans, but rather farmers and private individuals who were borrowing and lending.

At first glance, the contradictions here may seem insignificant, but they in fact challenge an influential belief in the social sciences that the top-down legal system of civil law countries is inefficient and therefore an obstacle to financial development and economic growth—what is known as the legal origins thesis (La Porta, Lopez-de-Silanes, Shleifer, Vishny, 1997, 1998; Levine 1997). In the legal origins thesis, the bottom-up, organic, and precedent-based approach of common law legal systems found in Britain and the United States allows new law to bubble up from judges' decisions as the economy evolves. The top-down civil law (so the argument goes) requires actual laws to be passed before there can be any legal change, because a judge's decision cannot veer off into unexplored terrain and create new law. With judges' hands tied and legal evolution dependent on passing legislation, the civil law system would be inflexible and unable to adapt, and it would therefore choke off financial development and economic growth. But if that argument is correct, the notarized letter of exchange should never have come into existence; it should have been smothered by the inflexibility of the civil law. That it did arise, and (as we shall see) developed and spread organically, and later disappeared without any new laws being passed contradicts the whole argument about the civil law. So does the active role that appellate judges played in its diffusion: they were not simply restrictive interpreters of existing law codes.

But that is not the only problem that the NLE singles out, for it also raises questions about much of the scholarship on networks.[2] This scholarship focuses on individuals with shared characteristics—people who are friends, for instance, or peasants who live in the same village. That focus is the power of this scholarship, but it is also a weakness, because it blinds us to the other connections individuals have. Seeing who all your friends are, for instance, will reveal little about where you will go for medical care, and knowing all the ties that connect villagers will say little about patterns of migration. Focusing on a single network formed by people who are linked in one way amounts to analysis with blinders, which will omit important things—in particular, connections between networks.

That is admittedly a shortcoming of our analysis of the network of correspondent notaries in chapter 4. Our analysis was important, because it revealed what notaries were doing, but we, too, zeroed in on a network of individuals with shared characteristics and ignored other financial intermediaries who interacted with the notaries—among them, bankers. One could undertake a similar analysis of the commercial bankers whom we will investigate in the next chapter, and that analysis would be open to a similar criticism: it would gloss over the bankers' connections to other financial intermediaries, such as notaries. And even if we examined both the network of notaries and the network of bankers and traced out the connections between them, it would leave out still other intermediaries, such as merchants who were also tied into the same interactions, as in Dumigron's letter of exchange, which instructed the wholesale merchant Duthil to make payments for Dumigron. The omissions here can be significant, because economically important networks are loci of exchange, and hence must bring together individuals who are different.

That is a second reason why it is worth looking at the NLE contracts in detail. They let us see the interactions between individuals in distinct networks—specifically, notaries in one network, and commercial bankers in another. They allow us to go beyond standard network analysis, which rarely looks beyond a single network. They do so because they name both the notary who drew up the loan, and the intermediary (typically a banker) who took care of the payment, revealing how intertwined the notaries and bankers' networks were. The lesson is that notaries and bankers in the South of France were cooperating to provide contracts that combined a medium-term loan and payment services over space. This cooperation reveals one important way notaries and bankers interacted and suggests that rather than being competitors, they cooperated or complemented one another. There were in fact other ways they complemented one another, as we shall see in chapter 6.

We will examine the rise of the NLE, the legal changes that made it possible, and the demand for such a financial instrument, in an analysis that will cast doubt on common assumptions about the inflexibility of the civil law. We will then analyze the interactions between notaries, bankers, and merchants in a way that breaks free from the limitations of focusing on a single network and, finally, explore why the NLE eventually disappeared.

The Strange Advent of the Notarized Letter of Exchange

Probably the most hallowed of all financial instruments, the letter of exchange has a long history. Its widespread use in Western Europe starting in the late Middle Ages is usually considered the first financial revolution (Lévy-Bruhl 1933; Roover 1953; Van der Wee 1963; Carrière 1973; Neal 1990; Mueller 1997). Because it was particularly important in securing long distance trade, the network of merchants and bankers who issued and accepted letters of exchange linked all the market places in Europe (Neal and Quinn 2001; Santarosa 2015). Those connections allowed individuals engaged in commerce to move funds safely and cheaply through a violent part of the world where trade was often endangered by wars and always complicated by political boundaries. The same network also permitted speculators to play in the international currency market from an early date (Flandreau et al. 2009; Nogez-Marco 2013). In the eighteenth century, a thick market for inland bills (letters of exchange within Britain, which are also known as domestic letters of exchange) had arisen in Britain and was tied to a network of "country" banks. That network, it has been argued (Neal 1994), played an important role in the financing of the Industrial Revolution. There were also markets on the continent for inland bills (Brennan 1997, Musset 2008), but scholars have usually argued that a lack of banks made the continental market thinner than in Britain.

Unlike obligations or annuities, the letter of exchange emerged from commercial law for merchants, not from the civil law, which governed private dealings between other individuals. It was, at least indirectly, the offspring of Colbert's 1673 commercial code (the Code Savary) and of earlier laws and existing customary practices among merchants. Under the Old Regime, this legislation restricted the use of letters of exchange to merchants and other people who were engaged in commerce; most farmers and agricultural producers (an enormous fraction of the population in what was largely an agrarian economy) were excluded. The letter of exchange was also subject to the usury restriction, but this restriction could easily be sidestepped simply by discounting the capital sum to cover interest (or, in the case of international bills, by picking an appropriate exchange rate). Because merchants and others involved in commerce had to keep account books, which served as evidence in commercial courts, they were literate, and thus the eighteenth-century market for the letter of exchange functioned without much intervention from notaries. There were a few exceptions, such as Lyon and areas further south, where notaries witnessed protested bills—in other words, bills that had not been paid on time—but otherwise notaries before the revolution did not meddle with letters of exchange.

The revolution, we know, rewrote much of French law with a goal of creating a uniform national legal system. When it came to debt, the new law made a sharp distinction between commercial law (enshrined in the 1807 Commercial Code) and civil law (summed up in the Civil Code). Along with other legislation, these two codes constituted the supposedly rigid French civil law.

The Commercial Code was designed to facilitate commerce and industry and to apply to individuals who were experienced and fully familiar with business dealings. It therefore left parties to contracts considerable leeway to frame business agreements as they saw fit. In particular, commercial contracts did not have to be drafted by a notary.

The Commercial Code also aimed to resolve cases of nonpayment of debt quickly without forcing a liquidation when businesses could not pay their bills. In contrast to the new Civil Code, which did not allow imprisonment for debts, merchants who failed to pay their bills were almost automatically thrown in jail under the Commercial Code, even if they were allowed to resume operation after the conclusion of the bankruptcy process. Thus someone willing to pledge his own freedom to secure a debt (perhaps in addition to mortgaging physical collateral) would want to write a letter of exchange rather than a simple note.

Although the Commercial Code was designed for merchants, it could not be limited to them alone; the French Revolution ruled that out. The Enlightenment had exalted liberty and equality, and thriving commerce had made a society based on these ideals acceptable even before 1789 (Sewell 2014). Revolutionaries then invoked liberty and equality to achieve their political goals and justify their reforms. Legislation during the revolution, and even under the autocratic Napoleonic Empire, therefore gave everyone access to most contracts and organizations—with the exception of corporations—and let individuals' actions define their standing under commercial or civil law. When a farmer (such as Dumigron, in our example) signed a letter of exchange, he placed himself under the Commercial Code, even though he was not a merchant. In doing so, he relinquished many of the protections that the Civil Code offered debtors; in particular, he could be jailed for nonpayment.

The principle that action defined an individual's standing under the Commercial Code or the Civil Code affected other transactions as well. Consider, for example, the Bouault family from chapter 4, who invested in the bank run by Felix David, cosigned the 1.1 million franc obligation that David had taken out in 1840, and backed his loan with their own property as collateral. Although their investments as silent partners in the bank were regulated by the Commercial Code, their pledges of collateral in David's obligation were regulated by the Civil Code. Once the 1.1 million franc loan had been paid off, the Bouault family had no further financial responsibility, and they could not be imprisoned when the bank subsequently failed in 1841.

Open access to letters of exchange had important implications for notaries, for if illiterate people wanted to borrow by issuing a letter of exchange, they would need someone to draw it up and guarantee that they had approved it. If the debtor could not read or sign the letter, then the only way it would stand up in court would be if it had been drawn up by a notary. The notarized letter of exchange was thus a logical outcome of the revolution's egalitarian legal reforms when they were viewed through the lens of a liberal interpretation of the Commercial Code.

From a more conservative legal perspective, though, the notarized letter of exchange was suspect, both because of the procedure it entailed and because of the identity of the parties who were involved. The parties to commercial contracts, a conservative would argue, were all supposed to keep books and so did not need a notary's help. Their commercial dealings should be a purely private matter, and drawn up as contracts *sous seing privé*—in other words, contracts that they drafted themselves. Illiterate farmers, who would be the only individuals requiring a notary's assistance, should simply not get involved in such transactions.

This dispute, however, could not be settled on the basis of what was in the written law, for neither the Commercial Code nor Civil Code said anything about notarized letters of exchange. The issue was thus left up to judges to decide, and they settled it—as we shall see—in a way that demonstrates the flexibility of the supposedly rigid civil law.

To see what was happening with the notarized letters of exchange, let us begin with two adjacent markets: the cantons of Valréas and Nyons in southeastern France. Valréas is unusual, for although it is administratively a canton of the department of the Vaucluse, it is separated from the rest of the Vaucluse and is totally surrounded by cantons in the adjacent department of the Drôme (figure 5.1). If the revolution's Cartesian principles had been scrupulously applied, Valréas itself would have been in the Drôme. But prerevolutionary political history subverted those principles. Before the revolution, Valréas (like much of the rest of the Vaucluse) had not actually been part of France; it belonged to the pope and was ruled from Avignon. The pope's lands in France were a discontinuous patchwork of territories scattered across the southern French provinces of Provence and the Dauphiné. In 1791, after the revolution was underway, France annexed the pontiff's possessions, and when the department of the Vaucluse was formed, it contained all of the papal holdings, including Valréas and the adjacent municipality of Suze-la-Rousse, which had been removed from the department of the Drôme to provide a bridge to the rest of the Vaucluse. Then, in 1800, Suze-la-Rousse was given back to the Drôme, leaving Valréas as the only canton in France that is an enclave in a different department.

Beyond that enclave, the closest canton to Valréas in the Vaucluse is Vaison-la-Romaine (figure 5.1), and we have credit data not just for it and Valréas, but also for two neighboring cantons in the Drôme—Nyons and Montélimar. These markets are all close: the two that were most distant from each other (Montélimar and Vaison-la-Romaine) are only sixty-five kilometers apart. But despite their proximity and similar terrain, they had

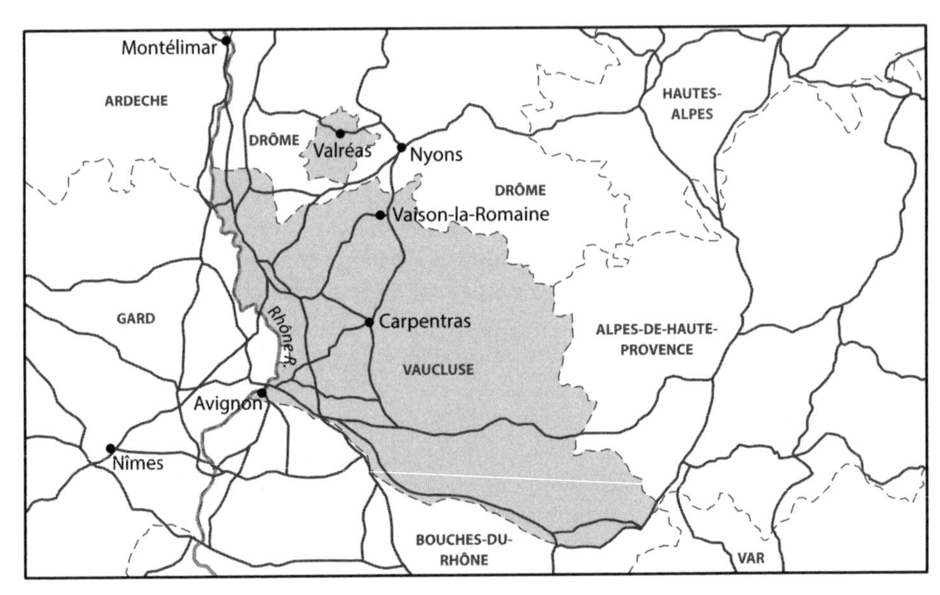

Figure 5.1. The canton of Valréas and the department of the Vaucluse.

a strikingly different penchant for NLE. Of 465 credit contracts drawn up during the year 1840 in Valréas and Vaison (the two Vaucluse cantons), some forty-six percent were NLE, but in Nyons and Montélimar (the two nearby Drôme cantons) there were—surprisingly—absolutely none. And it was not just in Nyons and Montélimar that the NLE were shunned; they were not used at all in the department of the Drôme or in the nearby department of the Isère either. Notaries in the two departments did draw up credit contracts called *billets à ordre* that were substitutes for NLE. Yet although notaries drafted both contracts, the billet à ordre was different from the NLE. Unlike the NLE, the billet did not specify where the debt had to be paid, and it did not involve a second intermediary such as a banker or merchant, which was one of the key features of the NLE. Furthermore, while notaries in the Vaucluse devoted roughly two-fifths of their business to NLE, those of the Drôme and the Isère spent less than a quarter of theirs on the billets, and of course no time at all on the NLE (the averages here are for all the cantons in the Drôme and Isère, not just Nyons and Montélimar). The NLE was important in the Vaucluse, but not at all in the adjacent departments of the Drôme and Isère.

The contrast between the Vaucluse and the Drôme was not just because people in the Drôme were unwilling to sign or accept notarized letters of exchange. In fact, twenty-seven percent of the 233 letters of exchange notarized in the canton of Valréas in 1840 or 1865 involved at least one party (borrower, lender, or correspondent) who resided in the Drôme. Those people in the Drôme were all willing to participate in dealings with NLE.

These unexpected differences have implications for the debate about the civil and common law. To grasp what was going on, though, and to understand what it implies about civil law, we have to keep in mind the ambiguous legal status of the notarized letter of exchange. As a financial instrument it was part of commercial law, but it was used primarily by people who were not explicitly engaged in commerce. That is exactly what we see in Valréas: although thirty-four of the NLE contracts involved borrowers in trade, crafts, or construction, who might be considered involved in commerce, 188 of the borrowers were not in commerce: ninety-eight of them were borrowers from agriculture, and another ninety borrowers simply identified themselves as proprietors.

Conceivably, the popularity of the NLE in Valréas could have stemmed from conflicting appellate court decisions. Valréas and the department of the Vaucluse were subject to the appellate court in the city of Nîmes, while the Drôme and the Isère were in the circuit of a different appeals court, in the city of Grenoble. One could well imagine that the two courts might have differed about who could use the instruments, with Grenoble reserving the NLE for people in commerce, while the Nîmes court was more liberal and let anyone use the NLE. If so, then cantons in the Vaucluse (which were subject to the court in Nîmes) would use the NLE, while cantons in the Drôme (which were within the jurisdiction of Grenoble) would not.

That sort of explanation is particularly appealing, because there were no striking differences between the economies of the cantons that might account for the sharp differences in use of NLE. The economies of Vaison (where NLE were common) and Nyons (where they were not) were quite similar: in the 1840s, for example, the primary cash crops in both cantons were wool and silk cocoons, produced for the market in Lyon. There is simply no economic reason why two-fifths of the contracts signed in Vaison were letters of exchange while seventeen kilometers away in Nyons not one of the credit contracts was a letter of exchange. So were different appellate court decisions the explanation? The only way to tell is to examine the jurisprudence.

The Codes and Jurisprudence

As we have pointed out, neither the Civil Code nor the Commercial Code mentions the notarized letter of exchange. The Commercial Code does have a section devoted to the principal commercial credit instrument, the letter of exchange, but, as we have noted, the code was designed to deal with commercial transactions, and so it presumed that participants would have the expertise and ability to draw up such contracts privately. The Commercial Code in fact aimed to create structures that would reduce reliance on notaries. As for the Civil Code, it laid out circumstances under which an individual could or had to use a notary, but it did not take up the legality of having a notary draw up a letter of exchange.

If the common misconception about civil law were true—namely, that what is not authorized by law codes is forbidden—then the NLE would never have arisen, for it was not only omitted from the Civil and Commercial Codes, but it was also never sanctioned by any legislation. The very legality of its existence was unclear, and appellate courts had to resolve the issue, which turned on two questions. First, to what extent could people not in commerce avail themselves of commercial institutions such as the letter of exchange? The second question was more specific: Was it legal to notarize a letter of exchange?

The debate over the first question (over the definition of "*commerçant*," or, in other words, who was engaged in commerce) raged throughout the nineteenth century. It was a burning issue, at least in part, because answering the question determined who fell under the rules of commercial bankruptcy (and so could be imprisoned) and who was subject to civil insolvency (and so could usually stay out of jail).[3] On one side of the debate stood parties who argued for a narrow interpretation of the Commercial Code; they maintained that it should apply only to individuals in commercial professions, such as merchants, artisans, or industrialists, but not farmers, rentiers, and civil servants. The other side of the debate rallied the partisans of open access to commercial legal rules, who invoked the democratic legacy of the revolution to bolster their position. The conservative party, of course, saw notarizing the letter of exchange as a deviation from the intent of the Commercial Code. The liberal side saw notarization as a natural consequence of open access to such letters. How, after all, could illiterate people sign letters of exchange without a notary?

From 1812 to the mid-1830s, the issue of the legality of the notarized letter of exchange appeared regularly in decisions of both the appeals courts in Nîmes and Grenoble, and also in the deliberations of the Cour de Cassation, which reviewed the decisions of lower courts. Here it is important to note that early nineteeth-century France, unlike the United States, did not have a supreme court that was the sole and ultimate arbiter in matters of jurisprudence. Instead, there were twenty-seven appeals courts (each for a different jurisdiction, as with federal appeals courts in the United States today) that provided final review of lower court decisions, plus the Cour de Cassation, which assessed cases mostly on procedural grounds and was not in any way a supreme court. The decisions of the appellate courts and the Cour de Cassation were published in newspapers such as the *Gazette des Tribunaux* and compiled in the *Journal du Palais*, a legal periodical; they were also discussed as an important source of jurisprudence in legal manuals. In contrast to the courts in countries with common law legal systems, such as Britain or the United States, the French courts cited only the codes or laws in their decisions, not prior decisions, because precedent was not supposed to be a source of legal legitimacy. But legal practice and actual jurisprudence were quite different from theoretical statements about legal legitimacy in the literature on the legal origins thesis. Indeed, legal manuals and commentaries make it abundantly clear that the appellate court decisions were regarded as setting precedent.[4] As a result, it did not take a new code or piece of legislation to modify the law. An appellate case could also change French law, and French law was thus far more pliable than scholars who contrast the supposedly rigid French civil law and the flexible common law believe.

All of the appellate decisions we have found affirm both the legality of notarizing a letter of exchange and non-commerçants' rights to use this instrument. Furthermore, there were no sharp differences between appellate courts on either matter, which casts doubt on contrasting appellate decisions as the explanation for the differences in the use of NLE. The basis of the legality of the NLE was that the Commercial Code enabled people to dispense with notaries but did not require them to do so, in the same way that legislation allowing individuals to trade a stock outside the stock exchange did not require them to do so. The courts provided no rationale for their decision that all individuals could use NLE. The cases that came up involved borrowers in agriculture, but the judges never questioned the validity of the contracts, as they would have if they believed that farmers could not engage in such transactions. The decisions simply affirmed that if the borrower had drawn up a letter of exchange, it could be endorsed without his or her consent, in contrast to what would have been the case with an obligation. It was, in short, the nature of the instrument that mattered, not the identity of the issuer.

The clearest affirmation of the legality of notarized letters of exchange comes from a Grenoble appeals court decision of 1836:

> Given that the legislator nowhere prohibits drawing up letters of exchange or payment orders before a notary ; to require otherwise would deprive illiterate individuals of the right and facility to participate in such negotiations. Given that the act of August 8, 1828, is nothing more than a payment order; but that in any case [Mister] Magand for whom it was drawn up and who mandates payment in favor of [Mister] Génard cannot be admitted to request the nullification of such an endorsement, which constitutes between Magand, a merchant, and [Mister] Génard, another merchand, a true commercial act.[5]

The Grenoble court made it clear that notarization of letters of exchange was legal. What matters most for us is that Grenoble was the appeals court for the department of the Drôme and thus included both Nyons and Montélimar, places where NLE do not appear (even though our data come from 1840, four years after the court decision). Clearly, the relevant appeals court allowed the NLE, but virtually no one adopted them in Nyons and Montélimar. The reason why no one employed them must be something other than a ruling by the relevant appellate court.

Further evidence that differences in use of the NLE were not caused by contrasting appellate decisions comes from markets further west, on the other side of the Rhône river, which runs through southeastern France. If appellate courts determined whether the NLE was employed, then its popularity should vary greatly across appellate jurisdictions but relatively little within each jurisdiction, provided we make the reasonable assumption that there was demand for the NLE wherever they were allowed. But that is not what we find. Consider, for example, the appellate jurisdiction of Nîmes, which included not just the Vaucluse, which was on the east side of the Rhône, but also the departments of the Gard and the Ardèche, which were west of the river. Although the Gard and the Vaucluse did adopt the NLE, the Ardèche did not. A bit further west lay the appellate circuit of the city of Riom, which encompassed the departments of the Allier and the Cantal. The notaries of the Cantal drew up lots of NLE, while those of the Allier did not. Still further west, we reach the circuit of the city of Limoges, which included both the departments of the Haute-Vienne and the Creuse. While there were hundreds of letters of exchange in the Haute-Vienne, we find only nine in the Creuse; we encountered similar contrasts within the jurisdiction of the appellate court of the port of Bordeaux.

Clearly, there was a northern boundary beyond which the notarized letter of exchange did not spread, and that boundary was virtually impermeable. North of it, only nineteen of the 30,733 loans in our 1840 cross section were NLE. South of it, by contrast, nearly half of the loans (10,701 out of 21,187 contracts) were NLE.

The boundary, however, was not dictated by appellate court decisions. The French appellate courts were in fact receptive to the NLE, and that is the important point here. The appellate decisions all affirmed that NLE were legal and that individuals outside of commerce could use them, even though neither the Civil Code nor the Commercial Code even mentioned the NLE. Clearly, the appellate courts were not simply hobbled interpreters of written law who could do nothing if the written law was silent, contrary to what much of the economics literature on legal origins and the civil law assumes. French appellate courts could in fact respond when issues arose and the law was unsettled. In the case of the NLE, the courts reacted to demands for access to the instruments by invoking the legal equality of the French Revolution and allowing everyone to use them. On that, none of the appellate courts differed.

Does Lack of Access to Banks Explain Use of the NLE?

Use of the NLE was neither dictated by appellate courts nor the result of individual notaries' decisions. Its prevalence seems to be the product of decisions made by borrowers, lenders, notaries, and correspondents in each department. Indeed, within our sample, if one market in a department has letters of exchange, then all the others in the department do as well. Exactly how this locally coordinated equilibrium was arrived at is unclear, but we can make some guesses and test if they fit our evidence.

Because the NLE was a substitute for a medium-term bank loan (or a short-term one that was regularly rolled over), one might assume that it arose in places where banks were rare. Could that be the explanation for the variation in its use? That is at least a hypothesis we can test, because we know the number of banks by canton for all of France both in 1840 and 1865, and can thus ascertain the extent of bank penetration in the NLE region relative to the rest of the country. We can do the same for another factor that could also have explained the prevalence of NLE's—literacy—since illiterate borrowers would have had to use a notary to draw up any commercial contract. As d'Auvilliers, a jurist, put it:

> If the drawer does not know how to write, it is mandatory that the letter of exchange be notarized. The act would then be an affidavit verifying that the letter of exchange was dictated by the drawer and that the the notary signed in his stead.[6]

Here we need to examine the correlation between literacy and the NLE, which we can do because we know literacy rates among army conscripts in the 1830s by canton for a large number of French departments. That should be a good measure of literacy (at least for males) in the cantons.

To test the effect of literacy and access to banks on the use of NLE, we can run two regressions. The first examines whether literacy and the number of banks predict the prevalence of NLE in particular markets, which we can run for the 1840 and 1865 cross sections. The volume lent through NLE per capita in each is the dependent variable, and banks per capita and illiteracy rate of army recruits in 1827–29 are the explanatory variables, plus a constant term and the reciprocal of the market population as additional controls.[7] The second regression is the same, except that it excludes markets north of the border which delimited the region where NLE was used, because those northern markets had no NLE lending.

Table 5.1. Regression of volume of notarized letters of exchange

Dependent variable	Volume of NLE per capita 1840 (francs per person) (1)	Volume of NLE per capita 1865 (francs per person) (2)	As in regression 1 but South of France only. (3)	As in regression 2 but South of France only. (4)
Independent variable				
Banks per capita in the year of the cross section	6,194* (2,408)	2,564 (2,377)	12,078** (2,762)	2,341 (2,241)
Illiteracy (percent of army recruits in 1827–29 who could neither read nor write)	0.1016** (0.0376)	0.1044** (0.0397)	0.0224 (0.0518)	–0.0031 (0.0543)
N	155	155	60	60

* $p<0.05$; ** $p<0.01$

Note: Since the dependent variable is often zero and never negative, the regressions are tobit regressions, except for regression (3), because all of the southern markets had a positive number of NLE in 1840. Besides the independent variables listed in the table, the regressions also included a constant term and the reciprocal of the market population. Standard errors are in parentheses.

Source: See text.

The regressions for France as a whole suggest that a lack of banks played no role in explaining the pattern of reliance on NLE. If a lack of banks had pushed borrowers to turn to NLE as a substitute, then we would expect the per capita number of banks to have a negative coefficient in the regressions, but it actually has a positive sign, both in 1840 and in 1865 (table 5.1, regressions 1 and 2). Running the regressions with the per capita volume of NLE in 1865 as the dependent variable and per capita banks in 1840 as the explanatory variable leads to similar results. And the results are much the same if we limit the regressions to areas in the South of France where NLE were widespread (table 5.1, regressions 3 and 4). One could of course worry about omitted variables, but even so it seems unlikely that NLE were a response to the lack of banks.

The same conclusion is clear simply from looking at maps. In the south, where NLE were widespread, they turn out to have been popular both in areas with many banks (such as the corridor from Avignon to the city Montpellier, about one hundred kilometers away) and in areas with few banks (such as the departments of the Cantal and the Gers, which were both even further west). They clearly did not arise as a way to compensate for the lack of banks, and the spread of banks did not diminish their popularity either, at least under the political regimes that prevailed in France in 1840 (the July Monarchy) and in 1865 (the Second Empire).

Illiteracy, on the other hand, did seem to spur demand for the NLE. In the regressions, the fraction of conscripts who cannot read or write always increases the prevalence of NLE, and the coefficient is statistically different from zero at the one-percent level, at least when we run the regression for France as a whole (table 5.1, regressions 1 and 2). Yet by itself illiteracy cannot explain variations in the use of NLE. If we rerun regression one in table 5.1 without banks per capita, we would predict that the north of France would have 1.6 francs of NLE per capita in 1840, while the south would have 2.2 francs per capita. Yet that small difference is dwarfed by actual contrast in the prevalence of NLE between the north and the south: zero francs per capita in the north in 1840, versus a much larger 4.7 francs in the south. Clearly, something besides illiteracy was at work in creating demand for the NLE in the southernmost part of France, and something besides banks was at work in stopping its northward spread.[8] We now turn to the operation of the NLE network of notaries and correspondents.

The Network of Notaries and Their Correspondents

The primary difference between a letter of exchange and the financial instrument that was a partial substitute for it—the billet à ordre—was that a letter of exchange had to name a correspondent who would pay the specified sum. That correspondent had to live in a municipality other than the one where the borrower lived. The billet à ordre, by contrast, had to be paid by the borrower himself, not by a correspondent, and although it could be transferred by endorsing it on the back, it ultimately had to be presented to the borrower, and not to a banker or merchant who was serving as the borrower's correspondent. The notarized letter of exchange thus gives us a window into a second network, one different from the network of referrals that underlay the market for annuities and obligations. This second network tied together the notaries who assisted in the creation of the NLE and their allies, the correspondents who made payments for the borrower and in the process usually extended him credit.

In this second network, the correspondents, as we shall see, were not by and large notaries. Yet their presence was important, even though it runs counter to most of the social science on networks.[9] That literature tends to leave out such outsiders, for networks are usually homophilic; in other words, they link people who are similar. This is true whether the network ties together expatriate Jewish traders, Chinese merchants, or immigrants in a trade. Social networking today is homophilic too, because it relies on the idea that people with similar characteristics associate. The data that firms like Google or Facebook extract from their sites derive their value from the fact that individuals with similar characteristics have common behavior—in particular, they like to buy similar goods and services. These firms then provide their information about this common behavior to firms that have goods and services to sell.[10]

The network of notaries is by definition homophilic. All members are in fact notaries, who referred clients to one another in order to arrange obligations. One could easily imagine that the referrals would have extended to notarized letters of exchange in a way that included only notaries as intermediaries. After all, there were notaries in every canton in France, so turning to one to act as a correspondent was certainly feasible. Adding NLE to referrals for obligations would also have increased the number of transactions that occurred within any single notary's network and so further reduced the temptation for fellow notaries in his network to engage in opportunistic behavior. And notaries could easily have acted like correspondents and funded or repaid medium term loans like NLE; they often maintained cash accounts for their clients, whether it was money held in escrow for an investment, or revenue collected in managing clients' real estate and private loan portfolios. They could conceivably have integrated the NLE into their own network of fellow notaries and so provided one-stop shopping that would have freed clients from ever having to use a banker or a merchant in order to get an NLE or have it paid off.

There were some cases where that happened, at least for a while.[11] But the vast majority of our markets did not fit that pattern, for the intermediaries engaged in NLE included bankers and merchants—not just notaries—and so the network was anything but homogeneous. In the cross sections of 1840 and 1865, we have 20,422 NLE, of which 17,444 list the occupation of the correspondent or payer, who extended credit by paying off the borrower's debt, as the wholesale merchant Jacques Duthil did for the farmer Jean Dumigron in our example at the beginning of the chapter. Notaries were in fact correspondents in only 4,380 of the NLE, or just over a quarter of the ones for which we can identify the payer. Bankers were correspondents in 3,549 or 20.3 percent of the contracts and wholesale merchants (négociants) like Duthil in 7,533 or 43.1 percent. These three occupations account for 88.6 percent of all the identified correspondents. Given that many négociants were in effect quasi bankers, the correspondents in the network were roughly two-thirds bankers and wholesale merchants, and one-third other individuals, including notaries.

What is clear is that the notaries who wrote up the NLE were not acting as bankers. Neither were the lenders who were overwhelmingly farmers and proprietors, just like the borrowers. But the medium-term NLE credit market functioned well because it brought in bankers and wholesale merchants, who could easily extend medium-term credit and make payments; in other words, it worked precisely because it was heterogeneous. Notaries did not have a comparative advantage in making medium-term loans, for although they did keep funds on account for clients, they were not supposed to engage in lending on their own account in their own offices. Neither were they supposed to use the funds they kept in escrow or on deposit to enter banking (Hoffman, Postel-Vinay, Rosenthal 2000, 2003). But notaries were ideally suited to be issuers of NLE, because there were notary offices almost everywhere, while banks and négociants cropped up mostly in towns and cities with over five thousand people. Illiterate borrowers (likely an important clientele for NLE) were concentrated in the countryside and could easily consult a local notary, who would draw up the NLE and bring a correspondent whom he knew into the transaction. It is thus not surprising that notaries became the issuers. The bankers and négociants would then take over the payment of the letter, because as correspondents they had an advantage: they formed the core of the interregional payment system. The resulting specialization makes eminent sense, because the different intermediaries—the notaries, bankers, and merchants—had complementary skills.

To see how the notary-correspondent network worked in greater detail, let us focus on two departments—the Vaucluse in southeastern France and the Haute-Garonne, further west—where NLE were common in 1840. For the 1840 cross section in the two departments, we gathered the name, residence, and occupation for the notaries and the correspondents in all the letters of exchange.[12] We can thus ask quite precise questions about the structure of the NLE network.

If we start with the issuing side of the network, then near Toulouse, the largest city in the Haute-Garonne, seventy-five notaries issued 3,104 NLE, drawing upon 173 correspondents. In the Vaucluse, eighty-six notaries drafted 2,173 NLE, involving two hundred correspondents. In both departments, the ratio of correspondents to notaries is virtually identical—two to three—and the business of issuing the letters was concentrated in the hands of a minority of local notaries. In the Haute-Garonne, half the NLE were drawn up by sixteen of the seventy-five notaries in the department. The sixteen notaries who did the least business with NLE accounted for only six percent of the letters. The notaries in the Haute-Garonne who drafted large numbers of NLE were in no sense specializing in that line of business; they did three times as much business in general as the notaries who issued the fewest letters.[13]

The figures in the Vaucluse are similar, even though the demand for NLE was lower than in the Haute-Garonne. In the Vaucluse, notaries issued on average twenty-four NLE a year, or only two-thirds the number drawn up around Toulouse.

As for the correspondents who paid most of these NLE when they were due, they were a slightly smaller group in the Haute-Garonne (where 58.7 percent of all NLE were payable by one of the top twelve correspondents) than in the Vaucluse (where the top twelve correspondents handled 52.8 percent of the NLE). Most of that difference stems from a single notary and a single banker who did more NLE together than any other notary-correspondent pair in the Haute-Garonne: the notary Olmade and the Toulousan banker Courtois. Olmade drew up 356 NLE, or twelve percent of the total in the Haute Garonne. Courtois was his correspondent in 301 of those, or ten percent of all NLE in the Haute Garonne. If we set them aside and also remove the most active pair in the Vaucluse (notary Giraud from the town of Pernes-les-Fontaines, who draws his forty-nine NLE exclusively on Fortunet, a négociant in the city of Carpentras), then the top twelve correspondents account for fifty-four percent of all the business in the Haute-Garonne and fifty-two percent in the Vaucluse.

As with the notaries, many correspondents rarely handled NLE. The median correspondent in both departments received two letters, both drawn up by the same notary. In the Haute-Garonne, correspondents who received at least five NLE account for ninety-four percent of all NLE. Among those active correspondents, the median number of letters received is thirty, from two notaries. The Vaucluse numbers are similar.

Overall, the NLE networks in the Haute-Garonne and the Vaucluse are qualitatively similar. In both departments, the number of notaries who relied on a single correspondent is small (ten of seventy-eight and fifteen of eighty-six), but notaries did prefer to send most of their business to a favorite correspondent. Eighty percent of all NLE in the Haute-Garonne and seventy percent in the Vaucluse occurred between a notary and his preferred correspondent. These principal correspondents were neither exclusively négociants nor exclusively notaries. In the Haute-Garonne, some were bankers, who accounted for 664 of the NLE (495 of these were for Courtois). Négociants handled 1,425, and other notaries, 509. Together, these three groups paid eighty-five percent of all the NLE in the Haute-Garonne. In the Vaucluse, bankers formed only six percent of the correspondents, versus fifty-two percent for négociants and twenty percent for other notaries. Again, the Toulouse banker Courtois alone explains the higher concentration of activities in the three core professions in the Haute-Garonne.

Having notaries and their correspondents arrange and pay NLE did carry risks and the possibility of untrustworthy behavior. In the example at the start of this chapter, the négociant Jacques Duthil, who followed the instructions in the notary's NLE and paid off Jean Dumigron's debt, was making a loan to Dumigron. What assured Duthil that he would be repaid and compensated both for the funds he had advanced and for his efforts in making the payments? Did he know Dumigron personally and deal with him repeatedly, even though Dumigron was a farmer and lived almost forty kilometers away from Duthil's home in Libourne? That seems unlikely. Or was he relying on assurances from the notary who had drawn up the NLE? And did that notary in fact suggest to Dumigron that he have Duthil take care of the payments? If so, how could the notary trust Duthil to make the payment and not pocket some of the money?

Similar problems could arise with other NLE. What, then, kept the notaries and correspondents from taking advantage of one another? To answer that question, let us return to the network of notaries discussed in chapter 4, because it faced similar problems. As we pointed out, the network of notaries could have resolved these problems in three broad ways, and the same three possible solutions apply to our new network of notaries and correspondents. The first solution is bilateral relationships, where two members of a network interact with one another exclusively and rely on the value of their reputations to encourage trustworthy behavior. In chapter 4, that involved two notaries who referred clients back and forth to one another; here, the partners would be notaries and their correspondents. The second solution involves what we will call a coalition of the whole. It consists of all possible partners who were close enough that dealing with them was not ruled out by the cost of travel. Each member of the coalition of the whole then shares business with all the others, because they would all learn of one another's misbehavior, as among Avner Greif's Maghribi traders (Greif 1989, 2006). With this second solution, we would expect clients to be referred to all of a notary's possible local partners in the notarial network. The same would happen with the NLE network: the notaries would interact with all possible local correspondents if we waited long enough. The third possibility is the kind of geographically specific network woven by the referrals among notaries that fit the evidence in chapter 4. Members of the network dealt with a subset of nearby partners only. They could observe one another and share information; that sufficed to prevent misbehavior. The same would happen in the NLE network. Only a limited subset of nearby notaries and correspondents would interact: more than two, but fewer than all.

Did any of these three solutions sustain the NLE networks of notaries and their correspondents? Let us consider bilateral relationships first. Could they ensure that notaries would draw up NLE for creditworthy individuals only? And could they guarantee that correspondents would pay on time? If so, then bilateral relationships between notaries and correspondents should have been common, but if we combine the data from both the Haute-Garonne and the Vaucluse, there is only one notary pair that behave as though they are locked into such a bilateral relationship—Piquier, a notary from the municipality of Fronton in the Haute-Garonne, and Pujos, a notary from nearby village of Bouloc—who acted as one another's primary correspondent. (Fifty-six of the fifty-seven NLE drawn up by Piquier were payable by Pujos, while sixteen of the thirty-two drawn up by Pujos were payable at Piquier's office.) All the other notaries who drafted at least fifteen NLE used someone who was not a notary as their correspondent. Clearly, the NLE simply did not just bind together pairs of notaries, as would have happened in a network based on bilateral reputations, and the chief reason was that most notaries used bankers or merchants as correspondents.

What about the coalition of the whole? Could that be the solution sustaining the NLE? To see if it was, consider the NLE network of notaries and their correspondents. Define a node in the network as a municipality with either a notary who issues NLE or a correspondent who pays NLE. A link between municipalities A and B is established when a notary in A (or B) draws up a NLE payable in B (or A). A link is symmetric if at least one notary draws up an NLE in A payable in B and at least one notary in B draws up an NLE payable in A. In other words, a link is symmetric if NLE flow both from A to B and from B to A. A link is asymmetric if the flow of NLE goes in only one direction. A notary in A may draw up NLE payable in B, or a notary in B may do the reverse, but not both.

This idea can be applied to our data from the department of the Vaucluse, to see if we can find evidence of a coalition of the whole. We will leave aside the enclave of Valréas, because some of the notaries there had correspondents from outside the department, whom we cannot observe. We can then map the connections between the remaining notaries and their correspondents and look for evidence of a coalition of the whole. We will do so in two steps, looking first at the symmetric links in the network and next at all the links in the network, including the asymmetric ones as well.

If we map the network of symmetric connections, where the flow of NLE goes both ways, we end up with a network that is sparse (figure 5.2). It has only six or seven important nodes (most clearly the cities of Avignon, Carpentras, and Orange), and most municipalities in the Vaucluse simply do not figure in this symmetric network. The numerous municipalities without links are not what we would expect with a coalition of the whole. Because they are nearby, we would expect them to be connected, too, at least if we waited long enough—all of which argues against the coalition of the whole.

What happens when we add the asymmetric links and graph the entire network? The network then includes municipalities (such as town of Ménerbes) where notaries draw up NLE but no correspondent receives

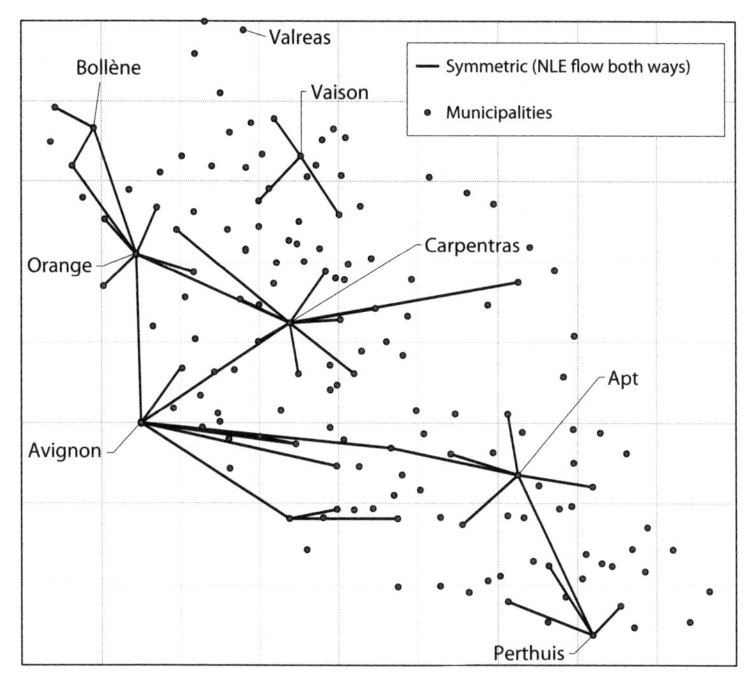

Figure 5.2. The symmetric notary correspondent network in the Vaucluse.
Source: Our denser sample for the Vaucluse. For details, see the text.

them. It also includes markets (such as Sainte-Cécile) with correspondents, but no notaries who are drafting NLE. The resulting graph (figure 5.3) bristles with far more connections than figure 5.2; it includes a large number of asymmetric links in the heart of the Rhône valley, where villages are connected to central nodes (such as the cities of Avignon, Bollène, and Orange) that stand out when the graph is limited to the symmetric segments of the network. This complex geography of connections casts doubt on the likelihood that there was any sort of coalition of the whole. To judge from their commercial connections, notaries and their correspondents simply were not in contact with much of the department, and they only cared about information concerning the behavior of intermediaries in nearby locations. In the northern part of the department, for example, no node except for Orange has a connection to any node south of the city of Carpentras. In other words, notaries and correspondents did not care about what was happening south of Carpentras, and they had no information about it either. Similarly, intermediaries in the southeast of the department (near the city of Apt) had no interest in what was going on north of Avignon. And while Avignon and Carpentras were

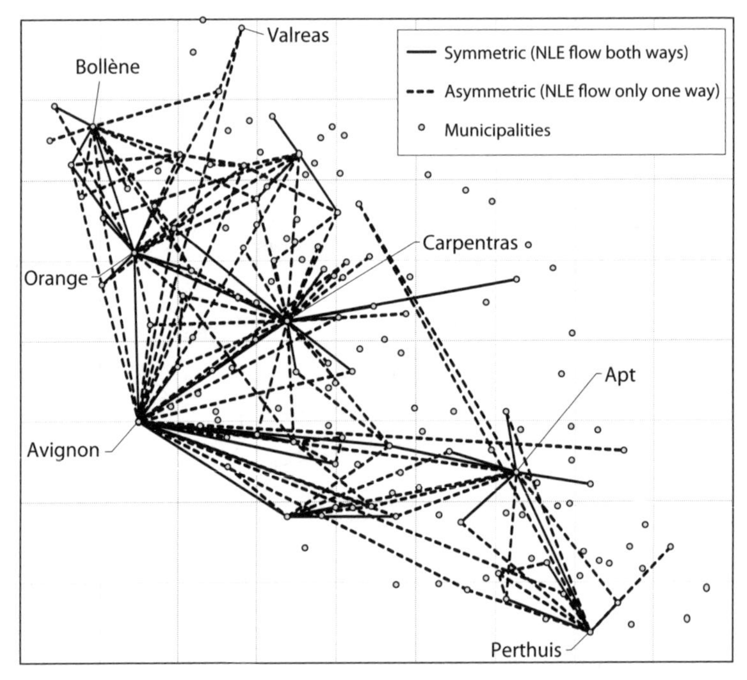

Figure 5.3. The notary correspondent network in the Vaucluse.
Source: Our denser sample for the Vaucluse. For details, see the text.

clearly central nodes, they themselves were scarcely connected at all. A coalition of the whole therefore seems highly unlikely.

There is another reason why a coalition of the whole was unlikely: the limits that geography imposed on information flow. Information about financial dealings could flow easily among the municipalities in the Rhône valley, because they nearly all had either a resident notary or a resident correspondent. But that was not the case for poorer municipalities in the mountains of the Vaucluse, which were far less likely to be part of the network. A coalition of the whole would involve 286 members, including these poorer municipalities, since they were close by, but maintaining such a coalition would be inefficient and thus unlikely. Doing so would require that each intermediary in the network be able to get timely information on all 285 other members, including those in the poor mountain municipalities.

In any case, the web of behavior traced in figure 5.3 does not match the broad net of links that would have been woven if the coalition of the whole had operated. Indeed, in our network, ninety-eight percent of the intermediaries interacted with fewer than ten counterparties, who were all located nearby. Rather than being a coalition of the whole, the notary correspondent network seems to rest on individual specific coalitions structured by geography—just as in the network we discussed in chapter 4 that made obligation lending possible by linking through referrals. In the case of NLE, the network is clearly not bilateral (most correspondents are not notaries), and it relies heavily on rural-urban ties with urban notaries (say, in the cities of Avignon or of Toulouse) using a correspondent nearby and rural notaries preferring a correspondent in a larger city.

Building such a network was probably easy, just as in the case of the notarial network of obligation referrals. Farmers who wanted NLE could all find notaries nearby, and although the farmers likely had few ties to bankers or merchants, the notaries did, and they could tap these connections to arrange an NLE for creditworthy clients, with a banker or merchant in a larger town.

Why might a farmer want an NLE rather than an obligation? There are several possible reasons. First of all, if he wanted to borrow, the NLE would increase the size of the loan he could take out by putting not just his wealth but his personal freedom at stake, because he would risk imprisonment if the debt were not paid. And, as with an obligation, he could add to the security of the loan by attaching a specific mortgage to it, if that was necessary to reassure his creditors and the correspondent.[14] For the creditors to whom the farmer owned money, the NLE was attractive too. In particular, it offered the advantage of liquidity, since the creditors could take the NLE to the correspondent to have the debt repaid. In contrast, an obligation loan would require creditors to wait until the borrower had enough cash to pay off the debt. The correspondent might even be willing to pay off the NLE in advance by discounting it, particularly if the creditors themselves endorsed the NLE, because that made them jointly responsible and thus put their own wealth and freedom at stake.[15]

By increasing the amount of debt that a borrower could take on, and perhaps even making loans liquid and therefore more appealing to lenders, the NLE made more credit transactions worth undertaking. They also facilitated the payment of bills in other places without having to make the trip in person to hand over the cash. It is no surprise, then, that the NLE grew in popularity, particularly in areas where illiteracy would keep borrowers and lenders from drawing up letters of exchange on their own. A network of intermediaries—from notaries to merchants and bankers—then grew up around the NLE. It emerged privately from other common transactions, as would-be borrowers consulted their local notaries, who put them into contact with the bankers or merchants whom they had dealt with and cooperated with in the past.

The ease with which these networks grew casts doubt upon the oft-repeated claims about the rigidity of the civil law. It also suggests that all sorts of financial networks may have little trouble growing, at least when property rights are clear and legal systems are flexible, as in nineteenth-century France. Under those conditions, financial networks may be likely to thrive so long as problems of asymmetric information can be overcome. Both the NLE networks and the network of notary referrals imply that it was quite possible to surmount these informational problems.

The Life and Death of a Financial Instrument

After popping up in the 1820s, the NLE spread rapidly in the south of France, reaching their greatest geographic range by 1830 and helping to make payments and medium-term loans available throughout much of southern France. Yet despite its utility, by World War I the NLE had disappeared. Their demise was gradual and varied from place to place. In some markets, the decline set in as early as the 1860s, but in others the NLE were still used regularly as late as 1900. Sometimes, the drop-off was precipitous, leaving only a trace level of NLE after 1870, while in others it was dragged out.

To understand both the diffusion and the decline requires a finer chronology than our four cross sections permit, for there are no NLE at all in 1807, and the remaining few in 1899 were concentrated in three departments. To understand what happened, we therefore had to go back to the archives and collect additional data at higher frequency in a small number of cantons: L'Isle-sur-Sorgues, a market in the department of the Vaucluse with a diversified economy; two cantons in the department of the Gard where vineyards predominated (Saint-Gilles and Vauvert); two more markets in the Gard where silkworm raising was the primary cash crop (Lasalle and Saint-Jean-du Gard); a neighboring canton to the Vaucluse (Villeneuve-les-Avignon); two markets in the department of the Aude (Castelnaudary, which is very close to the Haute-Garonne, and Lézignan, which is close to the Hérault); and, finally, a canton in the Haute-Garonne (Revel).

For each of these markets, we have a finer chronology, as we sampled a selection of the years 1820, 1825, 1830, 1870, 1875, 1880, 1890, and 1899, and read all of the credit contracts for January and February. The aim was to trace out the NLE diffusion in the 1820s and its disappearance in the 1870s and 1880s (table 5.2). As table 5.2 demonstrates, the NLE diffused swiftly. We found none of them in 1807 or 1810, but in the interval between 1820 and 1830, they began to crop up in all of our markets in the South. The pattern of diffusion does seem to follow the initial appeals

Table 5.2. The rise and fall of the notarized letter of exchange (number of contracts)

	Vaucluse	Gard			Aude		Haute-Garonne
Years	L'Isle-sur-Sorgues	Villeneuve-Les-Avignon	St-Gilles	St-Jean-du-Gard	Lézignan	Castelnau-dary	Revel
1807	0		0	0			0
1810		0		0			0
1820	0		107	2	0	44	
1825	0						7
1830	22	6	16	3	5	83	10
1840	46	12	140	7	12	127	21
1850	51						26
1860	30		135	5			26
1865	16	10	145	3	25	69	23
1870	28						24
1875	3		40		14	31	
1880	1	0	0	0			
1890	0	0	1	0	3	12	21
1899	0		0	0	3	12	14

Note: Each cell reports the number of NLE transacted in January and February of the given year. When that column is blank it is either because the data was not collected (e.g., in Revel in 1899) or the records are missing (e.g., in Revel in 1820). Saint-Gilles reflects the activity in the bureau of Saint-Gilles and Vauvert; Saint-Jean-du-Gard reflects the activity in the bureaus of Saint-Jean-du-Gard and Lasalle.
Source: See text.

court decisions to validate the NLE and to require immediate registration.[16] Once courts had recognized the NLE, typical users, such as illiterate farmers, were eager to adopt them to have access to more medium-term credit and to make payments in the era before widespread banks.

But demand for NLE cannot be reduced to a lack of banks and high rates of illiteracy in southern France in the early nineteenth century, as the example of the department of the Gard demonstrates. The Gard was a center of early adoption. All four markets we sampled in the Gard had NLE in 1820. But the Gard's appetite for creating the NLE was not the result of a lack of banks, because it already had twenty banks in the 1830s and thirty banks by the 1850s. Nor did it stem from a lack of commercial

Table 5.3. Literacy in notarized letter of exchange departments (percent of conscripts who can read and write)

Département	Circa 1830	1874	1899
Bouches-du-Rhône	37.8	86.3	94.1
Cantal	32	77.1	93.9
Dordogne	25.4	70.4	81.1
Gard	40	73.9	95.9
Haute-Garonne	30.8	75.2	95.7
Gers	48.9	83.2	94.9
Hérault	46.1	76.7	99.5
Tarn-et-Garonne	26.8	74.1	90.9
Vaucluse	37.7	74.5	96.9
Haute-Vienne	23.8	56.8	81.7

Source: The first column comes from the data base constituted from Archives Nationales, série F9 (150 à 261); see http://federation.ens.fr/wheberg/dataweb/conscription/yndex/. It reports average literacy for the years 1827, 1828, and 1829, and from d'Angeville in 1836, whose figures date from approximately 1830. For 1874 and 1899, the data come from *Annuaire Statistique de la France* for 1878 and 1900.

connections or from low levels of literacy. The department's chief city, Nîmes, was a center of the textile trade under the Old Regime, and the Protestant population in the north of the department could read and was plugged into a financial network that spanned Languedoc, Geneva, and Paris. To judge from conscripts who could read and write circa 1830, literacy rates in the Gard were actually among the highest, among departments where NLE were common (Table 5.3).

So what else besides illiteracy and access to bank-like payment services can help explain the invention of the NLE? Most likely, it was a local solution to a problem of increased demand for credit at a time when cultivation of cash crops (silk cocoons in Saint-Jean-du-Gard and wine in Saint-Gilles) was expanding but other sources of medium-term credit were scarce. In fact, since the alternative to the NLE was a less sophisticated financial instrument, the billet à ordre, one might surmise that the NLE diffused first in areas where there was already significant experience with credit and only later to more remote places like the Haute-Vienne or the Cantal.

If the spread of cash crops and the demand it created for credit help account for the rise of the NLE, what accounts for their demise? One explanation for their decline is increasing literacy; individuals who could sign their names would have likely opted for a private contract to spare themselves the notary's fees. Overall, from 1830 to 1899, the South of France saw a doubling of literacy; thus, by the 1870s, most borrowers and lenders would have been able to draw up NLE without the help of a notary (see the right side of table 5.3).

Growing literacy is no doubt part of the story, but it cannot be the full explanation, because the overall pattern masks differences that are not consistent with literacy as the sole driving force. If literacy alone killed off the NLE, we would expect them to have survived longest in the departments with the lowest literacy rates. The two laggards in literacy are the Dordogne and the Haute-Vienne, but the NLE had already vanished from those markets by 1899—not what we would expect if literacy alone were the sole cause here. Equally troubling is what happened in the Haute-Garonne: there, the NLE survived past 1899, but literacy rates in 1870s were almost identical to those in the Gard and the Vaucluse, where the NLE was on the wane. Furthermore, if growing literacy were doing all the work, then larger borrowers (who were more likely to be educated) would have disappeared from the NLE market, causing the average size of NLE to decline over time. Yet there was little change in their average size.

The pace of the NLE decline was also strikingly varied—far more than the general improvement of literacy in the Rhône valley would have led us to expect. In L'Isle-sur-Sorgues we sampled January and February once every five years. The NLE grew very rapidly from the late 1820s to the mid-1850s (since notaries in the bureau drew up fifty-one of them in January and February 1850 alone). Then a slow decline set in: sixteen letters of exchange were notarized in January and February of 1865. In 1870, for the same two months, notaries drew up twenty-eight. Afterwards, the decline was abrupt. We find only three NLE in 1875, one in 1880, and none in 1890 or 1899.

Elsewhere, the NLE exit followed a different rhythm, one dictated by the demand for credit in the local economy. In Saint-Jean-du-Gard and Lasalle in the north of the department of the Gard, where raising silkworms was important, the NLE crashed even earlier than in the Vaucluse, with only ten NLE in 1870, compared to more than seventy in 1840. The region may have been even more specialized in sericulture than L'Isle-sur-Sorgues, and it may thus have felt the shock of the silkworm diseases of the 1850s far more severely. Further south in the Gard, where farmers grew grain and cultivated grapes, NLE remained popular through the 1860s, most likely because farmers there did not depend on silkworms.

Further west, the decline began later, after 1870. In Lézignan in the eastern Aude, the number of NLE fell by forty-four percent from 1865 to 1875 and then by another seventy-nine percent between 1875 and 1890, although a few letters of exchange still cropped up in 1899. In Castelnaudary, a market in the western Aude that abuts the Haute-Garonne, the number of NLE dipped by half between 1865 and 1875 and by sixty-two percent between 1875 and 1890. But thereafter the number of NLE stabilized.

Revel, directly to the west of Castelnaudary, tells yet another story. The NLE cropped up there in the 1820s and reached a relatively stable plateau by 1840, one untroubled by the growth in literacy between 1840 and 1880. The NLE declined in the 1890s, but the process was slow. The same was true in the markets in the Haute-Garonne, Gers, and Tarn-et-Garonne: they all still had some notarized letters of exchange in 1899, albeit at a much lower level than in 1865.

Local credit, so this varied chronology suggests, was sensitive to the demand for credit in local markets. The NLE therefore rose and fell with the demand for medium-term financing and payment by local farmers. Thus, it was not just a response to a lack of banks or a solution for farmers who could not read. Rather, it arose in response to economic growth in the local economies in the 1820s. The civil law did not block this innovation; neither did appellate courts, who drew on the ideals of the French Revolution to make the new financial instrument available to all. The NLE made an exit that was just as complex: banks and literacy played a role, but they waned most rapidly when demand for the credit they provided itself faded away.

CHAPTER 6

The Diffusion of Banks

PEER-TO-PEER CREDIT MARKETS AS SUBSTITUTES FOR BANKS

For decades, most studies of financial markets in the eighteenth and nineteenth centuries have focused either on banks or on public finance. They have done so because many economic historians believe that banks play a decisive role in financing industrialization and that sound public finances are a prerequisite for developing a banking sector (Lüthy 1959–65; Gerschenkron 1962; Lévy-Leboyer 1964; Cameron 1961, 1967; Kindelberger 2015). Banks, in their view, are critical, and their arrival has often been hailed for breaking the shackles on capital markets that hold back economic growth.[1]

By contrast, we have focused on a different source of credit: notaries. Because notaries, as we know, only provided brokerage services, a lender who turned to them presumably had to forgo the benefits that a bank deposit would have yielded. That could mean that notaries offered illiquid and poorly diversified bond portfolios, because lenders might have had to take the entirety of each loan that a notary funded and hold it to maturity. If so, then investing in a bank or putting money on deposit would have provided greater liquidity and lower risk.[2] Banks would thus appear to be superior. So one potential explanation for the importance of notarial credit in France would be that the better alternative source of credit, banks, were scarce.

Economic historians have, by and large, accepted the argument that banks are necessary for industrialization and economic growth. They also believe a second important claim about banks, one that has major implications for the economic history of France: that banks there were slow to spread. To take one example, the most recent collection of scholarly articles on banks (Michel Lescure and Alain Plessis 1999) focuses on their tardy rise after 1860; implicitly, it concedes that there were few banks before then.[3] Quantifying the number of banks before 1860 is simply left aside, as it is in most of the rest of the literature. Apparently, the fact that banks were scarce before 1860 is so well known that it is not even worth counting how few there were.

There are two reasons why this claim about banks in France has endured for so long—longer, in fact, than is justified by the evidence. The first is simply that a lack of banks offers a convenient explanation for why nineteenth-century France was less industrialized than Britain. To be sure, France had cities, broad markets, secure property rights, and energetic entrepreneurs, but it did industrialize more slowly than Britain or Germany. Even at the end of the century, when it had begun to catch up, its industrial sector generated only thirty-four percent of GDP, versus forty-three percent in the United Kingdom and forty percent in Germany (Mitchell 1981, 840–57). Slower industrialization is just what one would expect if a country's banking sector was anemic, so no one had any reason to doubt the claim that France lacked enough banks.

The second reason this notion about the lack of banks in France survives is equally simple: there are, unfortunately, no official statistics for the number of banks in the nineteenth century, which makes it harder to actually count how many banks France had. Because banking was a free-entry business, there is no central record of a bank's establishment. The only exception was for banks seeking to organize as joint stock corporations, because that required special legislation until general incorporation was made possible in 1867. Tax records are also silent. Banks were admittedly subject to the *patente* (a business tax), but they paid no other special tax that could be used as an index of banking activity. The patente records would also omit bankers who ran other businesses (such as being a wholesale merchant) and who paid the patente for the second occupation in order to reduce their tax.[4] In addition, banks were not really monitored either, chiefly because the Banque de France (the central bank created by Napoleon) maintained an unchallenged monopoly on fiduciary or paper money. That monopoly reduced the need to watch banks closely in order to prevent monetary crises.

One could argue that the spread of banks in France was delayed by the lack of an appropriate legal structure. For banks to proliferate—so the argument would go—France needed joint-stock banks, and until the free incorporation law of 1867, founding a joint stock bank was difficult, which kept banks from entering markets in sufficient numbers.

That claim, however, seems wrongheaded. First of all, even if we accept that Paris did not make the corporate form available soon enough (a dubious assumption, since other European states were slow too, and even England did not allow general incorporation until 1844), there were still other feasible forms of organization that could have done the trick. In France, a bank could be open and operate as a sole proprietorship, a partnership, a limited partnership, or even a limited partnership with tradable shares (*commandite par action*). While these other legal arrangements did not offer potential bankers a joint stock entity with both limited liability and tradable shares, the *commandite par action* came close. And, as we shall see, the demand for the limited liability version of the joint stock firm was in any case low: both before and after it became freely available in 1867, most firms shunned it. Therefore, the lack of a joint stock limited liability firm was not a constraint that limited the creation of banks.

Economic historians writing in English thus tend to accept the lack of banks, and then invoke it to explain why France was slow to industrialize. For Rondo Cameron, "That [industrialization's progress was not more rapid in France] must be attributed in large measure to its banking system, characterized by an inadequate number and distribution of banking offices, an insufficient variety of specialized financial institutions" (Cameron 1967, 127). Economic historians have tried to find out, then, why the number of banks seemed so small. For some, such as Cameron, it was the failure to provide easy incorporation for banking firms before 1867, and limited access to secondary markets (the Bourse). For others, such as Antoin Murphy, the barrier to more banks was the long arm of history. For Murphy, the damage was done not only by the revolution's paper money (the assignats), but by the Law affair: John Law's failed 1716–20 attempt to create a central bank, remake government finances, and replace coins with paper money, which ended up triggering rapid inflation and a stock market bubble. Although both the assignats and Law's paper money were ways to eliminate the French obsession with gold, the inflation they unleashed only reinforced the fetish. As a result (so Murphy argues), "financial innovation was frowned upon and the banking sector, from 1720 until the 1930s, was only allowed to grow within the constraints of a specie-based monetary system. France's historical experience generated opposition to external finance that in turn led to internal finance and concentrated ownership."[5]

If taken at face value, what do Cameron's and Murphy's claims suggest? Presumably that France would only break free and begin to industrialize when banks were able to lend on a large scale. For the celebrated economic historian Alexander Gerschenkron (1962, 11), that turning point was the Second Empire (1852–70), when France was ruled by Napoleon's nephew, who in 1852 encouraged the creation of a big investment bank, Crédit Mobilier.[6] For other economic historians, the turning point came later, in the 1860s, when the large banks Crédit Lyonnais and Société Générale opened numerous bank branches (Bouvier 1961). Before then, the best thing one could say about the French credit system would be captured by Larry Neal's summary of our previous work: "Not so, claim the revisionist studies of private credit activities undertaken by the notaries that emerged from the ruins of public credit in 1723. . . . Hoffman et al. claim that the concentration of notaries in brokering long-term lending among private individuals thereafter was an effective 'third way' for financial intermediation. The French, under duress, had spontaneously discovered an alternative to banks and capital markets as means of financial intermediation—an information network managed by information brokers entrusted with the responsibility of placing either funds or loans among their clients" (Neal 2000).

On closer inspection, however, neither Cameron's claim about banks nor Murphy's can stand up to the evidence. Banks, as we shall see, did open their doors and make loans throughout France far earlier than any suspected. And there were in fact many more banks in the first half of the nineteenth century than other researchers have supposed. The claims about too few banks, particularly early on, simply overlook the numerous French banks that did exist and did make loans.

We base this argument on evidence derived from a neglected historical source—commercial directories—which we use to reconstruct a history of the diffusion of banks in France from 1800 to 1910. We then do the same for the United Kingdom from 1805 to 1857, so that we can compare the spread of banks in both countries. As we shall see, France did have fewer banks outside cities than Britain. But fewer rural banks did not mean a total lack of banks, and the corresponding greater number of banks in the British countryside may have had more to do with the lack of intermediaries in Britain who could play the role that notaries did in France, and arrange short- and medium-term loans for lenders in towns and villages. Britain, in short, may have had more banks because of failings in its own financial past. With fewer alternative sources of credit, Britain was far more dependent on banks than other countries.[7]

Elusive French Banks

The debate over banking in France was shaped by the country's slow industrialization, or at least its lag behind Britain, the first country to undergo sustained economic growth (O'Brien and Keyder 1978; Allen 2009; Kelly, O Grada, Mokyr 2014). The debate was also shaped by the French Revolution. Nearly everyone agrees that the revolutionary inflation and default on government debt harmed financial markets, and that Napoleon's policies hardly improved matters (Crouzet 1993). The revolution and slow industrialization are deeply intertwined, whether one views the revolution as the price to pay to cast off the shackles of the Old Regime or whether it is interpreted as a political catastrophe that hobbled economic growth for several decades (Lévy-Leboyer 1964, 29).The stakes in this debate were raised by economic historians writing in the immediate aftermath of World War II, but they overemphasized the role of investment in physical capital in spurring growth. Because this investment was expensive, these historians believed that the financial market was critical to the onset of growth.

Gerschenkron exemplifies this belief better than anyone else. For him, France's traditional banking system was too weak to support rapid industrialization, and its banks were simply too small to fund the large-scale enterprises a late-developing economy desperately needed. But when the Second Empire allowed the incorporation of universal banks (large banks with branches), France embarked on a path that would let it catch up with Britain.

The problem, however, was that Gerschenkron did not try to quantify differences in financial systems between Britain and France, either before or after the Crédit Mobilier or the universal banks were established. Rondo Cameron, in 1967, five years after Gerschenkron's influential essay, was the first to attempt to trace the expansion of banks in a way that could test Gerschenkron's claim quantitatively. The top panel of table 6.1 reproduces Cameron's data (table IV.2 of his *Banking in the Early Stages of Industrialization*). With that data, Cameron's conclusions seem unassailable. France seemed to have very few banks of any kind, universal or not. In 1810, when France was ruled by the Emperor Napoleon, there was only one bank office for 370,000 people, according to Cameron's figures. Even in 1870, at the end of the Second Empire, Paris apparently had only three dozen banks, and the provinces merely three hundred. Most people in France therefore had little access to banks, if Cameron is correct. With no banks to make payments or lend money, the French economy presumably suffered.

Cameron's table lists no sources, although his discussion suggests he relied heavily on Bertrand Gille's work (1959). For his part, Gille does not provide any systematic data either. But other work—by Maurice Lévy-Leboyer (1964)—casts doubt on the belief that lack of credit could explain France's slow industrialization. Lévy-Leboyer took a broader view of credit and finance than most, recognizing that credit (and in particular long-term credit) could flow through traditional networks just as much as through more "modern" intermediaries. Although Lévy-Leboyer never produced an alternative to Cameron's table, he did show a possible path in later work. "To be sure, we are not well informed, except for a case by case basis, on the origins of local banks, on their numbers (a hundred maybe in 1820, according to an almanac; about three times that in 1840), or on their roles or impact" (Lévy-Leboyer 1976, 371). The almanac Lévy-Leboyer refers to is probably the commercial directory published by Jean de la Tynna, one of the business guides that came out annually and listed banks and other useful information for businessmen and administrators in nineteenth-century France.[8]

To remedy the shortcomings of earlier studies, it is straightforward, albeit tedious, to plow through the volumes published by de la Tynna (and his successors the Bottin and Didot publishing firms) looking for banks and bankers. For Paris we had already done so up to 1870 while writing

Table 6.1. Banking in the early stages of industrialization

	Rondo Cameron											
	1800	1810	1820	1830	1840	1850	1860	1870	1880	1890	1900	1910
	Joint stock banks											
Paris	3	1	1	1	6	4	10	17				
Provinces	1	0	3	3	15	20	98	132				
Branches	0	3	0	0	3	25	48	100				
	Private banks											
Paris	10	15	25	30	30	25	25	20				
Provinces	50	60	100	188	250	200	200	200				
Total banks	64	79	129	222	304	274	381	469				
1,000 persons per office	430	370	234	176	112	130	98	82				

	Cameron corrected											
	1800	1810	1820	1830	1840	1850	1860	1870	1880	1890	1900	1910
	Joint stock banks											
Paris	1	1	1	1	1	2	2	5	5	5	5	5
Branches of Paris firm		0		0	7	10	62	92	225	329	582	1,196
	Private banks											
Paris	103	54	42	152	214	174	306	447			843	
Provinces	79	309	367	701	1,053	1,405	1,848	2,014	2,263	2,055	1,951	2,026
Total banks	183	364	410	854	1,275	1,591	2,218	2,558				
1,000 Persons per office	150.4	80.3	73.6	45.8	26.7	22.4	16.8	15.0				

Note: The source in 1801 do not provide a way to distinguish bankers from wholesale merchants (négociants) in Bordeaux, Lille, Marseille, or Nantes. Together these cities had 26 bankers in 1820 and surely had some in 1800, so the numbers above in panel B are surely biased downward early on.

Sources: The top panel reproduces Rondo Cameron's table IV.2 in *Banking in the Early Stages of Industrialization*, 111. Cameron provides no sources for that table. The bottom panel tabulates bankers listed in the Almanach-Annuaire du Commerce.

Priceless Markets (Hoffman, Postel-Vinay, Rosenthal 2000). Now we have extended that effort and tabulated the number of bankers outside Paris roughly twice in each decade from 1800–1801 until 1911.[9] Nonetheless, there are some challenges to deriving systemic counts of banks from the commercial directories. In 1800 and 1805, specifically, bankers are listed only for cities with commodity exchanges (bourse de commerce); furthermore, in many cities where there were banks (among them Marseille, Bordeaux, Lille, Nantes, and Amiens), the early directories do not differentiate them from wholesale merchants, who often engaged both in trade and banking. By 1810, however, the directories provide information for the individual arrondissements (the French administrative subdivisions just below the level of department) in each department, so we are relatively confident that banks would be included if their offices were located either in the arrondissements' chief towns (the subprefectures) or in the city that was the department headquarters (the prefecture).

The data that we ended up culling from the commercial directories does understate the number of banks, because being listed as a banker there depended on two actions. First, to be listed, wholesale merchants who discounted letters of exchange for their clients had to choose to identify themselves as bankers.[10] They might not do so if they spent more time as merchants than as bankers, or if their banking business depended more on making payments than on discounting letters of exchange. But even identifying oneself as a banker did not automatically generate a listing among the banks. Directories were compiled by local individuals; as a result, early on at least, for a bank to be listed, the directory's local correspondent had to decide whether to provide a separate list of banks, or to merge them either with wholesale merchants (négociants) or with the dominant type of local merchants (shipping firms in Calais, wine merchants in Bordeaux, or silk merchants in Lyon). If the correspondent put the banks among the merchants, he might append a distinction for those who were also bankers. But if he did not (as happened in Bordeaux until 1820), then the directory leaves all the local banks out. The bottom line, then, is that the directories clearly overlook some banks even after 1820, when lists isolating bankers begin appearing in all the major cities.

Despite the omissions, the directories yield the most comprehensive list of banks available, with the great advantage that it can be followed consistently over time. It is clearly an improvement over the Banque de France records used by Bertrand Gille (1959), which were incomplete.

The results of our counts from the almanac are displayed in table 6.1, panel B. They demonstrate that Cameron's numbers undercount the number of banks by a large margin. In 1800, for example, Cameron counted sixty-four bank offices (thirteen in Paris, fifty-one in the provinces). We found 202 in 1801 (126 in Paris and seventy-six in the provinces). Our

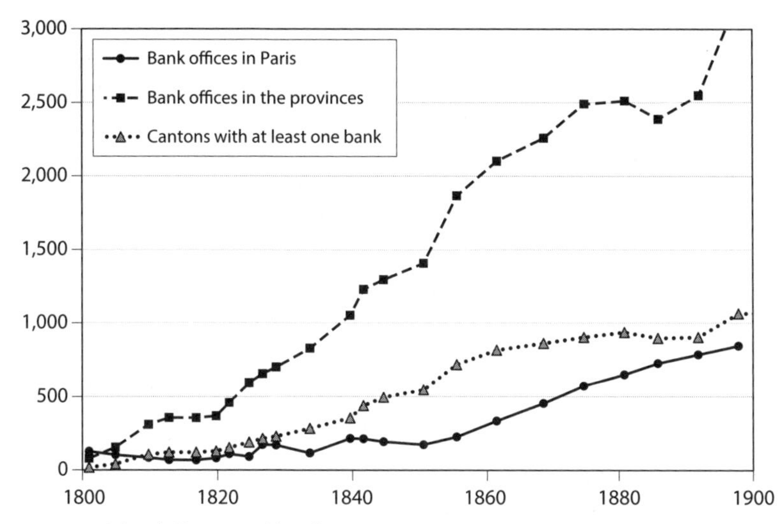

Figure 6.1. The diffusion of banks in France.
Source: For banks, see the text.

numbers are three times higher, which is close to the correction one has to make to all of Cameron's numbers up to the 1850s. Thereafter, the correction is larger, because Cameron is even further off. The consequences are dramatic. While our 1810 count implies about 100,000 French persons per office, according to Cameron's figures that level of service was not attained before 1870.

It is true, as figure 6.1 shows, that the diffusion of banks in France started from a very low point in 1801. The near absence of banks outside Paris is not surprising, given that the financial stabilization at the end of the revolution did not begin until 1795. Only then was the currency stabilized at one franc per 4.5 grams of silver, and there were more changes to come, with the public debt restructuring in 1797 and the establishment of the Banque de France in 1800 (Crouzet 1993). Inside Paris, the number of banks proved sensitive to political shocks. It hit a low in 1817, shortly after the 1815 final defeat and exile of the Emperor Napoleon, and again in 1833, after the 1830 fall of King Charles X, and the number of bank offices in Paris does not begin to rise regularly until the 1850s (figure 6.1). Outside Paris, the situation is different, with the number of banks growing quite steadily over time, except for a plateau from 1813 to 1820 and another from 1845 to 1856. Meanwhile, the number of cantons with at least one bank rose from nineteen (including Paris) to over one thousand in a century.

These banks spreading across France provided the short-term credit and payment services that had long been the speciality of bankers. The banks offered savers investments that were presumably more liquid, and they also funded commerce, agriculture, and industry. Some of the banks mobilized capital for longer-term investments, either by extending loans or taking equity position. In the city of Dijon, for example, Victor Felix David's bank put money into a textile mill and two iron foundries. When the investments soured in 1839, David and his relatives took out the huge 1.1 million franc notarial loan secured by family real estate that we discussed in chapter 4. In the countryside, the new banks helped support expansion of the food processing industry. In northern France, for instance, Louis Dumont's bank in the city of Valenciennes lent 100,000 francs to a sugar beet farmer to expand the factory he owned that processed the beets. To back up all these loans, the banks tended to rely less on the sort of collateral that secured the notaries' peer-to-peer credit, and more on cosigners and the borrowers' reputations.[11]

Clearly, we cannot invoke a shortage of banks to explain why notaries remained important midwives for credit throughout the nineteenth century. Such an argument might perhaps do for a small town such as Mirande, where banks did not arrive until the 1870s, but how can it ever account for the large amount of long-term credit arranged by notaries in cities such as Rouen or Amiens? In these large cities, there were already a dozen banks or more by the 1830s.

Perhaps we should think about the newly opened banks in a different way. Perhaps they did not replace notaries at all. In fact, rather than being substitutes for notaries, the banks might well have served different parts of the credit market, with notaries first focusing on long-term collateralized loans and banks on short-term commercial credit and interregional payment services. That is a possibility that we will return to in chapter 7.

But for now we leave that issue aside and take up other questions about banks that deserve attention. In particular, it may be that France had banks, but that they were not helpful to economic development because they were located in the wrong places. That is the topic we turn to in the next section, by comparing the distribution of bank offices in France to the distribution of bank offices in the United Kingdom.

The Diffusion of Banks in France and the United Kingdom Before 1852

We can compare the list of banks from the French commercial directories with similar data from commercial directories for United Kingdom.[12] Unlike the French list, which arose from a bottom-up process of individual firms entering the directories, the British list was produced by the government's

Inland Revenue office, because British banks were a source of government revenue. All bankers were subject to a bank tax (Marchant 1838). Moreover, the British directories report a complete list of banks for the British Isles as a separate table, in contrast to the French directories, where we must cull banks by examining the list of occupations for every city and town mentioned. If anything, this difference implies that fewer banks will be missed in the United Kingdom than in France.[13]

For economists who believe that financial development spurs economic growth, there are two testable hypotheses that link a lower number of banks in France to slower industrialization; both entail comparisons with the United Kingdom, because it industrialized earlier. The first hypothesis is that Britain simply had more banks that France. This could be derived either from the long-standing pro-creditor approach of English law or from the institutional and organizational changes ushered in by the Glorious Revolution. At bottom, this hypothesis posits that Britain had an "absolute advantage" over France in banking development. The second, more modest hypothesis assumes only that Britain had a relative advantage over France: its banking structure was more efficient because it gave people easier access to banks than did the banking system in France. It could have this greater efficiency either because more of the British population lived in cities, where banks tended to be located, or because British banks had a much greater propensity to open offices in small towns.

Let us begin with the first hypothesis. In 1810, the post office directory listed 771 banks in the United Kingdom (table 6.2). That is more than double the number in France, which had only 364 banks serving its larger population. By the late 1820s, the United Kingdom counted 862 banks and France nearly as many, 854. The numbers continued to grow in the 1830s and early 1840s, particularly outside of London and Paris, so that by the early 1850s, the United Kingdom had 1,721 banks versus 1,396 in France. The United Kingdom had an absolute advantage in access to banks but it was smaller than one might have presumed (about a twenty-five-percent edge in 1853), and the gap had narrowed since 1810.

Of course, France's population (about thirty million in 1821) was larger than the United Kingdom's (about twenty-one million). As a result, the United Kingdom had a clear advantage in access to banks. In fact, in 1820 the number of bank offices per inhabitant in the United Kingdom was over twice what it was in France (one bank office for every 69,000 people in France; one for every 28,000 in the United Kingdom). By the early 1850s, however, the gap in bank access had shrunk considerably: on average, there was now one bank for every 26,000 customers in France versus 16,000 in the United Kingdom.[14] Clearly, banks arrived earlier in the United Kingdom than in France, and there were more banks per person in Britain as well, which meant easier access.

Table 6.2. Bank diffusion in France and the United Kingdom

France								Great Britain (England, Wales, Scotland)							
1805	1810	1820	1829	1833	1842	1851	1856	1805	1810	1820	1828	1834	1843	1852	1857
Departments								Counties							
Percent with at least one bank															
41	70	79	94	100	100	100	100	75	81	79	88	95	99	98	100
Number of observations															
86	86	86	86	86	86	86	86	89	89	89	89	89	89	89	89
Number of banks (outside Paris and London) France vs. Great Britain															
154	309	367	699	1,044	1,224	1,253	1,408	455	691	655	757	930	1,423	1,460	1,547
Banks in Paris								Banks in London							
66	54	91	155	116	204	143	227	70	78	71	72	59	89	85	80
								Number of bank offices in Ireland							
								0	2	27	33	45	157	176	181

Source for France: Almanach du Commerce de Paris, des départements de la France et des principales villes du monde (1805–38); *Annuaire général du Commerce et de L'industrie* (1842–56). For the United Kingdom, Critchet and Woods, *Post Office Annual Directory*, for 1805–1843; Slater, *National Commercial Directory*, for 1846; Slater, *Royal National Commercial Directory*, for 1852: and Thom, *Irish Almanac and Official Directory of the United Kingdom*, for 1857.

The United Kingdom also led in the number of banked locations—in other words, in the number of towns and cities with at least one bank. Before 1820, when there were twice as many banks in the United Kingdom as in France, the number of banked locations in the United Kingdom was three times as large as in France. The United Kingdom's lead in banked locations declined more slowly than its advantage in the number of banks per capita, which fell rapidly. The chief reason, as figures 6.2 and 6.3 show, is that French bankers were much more likely to congregate in the larger cities than their counterparts in the United Kingdom. In both countries, all settlements with a population greater than 50,000 had banks, but French towns of that size had an average of eleven to fifteen banks while their British counterparts had four to five. The disparity is almost as dramatic in towns with populations between 25,000 and 50,000, where the number of banks in France grew from about four by 1810 to six or so by 1850, while in Britain that number remains between three and four during the whole period.

The result of French bankers' predilection for cities was that in the first half of the nineteenth century thirty percent of all banks in France did business in towns with at least 25,000 inhabitants (figure 6.4), while in Great Britain less than twenty percent were located in communities that were large (figure 6.5). By contrast, sixty percent of all bank offices in Great Britain were in towns with fewer than 10,000 inhabitants, a share not reached in France until after 1910.

One possible explanation for at least part of this contrast is that the French banks operated at a smaller scale than their British counterparts and that this scale did not rise as the population grew. More banks would therefore enter cities as their populations grew during the nineteenth century, which would account for the larger number of banks in French cities with over 25,000 inhabitants. What remains unexplained, however, is why bankers tended to stick to the cities that were already served and why they did not see any profit in smaller towns nearby. In Britain, bankers did find it profitable to open up in such towns. Why such a difference would exist is a question we will take up below.

Before we do so, however, let us distinguish between the effect that urbanization itself had on bank locations in Britain and France and the impact of the different propensity to open banks in small French towns. We will do so by considering two counterfactual exercises that isolate the contributions of urbanization and of the different propensity to open banks in France (table 6.3). The top panel tabulates the fraction of markets (districts in Great Britain and cantons in France) with banks in each country, conditional on the size of the chief municipality in each canton or district. The bottom left panel then estimates the number of French cantons that would have had banks if France had had the same urbanization

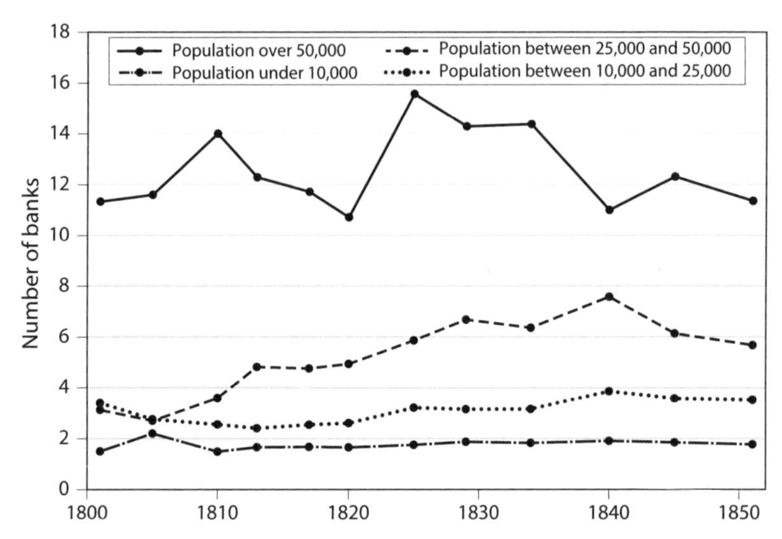

Figure 6.2. Number of banks by French canton chef-lieu (conditional on having at least one bank).
Source: For banks, see the text; for population, see http://cassini.ehess.fr/cassini/fr/html/6_index.htm.

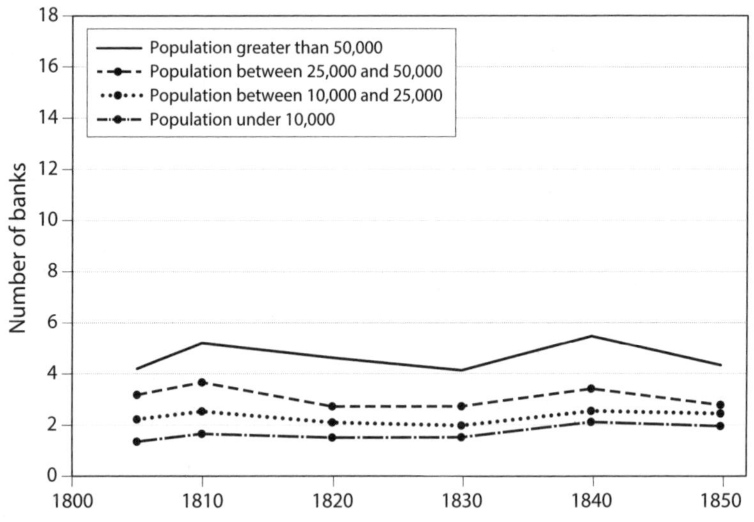

Figure 6.3. Number of banks in Great Britain by census subdistrict population (conditional on having at least one bank).
Source: For banks, see the text; for population, see http://www.histpop.org/ohpr/servlet/.

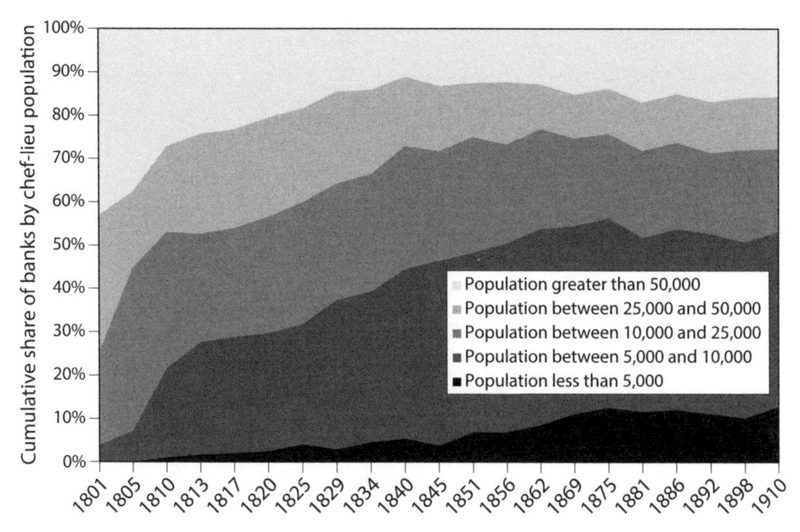

Figure 6.4. Share of French bank offices by canton chef-lieu population. *Source:* For banks, see the text; for population, see http://cassini.ehess.fr/cassini/fr/html/6_index.htm.

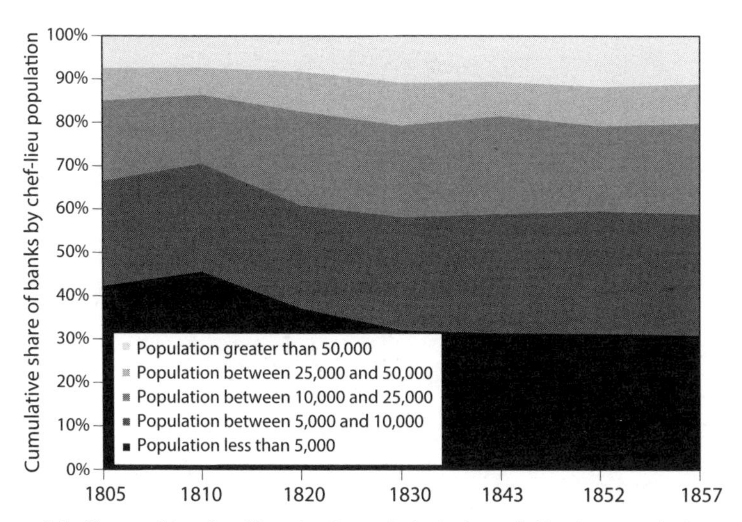

Figure 6.5. Share of bank offices in Great Britain by subdistrict population. *Source:* For banks, see the text; for population, see http://www.histpop.org/ohpr/servlet/.

Table 6.3. Counterfactual diffusion of banks in France

	Great Britain (England, Wales, Scotland)							France						
	Percent districts with at least one bank (by largest subdistrict population)							Percent cantons with at least one bank (by chef-lieu population)						
	1805	1810	1820	1830	1843	1852	1857	1805	1810	1820	1829	1840	1851	1856
Population > 50000	100	90.0	81.8	94.4	100	97.1	94.3	62.5	75.0	100	100	100	100	100
50000 > Population > 25000	78.6	78.6	87.5	89.3	90.9	97.4	97.4	52.6	85.0	77.3	95.7	100.0	96.6	100.0
25000 > Population > 10000	68.6	71.9	80.3	79.3	89.3	83.8	85.7	28.8	52.1	52.1	74.7	83.5	88.9	89.9
10000 > Population > 5000	56.0	68.4	62.3	76.6	84.2	87.3	86.7	2.3	12.5	17.1	32.8	43.3	49.6	54.3
5000 > Population > 2500	49.5	59.2	54.2	58.4	73.1	79.0	77.5	0.0	2.0	2.6	5.2	10.7	16.6	19.0
2500 < Population	17.6	29.7	21.9	23.6	39.7	44.6	42.0	0.0	0.1	0.4	0.8	2.7	4.0	4.7

	Counterfactual number of banked locations in France if France had													
	British urbanization rate							British banking propensity rate						
	1805	1810	1820	1830	1843	1852	1857	1805	1810	1820	1830	1843	1852	1857
Population > 50000	19	33	48	77	88	150	150	8	7	6	7	9	14	14
50000 > Population > 25000	32	52	81	115	122	161	167	15	16	19	21	17	28	32
25000 > Population > 10000	65	131	162	279	317	400	404	50	53	59	63	71	91	93
10000 > Population > 5000	10	64	110	216	263	353	385	119	153	142	185	171	222	224
5000 > Population > 2500	0	21	27	50	85	142	163	354	434	421	522	588	781	746
2500 < Population	0	1	3	5	11	19	23	327	543	389	372	518	634	601
	Counterfactual percent of banked locations in France													
France Counterfactual	4.4	10.5	14.9	26.3	36.7	43.5	45.9	30.2	41.8	35.9	41.5	56.8	62.9	60.9
France Actual	1.4	3.7	4.4	8.0	12.5	17.2	19.1	1.4	3.7	4.4	8.0	12.5	17.2	19.1
UK Actual	39.8	53.0	52.2	60.1	74.4	78.1	77.2	39.8	53.0	52.2	60.1	74.4	78.1	77.2

Source: For banks, see table 8.1. Population figures come from French and British censuses.

rate as Britain. In other words, it computes the effect that variations in urbanization rates alone had on bank locations in France.

This counterfactual exercise does increase the fraction of banked locations in France, as we can see in the third line from the bottom of the table, where the fraction of French markets with banks would roughly triple through 1843 and more than double thereafter. Nevertheless, a very large gap remains relative to Great Britain. Even with Britain's urbanization rate, France would still have a smaller fraction of markets with banks and a larger fraction (over twice as large) without banks (table 6.3).

The bottom right panel in table 6.3 leaves France's urbanization rate unchanged and then estimates what would happen if French bankers had the British propensity to open banks in markets of each size. The impact is even bigger than the effect of the urbanization rate; indeed, in the early years it increases the share of banked locations nearly tenfold (table 6.3, third line from the bottom). The lesson is simple: the British had greater access to banks not simply because Great Britain was more urbanized than France but because British banks were eager to open offices to serve semirural customers.

There is more to the contrast, though, than urbanization rates and the propensity to open banks in small towns. The anatomy of the banking sector was different in both countries. We assessed the industry's structure in 1856 for France and in 1857 for the United Kingdom. In 1856, there were 1,635 bank offices in France (table 6.2), with the Banque de France doing business in thirty-four towns, and the Crédit Foncier in eleven. Beyond these two establishments, which were both closely connected to the state, twenty-eight banks belonged to firms with more than one office. (None of these firms had more than two offices.) The rest, 1,562 so-called "unit" bank establishments, had only one office. Unit banks accounted for ninety-five percent of all bank offices. In 1856, therefore, France had a unit banking system, the same banking system that served most of the United States until 1994. In the United States, though, unit banking was the result of regulations and laws, usually on the state level. That was not the case in France.

In the United Kingdom in 1857, by contrast, banks with a single office accounted for only eleven percent of the establishments, and banks with an extensive branch system (twenty or more offices) accounted for 937 of the 1,804 bank offices outside London. Some of the disparity clearly reflected laws that facilitated bank incorporation in the United Kingdom, but branch banking was common even among unincorporated (so-called private) banks. Some twenty-eight percent of them had more than one office, a far higher figure than in France, where only one percent of private banks had branches. There was then a striking difference between British banking and its French counterpart, with the United Kingdom possessing a more extensive network of banks (and a more elaborate web of bank branches in particular) by the mid-nineteenth century. Moreover, our data may even underestimate the extent of the British network, for beyond the large number of branch banks, there were also clear ties between country banks and London banks. The sources providing our data in fact publish the names of the London bank that each country bank drew upon as a correspondent. Our list of branches, though, does not take those relationships into account.

This comparison of banking in France and the United Kingdom yields five conclusions. First, it is clear that banks were spreading in France even before Napoleon's regime ended and the monarchy was restored in 1814–15. By the 1820s their proliferation was making up for lack of banks in France. Second, the reason why France had fewer banks before the 1820s was probably the turmoil during the French Revolution and the restoration of the monarchy, not any difference in French and British institutions. Third, after 1820, large cities in France had just as many banks as in Britain, but small French cities were still more likely to be unbanked. Fourth, in the late 1850s, France had far fewer bank branches than Britain. With virtually no branch offices, France was stuck with what was essentially a unit banking system, and it is conceivable that small unit banks would have had a hard time making a go of it in small towns, where undiversified loan portfolios might be too risky. Finally, the directories we relied upon to count banks in France and Britain happen to exist throughout Europe. Systematic use of these directories to compile a census of bank offices in nineteenth-century Europe would provide us with a rich source of data for studying financial development, data that could profitably be put to use by economists, historians, and political scientists.[15]

The Growth of the Banking Network in France

So, what kept the number of branch banks in France so low? Did some obstacle restrict branch banking? Was it in turn the reason why so few banks opened in small cities in France? If so, then we would know what hampered bank access outside big cities in France.

One possible culprit was a lack of the institutional infrastructure needed to create large branch banks—in particular, easy bank incorporation, and ready access to primary and secondary markets for equity. Obstacles to incorporation were implicit in the arguments of Gerschenkron and Cameron, who stressed the lack of joint stock banks, particularly large universal banks with many branches. Other economists have made similar criticisms of the institutional infrastructure of the financial system in France and other countries.[16]

As Gerschenkron himself noted, the number of incorporated banks in France in the first half of the nineteenth century was small; of the few incorporated banks, only the Banque de France endured past 1850. But then institutions changed. Napoleon's nephew allowed a number of banks to incorporate when he was in power in the 1850s, and general incorporation became possible in the 1860s.

Did this easier incorporation spur bank diffusion and bank branching? To see if it did, we compared bank diffusion and bank branching before and after 1850. But before taking up that comparison, we should first consider how restrictive the limits to incorporation were before 1850. If they did not constrain bankers, or if there were legal alternatives that had the same effect as incorporation, then easier incorporation should not have helped banks spread and open branches.

Incorporation was limited by the government's reluctance to grant bank charters before the Second Empire (1852–1970). But, as we have seen, bankers could turn to legal alternatives to incorporation that had almost all the same advantages. In particular, entrepreneurs could have organized banks as limited partnerships with tradable shares (LPTS), an alternative joint stock form of the corporation, which lacked only limited liability for the managing partners. As a firm structure, it was widely used after 1825, with nearly 6,000 LPTS launched before the law permitting general incorporation in 1867. That was ten times the number of corporations.[17] And the LPTS was no mere passing fancy; famous firms such as the steel maker Schneider or the tire manufacturer Michelin were organized in this way for most of their existence. In Paris, from 1807 to 1863, a few dozen of the several hundred multi-owner banking firms were set up as LPTS, but even so, the form did not become popular among the capital's bankers. It was even less likely to take hold outside of Paris, where banks remained sole proprietorships, partnerships, or limited partnerships. The LPTS was available, but apparently few French bankers saw a profit to be made by turning their firm into a joint stock enterprise with tradable shares. That is a powerful argument from revealed preference that incorporation was not an obstacle to starting new banks.

But what, then, were the consequences of opening the door to general incorporation in 1867? And what was the effect of the other notable measure of state sponsored financial development at mid-century—the 1852 creation of both the Crédit Mobilier, the first large corporate investment bank, and the Crédit Foncier, the state-backed mortgage bank? As far as branch banking is concerned, the impact was limited, at least outside Paris. By 1869, banks with branches doubled their share of all offices outside Paris to eleven percent, but this was no sea change. In 1869, banks with branches only accounted for 14.5 percent of all provincial offices, and none of the large corporate banks founded before 1870 operated a large

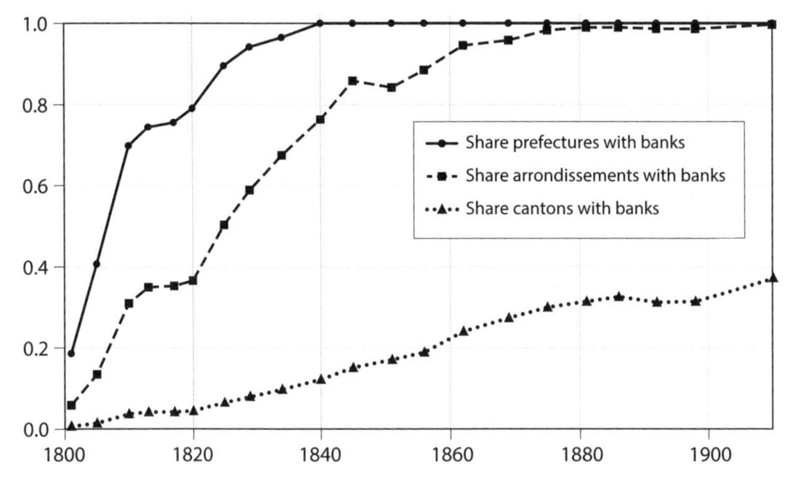

Figure 6.6.The diffusion of Banks in France.
Source: For banks, see the text; for population, see http://cassini.ehess.fr/cassini/fr/html/6_index.htm.

number of branches. Only the Société Générale had more than twenty, and it and the Banque de France remained the largest branch banks. Once again, revealed preference implies that generalized incorporation was not what kept bankers from opening branches. Otherwise, branches would have popped up in large numbers after 1867.

Although the rise of corporate banks under the Second Empire had only a limited impact on branching, the French unit banking system (to repeat, the same banking system that served most of the United States until 1994) continued to grow both in terms of numbers of offices and locations served. As figure 6.1 shows, there were some two thousand bank offices outside Paris by 1862, and the number increased steadily to 1910, as France's banks diffused through the administrative hierarchy of cantons and departments (figure 6.6). By 1840, all the prefectures had a bank, and nearly all arrondissements by 1869. And by 1910, so did forty percent of France's more than three thousand cantons. Urban cantons were still much more likely to have banks than rural ones (figure 6.6), and the cantons lacking a bank at the end of the nineteenth century were mostly places where the chef-lieu counted fewer than five thousand inhabitants.

Branching spread late, after 1870.The share of offices belonging to banks with branches rose to nineteen percent in 1875, 23.5 percent in 1881, twenty-seven percent in 1892, and thirty-six percent in 1898. By 1910, banks with branches finally dominated the French banking network, with sixty percent of all offices. Two-thirds of these offices belonged to the big national banks.

Table 6.4. Distance to nearest canton chef-lieu with at least one bank in kilometers

	1820	1840	1862	1898
25 percentile	20.0	13.7	5.8	4.5
Median	32.0	19.6	15.5	13.8
75th percentile	45.9	27.0	20.2	18.5
95th percentile	70.4	40.4	30.4	26.5
Average	32.4	18.6	13.3	10.0

Source: For banks, see table 8.1. The geographic data come from the Cassini data set.
Note: For each canton to obtain distance to a bank, we start with its surface area, compute the value of half the radius of a circle of the same area and then add the Cartesian distance to the nearest chef-lieu with a bank. Each canton is weighted by its population.

Did this expansion of branch banking ease access to banks? Let us focus on 1898, the last of our bank counts for the nineteenth century, when there were 2,560 bank offices outside Paris. To estimate access, we computed an average distance to a bank for each of our markets—first, to the main municipality in each canton (the chef-lieu), by assuming it was half the radius of a circle of the same area as the canton. If the chef-lieu had a bank, then that figure was the distance to the nearest bank. If not, we added to it the distance to the chef-lieu of the closest canton with a bank.

The resulting average distance to a bank declined from thirty-two kilometers (more than a day's journey by foot each way) in 1820 to eighteen kilometers in 1840, and down to thirteen kilometers in 1862 (allowing a hardy walker to make the round trip within a single day)—all before the diffusion of branch banking (table 6.4). By 1898, as branches spread, the average distance had fallen to ten kilometers, but clearly most of the decline took place before the rise of branch banking. It seems then that, just as in the United States, unit banking in France did not prevent a dense network of banks from forming.

One may well wonder why unit banks continued to dominate the sector until the beginning of the twentieth century. One potential explanation might point to France's slow industrialization and argue that it reduced the demand for interregional payment services and capital transfers. With demand limited, universal banks with branches would be slow to open their doors, and firms would be forced to seek financing from unit banks, which could not underwrite the large-scale enterprises that have long been considered necessary for rapid economic growth.

That argument would fit Antoin Murphy's claim that firms in France hesitated to take on debt because of France's tortured financial history (Murphy 2005). All the financial and political shocks France endured (from the Law affair in 1716–20, through the rapid inflation during the French Revolution, and the multiple changes of political changes in the nineteenth century) would make firms' reluctance plausible, particularly for industrialists. Why rely on a succession of short-term bank loans to fund long-term expansion when a renewable loan might be canceled right in the middle of the investment project because of a political shock? Such fears would rule out the sort of repeatedly renewed short-term loans that helped New England industrialize, even though it, too, was limited to unit banks (Lamoreaux 1994). Demand for such loans would simply be killed off (so the argument would go) in France because of the country's tumultuous political history.

Yet in the end, any argument like this that focuses on demand to explain the slow diffusion of banks seems suspect on three counts. First, there was a real demand for interregional payment services that was growing over time because of increased market integration and specialization. Second, French industrial firms were, in fact, interested in borrowing long term, for there were a growing number of bonds listed in the Paris Bourse price lists starting in the 1870s, and there was even greater array of such bonds in the portfolios of rich Parisians (Piketty, Postel-Vinay, Rosenthal 2014). Finally, the revolution was a great experience for debtors with long-term contracts, because they were able to repay with depreciated currency. Thus, the revolutionary experience actually tilted borrowers' demand away from short-term to long-term credit—*not* away from credit in general. And that preference pushed them into the arms of notaries, not bankers. Of course, the revolution tilted the preferences of lenders in the reverse direction—toward shorter-term loans. So the dearth of debt in the accounts of French firms is due to an equilibrium phenomenon, not a lack of demand.

In our opinion, unit banks prospered in France for very different reasons. First of all, their local knowledge remained valuable throughout the nineteenth century. Second, they likely had a greater supply of capital than unit banks in other countries. Local unit banks usually did have a local informational advantage over large universal banks, but that advantage was not overwhelming; otherwise it would be hard to understand the successful spread of branch banking in the long run. The key to understanding the persistence of unit banks is the tradeoff between their informational advantage and their higher cost of capital. Because unit banks are smaller and hold a locally concentrated portfolio of assets, they are more likely to fail (Carlson and Michener 2009, Bordo, Redish, and Rockoff 2011). They are thus individually riskier and likely face a higher cost of capital.

Moreover, even in the absence of significant default risk, they cannot balance local shocks to demands for funds, so they will have to hold a higher fraction of their assets in idle reserves.

The impact of this higher cost, however, depends on a bank's access to liquidity. Here the Banque de France's policy of opening branch offices created a critical difference between France, on the one hand, and both the United States and the United Kingdom, on the other, and it helps explain why French banks were less likely to open branches in smaller towns. When the first bank with many branches—Société Générale—was just beginning to build out its network of branches, the Banque de France was already spreading across the country, first into every prefecture and then into many subprefectures (Bazot 2014). As a result, by the end of the 1870s—and hence before the large scale diffusion of branch banking—most bankers, even if they were from small unit banks, had ready access to the discount window of a Banque de France branch. They could therefore be confident of surviving negative shocks to their assets simply by getting an injection of cash from the nearest Banque de France branch. Even if they operated small unit banks, these bankers' short-term cost of liquidity would be the same as for a large bank with many branches, and they would not have to hold a higher fraction of their assets in idle reserves. The competition between them and larger banks with branches would therefore be played out not over the cost of funds, but rather over the trade-off between the convenience of branch banking and the efficacy of the local banks' knowledge.

There is evidence to back up this claim in the way branch banks diffused. If we compare the location of banks in 1862 and in 1898, it becomes clear that branch offices opened only in towns that were already served by banks, and they did not seek to serve unbanked markets. In 1862, fully ninety-four percent of the branches of the big national banks (Société Générale, Crédit Lyonnais, and the Comptoir d'Escompte de Paris, the predecessor of the Comptoir National d'Escompte de Paris) operated in towns where there was already at least one bank, and most were located in places that had already multiple banks (figure 6.7). In other words, when the national banks expanded their networks in France, they were not using a lower cost of capital derived from an ability to diversify, in order to open branches in unbanked markets; nor, apparently, did savings from centralized management let them enter unbanked markets. Instead, they set up branches in already banked markets and competed for the same clients as more traditional unit banks. Presumably, that was where the convenience of branch banking had its greatest appeal. The same predilection for already banked markets held (see figure 6.7) for the government-backed banks (the Banque de France and the Crédit Foncier), and even for regional branch banks, which set up over eighty percent of their offices in markets that already possessed two banks in 1862. What allowed the

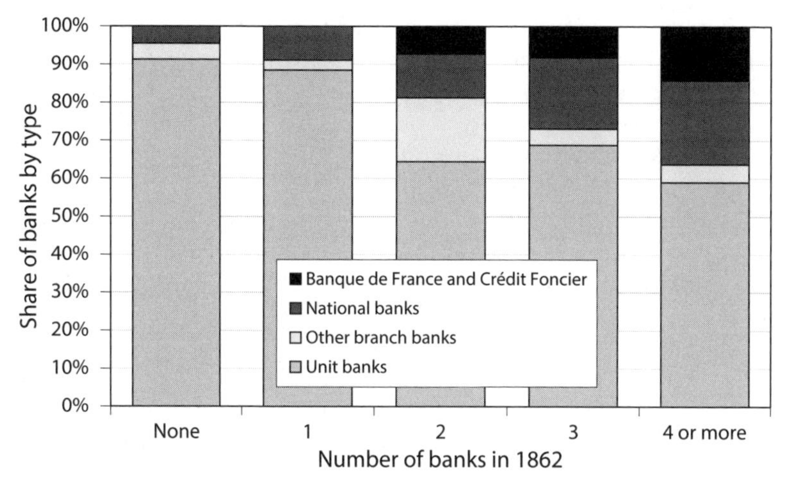

Figure 6.7. New banks in 1898, depending on the number of banks in that location in 1862.
Note: The national banks are Société Générale; Crédit Lyonnais; and the Comptoir d'Escompte de Paris, the predecessor of the Comptoir National d'Escompte de Paris, although it was not national until 1890.
Source: See text.

unit banks to compete against these behemoths was in all likelihood their continued easy access to the Banque de France's discount window and their superior information about the creditworthiness of their local clients. Their cost of funds would be no higher, and within the limits of their local markets, they could assemble a portfolio of loans with a lower risk of default.

Conclusion

Counting banks and analyzing where they locate are two ways to evaluate access to banking and the level of competition in financial intermediation. For all the achievements and growth of the French banking system, at the end of the nineteenth century about half of the French population lived in a canton where the nearest bank was in the next canton or the canton beyond that. Moreover, French banks tended to congregate in large cities. Had the city size/bank office relationship for France looked like England's, the rural population of France would have had much better access to banks (for it would have implied a fifty-percent increase in the number of cantons with banks by 1898).

The contrast between Britain and France was not the result, however, of the country's more contentious political history or the consequence of its slow embrace of incorporation. Instead, banks diffused slowly in France because of what traditional lending intermediaries—notaries—could do.

In making similar comparisons in the future, scholars will be well advised to consider the density of networks of such incumbent intermediaries. Even if banks were more efficient (and in the long run they did capture nearly the whole of local financial services), the presence of well-established and trusted long-term intermediaries, and networks for commercializing agricultural and craft output, must have slowed banks' entry into markets. The obstacles would be particularly forbidding if the traditional intermediaries offered long-term credit rather than the medium- or short-term loans in which banks specialized. In Western Europe, traditional intermediaries were common, even if they were not all notaries. Attorneys and scriveners arranged mortgages in Britain, for instance, much as notaries did in France.[18] However, there is no evidence that they built an informational structure like the French notaries. In fact, the lack of a well-established network of asset brokers like notaries probably spurred the proliferation of banks in Britain as the economy grew. One might well wonder whether the primary channels of causality run not from bank diffusion to economic growth but rather in the reverse direction.

One may therefore have some doubts about the accuracy of Neal's suggestion that financial convulsions in the early eighteenth century led France to discover notaries as an alternative to banks. In France and in much of continental Europe, notaries and bankers had long coexisted and provided different services. Although the financial crises may have slowed the diffusion of banks in France, the contrast between its banking network and Britain's likely had more to do with services offered by notaries and with the Banque de France's policies. Without notaries, bankers in Britain had had to shoulder a heavier demand for loans, creating a banking network that looked as if it were on steroids. Meanwhile, unit banks thrived in France, thanks to the Banque de France's willingness to provide liquidity. The network of peer-to-peer intermediaries is thus a major reason why banking in France and Britain diverged, and the same may be true in other developing economies.

The bank counts permit a final observation, about the relative size of bank lending and notarial debt. In 1898, loans and discounts by the Banque de France, the large branch banks, and all other banks totaled 4.6 billion francs; the Crédit Foncier's outstanding balance came to about 1.8 billion francs; and the stock of notarial debt was 6.2 billion. If we move back nine decades to the year 1807 and estimate bank credit from the number of banks in existence, then outstanding bank loans (whether from the Banque de France or any of the other banks) amounted to 210 million francs in 1807, while notarial credit outstanding was considerably larger, about 1.1 billion.[19] Between 1807 and 1898, bank credit thus increased at a 3.8 percent annual rate, or more than three times the growth rate of the French economy as a whole. The larger financial system, which includes notarized credit plus bank lending, expands from 1.3 billion francs in 1807 to 12.6 billion in 1898, for a more modest growth rate of 2.5 percent per year. This is a less dramatic number, but including peer-to-peer lending in credit totals is simply more realistic, and the idea that finance grew twice as fast as the economy seems reasonable.

If banks had been more efficient, then they should have replaced the notaries, but notarial credit still managed to grow at a 2.1 percent rate, almost two-thirds of what banks did. So there seems to have been little substitution of modern intermediaries for older forms of intermediation. Could it be that they were complements, and that growth required both more mortgages brokered by notaries and short-term loans intermediated by banks? The aggregate data seems to validate this view, but we still have to see how banks and notaries interacted in local credit markets.

In tracking the diffusion of banks in France, we have had to roam quite far from the notaries and their peer-to-peer lending. As the commercial directories make clear, the persistence of the peer-to-peer lending system cannot be explained by a lack of banks or by government policies that kept banks from spreading in France. Too many banks opened their doors in towns and cities throughout France for that to have been true. But if traditional notaries and banks were both doing local lending, then it remains to be seen how they divided the credit market. We take up that question in the next chapter.

CHAPTER 7

Banks and Notaries

As banks spread throughout France in the nineteenth century, what effect did their diffusion have on notaries? Did the banks opening their doors across France end up competing with them? The banks did offer a substitute for the notaries' mortgages—namely, mortgage-backed credit lines, such as the 11,000-franc loan that the Sagaire and Company Bank in the northeastern city of Epinal made to a local building contractor in 1865.[1] In addition, French bankers could (at least in principle) roll over short-term loans to create the equivalent of a medium- or long-term mortgage loan—something that banks did in the United States.[2] With these substitutes, it is conceivable that superior information or an ability to pool risks would allow banks to make loans at a lower cost than notaries could.

There were two conceivable ways that banks could have engaged in such lending. First, they could have entered the mortgage market as lenders but not relied on a notary to do anything except draw up the loan contracts. That might have been what a banker in the city of Lyon was up to in 1865, when he advanced four thousand francs to a local borrower. Perhaps the banker knew his borrower well, although it is certainly possible that the notary who drafted the contract also provided information about the borrower's creditworthiness.[3] Alternatively, bankers could have lent via contracts that were completely outside the mortgage market, such as short-term debts that were rolled over. In either scenario, the banks would have encroached upon the notaries' peer-to-peer lending. Bank entry would, in short, have cut peer-to-peer mortgage lending.

At the other extreme, banks might not have competed at all with notaries; rather, their short-term commercial loans might have complemented the notaries' business in arranging mortgages. A banker's short-term loans to merchants and manufacturers might have increased the demand for mortgages to build infrastructure or housing, and if the merchants and manufacturers purchased agricultural inputs, the commercial loans could also have augmented mortgage lending to farmers. A banker might also have tapped the notarial credit market to raise funds for his banking business, as a Lyon banker did in 1899, when he borrowed 350,000 francs secured by shares in the Tramways of Oran.[4] In all these cases, the diffusion of banks would have boosted notarial lending and reinforced the notaries' peer-to-peer system.

We examine both possibilities in this chapter, along with more realistic alternatives between the two extremes, including one in which notaries tried to compete with banks. As we will see, the banks were not superior substitutes for notaries. That was so even for the universal banks with branches that spread throughout France in the late nineteenth century. The only exception was the Crédit Foncier (CFF), the government-backed mortgage bank founded in 1852. But the CFF was a special case, because it had a monopoly on the issue of mortgage-backed securities, and its securities were widely thought to have a government guarantee. Even so, the CFF focused its lending on Parisians and the largest landowners in the provinces; as a result, in most places, it had almost no impact.

Notaries, in short, were not driven out of business by banks, at least before World War I. That is what our evidence shows, and, if anything, it was the banks that risked competition from notaries who entered short-term lending. Many notaries were in fact tempted to take money on deposit and start making short-term loans, at least until the 1880s, when the government enforced prohibitions on the practice. Thereafter, notaries and banks did not compete in the same market until well past World War I.

Instead of competing, banks and notaries complemented one another, and bank entry—surprising though it may seem—actually strengthened the notaries' mortgage lending. To make this case, we begin with a simple model of competition that will guide our empirical analysis.

Bankers and Notaries as Competitors in the Mortgage Market

Let us start with the extreme case in which banks are competing with notaries. We assume that banks can offer a lower-cost substitute for notarial credit, either because they have superior information or an ability to pool risks. Suppose for the moment that there is a single credit market, that all notaries in France have an identical and constant marginal cost of lending, that the total cost (interest and fees) of borrowing a franc through a notary is r, and that the notaries compete on price. The assumption of constant marginal cost for the notaries is reasonable because they all possessed lengthy records of past business doing lending and arranging other property transactions, from sales and leases to inheritances. Their costs of gathering information on creditworthiness and the value of collateral were therefore sunk, and they could hire clerks to write up loans at constant marginal cost.[5] Because all our markets (cantons) had at least three notaries, the value of loans in a given market before banks enter is

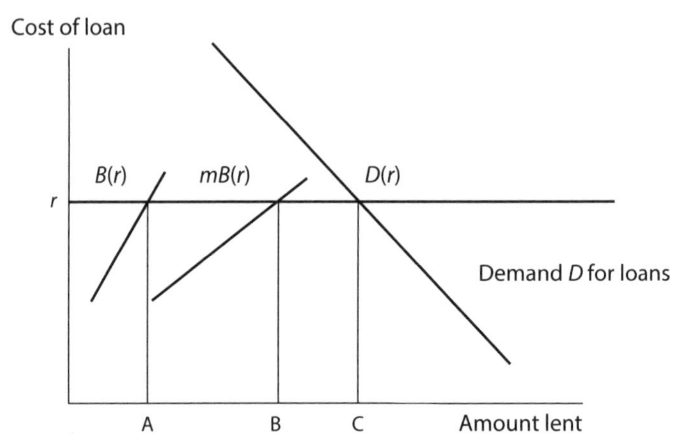

Figure 7.1. Demand D for notarial loans and supply of loans by notaries and banks.
Note: See text for details.

given by the amount of loans $D(r)$ demanded at the competitive price r. This price includes both the interest rate, which until the 1880s did not vary across space, and the transaction costs, which included the costs of drawing up the contract, verifying the collateral and the identities of the parties, and registering the mortgage if the parties required it.[6] In our simple model, markets with greater demand have more loans, but prices are the same everywhere. In terms of a simple supply and demand graph (figure 7.1), the notaries in a market have a horizontal supply curve at the competitive price r, and the amount they lend (C in the figure) is given by the demand $D(r)$ for loans at that price.

Our simple model here ignores much of the institutional detail at the core of chapters 3 and 4—namely, that prices did not clear local credit markets, that lenders and borrowers queued up to find bilateral matches, and that markets were only partly integrated because travel costs tended to restrict referrals to neighboring cantons. But the simplification is of far less consequence than one might imagine. As long as those costs are reasonably small, the local demand for loans in the model is just the loans sought by those borrowers whom local notaries deem creditworthy. The horizontal supply curve captures the willingness of local and more distant lenders to fund the loans of clients that notaries certify and the marginal cost of drawing up loans.[7]

So, with these assumptions, what happens if banks enter and compete with notaries? If, as the historiography would have it, banks are more efficient than notaries, it means they can offer loans to borrowers at a lower cost than notaries and still make money. In other words, the marginal cost of banks, $B(r)$, must be lower than that of notaries, r. The banks' costs advantage would be on the financial side. In particular, risk pooling or liquidity services could have reduced bankers' cost of capital relative to what was paid to lenders in notarial markets. Now, because banks were new to the long-term credit market, they had to acquire the sort of information about clients that notaries already possessed. The less bankers knew about a client, the more costly gathering information about creditworthiness and collateral would be. Hence, as banks expanded, they faced an increasing marginal cost. The fact that in France nearly all banks remained small suggest they had capacity constraints, which would have also produced an increasing marginal cost.

Now let a bank enter a market not served by other banks. The bank attracts clients by offering them a tiny fixed rebate, and it maximizes its profits simply by lending to the point where its marginal cost $B(r)$ equals that of notaries. That is the amount A in figure 7.1. If A is less than the lending C done before the bank entered, then total mortgage lending will be unchanged, but banks will be making the amount A of the loans, while the notaries will be reduced to lending only C minus A. The notaries' lending will therefore fall after the bank has entered, and if the single bank finds it profitable to make more loans than C, then the notaries will exit the market and stop lending altogether.

If m banks enter the market, then they will supply $mB(r)$ in funds at cost r. As long as that is less than $D(r)$, then total lending C will once again remain unchanged. The banks will now provide the amount B of the total loans, and the notaries will be reduced to providing only C minus B. Once again, bank entry will cut notarial lending, except in markets that are too small to justify bank entry.[8] And that will be the outcome whether the banks make mortgage loans directly or whether they provide a substitute by rolling over short-term loans.

One can build in more subtle assumptions about notaries that would allow for markets to differ in terms of the intermediaries' (notaries' or bankers') costs. Such heterogeneity will complicate the analysis, but as long as bankers are competing with notaries, and are more efficient than notaries, then bank entry should reduce notarial lending. It is true that the extreme situation we are modeling here is static and makes a number of simplifying assumptions about marginal costs and the role of prices. It also supposes that there is just one credit market, and not distinct markets for different types of credit, such as long-term mortgage loans or short-term lending. We will relax those assumptions below, but for the moment let us stick with them and see what actually happened to notarial lending when banks opened their doors.

Does notarial lending actually fall, as our assumptions lead us to expect? One way to find out is to regress the volume of notarial lending in each

Table 7.1. Selected coefficients: notarial lending regressions, 1865–99

	Regression 1	Regression 2
Dependent variable	Volume of new loans (francs)	Volume of new loans (francs)
Explanatory variable	Coefficient (standard error)	Coefficient (standard error)
Number of banks in market	96,307 (23,535)	135,518 (35,586)
Number of observation	198	198

Note: The regressions were run using first differences: regression 2 was estimated using an instrumental variable because of the endogeneity of the number of banks. Both regressions controlled for demand by including linear and quadratic terms in market population and average wealth; the wealth measure was per capita property taxes. For more on the wealth measure and the regressions, see the text and Hoffman, Postel-Vinay, and Rosenthal 2015.
Source: 105 markets from our sample; these are the same markets used for the regressions in Hoffman, Postel-Vinay, and Rosenthal 2015.

market in our data set on the number of banks in the market. If bank entry does reduce notarial lending—which is what we would expect if banks are superior substitutes for notaries—then the coefficient of the number of banks should be negative and sizable.

This naïve regression would be subject to a number of objections that we have to address. Most obviously, the number of banks in a market is correlated with other unobserved characteristics of markets—in econometric terms, our naïve regression suffers from omitted variable bias. To avoid that problem, we control for variations from market to market in the demand for loans. With these controls, the coefficient on the number of banks turns out to be positive, not negative. It is also sizable (see table 7.1, regression 1).[9]

The regression is still suspect, though, because bank entry is endogenous and so, therefore, is the number of banks, our key explanatory variable. In principle endogeneity could bias the regression results either for or against our hypothesis. We can leave aside the endogeneity problems that might lead to a downward bias (for instance, banks might enter markets where notarial credit is already on the decline because the economy is shifting away from agriculture, and the demand for bank loans is particularly high in this transition phase). What is more worrying is that banks might favor markets where they anticipate a rapidly expanding economy—something we cannot measure. In such markets, demand could expand so rapidly that banks and notaries would both prosper, while if banks had instead entered more average markets, then they would have dug into the business of notaries. If so, then the banks' choice of booming markets would blind us to the possibility that banks would normally compete with notaries. Although we consider that possibility unlikely because bank entry is predicted very well by city size, one of our explanatory variables, we did reestimate the regression using an instrumental variable to deal with the endogeneity problem. The coefficient of the number of banks is still positive, not negative, just as with the naïve regression (see table 7.1, regression 2).[10] Again, there is no sign that banks are competing with notaries.

Accepting that conclusion does depend on our assumptions holding. Two of them are major ones. The first is that a single credit market exists rather than distinct markets for different types of loans. Although the single market hypothesis is clearly an oversimplification, banks did offer substitutes for the loans notaries arranged (in particular, mortgage-backed credit lines), and the question of whether they could do so at lower cost than the notaries is certainly important. We will in any case relax this assumption below. Our second major assumption is that notaries had constant marginal cost. That assumption, too, seems justified, but we will relax it as well when we consider bank entry in greater detail later in the chapter.

There are also some other minor assumptions, and the results of our regressions are therefore not absolutely conclusive.[11] But there is also independent evidence that supports them. It comes from an exhaustive list of all the banks in France by canton for the years 1886–92 and data on the number of all French notaries who were forced out of office in each canton for fraud or bankruptcy in the years 1887–89.[12] Such a loss of office was presumably an unexpected shock to notarial lending that should have driven borrowers and lenders to other intermediaries. If so, and if banks were more efficient substitutes for notarial lending in the same credit market, then banks should have entered the market when notaries departed. But that was clearly not the case, as figure 7.2 shows.[13] When one or two notaries have to exit a market, the number of banks that enter the market is actually smaller than the number of notaries that go out of business. And when three or more notaries have to quit, there is no bank entry at all—absolutely the opposite of what we would expect if they were more efficient substitutes.

Crédit Foncier Loans and Mortgage-Backed Credit Lines

So we have reason to believe that banks were not competing against notaries. One might object, though, that our regressions fail to take into account lending by the Crédit Foncier (CFF), the government-backed mortgage bank that certainly did make mortgage loans. As we know from

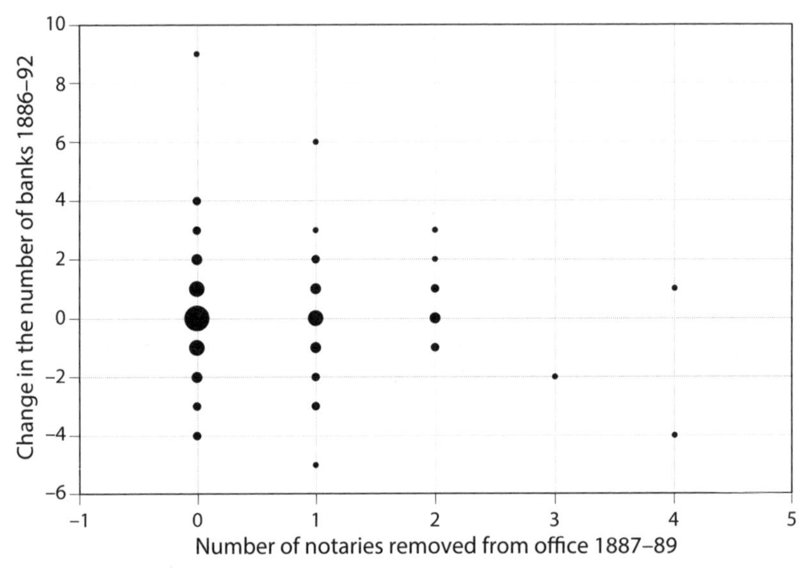

Figure 7.2. Change in the number of banks, 1886–92, and the number of notaries forced out of office for fraud or bankruptcy, 1887–89.
Note: The size of the dots is proportional to number of observations in each cell. The data here come from an exhaustive list (compiled by the authors) of banks and notaries removed for all the cantons in France, not just the cantons in our sample.
Source: See text and chapter 6.

chapter 6, it opened branches throughout France and could make loans anywhere in the country, but we did not include its branches outside Paris in the count of banks that we used in our regressions; the regressions may overlook other lending by banks as well.

Omitting the CFF is potentially serious, because the CFF might presumably have posed a major threat to the notaries' credit business. Launched in 1852, the mortgage bank was one of several new financial institutions created under the autocratic regime of Napoleon's nephew. The CFF had the advantage of being able to pool risks to fund mortgages. It did so by floating long-term bonds on the stock market. It was in fact the only mortgage lender allowed to raise money in that way, and the long-term bonds let it lend money out for longer terms than other mortgage lenders. For instance, in 1899, the CFF provided a Lyon corsetmaker a mortgage with payments stretching over seventy-five years. In addition to those advantages, government agents were involved in its administration (the CFF operated like a regulated monopoly), and it enjoyed an implicit government guarantee for its debt. Hardly surprising, then, that it grew rapidly in the early 1850s, particularly in Paris, where it made a quarter of all new mortgage loans between 1853 and the spring of 1855. After a slack period in the late 1850s, its growth resumed in the 1860s, and by 1899 it held an estimated twenty-four percent of outstanding French mortgage debt, much of it in huge loans. Its typical loans included a 650,000-franc mortgage for a couple of property owners in Paris, or, in the provinces, a 300,000-franc loan to La Protectrice, a real estate development company in Lyon.[14]

Rather than rerunning the regressions with the Crédit Foncier branches added to the count of banks in the markets outside Paris, we have added the actual volume of loans it made in each market as an additional explanatory variable. Adding the volume of its lending rather than a count of its branches is a more accurate measure of the threat it posed to notaries' lending, because its loans were large and had a long duration. We know what the volume is because its loans were drawn up by local notaries in each of our markets. If we assume that, like other banks, the CFF matched the notaries' marginal cost, then it is reasonable to simply add the volume of its lending as an additional explanatory variable. If the CFF was a superior substitute for notaries, then the volume should enter the regression with a negative coefficient; the coefficient would then represent the amount that each franc of notarial lending fell when the CFF extended a loan of one franc.

There is a similar problem with mortgage-backed credit lines opened by banks. The credit lines would count as mortgage lending (provided the borrowers drew upon them), and although the notaries were involved in the transactions, it would be reasonable to classify them as the banks' business. Unfortunately, the banks that opened the mortgage line of credit might not appear among those counted in a given market. The solution, as with the CFF, is to add the lending banks as yet another explanatory variable in our regression. We know how big the mortgage line of credit was and the market in which the loan was extended, because it was where the mortgage was registered. If bank lending through mortgage lines of credit is a superior substitute for notarial lending, then it too should have a negative coefficient.[15]

When we add these two variables and rerun the regressions, the coefficient for the number of banks is still positive, as is that for mortgage credit lines. The Crédit Foncier, though, does have a negative and statistically significant coefficient, which implies that one hundred francs of CFF loans cut notarial lending by thirty-two francs, but the coefficient becomes positive and insignificant when Paris is excluded. The results are similar if we use instrumental variables to cope with the endogeneity of these two added variables: the coefficients for the CFF and mortgage credit lines never turn out to be negative and significant.[16]

Although the results may only be suggestive because of the assumptions involved, banks do not seem to have offered a lower-cost substitute for notarial lending, either directly or via mortgage-backed credit lines. The only possible exception is the CFF, which had government backing and a monopoly on the right to issue mortgage-backed securities. Even then, the evidence is weak, for it disappears when we take into account the endogeneity of CFF lending, or exclude Paris from the regressions.

That any effect the Crédit Foncier had was limited to Paris is not surprising. To begin with, it only operated in a fraction of our markets, essentially Paris and the other large cities.[17] In addition, it relied on a government lien registration system to evaluate the collateral. Using that system involved sizable fixed costs, which would made it prohibitive for smaller loans. Notaries consulted the lien registration system too, but they could draw on other sources of information as well, which they derived from their own business doing lending and arranging a wide variety of other property transactions, from sales and leases to inheritances. Although they could turn to these other sources of information when making smaller loans, the CFF did not have that advantage. It therefore turned to the lien registration system and focused on big loans, but the large loans were rare outside of Paris and other large markets.

The CFF's strategy was risky, for lack of the sort of information notaries possessed had driven other earlier mortgage banks into bankruptcy, when they ended up making loans to less creditworthy clients with dubious collateral. Perhaps that is why the CFF took a long time to do much lending outside of Paris. In 1899, its loans averaged only 98,000 francs in markets other than Paris, compared to 953,000 francs for notarial lending in the same markets.

The regressions thus suggest that banks could not supply much in the way of lower cost substitutes for mortgages. The only possible exception was the Crédit Foncier, but like most mortgage banks in other economies, it depended on government backing.

The aggregate data from our sample tell much the same story: banks played little role in the mortgage market. The sample does omit any short-term loans that were rolled over regularly to substitute for long-term credit, because they would not be secured by a mortgage. But that category of loan was likely small. And our sample does include all mortgage loans, including any that were funded by banks. The reason was that for a mortgage to be valid, the loan had to be drawn up by a notary. If we therefore consider any loans with a bank or banker as lenders to have been arranged by a bank, then banks were originating 0.5 percent of the loans in 1840 and furnishing two percent of the funds lent. Under these same assumptions, banks (including the CFF) were responsible for almost two percent of all loans in 1865 and 3.4 percent in 1899. At this growth rate in the number of loans between 1840 and 1899, it would have taken French banks until the 1970s to furnish half of all mortgages. If we look at the volume of mortgages, then growth is more rapid, with the value of loans made by banks and the CFF reaching twenty-one percent of the total in 1899. At that rate, they would captured over half the market by the 1920s. Nonetheless, it is still clear that, despite their rapid diffusion, banks were not taking over mortgage lending.

Did Universal Banks Compete Against Notaries for Lenders?

Although banks generally did not supply a lower cost substitute for the notaries' mortgages, there was still one other way they could have competed against the notaries—namely, by offering potential lenders an alternative to investing in mortgage loans. If the alternative was more attractive than a mortgage (if, for instance, it yielded a higher return yet was just as secure, or if it allowed investors to diversify their portfolios), then potential lenders would leave the mortgage market. The supply of potential lenders would fall and the cost of retaining those who remained would rise. The effect would be to raise the notaries' cost of making loans and reduce the amount of lending they did.

How could a bank offer investors a higher risk-adjusted return or an investment that would diversify their portfolios? The easiest way, at least theoretically, would be to let clients open interest-bearing deposit accounts. With the funds from such deposits, the bank could make loans, pool the risks involved, and pay at least as much interest as an obligation would earn. The deposit account would presumably be safer than the obligation, because with the pooled risks the odds of the bank's failing would be less than the odds of default with a single obligation. And if the bank had branches in other parts of France, its interest-bearing account would let investors diversify their portfolios geographically.

That at least is the theory, but in reality banks did not offer such accounts on a wide scale until the 1860s (Bouvier 1961). Their primary business remained what it had traditionally been—granting short term loans to local merchants and businesses and making payments for them—and they restricted these services to clients whose reputation and past dealings they knew well. When, in 1825, Hugues Guerin opened a branch of his Lyon bank in the nearby city of Saint-Etienne, for example, he warned his nephew, who was in charge of the Saint-Etienne branch, to limit banking to customers who already had commercial dealings with Guerin. The nephew wanted to offer interest-paying accounts to some additional local businesses (and then only under the condition that the accounts "just about even out"), but he had to plead with his uncle for the right to do so.[18]

The first banks to provide interest-bearing deposits extensively were the Société Générale and the Crédit Lyonnais, whose branches began to spread throughout France in the 1860s. To judge from the Crédit Lyonnais, one of the chief reasons the two banks were opening branches was to mobilize savings held by clients whom local bankers did not serve. Local bankers, one of the Crédit Lyonnais's agents emphasized, simply did not seek out these savings, for they did not have the Crédit Lyonnais's goal of "revolutionizing individual investments."[19]

There were two reasons why unit banks would not seek out depositors on a large scale. First of all, a unit banker's comparative advantage lay in exploiting his information about his clients' creditworthiness (and his own reputation with other bankers) in order to make short-term loans and discount commercial paper and short-term letters of exchange.[20] Allocating his time to building up deposits would make poor use of this information and of his skills as a banker. Second, it would likely be difficult for a unit banker to make his interest-paying deposit accounts more attractive than a notary's obligations. Although unit bankers did pool risks, their assets were local and not geographically diversified, and their rate of failure was high.[21] Their deposits might thus be no safer than an obligation vetted by a notary, and if the deposits were demand deposits, it would be difficult to match the rate of interest paid on an obligation, because the unit banker would have to keep substantial cash on hand to meet withdrawals.[22]

The Société Générale and the Crédit Lyonnais would stand a much better chance of competing against the notaries for lenders' money. The two examples of what we have called universal banks established branches throughout France and aggressively sought out customers who opened interest-paying deposits. By 1881, the Crédit Lyonnais's liabilities included 380 million francs of deposits for one hundred million francs of paid in capital. Its chief rival in the deposit business was the Société Générale.[23] If this or one of the other universal banks opened a branch in one of our markets and competed against the local notaries for lenders' money, then the local notaries' cost of arranging loans would rise, and notarial lending would fall.

Figure 7.3 captures what would happen then. Universal banks like the Société Générale and the Crédit Lyonnais provided a wide variety of services through their branches, but the critical one for notaries was deposit banking, because it gave lenders an alternative. After such a universal bank enters a market, the cost of a notarial loan increases, and the amount of

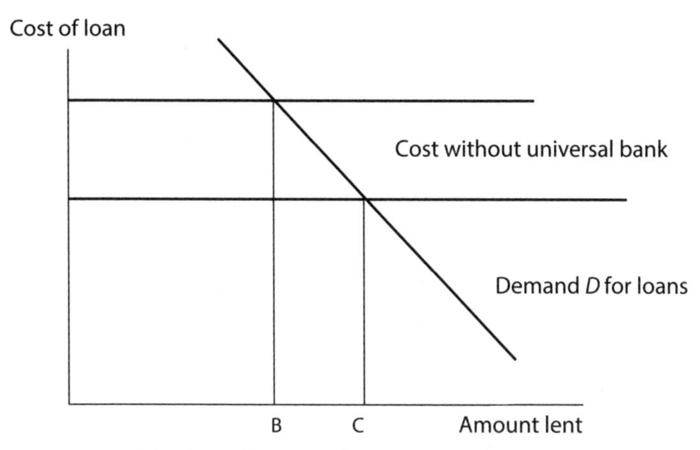

Figure 7.3. Notarial lending if notaries face competition for lenders' funds from universal banks.

notarial lending falls from C to B. Adding unit banks to the picture would lead to a similar outcome: once again, notarial lending would fall.

The implication is that we should add to our regressions a variable that distinguishes when there is a universal bank in our markets. The variable is one if the Société Générale or the Crédit Lyonnais opens a branch in the market; and it is also set equal to one if there is a branch of the Comptoir National d'Escompte de Paris, another universal bank whose branch network was not as extensive.[24] We include the dummy variable along with the number of banks that were not universal banks, plus linear and quadratic terms in wealth and population to control for demand. If competition from the universal banks raised the cost of a notarial loan by enough to greatly reduce notarial lending, then the coefficient of this dummy variable should be negative and significant, both statistically and economically.

Since the universal banks had not developed their network of branches in 1865, the dummy variable is zero in 1865, and we can therefore run the regression using first differences only between 1899 and 1865. (The first differences will also control for peculiar features of the demand for loans in each market, much like fixed effects.) When this first difference regression is run, the coefficient of the dummy variable is negative, but it is not statistically significant (table 7.2). It is not significant economically either, for in the average market, the presence of a universal bank in a market reduces notarial lending there by only 0.9 percent in 1899. Although the worry about bias caused by the endogeneity of bank entry applies to universal banks too, it is much less likely to affect the coefficient of our

Table 7.2. Selected coefficients: regression of lending on banking variables, 1865–99

Dependent variable	Volume of new loans (francs)
Explanatory variable	Coefficient (standard error)
Dummy variable for presence of a universal bank	–16604 (64895)
Number of other banks in market	–649 (42814)
Mean volume of new loans per market (million francs)	1.85

Note: The regressions were run using first differences; see the text for details. The regressions controlled for demand by including linear and quadratic terms in market population and average wealth; the wealth measure was per capita property taxes. For more on the wealth measure, see Hoffman, Postel-Vinay, and Rosenthal 2015.
Source: See table 7.1.

dummy variable, because universal banks competed primarily with local unit banks (they were extremely unlikely to enter unbanked markets) and not with notaries. Overall, it seems then that the universal banks did not have much of an impact on notarial lending. That conclusion also fits the qualitative evidence. The Crédit Lyonnais thought that it was simply too tough to compete with notaries for lenders' funds; it was much better to cooperate with them and use them as sources of information.[25]

Banks and Notaries as Complements

So far we have been working under an extreme assumption: that there is only a single credit market, one in which banks offer substitutes for notarial mortgages. That is clearly unrealistic. So is the other extreme assumption: that banks' short-term commercial loans complemented the notaries' business arranging mortgages, leaving bankers and notaries in distinct markets, without any competition between them. That is implausible because bankers did offer some substitutes for notarial credit—specifically, the mortgage-backed line of credit and the Crédit Foncier's loans. So there was some competition between banks and notaries, but to judge from the regressions, it was limited.

A more reasonable assumption allows banks to engage in this limited competition with notaries and lets their short-term commercial lending complement the notaries' business arranging mortgages. Bank entry could then increase the demand for mortgages, if the banks supplied only modest numbers of substitute loans for the notaries' mortgages; the substitution effect was therefore smaller than the complementary effect of commercial lending. The increased competition in the mortgage market would then be offset by more commercial lending.

It is easy to see how that could happen. Let us suppose that there are two types of loans—say, commercial and mortgage loans. Assume too that the technologies for certifying different types of loan requests are distinct and that the information needed for certifying mortgage loans is not useful to certifying commercial loans—an assumption that is not at all unrealistic. In Lyon, for instance, the Guerin bank kept detailed notes on clients' reputations, which were essential for making commercial loans. Although the notes contained some information about clients' wealth and occasionally even their real property, when bankruptcy threatened the Guerin bank could not rely on its notes but instead had to investigate to find out whether the debtor's real property had already been mortgaged [26]

Let us assume that borrowers in this credit market want to raise an amount *V*, which they can do either by pledging real collateral (with notaries) or movable goods and their reputation (with a banker). The two types of loans could be substitutes (which they presumably are at the margin, via loans such as mortgage-backed credit lines), but if so, then we are simply back in the previous case. So let us suppose that the two types of loans rely on different information and serve different purposes. The notaries, for example, could finance agriculture and real estate, where loans secured by mortgages dominated, while bankers could serve industry and trade, where what mattered were movable goods and reputation. If the geographic distributions of farms and industrial firms were independent (in other words, there was no relationship between the two distributions), then demand for notarial loans would be independent of demand for bank loans, once we controlled for wealth and population. A more reasonable assumption, however, would be that although banks would lend little to agriculture, the demand for their bankers' short-term commercial loans would rise with the value of agricultural output, as manufacturing firms dependent on farming expanded. There are clear instances where this happened—for instance, sugar refining in sugar-beet-growing parts of northern France.[27] In such cases, the value of agricultural output would be positively correlated with the demand for mortgage loans, and so would the demand for both the notaries' and the bankers' services.

Bank entry and notarial lending would therefore be positively correlated. Both should also be positively correlated with population and wealth, for one would expect larger and richer towns to have a higher demand for bank loans and for notarial lending. As towns get larger and wealthier, they should have higher demand for bank loans because they

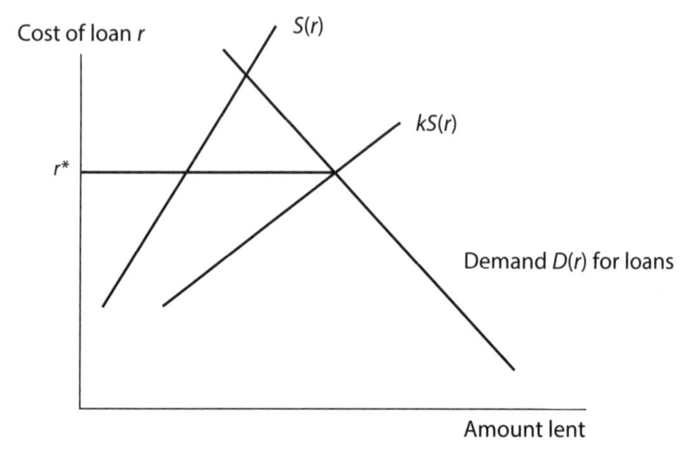

Figure 7.4. Loan demand and supply with increasing costs for k notaries in a market.

serve as regional trade centers and thus have growing demand for the payments and short-term loan services that bankers provide. At the same time, these larger towns would have higher real estate values, which would drive up the value of mortgages.

Bank entry could also reflect the number of notaries already in a market. As long as the notaries have constant marginal cost—an assumption we have maintained up to now—their number does not matter, because it would not change the cost of notarial lending. But suppose that assumption fails to hold, and that notaries have increasing marginal costs. Since there are always at least three notaries in each market, we will continue to assume that they compete and that (for the sake of simplicity) their marginal cost functions are identical. Let each notary's supply curve be the increasing function $S(r)$ in figure 7.4. If there are k notaries in the market, and no banks, then together they will supply $kS(r)$ in loans, at a competitive price r^* that satisfies $kS(r^*) = D(r^*)$, so long as r^* is greater than the notaries' minimum average cost. For a given market demand $D(r)$, a smaller number of notaries k will mean a higher competitive price r^* because the supply $kS(r)$ will be lower.

What would the consequences for bank entry be? In this more realistic scenario, they would depend on whether banks were primarily complements or substitutes for notaries. If banks were chiefly interested in providing substitutes for the notaries' mortgages, then for any given demand $D(r)$ for mortgages, we would expect banks to be more likely to enter a market when the number of notaries in the market was small. The banks would simply have more rents to earn if their marginal costs were less than r^*. If, however, the banks are first and foremost in the business of making commercial loans, and the commercial loans and mortgages are complements, then they would be less likely to enter markets with a small number of notaries, because the cost of a mortgage would be higher for a given level of demand.

Under this more realistic assumption, we can therefore determine whether banks were primarily substitutes or complements by regressing the number of banks that enter each market on correlates of demand for loans and a dummy variable for markets with a small number of notaries. The dummy variable's coefficient would have a positive sign if the banks were primarily substitutes, because it would mean that the dependent variable (the number of banks entering a market) would increase when there were few notaries in a market. A negative sign for the dummy variable would mean the reverse, and imply that banks and notaries were primarily complements. What constituted a small number of notaries? Again, there were always three, but in rural markets, regulations limited the number to a maximum of five. In cities, the number was essentially fixed at levels reflecting demand back in 1800.[28] A dummy variable for five or fewer notaries would thus be a reasonable yardstick in a market with a small number of notaries. Such markets were smaller on average, but it was not simply a matter of size, for their populations (in 1896) ranged from just over four thousand to nearly sixty thousand, while the markets with more than five notaries had populations from nine thousand to 2.5 million. As for the correlates of demand in these markets, we use the volume of lending that the notaries themselves were doing, plus linear and quadratic terms in wealth and population, which will capture residual demand met not by the notaries, but by banks.

Because the dummy variable for five or fewer notaries is virtually constant across time, we could not run panel regression with fixed effects or first differences. Instead, we ran a cross-section regression for 1840, 1865, and 1899. In the regressions, the coefficient of the dummy variable for a small number of notaries is always negative and significant.[29] The negative coefficient implies that fewer banks entered markets with a small number of notaries. That is what we would expect if the banks were not substitutes for notaries, but, rather, complements.

Conclusion

All of our evidence points to a single conclusion: in the mortgage market, banks—the modern intermediaries—were not more efficient substitutes for notaries and their peer-to-peer lending system. Banks were free to enter that market, and they did offer substitutes for the mortgages that notaries arranged, but they had at most a minimal impact on the amount of lending arranged by notaries and certainly did not drive any of them out of business. The reason was that banks were providing different financial services than notaries—short-term commercial loans instead of the long-term mortgages that notaries arranged. Demand for both sorts of loans was correlated, so the banks did enter markets where the notaries were busy, not because they expected to take business away from notaries, but rather because those were the places where the demand for the short-term credit they offered was high.

Our conclusion runs counter to what economic historians have long believed (Gerschenkron 1962; Cameron 1961, 1967; Kindleberger 2015; Ferguson 2001; Sylla 2002; Rousseau and Sylla 2003). In particular, economic historians' neglect of all the lending that transited through notaries' offices has led them to misread the financial history of France. They have mistakenly blamed delayed economic growth on what seemed like a lack of banks. Yet as we know, there was no shortage of banks, and the banks were not more efficient lenders.

One bank was a partial exception—the Crédit Foncier—but it had the benefit of government backing for its securities and a monopoly on the right to issue mortgage-backed securities. Even then, it only competed in the largest markets and only served the biggest scale borrowers. For most of the population, notaries remained the principal source of long-term loans until World War I. They were able to maintain such a position because they had the best information about the value of collateral and the creditworthiness of borrowers. In doing so, they helped integrate financial markets, and bankers could not simply sweep them aside, even though banks could pool risks and, if they were universal banks, give lenders a way to diversify their portfolios. The problem for the banks was that they did not have the information needed to sift through mortgage applicants, and the investments they could provide were not more attractive than the mortgages notaries arranged—indeed, even bankers invested in notarial credit. That is why they were not more efficient substitutes for notaries.

There is one more striking bit of evidence that reinforces this conclusion—namely, the fact that if anyone had to fear competition, it was the bankers themselves, because a number of notaries actually tried to enter the banking market. The evidence comes from Paris, where notaries—just like banks—were pooling funds and then lending the money out, up until the 1850s.

The funds came from interest-bearing deposit accounts that clients asked notaries to open. If the notaries then used the deposited money to make illiquid long-term loans or investments—which was likely, given their specialization in long-term credit—then their deposit banking carried huge risks, because clients could at any time ask that deposits be returned. Such unexpected withdrawals could push notaries into bankruptcy, which carried draconian penalties, including the loss of their valuable offices and possible criminal charges. Most notaries therefore shunned deposit banking, but some did not, and they attracted clients who wanted to earn money on deposit. That clients patronized these risk-taking notaries—rather than banks, despite the large number of bankers in Paris—suggests that banks in the first half of the nineteenth century did not have any enormous efficiency advantage over notaries, even in the business of deposit banking.

Moreover, notaries who took deposits were not the only ones to go bankrupt. Banks failed too, and, at least in Paris, they were, in fact, much more likely to go belly up than notaries. The truth is that bankers could not even drive notaries out of deposit banking in Paris, let alone in the provinces; only the government could do that. In 1843, it banned deposit banking by notaries after the catastrophic failure of the notary Lehon.[30] By itself, that measure did not bring notarial banking to a complete halt, either in Paris or the countryside, but it was reinforced by more stringent government regulation after more notarial bankruptcies in the late 1880s.[31] By 1890, all notaries throughout France had to keep scrupulous accounts that carefully segregated clients' money. Funds on deposit could not be held for more than six months, and sizable deposits (in Paris, anything over one thousand francs) had to be turned over to a public savings bank, the *Caisse des Dépôts et Consignations*.[32]

Notaries also competed against bankers in the business of trust management. In the rare instances when the notaries' account books have survived, they demonstrate that notaries received payments of interest and principal on obligations, railroad bonds, and municipal debt. These accounts also show that notaries sent off securities to be sold and dispatched funds to stockbrokers for purchases.[33] They were engaging in this trust management even at the end of the nineteenth century, when universal banks such as the Crédit Lyonnais were offering much the same service; in fact, the Crédit Lyonnais had to offer trust services for no fee in order to attract depositors.[34]

Therefore, notaries cannot simply be dismissed as archaic financial intermediaries who were unable to survive when faced with competition from modern banks. They did quite well even when confronted by the Crédit Foncier. They managed to do well, despite free entry for banks and enormous financial innovation, because they managed a treasure trove of information that they had accumulated over decades. That is what allowed them to originate eighty-five percent of the outstanding mortgage debt in 1865 and eighty percent in 1899, despite the growth of the Crédit Foncier.[35]

Nor were the notaries some quaint French exception. In Britain, Germany, and the United States—all economies with highly developed financial systems and large mortgage markets—between thirty-two and sixty-five percent of outstanding mortgage debt in 1900 was originated not by banks, but by traditional intermediaries who, like notaries, coexisted alongside banks.[36] The traditional intermediaries—for instance, attorneys in Britain—likely possessed valuable information about borrowers and lenders, and, as in France, the information or specialized services that they could offer likely made them the low-cost competitors.

The lesson here is that the survival of traditional intermediaries such as notaries is not necessarily proof of institutional failure. Rather, they may simply have had a cost advantage, such as private information, which new entrants—for instance, modern banks—could only slowly overcome. As a result, the diffusion of banks or other modern intermediaries may well be slow. We should not look at the absence of banks in an economy and jump to the conclusion that the financial system is malfunctioning. Traditional intermediaries may in fact be outcompeting the banks and slowing their diffusion. There is no unique path to financial development, and in a given economy, the first step may not be thriving banks in every market.

CHAPTER 8

Prices Return

By 1899, France, like much of the West, had taken giant steps toward the modern world. Just ten years earlier, Paris had drawn thirty-two million people to see marvels like the new Eiffel Tower at a world's fair. Visitors flocking to Paris for a second international exposition in 1900 were filmed and had their voices recorded. Railroads in France were speeding along 37,000 kilometers of track, and some two thousand motor vehicles were already plying French roads—more than in Germany or the United Kingdom. The French economy was thriving, with real output per person rising at 1.5 percent a year—faster than in the United Kingdom and about the same rate of increase as in Germany. Per capita incomes were at roughly the same level as in India or China in 2003, but financial markets were far more developed. With all the banks throughout the country, the French banking system counted more deposits relative to GDP than Britain or most of the rest of Western Europe. Stock market capitalization relative to GDP dwarfed that in Germany or the United States and was approaching what it was in the United Kingdom.[1]

One other momentous change was transforming the financial system. But unlike the growth of the stock market or the rise of the big universal banks, it has gone unnoticed, because it concerned the dark matter of mortgages that economic historians have long overlooked. The transformation did not take place overnight, but it did upend the equilibrium in the markets for all this credit, where the stock of debt continued to grow rapidly. What was this silent revolution in credit markets? It was simple: for the first time since 1740, our markets came to be cleared by prices.

For seven chapters we have ignored prices; we have in effect written a history of mortgage markets without concern for interest rates. The reason was simple: in our first five cross sections (from 1740 to 1865), interest rates do not vary at all. In the loan contracts, they are either omitted (as was the case for obligations in the eighteenth century) or almost invariably set at five percent (for rentes before 1807 and for obligations thereafter). But this changed radically by the end of the nineteenth century. In 1899, less than half the loans were paying that five-percent interest rate, instead of nearly ninety percent or more, as in the past. And the interest rate distribution in 1899 did not shift from five percent to another fixed figure, such as four percent, or to a bimodal distribution, with two interest rates. Instead, borrowers and lenders were agreeing on a whole range of rates, from three percent up to five percent. Since 1865, the mortgage market's long-standing equilibrium at a single interest rate had simply unraveled.

To understand this transition, we have to return briefly to the origins of the single price equilibrium in the seventeenth century, when the 5 percent usury ceiling was enacted. For our earlier study of credit markets in Paris, we gathered interest rates for perpetual annuities (rentes) in Paris for 1662 and 1670. Those two dates straddle the edict of December 1665 that reduced the maximum legal interest rate from 6.3 to 5 percent.[2] In 1662—three years before the edict—72 percent of all rentes were contracted at more than 5.1 percent interest, and only 26 percent of the rentes fell in the narrow band between 4.9 percent interest and 5.1 percent interest. By 1670—five years after the edict—fully 92 percent of the loans owed interest in this slender range.

The transition to a single interest rate was just as striking outside of Paris. In 1740, our sample contains 2,077 perpetual annuities with a reported interest rate. Of these, 86 percent were at 5 percent and 13 percent were at less than 5 percent. Of the remaining 15 contracts at more than 5 percent, 14 were in the exceptional southeastern territory of the Comtat Venaissin that belonged to the pope; he allowed interest rates among Christians to be up to 7 percent.[3] And by the time of our 1780 sample, 97 percent of all the rentes specified an interest rate of 5 percent.

What was happening was that virtually all loans were made at a five-percent interest rate. Debtors with better credit histories, more stable sources of income, or more collateral did not receive lower interest rates. Instead, they got larger loans and longer loan durations. After the turmoil of the revolution and the reimposition of the five-percent usury ceiling in 1807, the credit market returned to the same equilibrium, where better borrowers got bigger loans and extended durations, but not price discounts.

To explain the transition to a new equilibrium in 1899, this chapter will proceed in two steps.[4] We begin by reviewing some economics literature that deals with three different issues that arise in the transition from a single-price equilibrium to a range of prices. The first (most often associated with Stiglitz and Weiss 1981) suggests that when there is substantial asymmetric information, price competition in credit markets may be reduced, if not eliminated, in favor of credit rationing. Next we consider why the equilibrium in a credit rationing market may feature a single interest rate. There we appeal to the classic lemons problem (Akerloff 1970) for clues as to why such a single-price equilibrium may be sustained even if information improves. Finally, we examine a third approach (Grossman 1981; Milgrom 1981) that analyzes conditions under which such pooling equilibria may unravel.

This economics literature helps shed light on the transition from the near universal five-percent interest rate equilibrium to a regime with a distribution of rates in the late nineteenth century. In particular, it lets us frame our analysis of the transition using three sets of data: our cross sections in 1865 and 1899; additional, more detailed data from the department of the Aube (to the east of Paris) that ranges from 1865 to 1931; and, last but not least, a national survey of credit contracts for February of 1931. In our analysis using this data, we will emphasize three forces that each contributed to the transition: the rise of the government-backed mortgage bank, Crédit Foncier (CFF); the increasing availability of formal lien histories; and the negative demand shock associated with the agricultural recession of the 1880s. As we shall see, two additional forces also played a role, particularly after World War I: the government's direct intervention in credit markets and its monetary policies.

Theory: Unraveling a Credit Rationing and Pooling Equilibrium (CRPE)

For two hundred years, the mortgage market functioned with a credit rationing and pooling equilibrium (CRPE): loans could not exceed half the value of the collateral, and a single interest rate was charged. This type of market arrangement is not unique to that period, or to France. It is, in fact, relatively common in mortgage markets. Even today in the United States, France, and elsewhere, the typical conforming mortgage loan is capped at eighty percent of the value of the real estate pledged (Andrews et al. 2011). And in many countries nowadays, borrowers can find ways of borrowing in excess of that only by paying an additional cost for mortgage insurance or something similar. These additional costs are in effect risk premia that could have been imbedded in a higher interest rate, but were not.

Let us start with the credit rationing part of the institution: the loan-to-value ratio maximum (henceforth LTV). The common practice (as one of us has shown in earlier work) was to keep the loan value below half the value of the collateral (maximum LTV at fifty percent) (Postel-Vinay 1998, chapter 5). Someone with a property worth ten thousand francs, for example, could therefore borrow up to five thousand francs. But he or she could not offer to pay a higher interest rate and borrow six thousand francs—his or her ration of credit was effectively capped at five thousand francs.

But what if the borrower wants the six thousand francs for a really valuable project? The borrower may well be prepared to pay more for some flexibility. It would seem to be a good idea for lenders to offer a menu of interest rates that are increasing with LTV; the borrower then chooses the loan amount he or she prefers. Under perfect information, lenders could compute the borrower's risk of default conditional on loan size and charge an appropriate interest rate. In that case, however, there would be no reason to demand that collateral limit the size of the loans. The collateral only serves to induce the borrower to repay and to compensate the lender in case the borrower defaults. What really matters, though, is the borrower's ability to repay, and under perfect information, the lender will actually know that and be able to seize the borrower's future income and wealth; the lender will not need to rely on collateral. Thus, under perfect information, there is no need for credit rationing.

When the lender does not know the borrower's ability to repay—when, in other words, information about borrowers' wealth and income is asymmetric—then collateral pledges are valuable, because they can weed out borrowers who are not creditworthy. If the lender can evaluate the collateral, then the likelihood of default is negligible as long as the collateral's value exceeds the cost of repaying the loan. Default only arises if the collateral's value drops below the cost of repayment. That might happen if real estate prices fell or if the borrower used the loan to make special purpose investments in the collateral that did not produce returns.[5] To guard against such risks, LTV is usually less than one hundred percent.

Keeping the LTV well below one hundred percent has another effect, one that is even more important: it protects against adverse selection. For some borrowers, the lender's estimate of what the collateral is worth will be higher than what the borrower knows it to be. Such borrowers will have a large loan-to-value ratio, and they will be more likely to default if the price of real estate or other collateral collapses. In fact, default probabilities will rise as loan-to-value ratios grow closer to one. High loan-to-value ratios can therefore be sustained only if collateral prices (particularly real estate) are not volatile, and if estimates of the value of collateral are accurate and precise. Otherwise, severe rationing is the only way to sustain the market.

Historically, the loan-to-value ratio in France and elsewhere was fifty percent or less. On the US frontier in 1870, it was as low as thirty-three percent (Bogue 1955, 16, 84). For urban properties in the United States in the decade after World War I, it was fifty percent (Morton 1956, 175). The ratio remained at that level for the life of the loan because borrowers commonly owed interest only for the duration of the loan plus a single balloon payment of the loan principal at the end.

In such a world, where the LTV remained well below one hundred percent, it is conceivable that an individual borrower might be offered a menu of loan contracts with different interest rates reflecting different loan-to-value ratios. For instance, the borrower might be able to choose a loan-to-value ratio below thirty percent with a four-percent interest rate; an LTV between thirty and forty-five percent with a 4.5-percent interest rate; or LTV between forty-five percent and fifty percent with a five-percent interest rate. With the menu, the lender would be allowing the borrower to pledge more collateral in return for receiving a lower interest rate. If borrowers did not maximize their loan-to-value ratio, we might then see a range of interest rates.

Although menus of this sort are possible, they rarely occur, because lenders balk at reducing interest rates in return for more collateral. To see why, suppose that, using this kind of menu, a borrower took one loan at four percent and with an LTV below thirty percent, and a second one from a different lender at five percent, with an LTV for the two loans together that was still below fifty percent (the aggregate credit limit) on the same collateral. Although the initial mortgage would remain the senior loan as long as it was the first to be registered, the initial lender would certainly be concerned about the second loan. The reason is simple: the second loan eliminated the security of the extra collateral, which might well be a sign that the borrower was short of cash or that his net worth had declined. If lenders reasoned in this way, they would refuse to cut the interest rate in return for a lower LTV.[6] In reaction, borrowers would simply boost the size of their loans up to the credit limit allowed by the collateral they mortgaged.

The consequence of asymmetric information is to push lenders toward credit rationing, and in many cases to a single interest rate. For example, all loans would be made at the same (five-percent) interest rate and the same LTV (fifty percent). The mortgage market would then have a credit rationing and pooling equilibrium, or CRPE, with all borrowers getting the same terms. That is precisely what we observed in France from 1670 to 1870.

Can a CRPE be Self-Sustaining?

Asymmetric information seems to have motivated both rationing on loan value and pooling on interest rates—in other words, our CRPE. It is clear that asymmetric information is necessary to sustain such a CRPE equilibrium. We can see why by asking whether lenders or notaries would have an incentive to behave any differently if all loans were made at the same interest rate and rationed on loan value—in other words, whether CRPE would be an equilibrium, at least for the lenders and notaries.

Suppose a particular lender has exclusive information that makes him confident that a borrower will scrupulously adhere to the terms of the contract and hence be an above-average credit risk. It might seem that the lender would give the creditworthy borrower a discount because the borrower is better than average. But the lender actually has no incentive to do so, because he is the only one who knows the borrower is better than average. In other words, he would not deviate from the CRPE.

We will consider shortly what happens when this information becomes less exclusive, but the next step is to consider intermediaries—notaries. Suppose a notary knows that a particular borrower will scrupulously adhere to the terms of the loan contract. Suppose as well that lenders trust the notary; in other words, they believe the notary's recommendation that the borrower is better than average. In this situation, the notary might consider giving the lender a choice between making a loan to the better borrower at 4.75 percent or lending to a standard borrower at five percent. A lender who faces higher costs of recovering foreclosed collateral in case of default might be happy to take the lower interest rate from a borrower who would be less likely to cause trouble. But would the notary actually offer this option to such a lender, and thereby break the pooling equilibrium? The answer, it turns out, is no; the notary simply would not make this option available.

To see why, assume that the notary splits his creditworthy borrowers into two groups: the best borrowers (the ones who are most likely to repay and to observe the terms of the loan contract), and the rest the merely good borrowers. What the notary decides to offer the lender will depend on what other lenders and notaries infer about the rest of his borrower pool. It is true that his best borrowers are better than the good ones. But at the same time his remaining good borrowers who get five-percent loans are worse than the average. So now consider how lenders will react if a single notary starts offering lenders the option of making loans to his best borrowers at a lower interest rate. Lenders will have a choice between the notary who offers this option and other notaries who pool all their borrowers and arrange all their loans at five percent. Faced with such a choice, lenders will avoid any five-percent loans arranged by the notary who offers the lower interest rate option, because his five-percent borrowers are worse than average. Instead, lenders will pick borrowers from pooling notaries in the expectation that their five-percent borrowers are better than the ones from the notary who separates his best and merely good borrowers. The notary who offers the low interest option will therefore lose business, and as a result he will revert to making all his loans at five-percent. Notaries, in short, will have no incentive to deviate from the pooling equilibrium when they arrange loans.[7]

The same logic applies to the referrals notaries made. Referrals from notaries who separate would not be equivalent to those made by a notary who pools. And while the clients with 4.75 percent loans from the notary who separates would be better than average, his clients with five-percent loans would be worse than average. The other notaries will therefore spurn his five-percent referrals, which will cost him business, and the loss of business will keep him from deviating from the pooling equilibrium. The argument here, it should be stressed, does not depend on any loss of trust in a notary who deviates from the pooling equilibrium. The notary who deviates will be punished, but not because he is considered untrustworthy. Rather, it is because other notaries will find it more profitable to avoid doing business with him unless he sends them only his best borrowers. That, in turn, would have negative consequences for lenders willing to transact with the remainder of a separating notary's clients. In short, if information is privately possessed, then lenders and intermediaries are not likely to break an equilibrium of credit rationing and interest rate pooling, and that equilibrium is likely to persist.

What Might Make the CRPE Equilibrium Unravel?

The CRPE equilibrium is robust, but it could still break down for two different reasons. Both are the results of financial changes broadly defined. The first reason involves financial intermediaries' business practices; the second, information and borrowers. The implication is that financial modernization can destroy the interest pooling equilibrium—something we will test using our data.

The first hypothesis we call the business practices hypothesis. It explains the fate of the CRPE by focusing on financial intermediaries' concern for their reputations. Recall that in the information equilibrium described in chapter 4, honesty in referrals is enforced by the threat of exclusion. If a notary begins to separate his clients and offers some of them lower interest rate loans, he is doing something unexpected and might well be shunned by his colleagues. As a result, he would receive fewer referrals and be able to send fewer of his own clients out, and his business would presumably decline.

The force of that threat might diminish, however, if referrals declined in value, and referrals might well do just that in cities. It was in cities that new financial methods and new financing requirements were spreading, with burgeoning equity and bond markets and a growing demand for resources to finance infrastructure, urban housing, and industrialization (Lévy-Leboyer 1977). At the same time, urban wealth was growing rapidly in the second half of the nineteenth century, making capital more abundant (Piketty et al. 2006, 2014; Daumard 1973). It stands to reason that more subtle approaches to evaluating the cost of credit would start in the largest cities. Notaries there, as we have shown (at least in the case of Paris), were certainly tempted to participate in these changes, which would reduce the value of referrals.[8] In turn, the reduced value of referrals would allow innovators to disrupt the CRPE equilibrium in cities.

Moreover, in the largest cities, access to the referral network was not as important. To begin with, urban notaries were mostly receiving referrals from the countryside rather than sending them out and so were less likely to have clients whom they were unable to match. Competition from the Crédit Foncier would also cut the value of referrals in cities because it sought out the most qualified urban borrowers. In effect, the Crédit Foncier was already separating borrowers, reducing the risks for notaries who cooperated with that large bank. We might well expect the pooling equilibrium to collapse first in the largest cities and then see the new business practices diffuse down the urban hierarchy from large cities to smaller ones. Things would be different, however, in the countryside. For rural notaries, doing without referrals would have remained costly, because they (as our queuing model in chapter 3 suggests) would have found it very difficult to increase their supply of loanable funds. Thus the threat of being cut off from the traditional referral network would have been a powerful inducement for rural notaries to toe the line on the five-percent interest rate. Rural areas, therefore, would be most likely to maintain the pooling equilibrium longest.

The business practices hypothesis has other implications, particularly for the type of borrowers who would end up being referred. As urban notaries moved from a pooling to a separating equilibrium, rural notaries might interpret such a deviation from common practice as a sign that urban notaries no longer cared about their reputations. If so, then the rural notaries would stop sending borrowers who were as good on average as the ones they served at home. Whether they were in the countryside or in cities, the borrowers who considered traveling in search of better loan terms would face strikingly different incentives than when the pooling equilibrium prevailed everywhere. An area that continued to pool at five percent would only attract borrowers from the separating area who were willing to pay the high interest rate. The borrowers from the separating area who traveled would therefore look worse than their counterparts who took out loans at home, because the borrowers who took on debt at home in the separating area would be the ones who got the lower interest rates. As for the borrowers from the pooling area who traveled, they would be the ones who could get the low interest rate loans in the separating area and so would look better than their counterparts at home. In short, if the business practices hypothesis is correct, the borrowers who traveled from the pooling area would get loans at lower interest rates, while the borrowers who traveled from the separating area would pay higher interest rates. These are hypotheses we can test.

As for the other explanation for why the CRPE unraveled—our hypothesis about information—there is theoretical work we can appeal to (Grossman 1981, Milgrom 1981). It shows that as long as information is verifiable it should be disclosed by the party who possesses it. The information here might be a safety record, a credit history, or the quality of product; it is what in game theory is called a type. The individuals whose information makes them the most desirable type (in our case, a better than average borrower) want to reveal who they are. Doing so will allow them to stand out from the crowd and get better loan terms. But if they do, then the remaining borrowers have a lower average type. The best among these remaining borrowers will themselves want to reveal that they are better than the others and so they too will separate themselves from the crowd. In the end, all but the worst group of all announce their type.

Only one thing matters to ensure this sort of outcome: the type announcements have to be verifiable at sufficiently low cost. Without verifiability, everyone will want to state that they are the best type. If verifiability is costly, then some borrowers will likely misreport their type (just as people cheat on their tax returns). But if verifiability is cheap, then all borrowers will reveal their types.

A modern example from a different setting illustrates what can happen: restaurant cleanliness inspections in Los Angeles. For a long time, as Leslie and Zhin (2003) demonstrate, the outcomes of restaurant cleanliness inspections were private information. Patrons only knew that a restaurant had failed an inspection when inspectors shut it down until it cleaned things up. All that patrons knew about the other restaurants is that they had passed inspection, but not whether they were just barely passing or spotlessly clean. In the 1990s, though, Los Angeles County began to issue cleanliness rating cards to restaurants, which cut the costs of verifying restaurant cleanliness. Spotless restaurants earned an A, others a B or C. Each restaurant was issued a plastic card with their grade, and a website was launched with a list of restaurants and their grades. The city of Los Angeles, which is only a portion of the much larger county, required restaurants to display the marks they got, but other communities in the county did not impose that requirement. Yet within a few month of receiving their cards (so Leslie and Zhin found), the restaurants with low scores improved their cleanliness and did so regardless of whether they were in a part of the county that made posting of scores mandatory or in the part where it was optional. Since the only reason to make these improvements would be to display the cards, it is clear that restaurants everywhere were displaying their cards in their windows. Those with A cards wanted to crow about their cleanliness, while those with a B wanted to avoid being taken for a grubby C; no one wanted to look like they had something to hide. Easy verifiability made restaurants reveal their type, even when it was not required.

The same logic applies to credit markets. Suppose that credit ratings are verifiable but that borrowers have the choice to reveal them or not. Any borrower with the highest score will reveal that score because she will get a lower rate, faster service, or some other benefit from any lender that she encounters. The borrowers with the next highest score will also want to separate themselves from the group, and so on and so forth, until all borrowers *voluntarily* post their scores. The only thing that matters is that those benefits exceed the cost of revealing the verifiable information about credit ratings. The historical question, then, is this: When did borrowers get access to such information at low cost? When they did, they would reveal their creditworthiness, and that would be another reason for the CRPE to collapse.

Interest Rates and Information in 1899: France as a Whole

We can test our hypotheses about business practices and information using data about interest rates in our cross sections and in other sources of evidence we have consulted. Although, before the late nineteenth century, the records of the tax on notarial acts frequently do not report interest rates, there is abundant data on interest rates in 1899, and some data in 1865. Of the 14,652 contracts in our 1899 cross section, eighty-eight percent contain an annual interest rate. Of the others, 175 contracts (or one percent) say that no interest will be charged; another six percent specify that there is interest but do not specify the rate; and 638 or four percent of the contracts are silent on the matter. We could have just focused on the contracts for which we can compute an interest rate—in effect assuming that the reported rates are representative. Instead, we chose to recode all contracts that did not report an interest rate (about twelve percent of them) to five percent, and we did the same for the 1865 cross section. That procedure will bias the results against the hypothesis that the CRPE unraveled between 1865 and 1899.

Figure 8.1 shows the cumulative distribution of interest rates for 1865 and 1899 for France as a whole. These distributions reflect the data in our sample weighted by loan amounts and by the population for the market where the loan was arranged. The results should give an accurate picture of the distribution of mortgage interest rates in France in 1865 and 1899.[9] For 1865, the overwhelming majority of the loans (97.6 percent) were contracted at five percent. Clearly, 1865 is a pooling equilibrium. The data for 1899, by contrast, are strikingly different. First, the 1899

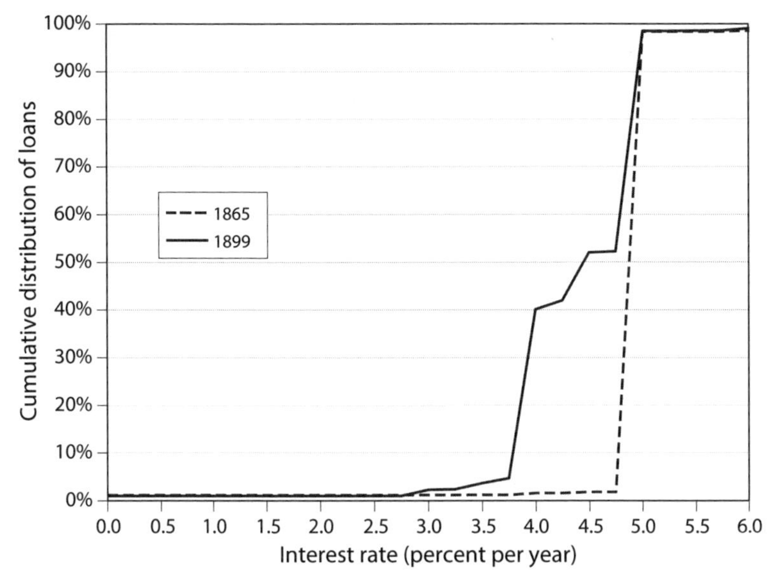

Figure 8.1. Distribution of interest rates, 1865 and 1899 (population and value weights).
Note: This sample includes only the 99 markets that are present in each cross section.
Source: See text.

cumulative distributions lie well to the left of the distributions for 1865; interest rates were much lower in 1899 than they had been thirty-five years before. In 1899, lending at five percent or more had in fact fallen to only fifty percent of the total volume of credit, halving the importance of these contracts between 1865 and 1899. That is a dramatic shift from the equilibrium in 1865.

This shift comes despite our assumption that all the contracts without interest were paying lenders five percent. In fact, if we drop that assumption and simply eliminate those contracts, then lending at five percent had fallen from sixty-six to thirty-three percent between 1865 and 1899.

Borrowing had clearly become much cheaper for most people by 1899. Moreover, the evolution was not simply a jump from pooling at five percent to pooling at four percent. A sizable share of the loans were contracted at one of four possible rates: four percent, 4.25 percent, 4.5 percent, and five percent, with larger loans more likely to receive the lower interest rates. Clearly, the pooling equilibrium on interest rates that had prevailed for two centuries had vanished by 1899.

The aggregate data cannot speak to our two hypotheses about why the pooling equilibrium unraveled—whether it was due to the intermediaries' business practices or the borrowers' verifiable information. Instead,

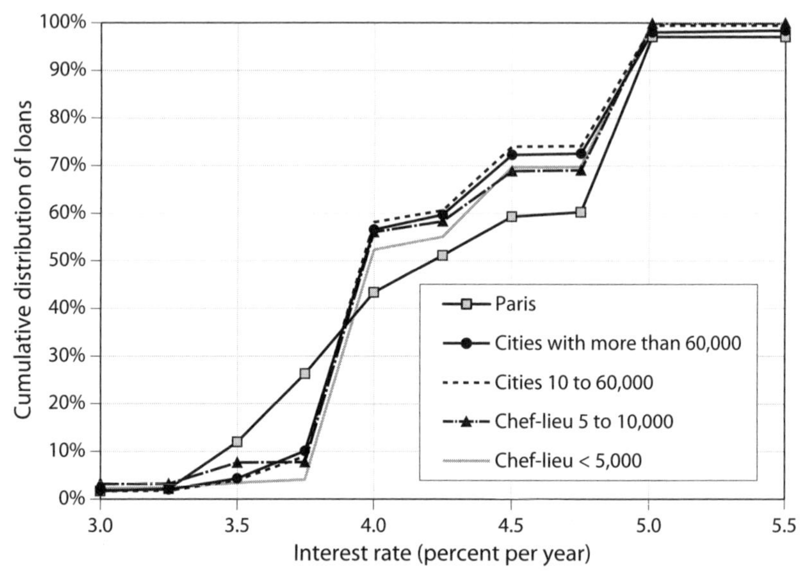

Figure 8.2. Distribution of interest rates in 1899 by bureau population (value weighted).
Source: See text.

we need to look across markets. To distinguish between the two hypotheses, we first graph the distribution of interest rates by market size for obligations in 1899 (figure 8.2). If the hypothesis about intermediaries' business practices is correct, the share of contracts at five percent or more should be small in cities and large in the countryside. But it is not. In fact, the share at five percent or more does not vary with population outside Paris, and it is larger in Paris, not smaller.

Paris is a particularly bad fit for the business practices hypothesis—such a bad fit that it deserves a digression. If the hypothesis about business practices is correct, then Paris should have the lowest cost loans, because, under the hypothesis, the separating equilibrium would take hold in the biggest city first. And with the Crédit Foncier dominant there, interest rates should be lower still. But Paris had the highest fraction of money lent at five percent (figure 8.2). In fact, once we remove the CFF, almost two-thirds of the loans (and funds loaned) were transacted at five percent. One might worry about our coding loans with no interest as though they paid five percent interest, and Paris does have a large number of notarized credit lines without information about interest rates. But if we consider only obligations with interest rates, then the share lending at five percent does decline to fifty-four percent of loans and thirty-seven percent of sums lent, but even then interest rates in Paris remain high.

Two additional pieces of evidence also argue against the hypothesis about business practices. The first is that the distributions of interest rates are virtually identical across the urban network of cities, from large to small. (See figure 8.2, where lending is weighted by value, without notarized credit lines.) That runs counter to the prediction of the business practices hypothesis, that the separating equilibrium would diffuse down the urban hierarchy and lead to differences in the distribution of interest rates by city size. Instead, interest rates were the same, which suggests that the new separating equilibrium operated in all cities, not just the largest ones.

The second piece of evidence against the hypothesis comes from comparing interest rates for loans where borrowers had to travel to find a lender and loans where they did not. If the business practices hypothesis is correct, and if (as it predicts) the countryside continues to pool while cities move to the separating equilibrium, then the borrowers who traveled from the pooling area—the countryside—would get loans at lower interest rates than their counterparts who stayed home. Presumably that would mean more borrowers would get loans below the pooling interest rate of five percent. As for borrowers who traveled from the separating area—the cities—they would pay higher interest rates on their loans: at least five percent.

That, however, is not what happened (table 8.1). Borrowers from villages or small towns (population under five thousand) who traveled ten to fifty kilometers actually had a trivially lower chance (58.0 percent versus 58.1 percent) of getting a loan at less than five percent than those who stayed home. And borrowers who traveled from bigger towns (population five to twenty thousand) or from cities (over twenty thousand) were slightly more likely to get a cheap loan, not less, contrary to the business practices hypothesis.

So we can rule out the business practices hypothesis, which would have the countryside remain in the pooling equilibrium and cities shift to the modern separating equilibrium. But it is not as if referrals disappear altogether in 1899, for, as table 8.1 makes clear, there were still large numbers of borrowers who traveled more than ten kilometers to find a loan. Referrals were in fact just as common in 1899 as they had been in 1865, according to the regressions used to analyze travel in table 3.4.

The pattern here points to a different outcome—namely, that the new separating equilibrium took hold everywhere. Referrals did not vanish; in fact, they continued to be used. But some borrowers had access to verifiable information that could prove they were creditworthy—hard information that they could pull from the Hypothèques registers. Borrowers of this sort could be found in all markets, large or small.

That outcome fits our second hypothesis, which turns on the verifiable information that borrowers possessed. Until the Hypothèques registers

Table 8.1. Share of loans paying less than 5 percent interest in 1899 by size of bureau and of borrower residence: borrowers who travel and borrowers who stay home

	Percentage of loans paying less than 5 percent interest		
Population of borrower's residence	Travel less than 10 km	Travel between 10 and 50 Km	Travel further than 50 km
5,000 or less	58.1	58.0	60.3
5,000 to 20,000	58.6	61.3	68.1
20,000 to 100,000	60.4	64.1	65.2
Number of loans	8,716	2,559	2,460

Note: We assume that a borrower who lived more than 10 kilometers from the lender had to travel. If a borrower lived less than 10 kilometers from the lender, we assume that the borrower stayed home even if he took out the loan in a bureau that did not serve his residence. Data for Paris is excluded.
Source: Our 99 market sample.

had acquired complete credit histories for individuals, the cost of communicating verifiable information was prohibitive. But once they did have complete credit histories, the cost of retrieval was rather small. Now the person who certified the information was neither the borrower nor his notary—instead, it was a government official in the Hypothèques registry. Information was in a sense standardized, creating confidence in transactions that had been impossible before. By the last third of the century, enough information had accumulated in these registers to make them reliable, and not just for the very top of the wealth distribution, but for a broad swath of the wealthy. Informing any willing lender would have cost a borrower very little, although informing a large number of potential lenders would have been expensive.

It is true that the verifiable information from the Hypothèques registers might not have been enough to break the pooling equilibrium, because the better borrowers would still have to get lenders to compete in making loans to them. Clearly, notaries would not have been eager to organize such a competition, for they would no longer be providing information and their fees would therefore drop. But here the Crédit Foncier likely played an important role; indeed, the bank's business plan explicitly targeted borrowers with large amounts of verifiable collateral. To induce these well-qualified borrowers to exit the traditional system, the CFF offered them loans that self-amortized over decades rather than the five-year balloon payment that was standard in notarial credit. It also offered an interest rate discount of a half or more percent per year. The CFF could offer such loans because it did not have to worry about the impact that separating the best borrowers would have on the rest of the market; after all, it had no intention of dealing with the rest of the market. The CFF also satisfied another condition emphasized in the models: the information must be cheap to communicate. Any borrower who knew he or she was qualified for a loan at the bank only had to apply there. Thus, a well-qualified borrower did not depend on a notary for a match and did not have to bear the cost of searching out a lender on his or her own.

Beyond the Crédit Foncier and the verifiable information from the Hypothèques, there were also market forces that were helping to destroy the pooling equilibrium. In the last quarter of the nineteenth century, the supply of funds to lend swelled, cutting the yield of French government bonds to less than 3.5 percent by the 1890s (Homer and Sylla 1991, 223). At the same time, a variety of shocks struck different parts of the agricultural economy, with the value of farm output as a whole falling eleven percent in the 1880s and remaining below trend until 1910 (Lévy-Leboyer and Bourguignon 1985, 321–2). That reduced the demand for credit in rural areas and strengthened the hand of well-qualified borrowers in other markets. Together, all these changes helped the best borrowers pressure their notaries to offer loans at low interest rates.

The changes also affected the lenders' strategy for dealing with the remaining lower-quality borrowers. Imagine that lenders considered government bonds as an alternative investment. In 1865, when government rates were at 4.5 percent, lenders might well have reacted to an attempt to separate the best borrowers from the rest of the pool by refusing to make any loans at all to individuals, because investing in government debt provided similar returns with greater liquidity. But by 1899, with government bond yields at 3.5 percent, a notarized loan at five percent to a lower-quality borrower might be attractive even if there was a possibility of default. The low government rates made lenders willing to take on those borrowers who did not have the highest level of collateral or the best credit histories.

Beyond 1899: The Department of the Aube

To check our argument and verify that 1899 was not a freak year, we collected three additional cross sections for the cantons of Arcis-sur-Aube, Bar-sur-Aube, and Troyes, for the years 1911, 1927, and 1931. All three cantons lie in the department of the Aube, to the east of Paris, and for each of them we gathered data from the tax on notarial contracts that was the source for all of our other cross sections. We chose 1911 because it was shortly before World War I, while 1927 came after a period of high

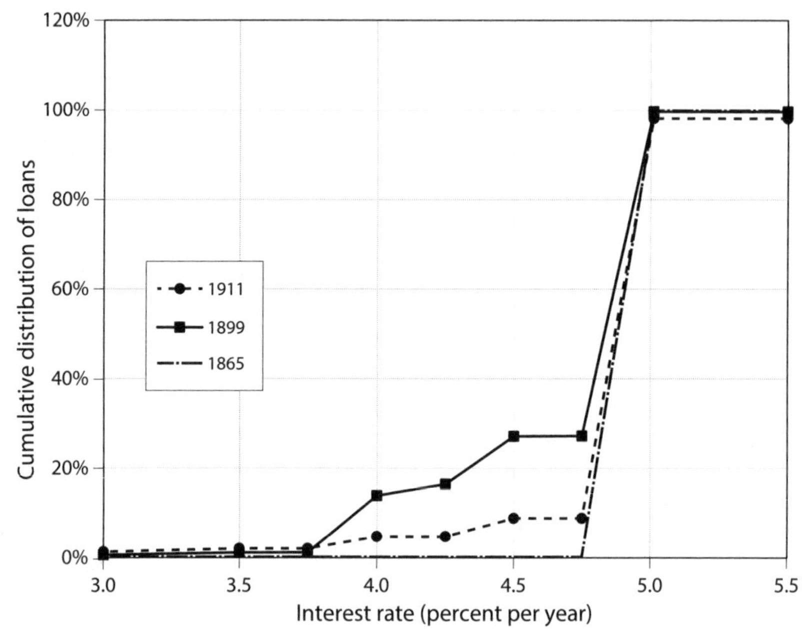

Figure 8.3. Interest rates in the Aube, 1865–1911 (value weighted).
Source: Our samples of notarized loans in the Aube.

inflation but before the Great Depression. 1931 was chosen to correspond with a national survey that we discuss in the next section.

Let us start with the distributions of interest rates from 1911 and, for simplicity's sake, focus on the distributions of the numbers of loans (figure 8.3). The leftward shift of the distribution we saw in the national data in figure 8.1 is repeated here. In 1865, the five-percent interest rate was so ubiquitous that in Bar the most common annotation in the source of our data is that the loan bore the "legal interest rate," while in Troyes the clerk simply ignored interest rates most of the time. By 1899, however, loans were made at a variety of interest rates. In 1911, when interest rates on government bonds had barely risen (to 3.1 percent from 2.98 percent in 1899), there was a move back to the right. In 1911, the share of loans with an interest rate lower than five percent dropped from thirty percent to twelve percent, in what was likely a response to local conditions that we unfortunately cannot observe.

While the variations in the distribution of interest rates between 1865 and 1911 would have astounded borrowers and lenders in the mid-nineteenth century, these variations pale when compared with what happened after World War I. As figure 8.4 shows, when we include the

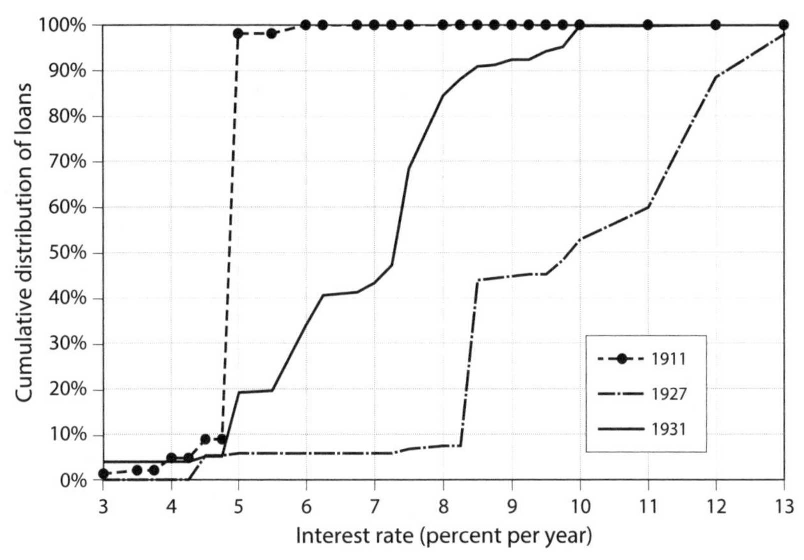

Figure 8.4. Interest rates in the Aube, 1911–31 (value weighted).
Source: Our samples of notarized loans in the Aube.

two distributions of interest rates from 1927 and 1931, the price revolution of the late nineteenth century seems to be merely a small scale disturbance. Indeed, if the median loan's interest rate in 1911 was about five percent, by 1927 it had jumped to nearly ten percent, a rate not seen for mortgage loans since the sixteenth century (Schnapper 1957). At the top of the range we have one loan negotiated at fifteen percent, while we also have a few loans at 4.5 percent.

To explain this startling range of interest rates, we can no longer rely simply on the evolution of market forces or benign government intervention. The yield of long-term French government bonds itself ranged between 4.15 and 5.05 percent in 1927 alone, and over the 1920s the highest yield was seven percent. In other words, most borrowers in the Aube in 1927 were paying two and half times the yield on government bonds. Had the same ratio applied in the 1910s, notarial loans would have paid 10.5 percent instead of the five percent that was the mode in the 1899 and 1911 data.

If the risk premium paid by private borrowers was about two percent in 1899 and 1911, then they should have paid about seven percent interest in 1927, which is a bit more than half what they actually did pay in that year. Clearly, the connection between government bond yields and private interest rates had changed drastically in 1927, leaving borrowers in the notarized credit market much worse off. Loan maturities had also collapsed, falling from six years to only two and a half years, which seems consistent with the notion that individuals were no longer confident of the stability of the mortgage market. But at the same time, inflation averaged about ten percent from 1912 to 1927, so a loan at twelve percent was paying a low real return to lenders—lower than what they had earned in the nineteenth century. In this light, the true surprise was the market for long-term government bonds, where real rates were persistently negative.

The second element worthy of note for 1927 is the arrival of new, specialized credit institutions. In the case of the Aube, it was the Société de Crédit Immobilier de l'Arrondissement de Troyes, a bank in the city of Troyes that focused on increasing the availability of rental housing. It made eighteen loans from January through early March 1927, all at 4.5 percent. At that rate, loans were a boon: interest paid represented a sixty-two-percent discount from the standard rate of notarized private loans between individuals, and it was slightly below the yield on government bonds in 1927 (4.6 percent). With inflation, the real rate was –0.5 percent. These loans obviously had an enormous appeal for borrowers who qualified for them.

The other banks in the Aube market were the Crédit Foncier at 10.5 percent, with a small fifteen-year loan, and the Banque Populaire de l'Aube, with three loans made to businesses. They are the three largest loans in the sample and on their own constitute thirty-eight percent of the funds lent, with an average maturity of two years and a variable interest rate of two percent above the Bank of France's discount rate, which at the time was 5.33 percent. If we include all the loans made by any bank, the total comes to fifty-three percent of funds lent in the sample. Mortgage credit was clearly moving out of the hands of notaries and into specialized institutions.

We collected a similar sample for 1931, during the Great Depression. In figure 8.4, the distribution of interest rates now lies further to the left of the graph. The highest interest rate we found was ten percent (instead of fifteen percent in 1927), and the median interest rate was 7.25 percent (instead of twelve). But this decline in interest rates must be put in context. After 1929 inflation gave way to deflation (from 1927 to 1932 prices were down by two percent a year), and the yield on government bonds dropped to 3.5 percent in 1931. Still, the median interest in 1931 was fifty percent higher than what had prevailed before World War I.

Banks had retreated from the market in 1931, which was hardly a surprise in the context of the Great Depression. Their share of lending fell back to thirty-one percent, even though they were making loans not just in the city of Troyes (as they had done in 1927) but also in the town of Arcis-sur-Aube. The banks' share dropped despite the fact that the same bank lenders (CFF, Banque Populaire, and Crédit Immobilier) were active in both 1927 and 1931, and 1931 also had loans from the Crédit Agricole bank. Our sample is too small for us to draw any significant conclusions about the role of banks and financial institutions in 1931 (we will return to this matter in the next section), but one thing is unmistakable: the world of notarial credit that is the focus of this book clearly ended with World War I.

France, February 1931

Our last data set comes from an unpublished survey of notarial credit compiled by the clerks of the Enregistrement administration, who enumerated all loans made in February 1931.[10] We recovered the loans they counted from the departments where we had collected credit samples for our earlier chapters. The survey does cover only one month instead of a full year, but it is more extensive, since it includes all the bureaus in a department, rather than simply the three or four that make up our typical departmental sample. Unfortunately, for some departments the survey provides little geographic detail.[11] We therefore limited our analysis to departments where we could allocate each loan to a registration arrondissement.[12] (As a reminder, arrondissements were the largest subdivision of French departments.) The resulting sample contains 5,977 loans from arrondissements that contained forty-five percent of the French population. If these arrondissements were representative, and if February was a representative month, then France would have had about 155,000 new notarial loans in 1931, a far cry from the 430,000 loans we estimated for 1740. The stock of outstanding notarial loans would also have been smaller than 1740: only 910,000 loans versus 1.7 million two centuries earlier. Yet, despite the Great Depression, the stock of outstanding loans had not completely collapsed (Michel 1908, 1934); our measure of debt stocks gives a debt to GDP ratio for mortgage loans of eighteen percent (eight percent for peer-to-peer credit and ten percent for banks).

To check that the sample was representative, we graphed the distribution of interest rates, using several different schemes: simple counts of loans with no weighting by value or population; weighting by value or arrondissement total population; and weighting by value and population. They all produced quite similar results, so we will focus on the cumulative distribution of interest rates weighted by loan size and arrondissement population (see figure 8.5).[13]

What is striking here is the very wide range of interest rates. Some loans pay one percent while others pay twelve or even fourteen percent. The explanation for this state of affairs is simple. On the higher side of the

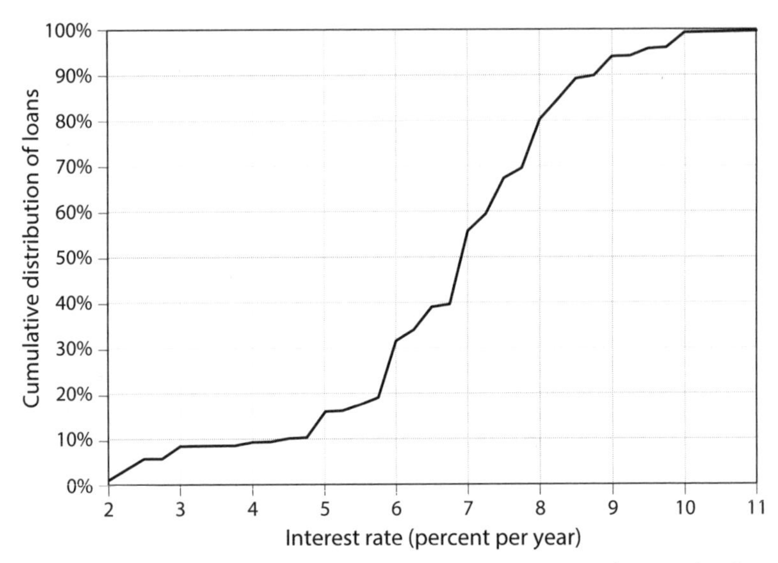

Figure 8.5. Interest rates for notarized loans, France, 1931 (value weighted).
Note: Loans below 2 percent or above 11 percent not shown on graph.
Source: Archives du Ministère des Finances (CAEF) B 39963.

distribution of interest rates were the loans between private individuals, ninety percent of which carried an interest rate of six percent or more. At the other end of the interest rates distribution were bank loans, with low interest rates made possible by generous state subsidies. As a result, nearly half the loans from banks were made at 2.5 percent or less. On average, borrowers with bank loans paid half as much in interest as borrowers with private mortgages (table 8.2).

By the winter of 1931, as table 8.2 shows, banks had become important players everywhere in France. If we break the loans down by the size of the market where they were registered, banks always accounted for at least nine percent of the number of loans, fifteen percent of the volume of lending, and forty-two percent of the stock of debt. The stock of debt was that high because bank loans were larger and had very long maturities (seventeen years on average, versus 4.4 years for private loans). In Paris, banks, continuing the early CFF lending, made twenty percent of the loans, which accounted for forty-six percent of the volume and a staggering seventy-seven percent of the stock of debt.

For France as a whole in 1931, banks were the lenders in 11.9 percent of mortgage loans, 24.7 percent of the volume of lending, and 56.8 percent of the stock of debt. By 1931, the modern credit revolution was clearly underway. With government assistance and the large and long duration

Table 8.2. Lending in February 1931

			Interest rate	Duration	Loan volume	Banks' share (percent)		
Population	Lender	Loans	Percent per year	Years	1,000 francs	Number of loans	Funds lent	Stock of loans
<5,000	Bank	13	3.6	16.6	29.8	9.15	17.24	45.1
	Private	129	6.4	4.2	14.4			
5,000 to 10,000	Bank	107	3.7	13.7	32.2	13.90	23.63	50.4
	Private	663	6.8	4.2	16.8			
10,000 to 70,000	Bank	302	3.2	16.6	40.6	11.47	16.35	42.1
	Private	2,330	7.3	4.4	26.9			
70,000 to 500,000	Bank	163	3.2	19.5	67.3	9.86	15.45	43.7
	Private	1,490	7.9	4.6	40.3			
Paris	Bank	112	5.1	20.0	502.7	20.44	46.43	76.5
	Private	436	8.1	5.3	149.0			
France	Bank	1,479	3.43	16.96	82.47	11.94	24.67	56.79
	Private	10,904	7.31	4.40	34.63			

Note: Estimates were extrapolated to all of France using the sampling rates for each market population category.
Source: Archives du Ministère des Finances (CAEF) B 39963.

loans they originated, banks now dominated the stock of outstanding debt, and they were starting to sideline notaries. Clearly, banks were very important for mortgage lending. Nonetheless, they had still not taken over the business completely, for even at the depth of the Depression in 1931, nearly ninety percent of borrowers continued to rely on the peer-to-peer lending system.

Conclusion

Prices returned to French mortgages in two phases. The first began in the 1880s, when cheap verifiable information became available and the centuries-old pooling equilibrium unraveled. This first phase was by and large a market phenomenon, but the government did play a role by developing a system of lien and title registration. Although it took time for the system to accumulate enough information to be useful, it did finally break the notaries' monopoly over mortgage lending credit information. Government sponsorship of the Crédit Foncier also contributed to this first phase, because the mortgage bank's strategy depended on breaking the pooling equilibrium.

In the second phase of the return of prices, the government took a much more active role. The second phase began during World War I, when the state inserted itself into the mortgage market in a wide variety of ways. As the 1931 survey makes clear, borrowers now had a powerful incentive to find projects that would benefit from bank loans. After all, interest rates for bank-financed mortgages were now usually half of what they were with private lenders. The outcome here was not the product of any greater efficiency on the part of banks, for, if so, then all borrowers would have sought mortgages from banks, and there would have been no notarized lending at all. Instead of being the heralds of greater efficiency, the banks simply acted as a pass-through for the government, which decided which lenders merited massive subsidies. The state was now directly involved in allocating loans to private borrowers—something completely unknown before the twentieth century.

Before this government intervention, though, the notaries were the ones arranging loans between private lenders and borrowers. They made loans big and small, and they did so in every corner of France, for two centuries or more. Even back in 1740, their peer-to-peer lending allowed a third of French families to borrow. Thereafter, the stock of debt they funded rose, reaching twenty-three percent of GDP in 1780, and, after a setback during the French Revolution, twenty-seven percent of GDP in 1840 (table 1). By then they were supplying as much secured credit as mortgage lenders were in the United States in the 1950s, provided that we measure debt relative to GDP. Although their lending relative to GDP slipped a bit thereafter, they were always able to supply credit equal to some twenty percent of GDP, despite the entry of hundreds of banks, including a government-backed mortgage bank. That is a phenomenal achievement, particularly for a credit market that has long remained hidden.

CHAPTER 9

Conclusion

The big debt we discovered pushes the rise of credit markets back at least a century before the rise of capitalism. It also rewrites the story of financial deepening between 1740 and the early twentieth century. To see why, consider French credit markets near the end of this period—say, in 1913, just before the start of World War I. In that year, France had all the trappings of modern finance: an active stock exchange, many banks large and small, and other specialized financial intermediaries, including the Crédit Foncier—the national mortgage bank. For mortgage debt, the Crédit Foncier was the visible part of a much larger market, one where most loans were dark matter, which was still not counted in conventional credit statistics. But apart from that lone anomaly in the usual source of data on financial markets, everything else would look familiar. In particular, borrowers paid a variety of different interest rates, just as they do today.

But as we move back in time, this familiar picture changes. The wide variety of behaviors, organizations, and institutions shrinks. By 1865, interest rate variation has shriveled up and nearly disappeared. By 1840, the Crédit Foncier has vanished. By 1807, nearly all banks have vanished. And by 1780, none of the modern finance institutions survive, apart from a stunted stock market. The only thing that persists, as we voyage back in time, are the huge number of peer-to-peer loans arranged by notaries. They endure, and when taken together, they already represent a large credit market in 1740, with one loan outstanding for every fourth household and a debt-to-GDP ratio greater than 16 percent.

As this voyage back in time makes clear, big peer-to-peer borrowing is more than just an astonishing historical statistic. It in fact has important implications for the social sciences and for understanding both modern credit markets and long-run economic change.

Let us start with its lessons for the social sciences, where in recent years researchers have grown more and more interested in history and how it shapes the present. The many social scientists engaged in this research could learn something important from our efforts to unearth the dark matter of notarial credit. The problem we faced was that the dark matter did not appear in banking statistics; it did not involve standard financial organizations, such as stock and bond exchanges, either, which would have made it easy to gather data from published histories and contemporary financial press. So, to estimate how much notarial lending there was, we could not turn to any readily available published sources or even to existing research. Instead, we had to collect data from the archives. The effort invested in the process was important—just as important as a novel instrument would be to an experimental physicist, or a new theory to a mathematical economist—for, without it, we would have skipped right over the most significant discoveries of our book. Published sources would simply have blinded us to what was actually happening. Only archival research would do—a lesson that social scientists doing historical research must learn.

They need to learn as well that archival research demands careful attention to three elements of the data collections process: how the original historical evidence was generated, how it was preserved, and how they go about collecting it. Ignoring any of those elements can cause enormous problems.

If, for example, we had simply accepted the conclusions in other published work on notaries, we would have assumed that the sort of contracts notaries drew up remained constant over time, as did the services that they provided to their clients. But that, we now know, would be a gross error. As chapter 3's discussion of literacy shows, the role notaries played in fact changed significantly. So did the sort of contracts they drew up, such as their innovative notarized letter of exchange, which we analyzed in chapter 5. Only research with original sources spared us those mistakes. We would have committed equally egregious errors if we had trusted Rondo Cameron's published data on banks. The implication here is inescapable. To understand the role of history, social scientists have to make a similar investment in archival inquiry or other primary sources. Only then will they have the high-quality data needed for a fruitful interaction between history and the social sciences.

A second lesson our discovery teaches concerns the relevance of history for present-day outcomes. In recent years, economists have taken the lead in documenting the long-run effects of history. They argue, for instance, that the slave trade's legacy continues to impoverish Africa (Nunn 2008). They aver that imperialism still hobbles economic growth in modern societies, particularly in those that suffered from severe inequality or that attracted few European settlers who could lobby for better institutions (Engerman and Sokoloff 1997; Engerman Sokoloff et al. 2012; Acemoglu Johnson and Robinson 2002; Acemoglu Robinson 2012; Dell 2010). Political scientists and sociologists make similar claims (Weingast 1995; Bates 2017; Tilly 2004). These efforts to tie current poverty to causes in the distant past do have enormous value, but if we are interested in growth we must be able to understand how economies can change. After all, Europe in 700 was neither the most prosperous nor the most politically stable part of the globe. The past matters, but so, obviously, does change.

We aimed to understand both historical inheritance and the process of change, and that goal argues for a deeper understanding of long-run change. To fully grasp the role that history plays in long-run outcomes, social scientists have to go beyond simply establishing a causal connection between social and economic outcomes today and events in the past; that is merely one step. Social scientists must then take a second step and actually uncover why institutions fail to change or why they successfully evolve. Only then will they understand how events of long ago can have enduring consequences, and why intervening forces may not dilute the influence of the past. The task, as we shall see, will require both general models and long-run data that cover the decades between the ancient causes and modern outcomes.

With these two lessons in mind, let us consider what the enduring system of peer-to-peer lending says about credit markets and long-run economic change. It turns out to tell us a great deal about banks, about mortgage markets, about modern peer-to-peer lending, and about the role that legal systems and political turmoil play in long-run financial development. It also highlights the importance of the informational infrastructure underlying credit markets—an unexplored topic where much more dark matter may lurk. The insights are important, particularly when they concern contemporary mortgage markets, which have an unrivaled potential to lay contemporary economies low (Gjerstad and Smith 2014; Mian and Sufi 2015).

Banks and Mortgages

In most developed economies, peer-to-peer lending played an important role in the mortgage market, but when it faded away, specialized lenders took over, such as Savings and Loans in the United States, or mortgage banks in continental Europe. They dominated the market until deregulation brought commercial banks into mortgage lending on a large scale.

That is the status quo, but the role that banks currently play deserves reconsideration, or so our high-quality historical data about peer-to-peer lending suggests. It is striking that peer-to-peer mortgage debt was large even in 1899, when banks covered France, and it was big way back in the mid-eighteenth century, well before most people had access to banks. The implication is that banks are not essential to mortgage lending; it can go on without them.

But our historical data do more than simply correct the history of financial development, by pointing out that mortgages were long made without banks, both in France and in other Western economies. The data also highlight the primacy of information flows in credit markets. The information flows, after all, are the reason why the peer-to-peer networks of notarial lenders credit survived so long in France and also why they could furnish so much credit. The usual story is that economies were starved for this sort of long-term credit until large universal banks arrived; they alone could provide the long-term loans that were essential for mortgage markets, which are typically one of the largest capital markets in any modern economy. But in both France and in other Western economies, banks—even universal banks—long shunned mortgage lending, and the mortgage market nonetheless thrived. The banks only entered the market in a significant way when the government intervened to support their efforts in what was effectively a private-public partnership.

In France, banks did admittedly dip their toes into mortgage credit in the second half of the nineteenth century. That was true in particular of the Crédit Foncier, but its mortgage business, and the mortgage lending by other banks, remained small before World War I and likely before World War II too. The limits to mortgage lending by banks was not for lack of entrepreneurs eager to have banks make mortgage loans. Schemes for modernizing the mortgage market in France go back at least to the reforms proposed by John Law in the 1710s (Perrot 1992). Although the bank he created (the Banque Générale) was focused on France's public finance, he authored a plan to also create a land bank and thereby help reestablish credit in France.[1] But his plan came to nothing. In the early nineteenth century, entrepreneurs actually founded private mortgage banks, but they all failed (Hoffman, Postel-Vinay, Rosenthal 2001, 326; Postel-Vinay 1998, 164–65). They were all undercapitalized and, worse yet, they simply could not overcome the notaries' informational advantage, which left them stuck with all the risky borrowers and mediocre collateral. With the help of government backing, the Crédit Foncier (CFF) did somewhat better, and it rapidly gained a dominant position in Paris by 1899. But it had far less impact outside the French capital. The CFF stayed mostly out of the provinces—and thereby limited the amount of lending it did—because it had learned a lesson from all the private mortgage banks that had failed in the past. It restricted its business to a small number of borrowers with huge amounts of collateral, most of whom were from Paris, and it left the bulk of mortgage lending to the better informed notaries.

Similar problems with risky borrowers and high default rates would arise if a big bank tried to originate mortgages on a grand scale and then used them to create mortgage-backed securities. If the bank funded a large number of mortgages, it would lack detailed knowledge of borrowers' creditworthiness, and it would then—as history shows—run the risk of falling victim to adverse selection or to a downturn in the real estate market.[2] The bank would be better off avoiding the mortgage market and choosing a different strategy. It could provide a wide variety of services to a small number of clients whom it knew well, as local merchant banks did in nineteenth-century France, or it could attract more clients but restrict the services it provided, as the universal bank Crédit Lyonnais did when it limited itself to drawing savings from the provinces and then invested the funds in Paris.

The bottom line here is quite simple, even though it runs counter to what most economic historians believe. For a long time, banks worked well for a limited number of financial activities (such as mobilizing savings in the provinces and investing them in Paris) or for a limited number of well-known clients (such as merchants who wanted to borrow short term, had good reputations, and could back up their loans with easily liquidated goods). But that left out an enormous demand for credit, particularly in the mortgage market, where, in the nineteenth century, private banks provided virtually none of the supply. The only exception was the Crédit Foncier, and even then it could only solve the information problem for the very wealthy, whose large loans covered the fixed cost of detailed collateral investigations (see chapter 7).

Because French institutions have been accused of stifling financial development, one might well think they kept banks from entering the mortgage market. Some state policies may (at least at first glance) seem to support that point of view: the restrictions on bank incorporation prior to 1867, the ban on issuing mortgage-backed securities (except for the Crédit Foncier), and credit rationing by the Bank of France (Lévy-Leboyer 1976; Homer and Sylla 1991; Lescure 2003). The accusation, however, is unjustified. To begin with, bank entry into mortgage lending was delayed almost everywhere into the twentieth century. In the United States, mortgages accounted for only thirteen percent of national bank assets in the 1970s.[3] In Germany, a slew of special purpose credit institutions called *Landschaften* funded mortgages as early as the eighteenth century. But they were not banks, and, like the Crédit Foncier, they depended on a partnership with the government (Wandschneider 2013). Finally, in the United Kingdom, late in the nineteenth century, building societies began to fund mortgages, but only a century after the rise of banks (Sheppard 1971). In all three of these countries, banks did not originate mortgages until (often quite late in) the twentieth century. There is therefore nothing peculiar to France about the delayed entry of banks in mortgage credit.

The implication of all this historical evidence is that mortgage markets impose large risks on banks and other lenders that carry mortgage debt on their books. That was true in the past—so our data show—and it is likely true today. Indeed, holding a diversified portfolio of mortgage-backed securities offers lenders little protection if there is a national downturn in real estate prices. The macroeconomic consequences of such a downturn can be devastating; by wiping out the net worth of huge numbers of private borrowers, it can drastically cut consumption spending and foist bigger losses on the financial system than a stock market crash would (Gjerstad and Smith 2014; Mian and Sufi 2015).

Letting the lenders fail and the economy tank is politically unacceptable too, at least in most modern democracies, and governments therefore cannot credibly promise to avoid intervening. So there will inevitably be government intervention in mortgage markets, and the key is making the regulation intelligent so that crises are avoided.[4] One option would be to require banks and other financial organizations that originate mortgages to keep a fraction of the loans on their books and to significantly bulk up the capital on their balance sheets in order to protect against potential losses. Holding on to the loans would encourage banks to take care when originating mortgages, and the additional capital would reduce the likelihood of bank failure. But it is not just banks that need the right incentives. Borrowers should also be obliged to put up equity of their own, so that their net worth will not be destroyed in a housing downturn. That would mean requiring a down payment of, say, ten to twenty percent and banning second mortgages that would reduce the borrowers' equity below that level. Demanding so much equity might seem draconian to lobbyists for the housing industry, but it was common in the United States, for instance, as recently as the late twentieth century. It would have to be put into law or into durable regulations, though, because lenders—so history demonstrates—cannot be trusted to maintain tough lending standards in a housing boom (Hoffman, Postel-Vinay, Rosenthal 2007).

What our Historical Evidence Reveals About Modern Peer-to-Peer Lending

Peer-to-peer lending is thriving today, thanks to the internet. Our historical evidence can help us understand it—in particular, some of the risks it entails.

Like notaries long ago, modern peer-to-peer lenders broker loans, and, as notaries did, they usually have information about creditworthiness that goes beyond what is readily available to other lenders. For notaries, the supplementary information derived from their records, and from their knowledge of clients' property and business dealings; it bolstered what they could learn from official lien registries. For modern peer-to-peer lenders, the additional information comes from data about credit risks that do not yet figure in the credit scores that other lenders have to rely on to estimate borrowers' riskiness. That additional information might, for instance, be a borrower's education and academic performance. For the peer-to-peer lender Upstart, these added bits of data help paint a clearer picture of a young borrower's creditworthiness than credit scores would on their own. The added information allows Upstart to make profitable loans to youthful borrowers, who usually have no credit score at all at the moment when they start working and would like to borrow to buy a car or purchase consumer durables such as furniture.[5]

But there are two striking differences between today's peer-to-peer lenders and notaries of the past. Unlike the notaries, the peer-to-peer lenders do not share information with one another and they can buy one another out.[6] Conceivably, one of the peer-to-peer lenders could end up dominating the market by gaining market recognition and thereby drawing in more and more users, as happened with Google's search engine. With more users than its competitors, the dominant peer-to-peer lender could make better matches than its competitors, and then cut its fees and absorb other peer-to-peer lenders. In the end, it could conceivably become a monopolist, protected from entry by name recognition and its huge proprietary database.

One could weigh the costs of such a monopoly, but a bigger risk might be the temptation for such a peer-to-peer lender—or any peer-to-peer lender—to become a shadow bank. It could do so by pooling the funds potential lenders want to lend out and paying them interest in return. It could do the same with other investors in, say, the commercial paper market. The peer-to-peer lender could then make loans with the pooled funds, just like a bank. Notaries, we know, faced this very temptation in the eighteenth and nineteenth century (Hoffman, Postel-Vinay, and Rosenthal 2000, 2003), but it carried big risks, because the maturity mismatch between long-term loans and short-term deposits made by investors left notaries vulnerable to what amounted to bank runs. Shadow banking would involve similar risks for peer-to-peer lenders today. As a shadow bank, a peer-to-peer lender might escape regulation, and with a maturity mismatch between its liabilities and its illiquid assets, it too could be vulnerable to a run, and to failure. The damage such a failure would do could be particularly large if the firm had come to monopolize peer-to-peer lending. It could in fact trigger a financial crisis, as with the insurance firm AIG's involvement in the credit default swaps and other securities lending in 2008. Both this danger and the possibility of a monopoly in peer-to-peer lending suggest that regulation of peer-to-peer lending might be necessary in the future.

Beyond the potentially dire consequences if peer-to-peer lenders slip into banking, another danger lurks in their lending that stands out clearly if we compare their business today with that of notaries one or two centuries ago. Like those notaries, modern peer-to-peer lenders earn more if they make more loans. They also rate borrowers, just as notaries did, but their rating involves nothing like notaries' referrals. Rather, it depends partly on observables, and partly on applying proprietary software to large data sets in order to produce more reliable indicators of risk. But that creates a powerful incentive for peer-to-peer lenders to relax their lending standards in order to make more loans; with relaxed standards, they will have higher match rates and attract more potential borrowers from competing lenders. With notaries, this incentive was kept in check by competition and the value of referrals, but there is nothing similar with which to discipline modern peer-to-peer lenders. How this problem will be resolved is unclear.

Legal Systems, Political Turmoil, and Financial Development

Today, we noted, economic historians often ask whether a particular past event caused a later outcome. Here, France should give them an important test case, particularly for measuring the effect of history on subsequent financial development. France suffered enormous political and social shocks that should have affected credit markets and left their marks on our archival data. It was rocked by political turmoil during the French Revolution, particularly in the years 1789–94, and by rapid inflation in 1791–96. And when the autocratic general Napoleon Bonaparte took over late in the revolution (in 1804 he was crowned emperor), he gave France a legal system—French civil law—that is supposed to have throttled financial development. Statistical tests suggest that both the revolutionary upheavals and the civil law had a causal effect on later outcomes.[7]

But what does our long-run archival data show? It turns out to raise serious doubts about claims that the revolution and the civil law held back France's financial development. It also reinforces our claim that understanding the role of history requires more than just establishing a causal connection between events in the past and outcomes today. That is merely one step, and there is a second step that is just as important—namely, uncovering why institutions fail to change or why they successfully evolve.

To see what this second step involves, let us start with the political ferment and inflation during the French Revolution. Presumably, they should have harmed financial markets. One might naturally ask whether they were the reason why France had fewer banks than England. Although establishing a causal connection there would certainly be important, it is more interesting to ask how French credit markets as a whole evolved after the revolution. After all, if we find countries that (like France in 1820) are underbanked, giving them the bad news that the cause of their problems lies with a revolution years or decades earlier is cold comfort. Instead, we need to offer poor countries ways to offset the damage done by the earlier political tumult. Here, learning how French credit markets overcame the revolutionary turmoil teaches important lessons about how economies recover.

As far as French credit markets are concerned, it is clear that they were expanding before the French Revolution and that the revolution simply interrupted their growth rather than bringing it to a complete halt. The revolution did overturn many things, but the way loan contracts were used in French credit markets had already been transformed before 1789, and the volume of lending was already growing at a fast pace. As for the effect of the revolution on banking in particular, it imposed no legal restrictions on banks, and memories of the revolutionary inflation did not seem to slow the development of banking either. The one thing that 1789 did do was to demonstrate the surprising resilience of the notarial credit system, since lending recovered in a generation or so. The continued large-scale credit activities of notaries diminished the demand for medium-term bank loans. Over the long nineteenth century, demand for branch banking was reduced by the Bank of France's willingness to open local branches, whose discount windows helped sustain unit banks. The Bank of France was itself a creation of the revolution, so by indirectly sustaining unit banks, the revolution may have delayed branch banking slightly in France. But the path between the revolution and the French financial system in 1899 is clearly more complicated than the simple claim that all the political upheavals shackled subsequent financial development.

What about the effect of French civil law on credit markets? Although Napoleon's system of civil law provided the legal rules governing credit markets, it in no sense stifled them. Such a claim does admittedly run counter to an influential argument that has gained traction in economics, political science, and law. The argument is that French civil law's rigidity cursed the economies and their financial systems wherever it held sway (La Porta et al. 1997, 1998). If that argument is correct—and statistical evidence seems to support it—then France was fated to suffer slow economic growth and halting financial development forever.

We do not quibble with the existence of a correlation between legal regime and the level of financial development in the last quarter of the twentieth century. But the correlation—so our research suggests—is simply not useful in explaining the history of French debt markets. For one thing, the civil law did not freeze financial innovation, even when the codes did not change, as we show with the history of the notarized letter of exchange. French law was supple enough to allow the notarized letter of exchange to diffuse even though it did not even have a place in the civil law. (It had no place because it mixed legal codes by having notaries—who normally dealt only with the Civil Code—draft a commercial instrument governed by the Commercial Code.) The jurisprudence was quite clear in its support of flexibility, which runs counter to claims about the civil law's rigidity. Appellate decisions affirmed that anyone could act as a merchant, at least as far as a letter of exchange was concerned. For the appellate judges, legal identity depended on actions, not on one's profession or social status, in keeping with the French Revolution's commitment to open access in law. So, if the notarized letter of exchange is an indication, then Napoleon's legal reforms actually made the legal system more flexible, which casts doubt on the arguments that French civil law constrained economic behavior.

The same applies to claims made about the damage done to debt markets by the restrictions that French civil law supposedly imposed on creditors' rights. The problem here is that scholars have mistakenly concluded that French civil law handicapped credit markets by giving debtors more protection than England's common law. It is true that, relative to the common law, the civil law did limit a creditor's recourse in three ways. First, it did not transfer real collateral directly to the lender in case of default; second, it did not let a lender imprison a borrower unless the borrower was engaged in commerce; and third, it gave the borrower's wife a senior claim on the couple's property up to the value of her dowry. These limits, which dated back to the Old Regime and survived virtually unscathed in the Civil Code, had been in place long enough to affect French credit markets. Presumably, they would make it harder for a French than a British lender to repossess collateral or to throw a defaulting borrower in jail. If so, then loan-to-value (LTV) ratios on secured loans in Britain should have been higher than the fifty percent common in France. There is little evidence, however, that British LTVs exceeded fifty percent. Furthermore, nineteenth-century French law was far more flexible than scholars believe. In the first half of the century, for instance, an individual borrower could easily add imprisonment to the penalty for default in a debt contract by choosing a commercial debt form. And if the borrower's wife cosigned the loan, then her claim would no longer be senior. In short, these limits on what lenders could do to protect themselves were easy to evade.

On a broader level, the judicial decisions make it clear that the Napoleonic Codes embodying French civil law were treated as enabling legislation, not restrictive legislation. Far from interpreting new forms of credit contracts, such as the notarized letter of exchange, as an illegal novelty because they had not been mentioned by the codes, the judiciary validated them because they had not been forbidden. The same approach also holds when we consider organizational forms for businesses (Lamoreaux and

Rosenthal 2005). The jurisprudence here is hardly surprising, because the Napoleonic Codes themselves are very brief (a few thousand pages). They could hardly examine and decide every possible detail in as complex and diverse a society as France in 1810; the judges therefore had to have considerable leeway to interpret the codes. It may be that the interpretation of the codes became more rigid after 1914, but again that hypothesis cannot be examined or tested without a historical approach.

The whole premise that the French financial system was somehow handicapped also seems dubious. Although France's financial system was a bit less developed than Britain's in 1900, it was not far behind (Rajan and Zingales 2003) and it had grown dramatically during the nineteenth century. If, rather than seeing the revolution of 1789 as a permanent setback, one sees it as part of a long-term process of change under adverse conditions (including additional revolutions in 1830 and 1848 and the Franco-Prussian War), then French financial performance may not seem so dismal after all.

As we shall see, Latin Americans would have had reason to envy the French financial system, even though they adopted French legal codes. The lesson, for their economies, is that the problem is not really the French legal codes they inherited. Instead, it was the repressive financial policies their governments enacted that eliminated the legal flexibility written into the original Napoleonic Codes. Rather than paying the immense costs of rejecting the law codes they have inherited, they would do better to restore the original flexibility of those law codes that France enjoyed in the nineteenth century.

If French credit markets are any indication, then the shackles that history supposedly puts on financial markets via the civil law are actually less important than the decades it takes to construct financial infrastructure. In mortgage markets, for example, it took time to establish methods for securing and transferring titles to property and to build up reliable sources of information about existing liens and property value. In France, while lien registration was set up during the revolution, its effect on mortgage markets was limited until the 1880s, and it only began to matter then because of the growth of the Crédit Foncier, which enjoyed government support.

Analyzing this sort of long-run change—either in financial systems or in the infrastructure that supports them—is the sort of project that economic historians ought to pursue, because it sheds light on why financial systems evolve. Historians have experience with assembling data sets from disparate historical sources that make it possible to analyze the change of financial systems across centuries; they can do the research and the economic analysis. The results would go a long way toward explaining why some economies have large financial markets, while others are stuck with small ones.

Long-run Financial Development

So if economic historians and other social scientists want to shed light on long-run financial development, what research should they do? Our experience with the historical data from peer-to-peer lending suggests that they start by identifying and measuring traditional credit markets. That is essential to avoid being misled by claims in the shortsighted secondary literature. They can then tackle three problems: analyzing the infrastructure of knowledge that lets parties to financial transactions overcome asymmetric information; determining the spatial scale of traditional financial markets; and explaining why some of these markets mobilized more money than others or involved more people. All three problems will help explain why financial institutions evolve or fail to change—an essential part of understanding long-run development of any sort.

These tasks do require a common method, one that combines developing long-run data sets relevant to an entire economy (not just one location) and models that can be generalized beyond that economy. Without the long-run data from an entire economy, we cannot measure how big traditional financial markets were or determine their spatial scale. And without the models, we cannot generalize beyond a single economy or understand how problems of asymmetric information were resolved. Combining data collection with theoretical models is critical here. In our case, we were forced to revise our model of information flows by the data we had gathered on the numerous loans between borrowers and lenders in different localities. Earlier scholars who focused on particular locations tended to leave loans with nonlocal borrowers or lenders aside. In effect, they were treating them as errors in a model of closed local credit markets. However, we realized that these errors had to be incorporated into our models. The revised models in turn led us to revise our data samples. In short, theoretical modeling goes hand in hand with archival research. We believe that the same lesson is likely to be true for research on long-run economic development in general.

The same lesson is likely to apply to the long-run evolution of information and contractual infrastructures. In eighteenth-century France, the information infrastructure was created by notaries, at least for medium- and long-term credit. It arose out of regulations dating back to the Middle Ages, long before the use of title and lien registries caught on in the nineteenth century. It then remained central to mortgage markets well into the twentieth century, despite the growing popularity of the lien registries and despite the entry of modern intermediaries like the government-backed Crédit Foncier. In this older infrastructure, notaries gained importance, because they had easy access to information about the wealth and indebtedness of clients. They garnered that information because they drew up marriage contracts, probate documents, and handled the legal paperwork for land sales and many other transactions. Their legal expertise also allowed them to design contracts to suit the particular needs of their clients. That was the information structure in France. It is the one that we modeled in chapters 3 and 4, and the one that shaped the dealings between banks and notaries that we analyzed in chapters 7 and 8.

We are not suggesting that France should serve as a direct model for research elsewhere. Indeed, that would simply repeat the myopic errors made by scholars who assume that financial markets in the past must have been moribund if their financial institutions did not resemble ours today. Although all societies need to overcome the problem of asymmetric information, they do not all have to do so in the same way. In theory, notaries outside of France could have drawn upon the information they possessed and arranged loans, just like their counterparts in France. But whether they did so (in other words, whether they, like the French notaries, turned their information into the infrastructure needed for the credit market) is unknown. As yet, we simply do not know whether notaries outside France used their store of information to become brokers in real estate and credit.[8]

Here, economic historians (and social scientists in general) should leap into the breach and try to explain differences in information and contractual infrastructure. The research involved would be rewarding, as even a cursory glance at the secondary literature shows. As this literature demonstrates, the differences in information infrastructure in Europe's eighteenth-century financial markets reflected the continent's wide variety of legal and political institutions. Britain, for instance, lacked notaries, but even on the continent, the role notaries played in credit markets varied greatly, either because their profession was organized differently or because other professions furnished similar services. In France, notaries always competed with one another, and there were always many notaries per jurisdiction. In other parts of Europe, by contrast, each notary was a local monopolist. In many places, a borrower's pledge of a piece of real estate as collateral could be written up simply as a purely private contract. Recourse to a notary was thus an option (much like using an attorney today to draw up a will), but not a requirement.

It is true that, in France, that option was used almost systematically. But in other places, there were substitutes for notaries—other ways to legalize loan contracts, such as village clerks in Germany and town secretaries in the Netherlands. And in the Netherlands, at least, private contracts dominated, even though Dutch town secretaries and notaries offered the same services notaries provided in France.[9] Research in the Muslim world of trade and credit also produces evidence of individuals taking up the role of notaries and connecting lenders and borrowers of different religions.[10] For credit, no one in Europe was ever required to use a notary to draw up loan contracts. In the late nineteenth century in the United States, there were also a large number of private mortgages, but mortgages were also funded by mortgage companies and insurance firms, which employed local agents to assess collateral and the creditworthiness of borrowers.[11]

Why information infrastructures differed so greatly from place to place (even when legal systems and political institutions are similar) remains a mystery that deserves to be resolved. To be sure, the development of this infrastructure was shaped by literacy rates; having a written loan contract makes it much easier to keep track of what is owed at any time, but if many people cannot read or write, then the question is how to give illiterates access to written contracts (Arnoux 1996). Clearly, there were a number of ways to resolve this problem, because we know that written contracts were not limited to the literate, either in Europe, the Islamic world, or in the rich parts of Asia. The solution made possible by notaries, who, as court-appointed recorders, kept authentic copies of contracts, is only one possibility, and perhaps an extreme solution, for in other places the state did not get involved and the scriveners' business was competitive. Beyond the case of French notaries, we do not know much about how loan contracts were drawn up for the illiterate and what the consequences were for the information infrastructure. That is an important agenda for comparative economic and legal history.

Scholars could then consider how credit markets interacted with the information infrastructure in other economies, so that their experience can be compared with what happened in France. Whoever accepts this challenge will have to start by looking into the past, because credit markets existed for centuries before modern financial institutions were established. The task will also require great care in using the historical sources. If one source does not mention loans, lending could still be common, as we discovered with the notarized letter of exchange. There were more than ten thousand of them in our data set, but someone reading notarial archives would scarcely find a single one. The reason in our case was that the borrowers and lenders in these contracts wanted to avoid the expense of an official notarial record (a minute), and so notaries did not keep copies. It was only because we relied on a fiscal source (the Enregistrement), which taxed all contracts, that we know the notarized letters of exchange existed and were in fact quite common in certain regions. The lesson, then, is that anyone who wants to analyze financial infrastructure has to combine the economist's thirst for systematic data with the historian's desire to tap a wide variety of quantitative and qualitative sources.

The second problem social scientists should examine is determining the spatial scale of these traditional markets: their geographic reach and the distances that separated parties in transactions. In a settled economy with limited long-distance mobility, like France, it is not surprising that individuals were loath to transact with individuals who lived more than a day's walk away, even in 1865, when railroads were spreading across the country. But at about the same time, European investors were willing to hold mortgage-backed securities issued by intermediaries on the US frontier (in the 1870s and 1880s in Iowa and Missouri, as Bogue 1955 and Snowden 1995 show). Such enormous differences in the spatial reach of financial markets are common. Today, for example, venture capital firms invest only in firms that are close at hand, but stock and bond markets are global. In the sixteenth century, international merchants already deployed letters of exchange to integrate payments across major markets in Europe (van der Wee 1977; Neal and Quinn 2001; Matringe 2016; Pezzolo and Tarrara 2008). By the seventeenth and eighteenth century, large numbers of such letters survive for a wide variety of locations, making it clear that a local mortgage market existed side by side with an international commercial credit system (Carrière 1973; Trivellato 2012, 2014). But were these two markets connected? If so, how? The historians' trope that successful merchants turned to purchases of land to secure part of their wealth and enhance their social status suggests that money moved from one to the other. But that is only a suspicion; as yet, we do not know for sure.

Equally important is determining how these markets functioned away from the core areas of Europe, in its more thinly populated and poorer outer reaches; this is an essential part of establishing their spatial scale. In the southern part of the Iberian Peninsula, and in Scandinavia, Poland, or many areas in the Austrian Empire, people were generally poorer, and the population was not as dense as in France, England, or the Low Countries. If our arguments about liquidity in chapters 3 and 4 are correct, credit markets in these areas should have been smaller, because the wait time and the travel costs required to complete a transaction were much higher. And since our French markets were supported by referrals among notaries and would collapse without relatively frequent future business, it is possible that many of these thinly populated areas in Eastern Europe would have no credit network, because interactions would be too rare to prevent misbehavior. There are certainly other ways that credit markets might arise—around major cities, or other different geographic structures. If so, then they might come to life and skirt the obstacle of market thinness. Only new research can tell.

The third issue social scientists should study is one that has cropped up throughout the book: explaining the heterogeneity of credit markets, or, in other words, their wide variation in size, whether we consider the amount or the frequency of lending. The problem is pinning down the relationship between the size of credit markets, on the one hand, and the wealth and the population of the biggest city in each market, on the other. Researchers will also have to analyze the effect of wealth and income inequality, since they affect ownership of collateral and ability to repay. The relationships at work here are complicated, for urbanization is correlated with both wealth and wealth inequality. Furthermore, in Europe, urbanization and economic development have long gone hand in hand, but the distribution of city sizes varies greatly. In Austria, France, and England, one capital city (Vienna, Paris, and London) dominates other cities, while Italy, Germany, and the Netherlands have a far more egalitarian urban network, with a large number of medium-sized cities. The size of a dominant large city means that credit transactions are frequent, but since big cities usually have very skewed wealth distributions, their lending tends toward huge loan amounts, but fewer loans overall, because many borrowers lack collateral. The result, typically, is a capital market that services elites, whether they live and work there, or simply meet there during, say, the winter season, as in nineteenth-century London (Goni 2017). In either case, elites in dominant large cities will find numerous potential counterparties and intermediaries devoted to elite service, from nineteenth-century bankers to modern-day hedge funds.

The historiography of modern capital markets privileges these dominant large cities, as is clear from all the literature devoted to London, Paris, or New York as financial centers. By contrast, the alternative pattern of urbanization and financial development in economies such as the Low Countries' has by and large been ignored, even though it might well be far more helpful to a burgeoning middle class. With less competition from a wealthy elite, the demand for financial services from this middle class might give rise to intermediaries and organizations that serve investors and borrowers of middling wealth. The intermediaries and organizations could harness wealth in nearby cities and allow middle-class borrowers to buy property or pay for education. Whether this actually happened, however, requires data from the rest of Europe; by itself, the French evidence data is not enough.

Sorting out the impact of inequality on the size of credit markets is particularly difficult here, although it should affect lending in mortgage markets by limiting the number of potential borrowers with collateral. Within our data set, we have not found much evidence that inequality plays a role (either positive or negative) in determining the magnitude of credit markets or their rate of growth. There are two reasons why inequality seemed to have no effect. First, it is correlated with city size and varies little within each size category. The solution would be to have far more cities for each size category and hence get some variation in inequality, but our sample was too small to do that. The second reason is that inequality is also highly correlated with average wealth levels. Unequal cities were simply richer, and so did more borrowing and lending. Nonetheless, we suspect that high levels of wealth inequality are inimical to mortgage markets, because they reduce the frequency of interaction and lead most financial intermediaries to focus on satisfying the intermediation demands of the very rich.

Evidence from outside Europe lends credence to this suspicion. Latin America has long suffered from high levels of inequality, and when we compare the level of mortgage lending in Latin American cities with lending in similarly sized cities in France, the contrast is striking: there is simply much less lending in unequal Latin America. A pair of examples illustrates the disparity—the cities of Merida in Mexico and Limoges in France, both of which had about forty thousand people in 1850. Despite the similar populations, Merida had only some seventy mortgage loans per year (Levy 2004). In Limoges, the number was twenty times higher: nearly 1,400 loans a year. One might simply attribute the difference to higher per capita incomes in Limoges, but the average loan size there was actually much smaller than in Merida: under one thousand francs in Limoges, versus over five thousand francs in Merida, just as we would expect if the local credit market was devoted to serving the rich.

Results from Lima, Peru, tell the same story (Zegarra 2015). With a population of about 100,000 in the 1860s, we can compare it to Toulouse in 1865, which had a population of 127,000. In Lima, the number of loans ranged from 550 to 460 per year, with an average loan value of 15,000 francs. In Toulouse in 1865, there were three times as many loans (1,500 per year), and the average value (3,500 francs) was again much smaller—less than a quarter the size of the average loan in Lima.

The same holds true for the larger but still medium-sized cities of Lyon and Rio de Janeiro. They had roughly comparable populations in 1870 (318,800 for Lyon and 228,743 for Rio). In Rio, only four hundred loans were arranged in 1870—a mere 1.75 loans per thousand inhabitants (Ryan 2007). In Lyon, at about the same time (1865), the number was far larger: 2,032 loans a year, or 6.62 loans per thousand residents, a figure nearly four times what it was in Rio. Again, the average loan size was smaller in Lyon: 9094 francs, versus 44,650 francs in Rio.

The conclusion is inescapable: mortgage markets in Latin American cities served a much smaller population of what were likely much wealthier borrowers and investors. In earlier work (Hoffman, Postel-Vinay, Rosenthal 2007), we blamed this stark difference on wealth inequality in Latin America. Were other causes at work too? That remains to be seen, but it is clear that the difference probably does not stem from differences in banking systems. The reason is simple. Banks, we know, played little role in the French mortgage market, and they may in fact have played a larger role in Latin America in the 1860s than in France. Also, mortgage markets in Latin America were small before mortgage banks and remained so afterwards after mortgage banks opened their doors. It appears that a lack of banks did not cripple Latin American mortgage markets and that inequality was instead the culprit. But researchers will have to check before we can be sure.

Big Debt and the Lasting Significance of Mortgage Markets

Mortgage markets teach all these valuable lessons, but—somewhat surprisingly—they rarely occupy the limelight. The spotlight shines instead on innovative venture capital, or the exotic engineering of derivative securities or IPOs that investors are eager to snap up. Yet mortgages really do matter, and they matter because they are big. For most households a mortgage is the largest debt they will ever take on. And when a firm needs to take on a lot of debt it will collateralize it with real assets. That was true of railroads in the nineteenth century and was still true of the Ford Motor Company in 2006 (Vlasic 2009). Mortgage markets are big in the aggregate, accounting for a large share of the debt taken on by households and firms in many economies (see figure 9.1 for the case of the United States). Thus, they play a very important role in credit mobilization, and they do so because they underpin both the market for real assets and investment in real assets.

In the eighteenth and nineteenth centuries, the largest real asset in terms of value was agricultural land, and mortgage markets had an enormous role to play in financing agriculture. That role loomed larger in frontier economies such as Canada, Argentina, and the United States than in more settled economies like Europe, because improvements embodied in creating new farms had to be financed, but mortgages were important everywhere. Later in the nineteenth century, when infrastructure investments like railroads required huge amounts of capital, mortgages proved critical for their financing too, along with the sale of land grants these railroads had been given. Later still, with the enormous development of urban housing, large mortgage markets arose in that sector. Mortgages then took on a social policy role, because politicians started to view high rates of homeownership as an important policy goal.[12]

While the characteristic of a mortgage as a loan backed by real estate has remained with us for centuries, everything else has changed. Of the fifty-percent loan-to-value ratio, five-percent interest rate, and five-year balloon payment loan that was the standard in the 1850s, little remains. Innovation has conjured up a slew of options for borrowers, including acceptable loan to-value-ratios ranging from fifty percent to more than ninety-five percent, accommodation for borrowers with poor credit

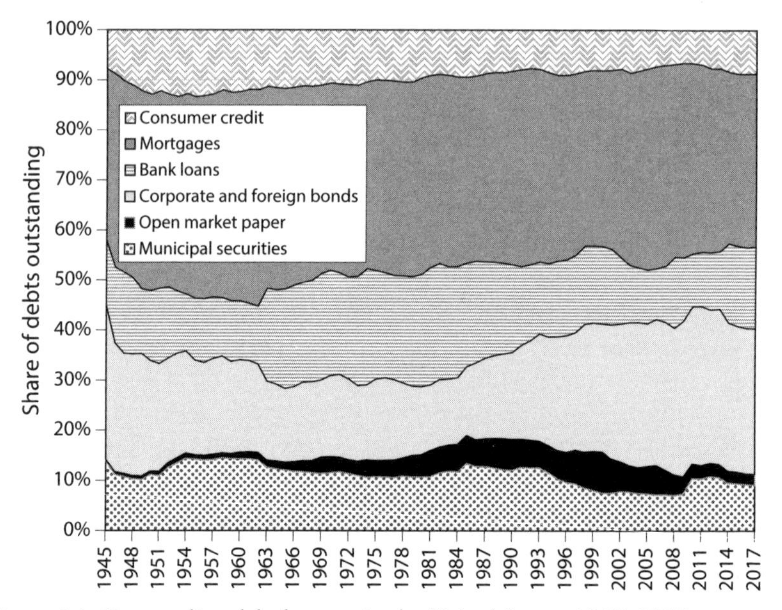

Figure 9.1. Outstanding debt by type in the United States, 1945–2017. *Source:* Federal Reserve Bank Board of Governors Flow of funds tables (1945–2017) at https://www.federalreserve.gov/releases/z1/current/ (consulted November 13, 2017).

histories, adjustable interest rates, varying terms, and self-amortization. Investors no longer fund loans directly, as they had for centuries. Instead, borrowers get their credit from banks or other organizations that are often subsidized by governments and whose sources of private funds are extraordinarily variable. Once issued, the mortgages can embark on a complicated trajectory: they can be bundled, sold, chopped up into tranches, or serve as ingredients for concocting new securities, whose price and return depend on the performance of the underlying mortgages.

Large though these innovations are, they are dwarfed by the structural changes imposed on financial markets by the shocks of World War I, the Great Depression, World War II, and they all accompany political upheavals. Before World War I, credit developed along a path that was shaped primarily by the growth of private institutions (with some state monitoring) in segmented financial markets. Elite investment banks and stock exchanges offered financial services to governments and to very large firms; smaller banks provided short- and medium-term loans to firms and individuals; and in France, the Crédit Foncier and notaries supplied mortgages. On the eve of World War I, anyone with a crystal ball could have predicted something like the status quo—perhaps notaries being slowly replaced by specialized mortgage lenders. No one, however, would have foreseen the state's wholesale entry into mortgage credit markets. In France, the state continued to play a preponderant role in credit until the mid-1980s. Since then, the reprivatized credit market of the last thirty years has given banks the lion's share of all lending. In 1914, the recent past was definitely not the future, and it may not be the future today either.

Although mortgage markets have long been forgotten as part of the financial system, they have played an enormous role for centuries particularly in wealthy countries. Yet despite their importance, it is worth keeping in mind how fragile they are. In fact, mortgages are the glaciers of credit, gliding silently through time until some large crisis triggers a surge in default at the same time as the real estate market crashes. As many of us have learned with dismay, when mortgage markets go sour (as they did in Spain, the United Kingdom, and the United States in 2007), the economy suffers. To avoid such catastrophes, lending standards must be maintained. One might think that this would be made easier in the internet economy, where mounds of data are available to evaluate default probabilities, the value of real assets, and any other characteristic of the loan. But as the early part of the twenty-first century warns us, even the most sophisticated financiers can get things horribly wrong. They trip up either because they ignore history ("it's a new economy") or because they forget that things can change ("housing prices have never declined in the aggregate in the United States").[13] Understanding the evolution of finance, in fact, requires an economic history that deciphers both what remains immobile and what changes over time.

Appendices

APPENDIX A

Appendix to Chapter 2

Table 2A.1. Descriptive statistics for markets and lending, 1740–80

	Loan duration (years)		Population (1,000s)	
	1740	1780	1740	1780
Paris	11.08	8.51	576	604
Chef-lieux pop >60K	5.31	5.15	421	510
Chef-lieux 10 to 60K	5.45	5.07	1920	2574
Chef-lieux 5 to 10K	4.14	3.68	2205	2445
Chef-lieux pop <5K	3.56	4.10	19480	21420
Total	3.89	4.28	24,602	27,552
	Number of loans (thousands)		Loans per 1,000 population	
Paris	6.2	9.3	10.7	15.4
Chef-lieux pop >60K	5.6	6.8	13.4	13.4
Chef-lieux 10 to 60K	30.7	28.9	16.0	11.5
Chef-lieux 5 to 10K	45.2	25.9	20.5	10.6
Chef-lieux pop <5K	349.5	296.6	17.9	13.8
Total	437.1	367.43	17.8	13.4
	Volume of lending (million livres)		Loan volume per person	
Paris	44.1	152.0	76.6	251.7
Chef-lieux pop >60K	8.8	20.9	20.8	43.9
Chef-lieux 10 to 60K	21.7	33.9	11.3	12.9
Chef-lieux 5 to 10K	15.7	15.1	7.1	6.2
Chef-lieux pop <5K	70.8	114.0	3.6	5.3
Total	161.1	335.9	6.5	12.2

(*continued*)

Table 2A.1. (*continued*)

	Loan value stock (million livres)		Stock of outstanding loans per person	
Paris	522	1,110	906	1,838
Chef-lieux pop >60K	74	168	176	345
Chef-lieux 10 to 60K	239	304	124	115
Chef-lieux 5 to 10K	133	88	60	36
Chef-lieux pop <5K	458	728	34	34
Total	1,426	2,398	58	87.0

Note: The loan durations are estimated using the population weights of our stratified sample; they are not weighted by loan size. Durations for some loans have been interpolated. Population totals are estimates; for details, see chapter 1.
Source: Our sample.

APPENDIX B

Appendix to Chapter 3

This appendix models how queues develop and when borrowers and lenders decide to travel in order to shorten the queues they face. It assumes that readers have read the verbal description of the model, which motivates the formal reasoning here. The appendix proceeds in two steps: first by analyzing a single isolated market, and then by considering two or more markets.

Model 1: A Single Isolated Market

Consider, first, a single market, isolated as though it were an island. In this market, borrowers and lenders queue up to match, and for a given loan type, the person in line for the longest time gets served next—the so-called FIFO ("first in, first out") principle. Let us assume that p is the instantaneous probability that a new borrower (or lender) arrives per unit of time. Then the probability that a borrower or lender arrives over an interval of length t is simply pt. If we fix the time period t of interest (a day, week, or month), we can ignore t and assume that a new person arrives with probability p and is equally likely to be a borrower or a lender. In a market of population n, the expected number of borrowers arriving during our fixed period is thus $\frac{np}{2}$; the expected number of lenders is the same. If the period is long enough or the population of the island is large enough, $\frac{np}{2}$ will be larger than one so that more than one person is expected to arrive during that time interval. Nevertheless, at the instant when a new player arrives, he or she receives all the information about the length of the queue and decides what to do before anyone else arrives. The game here is thus strictly sequential.

To get a sense of magnitudes involved, about 354,000 loans were drawn up in France in 1807, for a French population of twenty-nine million. If the average household size was four and we assume (somewhat incorrectly) that individual borrowers and lenders entered the credit market only once a year, then eighty-nine households out of a thousand were involved in the credit market in 1807, either as a borrower or lender. In other words, each household had about a one in ten chance of borrowing or lending during the year.[1] If the period was only a day, p would be roughly three in ten thousand. Clearly, these credit markets were not as active as the daily markets for food or even periodic markets for consumption items. They were, in short, thin.

Returning to the model, we assume that random shocks lead households to decide that they should borrow or lend. To do so, the household sends a request to a notary. The notary is in effect a market maker, who holds the order book, which in our case is simply a queue. The order book can be summarized by an integer. At time t, a queue of length $k_t > 0$ says that k_t households who want to lend were not matched at the end of period $t-1$; a queue of length $k_t < 0$ says that $-k_t$ borrowers remained unmatched. When $k_t = 0$, the queue is empty.

Let us suppose that when a borrower enters a market and gets a loan, he or she receives V_b. When a lender enters and makes a loan, he or she gets V_l. But the borrower or lender may have to wait to receive this undiscounted value. If the potential lender decides not to wait, she can exit the market and consume the funds she would have lent, which will gain her $U_l < V_l$. Similarly, a potential borrower can decide not to wait for a loan and receive $U_b < V_b$. The reservation values U_l and U_b are important, because they put upper limits on how long lenders and borrowers are willing to wait for a loan. The expected inefficiency of these markets is thus bounded by the difference between the benefits of a match V_i (for $i = b$ or l), which will have to be discounted by the wait time if the borrower or lender has to wait for a match, and the reservation value U_i.

The notary updates the queue in a very simple way. If new borrower arrives, the queue moves from k_t to $k_{t+1} = k_t - 1$. In other words, if there were already were too many borrowers, no matches can be made and the queue of borrowers lengthens by one. On the other hand, if there were excess lenders, a match is made, and the queue shortens by one lender. If a lender arrives, the queue moves in the opposite direction. We can also compute wait time for a household. The instantaneous probability a borrower arrives is $\frac{np}{2}$ and the expected interval between lenders (or borrowers) is $T = \frac{2}{np}$. If a new lender arrives and faces a queue of length $k_t > 0$, then the queue lengthens to k_{t+1}, and our new lender can expect to wait $2\frac{(k+1)}{np}$ until enough borrowers show up for her to be matched. The wait time for a queue of a given length will therefore fall as the market's population increases.

The probability that we have no queue at the end of period of time t can be made arbitrarily small by making t long enough; it will also be arbitrarily small if markets are large.[2] So if we wait long enough or have large enough markets, there will almost always be queues. If we ignore the outside option, the length of the queue could grow arbitrarily large. But because both the borrowers and the lenders have outside options, the maximal length a queue can take is the largest integer k such that $d^{\frac{2k}{np}} V_i \geq U_i$, where d is the discount rate for borrowers and lenders. Clearly, as the island population grows, the maximal queue length increases. Even though the maximal queue length will increase with the island's population, the expected wait time can be made arbitrarily small by increasing the island's population.[3]

The lesson the island model teaches should be reassuring to economists: the market is inefficient because unserved borrowers or lenders queue up to wait. But the expected wait time conditional on queue length declines with market population. That points to a solution to the inefficiency revealed by the island model: allowing individuals to travel from markets with long queues to markets with shorter wait times for the same queue length—in particular, larger markets. The gains from the move would have to be balanced against the costs, of travel itself and of foregone time.

Model 2: Two or More Markets

To model this sort of travel, let us start by considering two towns, Y and X, with Y having a larger population n_Y than X (n_X). When a borrower or lender from Y decides to seek a counterparty from X, we will assume that he or she has to pay travel costs c upon completion of the transaction. If the value of the transaction gross of travel costs is V_1, then a lender from Y who completes a transaction at X gets $V_1 - c$, and the same is true for borrowers from X. If d is the discount rate for borrowers and lenders, there will be a waiting time γ such that $d^{\gamma} = \frac{V_1 - c}{V_1}$. Beyond that waiting time γ in market Y, it will be worthwhile traveling to market X if a transaction is immediately available there. Note if transportation costs c are constant and V_1 increases, γ will decline. If V_1 rises with loan size, then larger loans will encourage travel.

A strategy for the lender is a function that maps the queue lengths at X and Y into probabilities of lending at X and Y. Because the model is perfect information and only one player moves at any instant in time, there is an optimal pure strategy.[4] The same argument applies to borrowers. For the sake of simplicity, we will focus on the case of a lender in what follows; the argument for borrowers is identical.

To determine the optimal strategy, first suppose that the queue at Y is negative; in other words, there is at least one borrower already waiting at

Y. The payoff for a new lender at Y is then V_l, because the lender is served immediately. The lender therefore makes the loan at Y, because the best she can get at X is

$$d^{\gamma}V_l = V_l - c$$

Suppose, then, that the queue at Y is non-negative (k_Y) so that there are lenders already waiting at Y. When our lender shows up at Y, she can expect a wait of $T_Y = \frac{2(k_Y+1)}{n_Y p}$. Her alternative is traveling to X, where the queue is k_X. We must consider two cases that depend on the sign of k_X.

If $k_X < 0$, the lender will be served immediately at X. She will therefore compare the gains from staying at Y, $\Pi_Y = d^{T_Y}V_l$ with the outside option U_l and with the gains from traveling to X, $\Pi_X = d^{\gamma}V_l$. If travel costs are high enough, then the lender will prefer the outside option to moving, and the markets will not be integrated. But if travel costs are low enough to make moving to X preferable to the outside option, then the lender will move to X if $\Pi_X > \Pi_Y$ or $\gamma < T_Y$. So, with low travel costs, the lender will move to X every time there is a borrower waiting there and no borrower at Y. Large loans will also encourage travel in this case, because γ will be smaller.

The decision is similar when there are lenders waiting at both X and Y—in other words, positive queues in both markets. Let the expected wait times for a newcomer in both markets be $T_Y = \frac{2(k_y+1)}{n_Y p}$ and $T_x = \frac{2(k_x+1)}{n_x p}$. If the lender is from Y, she now compares the outside option with $\Pi_Y = d^{T_Y}V_l$ and $\Pi_X = d^{T_X}(V_l - c) = d^{T_X+\gamma}V_l$ The lender will exit the market if the outside option is better than waiting at X and at Y.

For the sake of simplicity, let us ignore the outside option and assume that waiting at both markets is preferable to exiting. Under this assumption, moving to X is profitable if

$$\Pi_Y < \Pi_X \leftrightarrow d^{T_Y} < d^{T_X+\gamma} \leftrightarrow T_Y > T_X + \gamma$$

Once again, travel to X will be preferable if travel costs are low or loan sizes are large; both will reduce the size of γ.

If γ is small enough, then traveling to X is profitable as soon as $\frac{(k_Y+1)}{(k_X+1)} > \frac{n_Y}{n_X}$. So an optimal strategy for the lender involves always staying at Y unless the waiting time at Y exceeds the sum of the travel costs plus the waiting time at X.

Recall that the population at Y is assumed to be larger than the population at X. This assumption is unimportant when the two markets have queues of opposite sign, because a prospective lender who faces a wait at Y can immediately be served at X; the same has to be true for lenders at X, because travel costs have to be roughly symmetric. The populations are important, however, when the queues have the same sign, for with queues of the same length in both markets, the wait time in the market with the larger population, Y, is less than at X. Lenders may therefore move from X to Y but not from Y to X even though the queue lengths are the same in both markets.

We can extend the model to more than two locations. Consider locations on a lattice such that a location λ_{ij} has now two integer Cartesian coordinates (i,j) and that a lender is born at a given location that for convenience we denote location λ_{oo}. Location $\lambda_{ij}=(i,j)$ is such that travel costs are $c\sqrt{i^2+j^2}$. The lattice is large but for the lender born at λ_{oo} there is a finite set of relevant locations where she might go to seek a match with a borrower. The furthest locations the lender might consider are those where she would go and get an instantaneous match and do better than her reservation utility $(U_l < V_l - c\sqrt{i^2+j^2}$. Denote that distance by m; then the set of relevant locations are contained in a circle of radius $m=\frac{V_l-U_l}{c}$. The number of locations contained in that circle is finite, though it grows as c falls. More important, the number of relevant locations is fixed by travel costs alone and by loan sizes, and as long as costs c are not trivial, this number is not very large. Thus the lender observes all the relevant queues, and then computes the return (net of wait time and travel costs) and again makes a decision as to where to go to find a borrower. This implies that there is an optimal pure strategy where the lender minimizes travel costs as a way to break ties. The strategy for borrowers is similar.

If our assumptions are correct (if, in particular, there are no problems of asymmetric information), then our model of queues and travel therefore leads us to the following conclusions, which are all listed in the chapter:

- Travel costs will limit the distance borrowers and lenders will go to find a match. If travel costs are high enough, travel will be rare.
- Traveling to find a match will be more likely for large loans.
- Borrowers and lenders will prefer traveling to larger markets than to smaller ones, because with queues of the same length, the wait time in the larger market will be shorter.

APPENDIX C

Appendix to Chapter 4

This appendix lays out the formal model of how notaries shared information across space. It assumes that the reader is familiar with the intuitive description in the body of chapter 4, and formalizes those intuitions to explain what makes notaries' referrals reliable. The explanation, we know, is not reciprocity, because notaries accept referrals from locations that are quite different from those to which they send referrals. Furthermore, the notaries' interactions are complicated by the geography of their offices, which form a network. Because of the costs of travel, a notary will only refer clients to nearby notaries—notaries in his neighborhood. We want to explain why these referrals are limited to a proper subset of these neighboring notaries—the ones we call his correspondents.

The simplest geography with a realistic network puts each notary at the center of a hexagon of correspondents. But before we analyze the hexagon, we will show why a simpler geography—a line—is not interesting. We will then explore what can happen with a hexagon.

The Line

The simplest scheme involves locations on a line at integer intervals. Without loss of generality, we focus on the notary at 0 and call him Home. He has two correspondents: C_1 whose address is 1 and C_{-1} at -1.

Borrowers come in two types: "good" with probability p and "bad" $1-p$. Home knows that quality, and can certify quality to his lenders or to a corresponding notary. His certification fee is $X>0$. When the borrower is good, the notary who completes the transaction earns $Y_G>0$. If the borrower is bad, the transacting notary earns $Y_B<-X<0$.

When a borrower arrives, Home has up to four options: (1) find a lender among his own clients; (2) refer the borrower to C_1 or (3) to C_{-1}; or (4) turn the borrower's request down. If Home completes the transaction with a local lender, he earns $X+Y_i$; because $X+Y_B<0$, Home only completes transactions locally when borrowers are good. Home earns X for every referral C_1 or C_{-1} accepts. If a referral is refused or if he turns the borrower down, he earns nothing.

Of course, making a match at home requires that a lender be available. This occurs with probability q_o (and is known as having slack—shorthand for excess supply of lenders). If Home has no slack, he only has three options (refer to C_1, refer to C_{-1}, or turn the borrower down). Let q_i be the probability that notary i has slack when Home has no slack. For simplicity and without loss of generality let $q_1 = (1 - q_{-1}) > q_{-1}$. Although C_1 and C_{-1} know the probabilities p, q_0, q_1 (these are independent of each other) and the payoffs X, Y_B, Y_G, actual borrower quality and notary slack are private information.

The repeated game has an equilibrium we obtain by construction. Assume that the correspondents use trigger strategies. Therefore, they will turn down all referrals from a notary who has made a bad referral and accept all referrals from notaries who have been honest in the past. We start at a point when Home has already cheated C_{-1}. From this point on, Home can only refer clients to C_1. Assume that home has a bad borrower; if Home is honest and does not send that borrower to C_1, he earns nothing in this period but keeps the value of being honest in the future, which is (here r is the interest rate):

$$\pi_h^2 = \frac{p\left[q_o(X+Y_G)+(1-q_o)q_1X\right]}{r}.$$

Or Home can cheat C_1 and earn X today and have to go at it alone in the future:

$$\pi_c^2 = X + \frac{p}{r}q_o(X+Y_G).$$

Clearly, the notary is honest with C_1 if and only if

$$\pi_h^2 > \pi_c^2 \text{ or } q_1 > \frac{r}{p(1-q_o)}. \tag{1}$$

Condition 1 ($q_1 > \frac{r}{p(1-q_o)}$) simply says that the probability C_1 has slack when Home does not (q_1) is greater than a threshold value $\frac{r}{p(1-q_o)}$. It turns out that all the decisions of the notary regarding honesty involve comparing different probabilities to this same threshold value $\frac{r}{p(1-q_o)}$.

For example, if we step back and consider the incentives to cheat C_{-1}, given that Condition 1 holds (Home will not cheat C_1 in the future), then the additional probability of completing a transaction is q_{-1}. It pays for Home to be honest with C_{-1} if and only if condition 2 holds:

$$q_{-1} > \frac{r}{p(1-q_o)}. \tag{2}$$

Because $q_1 > q_{-1}$, Condition 2 implies Condition 1. Thus, if Condition 2 holds, Home's best response to two correspondents who use a grim trigger strategy is to be honest with both of them. Now suppose that Condition 1 holds but not Condition 2 ($q_1 > \frac{r}{p(1-q_o)} > q_{-1}$). In that case, Home is honest with C_1, who plays grim trigger, but C_{-1} refuses all of Home's referrals. Finally, suppose both conditions fail; then neither correspondent will accept referrals.

We now have to confirm that refusing referrals forever is the best response to a notary who is dishonest. If not, then Home will make referrals whenever he either has no slack or has a bad borrower and the correspondent's per-period payoff will be $q_i(p(1-q_o)Y_G+(1-p)Y_B)$. As long as that payoff is negative, punishing forever a notary who cheats is rational.

There are parameter values such that the trigger strategy is rational for correspondents ($p(1-q_o)Y_G+(1-p)Y_B \leq 0$) and such that Home makes referrals to two ($q_{-1} \geq \frac{r}{p(1-q_o)}$), one ($q_1 \geq \frac{r}{p(1-q_o)} > q_{-1}$), or no ($\frac{r}{p(1-q_o)} > q_1$) correspondents. If ($p(1-q_o)Y_G+(1-p)Y_B > 0$), then the correspondents willingly accept the bad borrowers and Home is honest with no one.

So far, we have implicitly assumed that correspondents do not communicate. But if Home can refer to C_1 and C_{-1}, neighbors can communicate. Does this matter? On the line, being able to communicate with direct neighbors does not change the equilibrium. Indeed, C_1 would like to communicate Home's behavior to C_{-1}, but his neighbors are C_2 and Home. So the only way a message could get to C_{-1} would be if it was relayed by Home. For communication to matter, correspondents need to communicate with each other and be able to influence access to referrals both by Home and by other correspondents. This requires a more complicated geography than the line.

The Hexagon Model

Let us start with Home and number each of his correspondents C_1 through C_6. Again, define q_i to be the probability that notary i has slack when Home has no slack. Slack now has to be defined relative to the set S of correspondents who accept referrals from Home. Let A denote the case where all correspondents accept referrals from Home and $-j$ be the case where all correspondents except j accept referrals from Home. θ_i^S is the probability notary i has slack when Home does not and none of the correspondents in S have slack. Henceforth, we call θ_i^S exclusive slack because in these events, notary i is a monopolist in lenders. The superscript will be used to index the set of notaries that are still willing to deal with Home.

On the hexagon, each individual has six neighbors, and each of his neighbors shares two neighbors with him. So when we consider the relationship between Home and C_1, we must also consider the role of their two joint neighbors C_6 and C_2. (Home does have three other correspondents, but these never interact with C_1, so we can ignore them, at least initially). Denote by Q_i the probability that i and his two neighbors have slack and let Θ_i^{Ht} be the probability that i and his two neighbors have exclusive slack—again, conditional on the set t of correspondents accepting referrals from H. (The capital letter theta here distinguishes Θ_i^{Ht}, which concerns i and his neighbors who deal with H, from lower case θ_i^S, which concerns i's own exclusive slack in dealings with H.) At issue is what kinds of coalitions can be sustained. Let us focus on the following trigger strategy for correspondents: "Accept referrals if Home has been honest with me and with both my neighbors in the past. Otherwise, refuse all referrals from Home. Do not punish notaries who refer bad borrowers to notaries who have been dishonest or have refused to punish bad borrowers in the past."

Given our structure, one can compute both subgame perfect (SGP) and renegotiation proof (RP) equilibria. The subgame perfect equilibria give the largest sustainable network. But the SPG equilibrium is too optimistic. Indeed, after misbehavior, notaries who should punish might not want to do so. The renegotiation proof equilibrium addresses this concern by requiring that Home compare the value of the current network to the value of the largest stable (LS) network that can be sustained after a deviation and renegotiation. While SGP and RP are characteristics of equilibria (and thus of the strategies of the players), we will call the set of correspondents who accept referrals from Home under a SGP (RP) equilibrium a SGP (RP) network. RP networks are typically smaller than SGP networks, because the punishments imposed on cheaters are weaker. In both cases, the cardinality of the largest network depends on how much one correspondent is a substitute for another. Intuitively, if correspondents are all valuable ($\theta_i^A \approx \frac{1}{6}$), then the whole network may be sustained. But if many correspondents are not very valuable (θ_i^A is small), then the largest network will shrink. For example, suppose one correspondent can meet all of Home's referral needs; in that case, Home will be tempted to cheat every one of the others, leaving only the useful correspondent to accept referrals. We illustrate these concepts with some examples.

Example 1: High Exclusive Slack

Assume ($\theta_i = q_i = \frac{1}{6}$). Then, independent of the set S, $\Theta_i^S = 0.5$ for each correspondent who has two neighbors who accept referrals, $\Theta_i^S = \frac{2}{6}$ for each correspondent who has one active neighbor, and $\Theta_i^S = \frac{1}{6}$ for each correspondent who has no active neighbors. Henceforth, we suppress the superscript S. Here and in all the other examples, the structure of the network will depend on the size of various probabilities relative to our threshold value $\frac{r}{p(1-q_o)}$.

If $\frac{r}{p(1-q_o)} > 0.5 > \Theta_i$, then no network can be sustained, because Home prefers to cheat even the most valuable correspondents.

If $0.5 \geq \frac{r}{p(1-q_o)} > \frac{2}{6}$, only the network of the whole can be sustained. Indeed, any other network has to have at least one correspondent with less than two neighbors ($\Theta_i \leq \frac{2}{6}$). Because that correspondent anticipates that he will be cheated he will drop out, leaving a smaller network with at least one correspondent with less than two neighbors. The network of the whole is then the only SGP and RP network.

If $\frac{2}{6} > \frac{r}{p(1-q_o)} > \frac{1}{6}$, all correspondents in SGP networks have to have at least one active neighbor, for $\frac{r}{p(1-q_o)} > \frac{1}{6}$ implies that Home cheats isolated correspondents. Networks of two, three, four, or five and six members are SGP. The LS coalitions are two pairs of contiguous correspondents and one pair of contiguous correspondents (if Home cheats either member of the pair, certainly the other will not renegotiate). So, now starting with the complete network, when Home thinks of cheating, he compares the value of the whole network $\pi_h^6 = \frac{p\left[q_o(X+Y_G)+(1-q_o)X\right]}{r}$ with the value of cheating now and then having access to the LS network of four correspondents $\pi_c^4 = X + \frac{p\left[q_o(X+Y_G)+(1-q_o)\frac{4}{6}X\right]}{r}$. $\pi_h^6 > \pi_c^4 \Leftrightarrow \frac{2}{6} > \frac{r}{p(1-q_o)}$, which is true by assumption. For a network of five to be sustained requires $\pi_h^5 > \pi_c^4 \Leftrightarrow \frac{1}{6} > \frac{r}{p(1-q_o)}$, which in this case does not hold. If we start with a network of four contiguous correspondents (or two pairs), the negotiation proof reversion is the two-correspondent network $\pi_h^4 > \pi_c^2 \Leftrightarrow \frac{2}{6} > \frac{r}{p(1-q_o)}$. But a network of three is not renegotiation proof $\pi_h^3 > \pi_c^2 \Leftrightarrow \frac{1}{6} > \frac{r}{p(1-q_o)}$. So in this case, networks of six, four, or two correspondents may be sustained.

If $\frac{1}{6} > \frac{r}{p(1-q_o)}$, all correspondent subsets are SGP and RP. The LS network is the singleton, but this case is uninteresting because the network has no strategic value.

Example 2: Low Exclusive Slack

Assume ($\theta_i = 0$; $q_i = \frac{1}{3}$). In this case, slack of C_i occurs at the same time as that C_{i-3}.

In a complete network, $\theta_i = \Theta_i^A = 0 \ \forall i$, so it cannot be sustained. The same holds for a network with four or five members, since at least one correspondent with a single active neighbor will have $\theta_i = \Theta_i^A = 0$. The network with three contiguous members (C_{i-1}, C_i, C_{i+1}) is efficient. (In other words, it provides the maximal referrals.) $\Theta_{i-1}^3 = \Theta_{i+1}^3 = \frac{2}{3}$; $\Theta_i^3 = 1$.

If $\frac{r}{p(1-q_o)} > \frac{2}{3}$, no network can be sustained.

If $\frac{2}{3} \geq \frac{r}{p(1-q_o)} > \frac{1}{3}$, the network with three contiguous members is SGP but not RP. The LS network has two contiguous members. So comparing $\pi_h^3 > \pi_c^2 \Leftrightarrow \frac{1}{3} > \frac{r}{p(1-q_o)}$, which in this case does not hold. The network with two contiguous members is SGP and RP.

If $\frac{1}{3} \geq \frac{r}{p(1-q_o)}$, networks with two or three contiguous members are SGP and RP. The LS network is the singleton. This case is uninteresting because the network has no strategic value.

Example 3: Locally Correlated Slack

Assume $\theta_i = \frac{1}{12}$; $q_i = \frac{1}{4}$. In this case, some of the slack of C_i occurs at the same time as $C_{i-1}\left(\frac{1}{12}\right)$ and $C_{i+1}\left(\frac{1}{12}\right)$ have slack. When the network is complete, $\Theta_i^A = \frac{4}{12}$.

If the network has five members (j is no longer accepting referrals from Home) $\Theta_{j-3}^{H-j} = \Theta_{j-1}^{H-j} = \Theta_{j+1}^{H-j} = \frac{3}{12}$; $\Theta_{j-2}^{H-j} = \Theta_{j+2}^{H-j} = \frac{4}{12}$.

If the network size is four, there are three architectures to consider.

1. j and $j+1$ no longer accept referrals $\Theta_{j-3}^{H-jj+1} = \Theta_{j-2}^{H-jj+1} = \frac{4}{12}$; $\Theta_{j-1}^{H-jj+1} = \Theta_{j+2}^{H-jj+1} = \frac{3}{12}$.
2. j and $j+2$ no longer accept referrals $\Theta_{j+1}^{H-jj+2} = \Theta_{j-3}^{H-jj+2} = \Theta_{j-1}^{H-jj+2} = \frac{3}{12}$; $\Theta_{j-2}^{H-jj+2} = \frac{5}{12}$.
3. j and $j+3$ no longer accept referrals $\Theta_{j+2}^{H-jj+3} = \Theta_{j+1}^{H-jj+3} = \Theta_{j-1}^{H-jj+3} = \Theta_{j-2}^{H-jj+3} = \frac{4}{12}$.

If the network size is three, there are three architectures to consider.

1. $j, j+1, j+2$ no longer accept referrals $\Theta_{j-3}^{H-jj+1j+2} = \Theta_{j-1}^{H-jj+1j+2} = \frac{3}{12}$; $\Theta_{j-2}^{H-jj+1j+2} = \frac{4}{12}$.
2. $j, j+1, j-2$ no longer accept referrals $\Theta_{j+3}^{H-jj+1j-2} = \Theta_{j-1}^{H-jj+1j+2} = \frac{4}{12}$; $\Theta_{j+2}^{H-jj+1j+2} = \frac{3}{12}$.
3. $j,\ j+2,\ j-2$ no longer accept referrals $\Theta_{j-1}^{H-jj-2j+2} = \Theta_{j+1}^{H-jj-2j+2} = \Theta_{j+3}^{H-jj+2j-2} = \frac{3}{12}$.

If the network size is two, there are two architectures to consider.

1. $j, j+1$ only accept referrals $\Theta_{j}^{Hjj+1} = \Theta_{j+1}^{Hjj+1} = \frac{4}{12}$.
2. $j, j+2$ or $j, j+3$ only accept referrals $\Theta_{j}^{Hjj+2} = \Theta_{j+2}^{Hjj+2} = \frac{3}{12}$.

If $\frac{r}{p(1-q_o)} > \frac{4}{12}$, no network can be sustained.

If $\frac{4}{12} \geq \frac{r}{p(1-q_o)} > \frac{3}{12}$, any network with at least one correspondent with $\Theta_{i}^{Ht} = \frac{3}{12}$ will be eliminated. That leaves the network of six correspondents, networks of two pairs of correspondents, and networks of pairs of correspondents as the only SPG networks. The LS network is two pairs of correspondents, because $\pi_{b}^{6} > \pi_{c}^{4} \Leftrightarrow \frac{2}{12} > \frac{r}{p(1-q_o)}$, which does not hold. The only RP networks are networks of two pairs of correspondents and networks of pairs of correspondents.

If $\frac{3}{12} \geq \frac{r}{p(1-q_o)}$, all correspondent subsets form a subgame perfect network of correspondents. The LS network is the singleton, so all correspondent networks are RP.

Implications

The model makes it clear that it is possible to sustain a geographically realistic network—one where the notaries are not all connected with one another. Although all neighbors can be sustained as correspondents for some parameter values, those cases are uninteresting, for they are unrealistic and the network has no strategic value or collapses as soon as Home cheats once. When we look at renegotiation proof rather simply as subgame perfect equilibria, only a fraction of the neighbors can be sustained as correspondents. The incompleteness of the realized network is the most important prediction the model makes.

APPENDIX D

Sources and Methods

The two principal sources we used were: the *Contrôle des actes civils et des actes sous seing privé* (1740–80), which is usually series 2C of the departmental archives, and the *Enregistrement des actes civils publics (1807-1840-1865-1899)*, which is the series Q (often 3Q) of the departmental archives. When these were lacking, we supplemented them by going to the notarial minutes of relevant notaries.

We collected data in three samples:

1. Core sample: ninety-nine bureaus where all years were collected, by department, with department names in italics.

Aisne: Château-Thierry; Hirson; Vervins; *Allier*: Dompierre-sur-Besbre; Montluçon; Moulins; Varennes-sur-Allier; *Ardèche*: Privas; Rochemaure; *Aube*: Arcis-sur-Aube; Bar-sur-Seine; Troyes; Vendeuvre-sur-Barse; *Calvados*: Argences; *Cantal*: Aurillac; Mauriac; Salers; *Charentes*: Angoulême; Montignac-Charente; *Cher*: Bourges; Dun-sur-Auron; Saint-Amand-Montrond; *Côte-d'Armor*: Belle-Isle-en-Terre; Saint-Brieuc; *Côte-d'Or*: Dijon; Montbard; Nuits-Saint-Georges; *Creuse*: Chénérailles; Guéret; *Dordogne*: Excideuil; Périgueux; *Doubs*: Baume-les-dames; Besançon; Pontarlier; *Drôme*: Chabeuil; Montélimar; Nyons; Valence; *Eure*: Evreux; Louviers; Rugles; *Gard*: Génolhac; Nîmes; Saint-Gilles; Sauve; *Gers*: Auch; Lectoure; Mirande; *Haute-Garonne*: Toulouse; Villefranche-de-Lauragais; Villemur-sur-Tarn; *Haute-Vienne*: Bellac; Limoges; *Haut-Rhin*: Sainte-Marie-aux-Mines; *Hérault*: Lunel; Montpellier ; *Indre*: Buzançais; Châteauroux; La Châtre; Saint-Gaultier; *Isère*: Grenoble; Tullins; Vienne; *Loir-et-Cher*: Blois; Bracieux; Mondoubleau; Montoire; Romorantin; *Mayenne*: Château-Gontier; Laval; Mayenne; *Morbihan*: Auray; Pontivy; Vannes; *Rhone*: Lyon ; *Saône-et-Loire*: Autun; Couches; Macon; Montcenis; *Sarthe*: La-Flèche; Le-Mans; *Seine*: Paris; *Seine-Maritime*: Elbeuf; Rouen; *Somme*: Ailly-sur-Noye; Amiens; Corbie; Rosières; *Tarn-et-Garonne*: Moissac; Montauban; *Vaucluse*: Apt; Avignon; L'Isle-sur-la-Sorgue; Orange; *Vosges*: Epinal; Mirecourt; Remiremont.

2. Additional bureaus, twelve bureaus where information is missing for some years (in parentheses). Again, department names are in italics.

Aisne: Villers-Cotterêts (1865–99); *Bouches-du-Rhône*: Salon-de-Provence (1780); *Calvados*: Caen (1840, 1865, 1899); Falaise (1865); *Charentes*: Jarnac (1899); *Côte-d'Armor*: Tréguier (1899); *Gard*: Portes (1807–99); Saint-Jean-du-Gard

(1780, 1840, 1865, 1899), Saint-Ambroix (1780); *Nord*: Bavay (1740, 1780), Maubeuge (1740, 1780); *Somme*: Moreuil (1840, 1865, 1899) .

3. Sixty-six bureaus where we only collected data for 1840 and 1865 (department names in italics).

Aube: Bar-sur-Aube; Brienne-le-Château; Estissac; Lusigny-sur-Barse; Nogent-sur-Seine; Piney; Romilly-sur-Seine; Soulaines-Dhuys; *Eure*: Amfreville-la-Campagne; Breteuil; Conches-en-Ouche; Le Neubourg; Verneuil-sur-Avre; *Gard*: Aigues-Mortes; Alès; Marguerittes; Remoulins; Roquemaure; Saint-Chaptes; Uzès; Vauvert; Villeneuve-lès-Avignon; *Haute-Garonne*: Auterive; Caraman; Fronton; Grenade; Léguevin; Montastruc-la-Conseillère; Montgiscard; Muret; Revel; *Hérault*: Aniane; Béziers; Castries; Clermont-l'Hérault; Gignac; Lodève; Pézenas; Sète; *Morbihan*: Baud; Grand-Champs; Locminé; Rohan; *Sarthe*: Brulon; La Suze-sur-Sarthe; Loué; Malicorne; Sablé; *Seine-Maritime:* Caudebec-en-Caux; Dieppe; Fécamp; Pavilly; Yvetot;*Vaucluse*: Bollène; Bonnieux; Cadenet; Carpentras; Cavaillon; Gordes; Malaucène; Mormoiron; Pernes; Pertuis; Sault; Vaison-la-Romaine; Valréas.

As noted in chapter 1, the Contrôle covered the whole country except in Paris and some recently acquired provinces (our markets of Bavay, Maubeuge, Avignon, and L'Isle-sur-la-Sorgue). These gaps were filled after the revolution, but for the eighteenth century we had to rely on the notarial archives. For Paris, where there never was a Contrôle, we collected data from every fifth box of notarial minutes in the *Minutier central des notaires* at the *Archives nationales*. We are very grateful to Marie-Françoise Limon-Bonnet, chief archivist at the Minutier central des notaires, for helping us gather this data efficiently.

The archival call numbers at the Minutier central for 1740 are: I-397; I-402; II-480; II-481; IV-506; V-393; VI-691; VIII-1037; XI-541; XII-460; XIV-307; XV-609; XVI-699; XVII-722; XVIII-551; XIX-697; XXI-339; XXIII-510; XXIV-680; XXVI-406; XXVII-213; XXVIII-266; XXX-277; XXXI-119; XXXIV-525; XXXV-616; XXXVIII-312; XXXIX-362; XLI-472; XLIII-374; XLIV-354; XLVI-287; XLVII-86; XLIX-606; XLIX-648; LI-917; LII-291; LII-296; LIV-808; LVI-256; LVIII-321; LIX-317; LX-268; LXI-407; LXIV-316; LXV-281; LXVI-441; LXVIII-413; LXX-323; LXXII-289; LXXIV-7; LXXVI-282; LXXVII-217; LXXIX-28; LXXXI-287; LXXXII-238; LXXXIII-370; LXXXV-476; LXXXVI-603; LXXXVII-935; LXXXVII-940; XC-352XCII-505; XCIV-222; XCVI-338; XCVII-281; XCVIII-473; XCIX-467; CII-324; CVI-285; CVII-434; CXIX-261; CXI-198; CXII-682; CXV-519; CXV-524; CXVI-310; CXVII-434; CXXII-644.

The call numbers for 1780 are: I-580; II-694; III-1114; III-1115; III-1120; IV-758; V-717; VI-823; VII-447; VIII-1244; X-685; X-690; XII-693;

XII-694; XIII-407; XIII-412; XV-931; XV-932; XV-937; XV-938; XVI-836; XVII-1004; XVII-1005; XVIII-808; XVIII-813; XIX-844; XXI-493; XXI-498; XXIII-769; XXIII-774; XXIV-913; XXVI-684; XXVI-689; XXVII-409; XXVII-414; XXVIII-483; XXX-465; XXXI-223; XXXIII-651; XXXIV-720; XXXV-848; XXXVII-123; XXXVII-124; XXXVII-852; XXXVIII-627; XXXVIII-631; XXXVIII-632; XL-58; XL-59; XLII-603; XLIII-499; XLIV-544; XLIV-545; XLIX-848; L-655; L-656; LI-1144; LI-1149; LII-556; LIII-553; LIV-984; LIV-989; XLV-568XLV-571; LV-36; LVI-250; LVI-251; LVI-256; LVI-257; XLVII-310; XLVII-315; LVII-550; XLVIII-261; LVIII-499; LIX-317; LX-432; LXI-582; LXI-583; LXIV-457; LXV-412; LXVI-643; LXVII-747; LXVIII-584; LXVIII-587; LXVIII-588; LXX-531; LXX-532; LXX-535; LXX-536; LXXI-27; LXXII-441; LXXII-442; LXXIII-1008; LXXIII-1009; LXXIII-1014; LXXIX-222; LXXIX-227; LXXV-754; LXXV-755; LXXVI-474; LXXVII-399; LXXVIII-853; LXXVIII-858; LXXXI-481; LXXXII-574; LXXXII-579; LXXXIV-560; LXXXVI-809; LXXXVII-1183; LXXXVII-1188; LXXXIX-743; LXXXIX-744; LXXXIX-747; LXXXIX-748; LXXXIX-753; XCI-1183; XCI-1188; XCI-1189; XCI-1192; XCI-1193; XCII-821; XCII-822; XCII-826; XCII-827; XCIV-446; XCIX-645; XCV-365; XCV-366; XCVII-511; XCVII-512; XCVIII-633; XCIX-650; C-828; C-833; CI-645; CI-646; CII-504; CII-324; CIII-20; CIV-1362; CVI-285; CVI-561; CVII-434; CVIII-688; CIX-752; CIX-753; CIX-756; CIX-757; CX-480; CXI-344; CXI-198; CXII-682; CXII-795B; CXIII-515; CXIII-518; CXIII-519; CXIII-520; CXV-917; CXV-918; CXVI-521; CXVII-892; CXIX-4543.

In the last cross section (1899) of the acts recorded in the bureau of Sainte-Marie-aux-Mines (in the department of the Haut-Rhin), the summaries are in German, because Alsace was annexed to Germany between 1871 and 1919.

Sources for Collateral and Literacy: Eighteenth and Early Nineteenth Century

For Paris in the eighteenth century, we relied on our 1/5 sample of the notarial acts of 1740 and 1780, which are preserved at the Archives Nationales, Minutier central des notaires, in Paris. These samples are described above.

For the Department of the Aube, we read the notarized loans in Arcis-sur-Aube, Bar-sur-Seine, and Troyes in 1740, 1780, 1800, and 1807 at the *Archives départementales de l'Aube*. We also used parish registers (online) to estimate the proportion of illiterates at marriage.

Sources for Notarized Letter of Exchange

To more precisely measure the rise and fall of the notarized letter of exchange over the nineteenth century, we relied on the Enregistrement des actes civils publics of the following bureaus: Castelnaudary and Lézignan (Aube), Revel (Haute-Garonne), Saint-Gilles, Saint-Jean-du-Gard and Villeneuve-les-Avignon (Gard), and L'Isle-sur-la-Sorgue. Here, each bureau is followed by the department in which it is located.

Sources on the Evolution of Peer-to-Peer Credit in the Twentieth Century

To assess the evolution of peer-to-peer credit in the twentieth century we used:

- The Enregistrement des actes civils publics for the bureaus of Arcis-sur-Aube, Bar-sur-Seine, and Troyes in 1911, 1927, and 1931, all at the Archives départementales de l'Aube.
- In the Archives du Ministère des Finances (CAEF), the document with the call number B39963: "Direction Générale des Contributions Directes et de l'Enregistrement, Relevé des obligations hypothécaires enregistrées dans les bureaux dépendant du département xxx pendant le mois de fév 1931, Réponse à la circulaire du 12/3/1931."

Source for Obligation Maturities

Our sources for 1740, 1780, and 1807 often leave out the duration of obligations. We therefore estimated how long the obligations lasted in these years by drawing additional evidence about obligation durations from the notarial records preserved in the departmental archives where we were collecting data.

APPENDIX E

National Totals and Their Accuracy

Our sample is aggregated to national totals by weighting up the populations of bureaus within size bins defined by the populations of the chefs-lieux; for the weights and populations, see table E.1.

This method of estimating national totals leads to results that are very close to the national totals for notarized loans reported in Alline (1983), which are based on government tax receipts. As the appendix figure shows, our ninety-nine markets provide a very good picture of the long-run evolution of notarized credit.

Table E.1. Bin weights and populations for sample cross sections

		Cross section					
		1740	1780	1807	1840	1865	1898
		French population by bin size					
Paris	Pop	576	604	649	935	1825	2536
	N	1	1	1	1	1	1
Chef-lieu pop>60K	Pop	420.5	509.63	567	950	2052	4287
	N	5	5	6	8	15	29
60K>chef-lieu>10K	Pop	1920.3	2574.1	2564	3696	5246	6755
	N	59	82	88	114	157	189
10K>chef-lieu> 5K	Pop	2204.7	2444.6	3218	3808	4068	4207
	N	134	151	213	237	255	248
5K>chef-lieu pop	Pop	19480	21420	22501	24494	24100	22056
	N	2498	2481	2445	2311	2303	2295
		Sample population					
Paris	Pop	576	604	649	935	1825	2536
	N	1	1	1	1	1	1
Chef-lieu pop>60K	Pop	197.6	245.25	200.8	409.8	704	1356.3
	N	2	2	2	3	5	10

(continued)

Table E.1. Bin weights and populations for sample cross sections

		Cross section					
		1740	1780	1807	1840	1865	1898
		Sample population					
60K>chef-lieu>10K	Pop	570.89	666.07	719.2	999.2	1271.1	1089.4
	N	16	19	22	30	33	29
10K>chef-lieu> 5K	Pop	262.75	291.38	378	335	311.1	277.7
	N	16	18	24	19	19	17
5K>chef-lieu pop	Pop	491.24	500.52	556	570.1	520.9	460.5
	N	63	58	49	45	40	31
		Weights					
Paris		1	1	1	1	1	1
chef-lieu pop>60K		2.13	2.08	2.82	2.32	2.91	3.16
60k>chef-lieu>10K		3.36	3.86	3.57	3.70	4.13	6.20
10K>chef-lieu> 5K		9.77	8.39	8.51	11.37	13.08	15.15
5K>chef-lieu pop		39.66	42.79	40.47	42.96	46.27	47.90

Note: For each table, "pop" is population of the chef-lieu in thousands, N is the number of cases, and K is 1,000. The chef-lieu refers to the chief municipality in the cantons that are our markets. Usually, the chef-lieu was the town or city in the canton with the biggest population.
Source: Our sample.

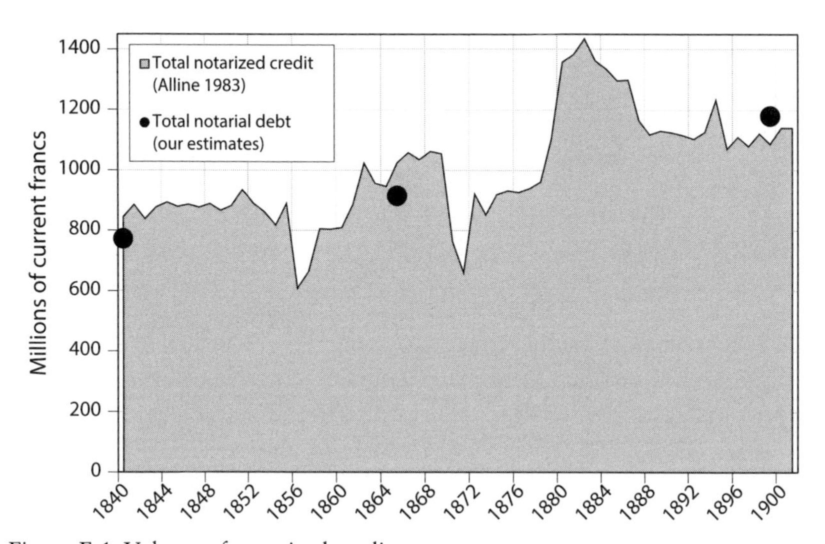

Figure E.1. Volume of notarized credit.
Note: The three dots are our estimates of the volume of credit in France.

Notes

Introduction

1. See Ross Levine (1998) for the data linking economic growth to financial development, which includes the growth of credit markets. In his view, better financial systems "ease the external financing constraints that impede firm and industrial expansion" in developing countries (Levine 2005, 868). For a persuasive example of how an underdeveloped credit market slowed the early economic growth of countries that are now rich, see Temin and Voth (2013). They conclude that a thriving market for government debt in eighteenth-century Britain stifled private credit and thereby slowed economic growth during the Industrial Revolution. For other influential histories emphasizing the role that financial development plays in economic growth, see Gerschenkron (1962), Kindleberger (2015), Neal (1994), Quinn (2004).

2. For evidence that much of Europe was rich early on, consider the real wages of what were typically the lowest income workers in premodern economies—unskilled laborers. In 1750s—well before banks spread throughout Europe—laborers' real wages in many parts of Europe were much higher than in South and East Asia. If we compare with Shanghai in the prosperous Yangtze Delta in China, then in the 1750s, real wages in Leipzig were 42 percent higher than in Shanghai, 140 percent higher in London than in Shanghai, and 154 percent higher in Amsterdam than in Shanghai. Real wages in Japan and India were even lower than in Shanghai. The data here come from the file for Beijing prices 1738–1923 at the Global Price and Income History Group website, http://gpih.ucdavis.edu/ (accessed February 17, 2017); further documentation is Allen et al. (2005). It is worth pointing out here that the wage data is subject to debate, that wages are not the only source of income, and that similar real wages could mask huge differences in personal income and wealth. Still, the high real wages do suggest that by 1750 the poorest workers in Europe had relatively high incomes. Although reliable GDP figures would be better, they are not available for the 1750s; in the 1820s, though, per capita GDP seems to have been 86 percent higher in the Netherlands than in the Yangtze Delta (Li and van Zanden 2012, table 5). The comparison here involves a rich area in Europe (the Netherlands) and a wealthy section of China—the Yangtze. The difference is large, even though the Netherlands suffered severely during the revolutionary and Napoleonic wars.

3. In the 1750s, for instance, real wages in Paris were 12 percent higher than in Leipzig. The data here come from Robert Allen's European data for laborers' relative wages at http://gpih.ucdavis.edu/ (accessed February 17, 2017) and are based on a slightly different market basket than the international real wage data. In 1820, French per capita GDP apparently ranked 8th in the world (Maddison 2007, table A.7), if one is willing to trust such early international comparisons of GDP.

4. See chapter 1 for the calculation of the fraction of French families borrowing in 1740. In 1840, the stock of debt mobilized by the shadow credit system amounted to 27.2 percent of GDP, according to table 1. Compare that with the stock of mortgage debt in the United States, which averaged 31 percent of GDP in the 1950s, according to the Federal Reserve Bank data at http://www.federalreserve.gov/releases/z1/Current/data.htm.

5. For an example of this sort of implicit assumption that countries without banks have little credit, see Cameron (1967). Botticini's study of Jewish lending in Italy (2000) is one of the rare exceptions to this pattern of glossing over personal lending before banking was widespread. Observers in the nineteenth century knew that this peer-to-peer debt market was big and they gathered evidence about it from fiscal records. See appendix E for aggregate totals derived from this evidence, which are very close to our figures.

6. Indeed, we left out seller-financed loans in real estate transactions because the seller might have better information about the value of the collateral than the typical lender. And we could not count privately contracted debt because it left no trace in the archives.

7. Hoffman, Postel-Vinay, and Rosenthal (2000). The evidence there came not from fiscal records, but from notarial archives. Employing notarial archives was feasible for Paris, but it would be far too costly to estimate lending for an entire economy.

8. See Lopez-de-Silanes, Shleifer, Vishny (1998, 1113–17), for the seminal article on the subject.

9. Rajan and Zingales (2003). For additional evidence, see the introduction to chapter 8.

10. The reason, as we show in Hoffman, Postel-Vinay, and Rosenthal (2015), is that peer-to-peer lending prospered in France as banks profilerated. The actual growth in total lending is therefore larger than figures based on bank lending alone imply, and GDP growth is correspondingly less sensitive to true total lending.

11. The most influential version of this argument is due to Gerschenkron (1962), who stressed the role of universal banks. His work spawned a number of historical studies of banking and the development of financial markets, including Sylla (1969), Cameron (1967), Davis (1963), Kindleberger (1984; reprint 2015), Haber (1991), and—more recently—Haber and Calomiris (2014) and Fohlin (2007), who does criticize the Gerschenkron hypothesis about universal banks. Gerschenkron's influence did, though, have unfortunate consequences: it condemned any lending before banks to utter irrelevance—an enormous mistake—and it also belittled significant sources of bank credit that competed with universal banks. For an outstanding effort to correct that second mistake, see Guinnane (2002).

12. The evolution of the stock of debt relative to GDP in table 1 makes this clear. For a discussion of the growth of credit over this long period between 1740 and 1931, see chapter 8.

Chapter 1

1. Archives départementales (henceforth AD) de la Haute-Vienne, 2 C 168 (January 28, 1740). From 1726 to the revolution, the French unit of account was

the *livre*. It is the currency with which all of our markets' transactions were denominated except in the Vosges and the Nord. It was worth 4.45 grams of silver. The postrevolutionary currency, the franc, had the same unit value of silver. In 1740, Jean Pajot's loan for 40 livres would have paid an unskilled day laborer for 40 days of work in Paris, and probably even more in Bellac; see the French wage figures at the Global Price and Income History Group website at http://gpih.ucdavis.edu/.

2. The French crown outsourced the collection of indirect taxes to the General Farm in return for what amounted to a gigantic loan. The loan was the crown's most significant source of short-term funds (Durand 1971; Johnson 2006).

3. For the experiment with paper money and the 1720 stock market panic—the so-called John Law Affair—see Hoffman, Postel-Vinay, and Rosenthal (2000, 69–95), and Neal (1990, 2012).

4. Beyond the particular peer-to-peer credit markets we examine, there were other sorts of lending as well, both in France and other countries, back into the Middle Ages. See, for instance, Botticini (2000, 2012); Gelderblom, Jonker, and Kool (2016).

5. Lenders had long been aware of this problem. In 1614, for example, the jurist Charles Loyseau complained about the difficulty of getting any sort of guarantee of repayment for perpetual annuities—a major problem, he claimed, because many families had defaulted after having been impoverished during the sixteenth-century wars of religion (Loyseau 1614, 3–4).

6. Here we employ Britain as a shorthand for England, Wales, and Scotland. When we have to be more precise, we will use England to refer to England and Wales; Great Britain to refer to England, Wales, and Scotland; and the United Kingdom to refer to Great Britain plus Ireland.

7. When we began the project, the delay was 100 years, which explains our end date of 1899.

8. For example, 7 kilometers in the department containing Marseille, 4 kilometers in Lyon's department.

9. The law itself made this clear, as legal handbooks pointed out. "Par l'édit du mois d'octobre 1706, il est ordonné que tous les actes passés sous seing-privé seront contrôlés avant qu'ils puissent être employés à former aucune demande en justice, et les droits payés . . . comme s'ils étaient originairement passés devant notaire, à peine de nullité." Merlin (1812–25, 1: 84–85). See also Guyot (1765–83, 1: 265–66).

10. AD Haute-Vienne, 2 C 168 (January 28, 1740).

11. Since we did not count the tied contracts, we do not know how much larger actual lending would be if they were added to our totals.

12. Much of the short-term credit that financed trade was not subject to the restrictions, and the same holds for certain lending by Jews. In the Comtat Venaissin (the enclave in southeastern France that in 1740 was ruled not by the king of France, but by the pope), for instance, Jews could make short-term loans at high interest rates (Rosenthal 1993). It is impossible to determine what the total was of all this short-term lending outside the restrictions, because most of it has left no trace in the archives.

13. In the actual loan contracts, borrowers often used abbreviations "s'obligeant, etc." that amounted to pledging all the borrower's goods. Such abbreviations made

the boundary between a borrower's pledging all his goods and mortgaging a specific asset a bit vague. See Guyot (1784–85, 1: 59, s.v. "abbréviation").

14. See Guyot (1784–85, 8: 616–82, s.v. "hypothèque") for details here and exceptions to our general account of securing loans under the Old Regime. The law here was full of complications, which our account glosses over. Guyot goes into much greater detail, but he himself likely downplayed the value of the specific mortgage. Originally, the late medieval Church required that annuities be guaranteed by specific real property, but even in the late fifteenth century, nearly all annuities in Paris combined a specific guarantee with a general one (Schnapper 1957, 55).

15. For an eighteenth-century case that reveals the advantages of option 1, see Guyot (1784–85, 8: 675). The added security of the first option when a mortgaged asset was sold was clear by the fifteenth century, if not before (Schnapper 1957, 58–59). Going to court to sue delinquent debtors was costly under the Old Regime, but as judicial records show, creditors did seek repayment in the courts, and they could interefere with a borrower's attempts to sell off pledged collateral. As is the case today, the costs of suing and collecting debts were likely prohibitive for the smallest loans.

16. Guyot (1784–85, 8: 627).

17. 53 departments have their inventories on line. We culled the rest of the information from the collection of departmental inventories at the French National Archives and by contacting the last dozen archives directly.

18. The French administrative structure has four levels. At the lowest level, some 40,000 municipalities are organized into about 2,700 cantons. The cantons are grouped into some 400 arrondissements, which are in turn amalgamated into 90 departments.

19. The Vaucluse did have a few bureaus in what was the province of Provence, but it lacked them in territory that was not part of France in 1740—the the Papal States and the Principality of Orange. Some parts of the Pas-de-Calais also had bureaus, but most territory in the department was exempt until the revolution.

20. In the typical department, our task entailed requesting at least 150 volumes of stored records and then taking over 10,000 photographs to complete the samples for the department—a task that usually took 3 to 4 days.

21. Departments of the Aisne, Allier, Ardèche, Aube, Bouches-du-Rhône, Calvados, Cantal, Charente, Cher, Côte-d'Or, Côtes-du-Nord, Creuse, Dordogne, Doubs, Drôme, Eure, Gard, Haute-Garonne, Hérault, Indre, Isère, Loir-et-Cher, Mayenne, Morbihan, Nord, Haut-Rhin, Rhône, Saône-et-Loire, Sarthe, Seine (Paris), Seine-Inférieure, Somme, Tarn-et-Garonne, Vaucluse, Haute-Vienne, and Vosges.

22. The data collection effort behind this book first began in 1992, when digital cameras were at best an exotic dream. Initially, some records were collected on paper; others were microfilmed. It was not until 2001 that affordable digital cameras were sufficiently flexible that they could reliably photograph double pages of the registers in the often dim light of the archives.

23. This is a problem the departmental archives' research guides make quite clear. See, for instance, Georges and Droguet (1993, 295–330).

24. We do have an example of this, from the Morbihan, the French department that included Pontivy. In 1740, the notary in Baden (a municipality in the canton of Vannes in the Morbihan department) registered his contracts not in Vannes, but in another canton, Auray. We did net him out of Auray but did not add him back into Vannes.

25. For the creation of the cantons, see Woloch (1994, 27, 36, 114–27).

26. Urban historians provided the population of cities with over 10,000 inhabitants and of towns with between 5,000 and 10,000 inhabitants (de Vries 1984; Bairoch 1988; Lepetit 1988; and the online data cassini.ehess.fr).

27. The difference in the assigned percentages simply reflect the more rapid growth between 1740 and 1806 of towns with more than 5,000 people.

28. The major reason for the plus or minus 10 percent uncertainty comes from the poor population figures available for the Old Regime. By 1807, that is no longer a problem. As for why our sample might underestimate lending, it is because of the possibility (noted above) that some notaries might have reported to bureaus outside their cantons. In any case, the error involved in our figures is likely to be much smaller than 10 percent, because estimates of debt levels using very different sources lead to numbers that are very close to ours. For details, see appendix E, "National Totals and Their Accuracy."

29. There is a vast literature on credit rationing. The basic model is Stiglitz and Weiss (1981); see, more recently, Arnold and Riley (2009).

30. If short-term credit was limited before the nineteenth century, there were gains from entering the banking market for short-term borrowers whom bankers would not serve. Some notaries tried to move into this market, but it entailed high risks. We touched upon this subject in Hoffman et al. (2000) and will take it up again in future work on the notorious 1744 bankruptcy of the Parisian notary Antoine-Pierre Laideguive. For eighteenth-century banking and short-term lending, see Lüthy (1959–61, 1:111–12, 2:37, 160, 246–51); Brennan (1997, 2004); Carrière (1973); Meyer (1969). Chassagne (2012) has little on the eighteenth century but points to similar practices in early nineteenth-century Lyon. Another example of tied transactions in the eighteenth century were the short-term loans merchants made to well-known nobles, some of which were then converted to medium term notarial debt. For examples, see Forster (1971, 50–51, 129–38, 205). Although Forster suggests that nobles also got short-term loans from bankers, the lenders he mentions were actually government financiers, and they were not listed as bankers or as *agents de change* (stockbrokers, who might also operate as bankers) in the 1765 *Almanach Royal*—the year they were making loans. Private short-term credit also seems to have been limited in London (Temin and Voth 2013).

31. See Snowden (1995), for a US example; Hoffman et al. (2000) for French examples; and for an early instance of success, Wandschneider (2013).

32. For the examples in this paragraph, see Hoffman, Postel-Vinay, and Rosenthal (2014).

33. The population of France was 24.6 million in 1740. With roughly 4 people per household and 2 distinct parties to every loan, the 430,000 new loans per year would involve more than 10 percent of the households each year. And if we take outstanding loans at 1.7 million, it leads to almost 30 percent of households involved in credit.

34. The number of loans is smaller than the sample that we have used to create the estimates for table 1.1 because for several markets where the rest of the social information was missing we did not gather information about gender. The omission concerns a tiny number of markets and only 4.7 percent of the loans in the sample.

35. See chapter 4 for data on third party guarantors, both in 1740 and in our other cross sections.

36. Public officials of any administration are classified in public administration; noble includes all individuals who give a title and no other detail. Thus the baron who is a maréchal de camp is classified as a military officer and subsequently in public administration. Women are classified with an occupation if they report one for themselves or their husband or father.

37. Mitchell and Deane (1962, 401). The debt was 47 million pounds or 1,175 million livres.

Chapter 2

1. Between 1740 and 1780, the frequency of the word "philosophe" increased by a factor of 27 in French books, according to a Google ngram search conducted December 27, 2016. The frequency was measured relative to books scanned by Google, and it was based on the 3-year average frequency centered on 1740 and 1780. For the popularity of social criticism by major philosophes and their lesser-known imitators, see Darnton (1979, 1994). For signs of the declining hold of organized religion, see Vovelle (1973) and Norberg (1985).

2. For our interpretation of the coming of the French Revolution, see Hoffman, Postel-Vinay, and Rosenthal (2001, 221–24), and Sargent and Velde (1995). Although, today, most histories of the French Revolution do mention the fiscal crisis, they focus on the iconoclastic ideas, and they overlook how important the crisis was in giving reformers a way to push for constitutional reforms that went way beyond what the monarchy wanted.

3. The populations here, as in chapter 1, are those of the chef-lieux of the 1806 cantons that define our markets. See chapter 1 for details of how we estimated populations and why we chose 1806 cantons to define our markets. It was not just notarial credit that was ubiquitous in the late eighteenth century; the same was true of the short-term lending among merchants and traders, which, thanks to expanding trade, popped up with surprising frequency even in remote corners of France (Rothschild 1998, 2014).

4. For the claim that banks were slow to diffuse in France and that French economic growth suffered as a result, see Cameron (1967, 127). For bankers in later eighteenth-century Paris, the 1780 *Almanach royal*, ed. Laurent-Charles d'Houry (Paris: d'Houry), lists 71 of them, not counting *agents de change* (stockbrokers) who also engaged in banking. Wholesale merchants acted as bankers as well. Elsewhere in France, there were also merchants who provided shorter-term credit, and some bankers too, particularly in large cities such as Lyon (Rothschild 1998, 2014; Vigne 1903, 231–34).

5. Until 1780, there were 60 general farmers with wide authority. Necker reduced them to 40 and created another two organizations: "the régie générale" with 25 bonded administrators and the "administration des domaines" with

another 25. Each was required to pony up a million livres. The restructuring increased the total advance from 90 million to 110 (see Durand 1971). Income from the General Farm ranged between 22 and 53 percent of royal revenue in 1781 and 1789, if we include both the *régie générale* and the *administration des domaines*. The numbers here come from figures revealed in the public debate over royal finances on the eve of the French Revolution (Marion 1968 [1914–31], 1: 464–68). The accounts—by opposing ministers Necker and Calonne—have been much debated, and they differ, but not in a way that affects our numbers.

6. Lavoisier (1893, 6:158) : "Il faut qu'ils prélèvent l'intérêt de l'emprunt de 1,560,000 qu'on doit porter au moins à 6 percent, si l'on fait attention que plusieurs d'entre eux empruntent à ce taux, qu'il en coûte à tous des frais de notaire qui peuvent être estimés à 1.5 percent pour la première année."The quotation comes from Lavoisier's 1774 analysis of the General Farm.

7. Lavoisier (1893, 6: 392–93) : "Les membres des compagnies de finance et les comptables sont presque tous dans ce même cas, il en est peu qui soit propriétaires de la totalité de leur fonds d'avance: ces fonds ont été fournis par des prêteurs auxquels ils ont passé des obligations qui échoient à la fin du bail ou de la régie . . ." From the supplement to Lavoisier's 1790 "Réflexions sur les assignats."

8. "La plus part de ceux qui ont obtenu des croupes, n'étant pas en état de faire des fonds, ont été obligés de faire des traités avec des notaires ou autres particuliers"(Lavoisier 1893, 6: 160).

9. If we take a broader view of exactly who was a general farmer and include in their number the 50 administrators of the Régie and the Domaines, then the sample total comes to 9.4 million livres. This suggests that Parisian notaries provided lenders with 47.2 million of the global advance's 110 million. Because Paris was exempt from the Contrôle des Actes tax, we had to sample the actual notarial records to gauge lending in both 1740 and 1780.

10. We use the 1806 canton boundaries to define our markets, even though the terminology may seem anachronistic. Their clear boundaries argued in their favor, as we explain in chapter 1.

11. Diderot and d'Alembert (2016 [1751–72], 15:509, sv "Stellionat," consulted August 15, 2016); Guyot (1765–83, 59:157–62, sv "Stellionat, stellionataire"). According to both sources, criminal prosecution of stellionat in France was rare unless the fraud was large.

12. AD Côte d'Or E 1759; Forster (1971, 55–64). The family also employed lawyers who seem to have been professional stewards.

13. This is clear from the rare notaries who preserved not just the documents they drew up (these minutes they had to keep) but their accounting papers. See, for instance, Archives nationales (henceforth AN), Minutier Central (henceforth MC), Etude XXIII, CT XXIII/27, 28, 58 (1860–99). By the late nineteenth century, many other notaries kept accounts client by client but the records have not survived (*Guide de la comptabilité notariale*, 1890).

14. We compute the median for each market in 1740 and 1780, take the ratio, and then compute the average over all the markets.

15. Specifically, we assign our cantons to size categories based on the population of their chef-lieux. We then give each canton a weight that is proportional to

the number of markets in its category in France as a whole. With these weights, each market with population less than 5000 in 1740 gets a weight of 39.6 while Paris gets a weight of 1.

16. For per capita GDP, see table 1 in the introduction. The same conclusions would hold if one were to carry out these calculations on the basis of nominal wages or nominal income because the movements in loan size simply dwarf any changes in nominal income.

17. This would correspond to $50,000 for the United States and $41,000 for France today.

18. The most likely cause of rising inequality in the eighteenth century would be the increase in agriculture rent, which (according to David Weir's estimates in Weir 1991, 935–36) rose 43 percent relative to wages between 1726–50 and the 1780s. Even if we were to assume that the poor earned only wage income and the increase in rent all went to the rich, it would still not be enough to explain a doubling of median loan size. In fact, many residents of the countryside owned property (and hence benefited from the increase in rent), even if they were not rich.

19. As we explained in chapter 1, the acts en brevet were the less formal contracts that notaries could draw up without preserving a copy. One reason the fee for an act en brevet was lower was that the Contrôle imposed a lower tax.

20. The evidence here comes from a sample of marriage contracts from the years 1738–40 and 1778–80 in Arcis-sur-Aube and Bar-sur-Seine. They show a signature rate for men of nearly 70 percent in 1778–80, which implies that over 50 percent of the loans would have at least one illiterate party if borrowers and lenders were chosen at random. The signature rate was even lower (61 percent) in 1738–40.

21. There is also some indirect evidence that borrowers and lenders in the Aube were more likely to turn to notaries to secure their loans in 1780 than in 1740: the ratio of the number of loans preserved in the notarial minutes to the total number of loans in the Contrôle des Actes rose from 0.16 in 1740 to 0.26 in 1780. Again, though, the change is small, and it could have resulted from other trends that raised the average loan size and pushed more loans over the threshold of 300 livres where they could no longer be brevets. On this, see Guyot (1784–85, 2: 547–55).

22. The non-real estate assets pledged as collateral in these loans include the government offices, and government debt in the form of annuities paid by the Hôtel de Ville, the Aides et Gabelles, and provincial estates. For the loans the general farmers took out, they pledged the forthcoming revenues from their share of the tax farm.

23. Etude CXIII, fol. 510 (November 1, 1780).

24. For France as a whole the duration of the obligations across loans in our sample increased from slightly over 1 year in 1740 to nearly 2 years in 1780. The durations here are calculated using the population weights of our stratified sample, but are not weighted by loan size.

25. See the figures in appendix A to chapter 2.

26. Borrowers and lenders who in this case would go to Avignon might include people from the eastern half of the province of Languedoc, which included Nîmes,

and from the northern portion of the region of Provence, which surrounded Avignon. Before the French Revolution endowed France with a uniform legal system, the law varied from place to place, as did the court system. Precisely how this might affect credit markets, though, is unknown.

27. AD Rhône, 10C 1210 Photo 68, April 19, 1780.

28. In Paris, the Bourrée de Corberon relied on a particular notary AN MC ET XXXIII, In Nuits-Saint-Georges they relied on a variety of notaries, see AD Côte d'Or C9810–9888.

Chapter 3

1. For legislation affecting the 5 percent cap, see Hoffman, Postel-Vinay, and Rosenthal (2000, 9).

2. Hoffman, Postel-Vinay, Rosenthal (2001, 221–63); Hoffman, Postel-Vinay, Rosenthal (2007, 149–52); Lüthy (1959–61, 2: 464–592); Velde and Weir (1992).

3. Postel-Vinay (1998); Hoffman, Postel-Vinay, Rosenthal (2000).

4. Merlin (1825–28, 14:1–16, 122–66; 15:1–170; 22:240–41; 25:173–225); Griolet and Verge (1910–26, 9; 1922, 589–90); Grenier (1824, 1:105–108, 122–51). As these handbooks make clear, the law concerning the seniority of liens registered with Hypothèques was still being worked out in the early nineteenth century. That uncertainty may have also led borrowers and lenders to avoid the fee for the registration and stick with the notary instead.

5. The abolition of venality certainly reduced the demand for notarized loans (as did the end of the General Farms). More broadly, after the revolution, government debt was legally a movable asset, and thus no longer the basis of a mortgage.

6. Although one might well think that the survey was a national effort, we have only found its remnants in the Gard, after having looked in more than thirty departmental archives.

7. For 115 notaries in the Gard, we have complete tabulations from 1779 to 1808; for 63 others in the department, we have only partial totals. Of the 54 notary offices whose tabulations are entirely missing, 50 were eliminated by the Revolution. AD Gard M6 1728–1731.

8. See Hoffman, Postel-Vinay, and Rosenthal, "Contracts and Revolution" (2011).

9. The average maturity figures here are weighted by loan value; unweighted maturities fell by over 40 percent. Henceforth, all average maturities are weighted by loan value unless the text specifies otherwise.

10. The one exception might be investing money in a life annuity in return for a stream of income that would last as long as the lender lived. In an era before pensions, such an annuity would provide income in old age no matter how long a lender lived, but it would also mean giving up the possibility of making any bequests to heirs.

11. Our eighteenth-century data leads to similar conclusions.

Chapter 4

1. The information is asymmetric because the borrower knows whether he is creditworthy, but the lender does not. That happens with both adverse selection (for example, the lender is unaware that the borrower's collateral is of low value) and moral hazard (for example, the borrower uses the loan to make risky real estate investments). Problems with asymmetric information bedevil credit markets and they have given rise to a large literature, beginning with Stiglitz and Weiss (1992).

2. The national income figures are from Toutain (1987); for the national debt, Annuaire Statistique de la France (1966, 494). All the lending data come from our sample.

3. For a benchmark comparison, the median home price in the United States in 2012 was about $200,000, or four times per capita income.

4. The Archivists of the Minutier Central are to be thanked for their extraordinary assistance here. Without it, these data would never have been collected.

5. As we explained in chapter 1, the nominal currency used in 1740 and 1780 (the livre) had the same silver value as the currency used in the later cross sections (the franc).

6. For details, see Hoffman, Postel-Vinay, and Rosenthal (2000, 226). Their wealth was dispersed even though borrowing involving offices had become centralized in Paris.

7. AD Côte d'Or, bureau de l'enregistrement et des domaines de Nuits-Saint-Georges, Actes civils publics, registres de recettes, 3Q22/207 folio 31; Jobert (1975, 1999). Although the Enregistrement does not indicate whether the lenders came to Dijon, the odds are that they sent trusted agents. The lenders agreed to the terms of the loan by a notarial act passed in Neuchâtel, and they empowered officials from the city of Neuchâtel (who were themselves lenders) to remove the liens on the borrowers' mortgaged property when the loans were repaid.

8. One example involving the banker David himself illustrates just how hard it can be to tell what real property is worth, particularly during a downturn. In the 1830s, he had purchased 700 hectares of land in northern France, but he ended up losing heavily on this investment (Jobert 1975, 349, 353).

9. Personal ties between borrowers and lenders in Paris (being relatives, having the same occupation, or living in the same parish) were rare by the eighteenth century (Hoffman, Postel-Vinay, Rosenthal 2000).

10. If most secured loans were registered, then a borrower who balked at registration would be signaling that he was more likely to be a bad credit risk, so borrowers themselves would have an incentive to register.

11. For the earlier tests, which used actual measures of social capital, see Hoffman, Postel-Vinay, Rosenthal (2009). If social capital solved the problem of asymmetric information, then markets with more social capital should have had high levels of per capita debt and more rapid growth of per capita lending. Regressions of growth rates of lending on past levels of lending using our full sample detect no such effect. The low R^2 in the regressions implies that, at worst, social capital diffuses within one generation and so confers no long-term advantage, which is consistent with our earlier results with actual measures of social capital.

12. Results are similar if loan maturity is regressed on the log of the loan size and the distance between the borrower's and lender's residence. The regression yields a very small coefficient and no significant relationship:

	Coefficients	t Statistic	Observations	27324
Intercept	−1.23	−19.8	Adjusted R^2	0.15
Ln (loan size)	0.64	69.8		
Ln(distance)	−0.0003	−1.4		

13. Notaries were not obliged to keep their correspondence or the accounting papers of their businesses, in contrast to their minutes (the contracts and other documents they drew up), which they had to preserve. In one exceptional instance—the notary of Etude XXIII in Paris—the notary's accounting books have survived, and they demonstrate that notaries did interact with one another, because the notary's books show that other notaries kept accounts with him. Furthermore, the accounting papers also contain three examples of letters exchanged by notaries. The letters concern the settlement of an estate, sharing fees, and—in one of the letters—a request that the Parisian notary carry out transactions in the Parisian credit market for a provincial notary. In that letter (CT/XXIII/73, February 10, 1878), A. Jumain, a notary in Guérard (Seine-et-Marne), asks the Parisian notary to sell an annuity for one of his clients and purchase three obligations issued by the Crédit Foncier. Although Jumain was not asking the Parisian notary to find creditworthy borrowers in these transactions, his request did assume that the Parisian notary would not take advantage of him by, say, selling the annuity quickly at a lower price. See AN MC, CT/XXIII/73 and DC/XXIII/333bisMAF.

14. AD Côte d'Or 5 NUM 6503, "Livre de créances, obligations et capitaux de Jean Etienne Demartinécourt, notaire à Selongey, 1814–1826," fols. 285, 288, 294.

15. The additional data come from cantons in the following nine departments: Gard, Haute-Garonne, Hérault, and Vaucluse in the south; Aube, Eure, Morbihan, Sarthe, Seine-Maritime in the north. We are grateful to the personnel at these archives for facilitating the delivery of all the documents we had to consult.

16. With the likelihood of referrals weighted by population, the probability of getting such a large number of cantons without referrals was $2.7*10^{-9}$. Without the population weighting, it was nearly the same, $3*10^{-9}$. One might also worry that cantons with more notaries would be more likely to get referrals, but the number of notaries per canton varied little in our denser samples—from 3 to 5. Furthermore, the number of notaries was correlated with population, so this concern would also be eliminated by the tests of referrals weighted by population.

17. For a similar point, see Goldberg (2012, chapter 5).

Chapter 5

1. Villargues, *Jurisprudence du notariat,* 1er cahier, tome 9 (January 1836, 140–41).

2. For an illuminating overview of the scholarship on networks and their use in economics, see Jackson (2010).

3. Lemercier (2003); Levratto and Stanziani (2011, 143–71).

4. The same is true for corporate governance jurisprudence from the Commercial Code to 1914. See Lamoreaux and Rosenthal (2005).

5. "Attendu que le législateur ne défend nulle part de faire des lettres de change ou des billets à ordres par devant notaire ; admettre le contraire ce serait priver les personnes illettrées du droit et de la faculté de faire de pareilles négociations ; Attendu que l'acte du 3 Août 1828 n'est autre chose qu'un billet à ordre ; mais que dans tous les cas Magand au profit duquel il a été souscrit, et qui a passé ordre au profit de Génard ne saurait être recevable de demander la nullité d'un pareil endossement, qui constitue entre Magand, négociant et Génard aussi négociant un véritable acte de commerce." Ledru-Rollin (1842, 27:1655).

6. "Si le tireur ne savait pas écrire, il serait indispensable que la lettre de change fût notariée. Alors l'acte serait un procès verbal constituant que la lettre de change a été dictée par le tireur dont la signature serait suppléée par le notaire. D'Auvilliers (1850, vol. 9:52, sv "lettre de change").

7. Suppose that the volume y of NLE equals the expression $a_0 + a_1 p + a_2 b + a_3 i + u$, when this expression is positive, and zero otherwise, where p is the market population, b the number of banks in the market, i the number of illiterate people in the market, and u the error term. If we divide both sides by p to reduce problems of heteroscadicity, then we end up with the regression that we have run.

8. The archives of the departmental chambers of notaries in the 1820s and 1830s might hold the key to what seems to have been a set of collective decisions.

9. For the literature on social networks, see Jackson (2010), for the perspective from economics, and, for a different approach, Wasserman and Faust (1997).

10. One might of course wonder here whether it is the homogeneous relationships among Facebook friends that matter or the heterogeneous relationships between buyers and sellers of information (in particular, the social media firms and the suppliers of goods and services), or even the heterogeneous relationships between buyers and sellers of goods and services.

11. For example, notary Crouzet in the town of Castelnaudary used the notary Lieusson as the correspondent in 18 of the 19 NLE that he drew up in January and February 1820 (AD Aude 3 Q 73).

12. The only exception was for the NLE from the bureau of the city of Cavaillon in the Vaucluse, because the clerk there did not record any detail about correspondents, not even their names.

13. Combining both departments, notaries who drew up more than 50 NLE in 1840 drew up an average of 545 contracts in all of that year. Notaries with between 30 and 49 NLE in 1840 produced an average of 435 contracts that year, and those with between 10 and 29 NLE managed 329 contracts. Finally, notaries who drew up less than 10 NLE were only drawing up about 240 contracts a year.

14. See, for example, AD Aude 3 Q 8 214 (February 2, 1875; January 21, 1890); and AD Tarn-et-Garonne 2 Mi 29R3 (November 9, 1840).

15. For examples, see AD Tarn-et-Garonne 2 Mi 29R3 (November 6, 9, 16, and 19, 1840).

16. D'Auvilliers (1850, 9:52, sv "lettre de change," chapter 1, number 10–12).

Chapter 6

1. There are certainly some economic historians who are free from this near-obsession with banks, including Neal (1990); Botticini (2000); Guinnane (2001); and Jonker, Gelderblom, and Kool (2016).

2. We say "might" here, because notaries could divide up large loans and sell parts to different clients, thereby allowing them to assemble a diversified portfolio. We know that notaries did in fact divide up large loans; for an example, see the discussion of the Bouault Bank loan in chapter 4.

3. Only two articles in the collection look at banks in the first half of the nineteenth century. One covers the exceptionally long-lived Courtois bank in Toulouse; the other tells the story of the failed Bouault bank in Dijon that we encountered in chapter 4.

4. A fictional but extremely realistic example of such a banker appears in Honoré de Balzac's novel *Illusions perdues*, which was published between 1837 and 1843. In the novel, the Cointet brothers, who are also printers and paper merchants, carefully avoid paying the higher patente for their banking business. See Balzac (1990, 486).

5. Murphy (2005, 185–222). The quotation is from p. 217.

6. Crédit Mobilier had subsidiaries in other cities (Gille 1970), but widespread branch banking had to wait until Crédit Lyonnais and Société Générale opened offices across France.

7. Evidence that public borrowing in Britain crowded out private credit (Temin and Voth 2013) would be consistent with this argument, as would the lack of crowding out in Paris (Hoffman, Postel-Vinay, Rosenthal 2000, 54–56, 100–103). The evidence is from the eighteenth century, not the nineteenth, but it underscores Britain's lack of intermediaries who could arrange loans as notaries did.

8. After 1818 or so, the almanac was published by Sébastien Bottin until the 1850s, and finally by the publishing firm founded by Firmin Didot. For 1911, Guillaume Bazot kindly shared his data set with us. See the list of commercial directories in the bibliography.

9. To be specific we do not count multiple offices of the same bank in the same municipality—this is an issue that only begins to matter in the 1880s.

10. This point was made by Bergeron (1978, chapter 10).

11. David's bank is discussed in chapter 4; for other bank loans, see Postel-Vinay (1998, 240–80). The example of Dumont's bank is taken from pp. 256–57.

12. We started this collection with the 1805, 1807, 1812, 1814, 1817, 1820, 1830, and 1834 post office directories. We supplemented that list with Pigot's national commercial directory for 1818–20, 1828–29, and 1837; with the directory of his successor Slater for 1846 and 1852; and with the bank lists published by Thom's directory of Ireland (which give lists for the entire British Isles) for 1857, 1875, and 1883. See the list of commercial directories in the bibliography for details.

13. The British directories did miss some banks. The Rothschild bank in London, for instance, was listed under merchants. Still, the directories for both countries provide an accurate census of nineteenth-century banking, which could be used to assemble valuable panel data sets for analyzing financial development.

14. Here, an ardent defender of the hypothesis that a lack of banks slowed France's industrialization might argue that the relevant comparison is not France versus the United Kingdom, but France versus England alone, since Ireland and northern Scotland were slow to industrialize. But one could make similar arguments about southwestern France, which was also slow to industrialize.

15. The data would be even more useful if future researchers combined data from the bank directories with a stratified sample of banks' published balance sheets, when they appear after the middle of the nineteenth century.

16. Levine (1998, 596–613); La Porta et al. (1997); Rajan and Zingales (2003).

17. For more details, see Lamoreaux and Rosenthal (2005) and Guinnane et al. (2007).

18. Anderson 1969ab; Habakkuk (1994); Miles (1991).

19. The figures on bank lending in 1898 come from new data assembled by Eric Monnet and Angelo Riva, which will appear in Patrice Baubeau, Eric Monnet, Angelo Riva, and Stefano Ungaro, "A New History of French Banks in the Interwar," working paper, Paris School of Economics. Their numbers are similar to those in Saint-Marc (1983), and they both supersede the estimates for France in Goldsmith (1969), table D-8, which seem exaggerated.

Chapter 7

1. AD Vosges 3Q15 116 (July 14, 1865).

2. In the years 1885–1905, for example, the bank of A. Levy in California rolled over unsecured one-day loans for an average duration of 279 days (White 2001).

3. AD Rhône, 46Q 129 (March 14, 1865). In other cases, it is more likely that bankers were simply investors, and the notary was assuring creditworthiness. See, for example, AD Rhône, 3Q18 9 (May 20, 1840), where a banker is among seven lenders from Lyon in a 70,000-franc obligation loan made to a lawyer, a notary, a propriétaire, and their wives. The borrowers had all traveled from the adjacent department of the Ain, so it is more likely that the notary was relying on a referral to provide information.

4. AD Rhône 46Q331 (May 30, 1899): the banker is "empruntant pour les besoins de son commerce." The lenders included another banker, a stockbroker, and a propriétaire. In this loan, the notary's legal services likely mattered more than any information he had, because the lenders themselves could probably have better assessed the borrower's creditworthiness and the value of the collateral than the notary could.

5. One might worry about the cost of supervising all the clerks, but that seems not to have been a problem. In Paris, a busy notary could hire enough clerks to draw up over a thousand contracts a year both in the eighteenth and nineteenth century.

6. After our 1865 cross section, interest rates began to vary across space, for reasons we will discuss in chapter 8.

7. The value of this competitive model is that it eliminates the complications from the distribution of travel costs that would make the supply curve a step function.

8. For a detailed formal model, see Hoffman, Postel-Vinay, and Rosenthal (2015).

9. Hoffman, Postel-Vinay, and Rosenthal (2015), table 4, regression 1. The coefficient was estimated using a first difference regression with a panel of 105 of our markets over the years 1840–99 (the 99 core markets and six others that are present in those three years). In the regressions, notarial lending excluded CFF loans and mortgage-backed credit lines offered by banks, both of which we discuss below. To control for demand, the regression included quadratic terms in population and wealth plus fixed effects for time periods. Lack of data for these controls ruled out adding the 1807 cross section to the panel. The results were similar if Paris was dropped, if the regression was restricted to the core sample, or if it was estimated using fixed effects for each market instead of first differences.

10. Hoffman, Postel-Vinay, and Rosenthal (2015), table 4, regression 2. The instrument was the first difference of the number of banks measured over the decade that preceded each cross section. It is a plausible instrument because there were no barriers to bank entry and banks could be formed or dissolved in a year or two. The instrumental variables estimates were similar if Paris was dropped from the panel.

11. Because our estimation strategy is static, we are in effect presuming that we can ignore dynamic effects, such as the option value for a bank of learning about the profitability of a market, which could cause a bank to wait a long time before exiting. That seems justified, since at the individual bank level turnover was empirically substantial. Our regressions also suppose that future wealth and population levels could be little affected by current lending. See Hoffman, Postel-Vinay, and Rosenthal (2015) for a discussion.

12. The bank data come from the same commercial almanacs used to construct our panel data set of banks. The list of all notaries who were forced out of office for fraud or bankruptcy in the years 1887–89 was taken from AN BB19/700, "Etat statistique des notaires suspendus, ayant reçu injonction de céder ou destitués de 1888 à 1898 par ressort de cour d'appel."

13. Regressions (available from the authors) that also take into account change in canton populations lead to a similar conclusion.

14. For a brief history of the Crédit Foncier, see Hoffman, Postel-Vinay, and Rosenthal (2000, 258–71). For more detail, see Allinne (1983) and Dupont-Ferrier (1925). For the examples in this paragraph, see AD Rhône 46 Q 335 (December 5, 1899) and 3 Q 18 339 (October 14, 1899) for the corset maker and La Protectrice; and Archives de Paris DQ7 20297 (June 1, 1865) for the 650,000-franc mortgage.

15. We do not know, however, whether the borrower actually tapped the line of credit, nor how big a loan he actually took out if the line was used. So the volume of mortgage lines of credit is measured with error. If it is the only variable measured with error, then this coefficient will be biased toward zero.

16. See Hoffman, Postel-Vinay, and Rosenthal (2015) for the instruments and the regressions, which all involved first differences.

17. In the 105 markets used in our regressions, the Crédit Foncier made loans in 17 of them in 1865 and 60 of them in 1899.

18. "Se balancent à peu près": Chassagne (2012, 86).

19. "Révolutionner les placements": Bouvier (1961, 1:115–17, 121, 150–55, 316–22). The quotation comes from 1:319.

20. That is what the Guerin bank did, and the same was true of the Courtois bank in Toulouse. Rather than "se risquer dans des affaires nouvelles," it stuck to the business of buying up commercial paper from local clients it knew well and then using its own reputation to sell the paper in Paris, where interest rates were lower than in Toulouse (Lescure and Plessis 1999, 56).

21. Between 1829 and 1898, the annual exit rate for French banks varied between 5 and 14 percent; see Hoffman, Postel-Vinay, and Rosenthal (2015). The exit rate is for all banks, including those with branches, but as we know, the overwhelming majority of French banks were unit banks. As we have explained, the Bank of France did make unit banks safer by buying assets from unit bankers who were confronted by negative shocks. As the yearly reports by the inspectors of the Bank of France make amply clear, these assets were not geographically diversified (Archives de la Banque de France, Rapports d'inspection de la succursale de xxx).

22. When the Crédit Lyonnais first opened in Lyon in 1863, it was still a unit bank, it paid 3 percent interest on demand deposits, and 5 percent on 1 to 3 month certificates of deposit (Bouvier 1961, 1:150). Obligations in Lyon in 1865 typically paid 5 percent.

23. Bouvier (1961, 1:150–55, 322).

24. Bouvier (1961, 1:322–23). There is also the Union générale, but it opened after our 1865 cross section and failed before the 1899 one.

25. Bouvier (1961, 1:308, 316). Although one of the Crédit Lyonnais's agents did suggest that the bank might be able to compete with notaries in offering credit, his viewpoint seems to have been isolated and was rejected by the management, which never engaged in that sort of competition against provincial notaries, or against provincial banks either. Société Générale seems to have pursued a similar policy. See Bouvier (1961, 1: 316, 346–47).

26. Chassagne (2012, 108–110, 165–71).

27. Postel-Vinay (1998, 251–69).

28. Notaries decided how much effort to put into their business, but they could not actually close up shop. When a notary wanted to retire, the normal thing for him to do was sell the office to a successor who had to meet competency and wealth requirement to be accepted by the state. When there was insufficient business to keep all the notaries in the canton busy, a retiring notary sold his archives to a competitor.

29. The regressions were negative binomial regressions that allowed one to calculate the expected value of the number of banks conditional on covariates that included the volume of notarial lending and linear and quadratic terms in population and per capita wealth. The 1807 cross section was omitted because the number of banks was often zero. See Hoffman, Postel-Vinay, and Rosenthal (2015) for the results. The same article addresses worries about the endogeneity of the explanatory variables, the robustness of the results, and the effect of adding additional explanatory variables.

30. See Hoffman, Postel-Vinay, and Rosenthal (2003) for a detailed account of the notaries' entry into banking, with formal model and data on bankruptcies by notaries and bankers in Paris.

31. Along with notaries guilty of fraud, these failures were the reason why the notaries in figure 7.2 were forced out of office.

32. *Guide de la comptabilité notariale* 1890; Postel-Vinay (1998, 71–72, 163–64).

33. AN MC CT XXIII 58 (1861–64), 69 (1864–69), and 80 (1897–99). These account books are from one Parisian étude, XXIII. Since notaries had no reason to preserve their account books after the accounts had been closed, virtually none of the notaries' accounting has survived, unlike the notarial records themselves (the *minutes*). The notaries had to preserve the *minutes,* which were not only an official record of past transactions but a valuable source of information.

34. Bouvier (1961, 1: 389–90, 2: 780–83, 796.

35. Hoffman, Postel-Vinay, and Rosenthal (2015), table 1.

36. Hoffman, Postel-Vinay, and Rosenthal (2015, 3). Although they arranged mortgages, British attorneys may have had a much more limited scope of operation than French notaries. As we argued in chapter 6, that might be one reason why banks were overdeveloped in Britain.

Chapter 8

1. Maddison (2007, tables A.7 and A.8 [GDP per capita in 1990 international dollars in 1913, growth rate of per capita GDP 1870–1913]); Mitchell (1981, 611–12, 668–70 [railway lines open and motor vehicles in use in 1899]); Rajan Zingales (2003b [bank deposits and stock market capitalization relative to GDP in 1913]); *The Encyclopaedia Britannica* (18: 914–30, s.v. "Motor Vehicles" [motor vehicle production and number of cars in use]). Mitchell's figures for motor vehicles in use do not begin until 1904 for the United Kingdom and 1906 for Germany, but France had slightly more cars than the United Kingdom in 1904 and substantially more than Germany in 1906. According to the 1910–1911 edition of the *Encylopaedia Britannica*, France produced more automobiles than any other country in the world up to 1906.

2. Isambert (1822–33, 18: 69–17 [Edict 471]); Hoffman, Postel-Vinay, Rosenthal (2000, 52).

3. Jews could charge up to 9 percent (Rosenthal 1993). As this case of lending in the papal Avignon shows, interest rates varied from country to country. For other examples, see Servais 1982; Dormard 2005; and Gelderblom, Jonker, Kool 2016.

4. An equally interesting question that lies beyond the temporal bounds of this book is why the 5-percent equilibrium arose in France. It does not seem to have taken hold elsewhere (see, for instance, Servais 1892; de Madalena 1988; Gelderbloom and Jonkers 2016; and Milhaud 2017).

5. For example, the borrower could use the loan to construct a large residence on productive agricultural land that had served as collateral. With the agricultural land out of production, the value of the collateral would fall unless buyers were willing to purchase the residence.

6. Second mortgages of this sort did crop up in our sample of contracts, and borrowers never promised to refrain from burdening collateral with additional mortgages. But the second mortgages were never made at a higher interest rate than the first mortgages, at least as long as the CRPE prevailed.

7. The key here is that the better borrowers are in effect subsidizing the worse ones. Relative to the alternative investment, in a pooling equilibrium the lenders with the better borrowers make a little money and those with the worse ones loose a little. Ex ante, lenders are willing to accept the average return of 5 percent. After separation, they will no longer be willing to do so for the worse group.

8. Hoffman, Postel-Vinay, Rosenthal (2003). See also chapter 7.

9. There is little difference between the weighted distribution in figure 8.1 and the distribution one obtains directly from the sample.

10. Archives du Ministère des Finances (CAEF) B 39963. Direction Générale des Contributions Directes et de l'Enregistrement, Relevé des obligations hypothécaires enregistrées dans les bureaux dépendant du département xxx pendant le mois de fév 1931, Réponse à la circulaire du 12/3/1931.

11. For the departments of the Aisne, Aube, Cantal, Indre, and Nièvre we have the data but no information about where loans were made. Data for the departments of the Charente, Haute-Vienne, and Vosges are missing altogether.

12. These departments were the Allier, Ardèche, Aude, Bouches-du-Rhône, Cher, Corrèze, Côte-d'Or, Côtes-du-Nord, Creuse, Dordogne, Doubs, Drôme, Eure, Gard, Haute-Garonne, Hérault, Isère, Loir-et-Cher, Mayenne, Morbihan, Nord, Haut-Rhin, Saône-et-Loire, Sarthe, Seine (with Paris detailed), Seine-Inférieure, Tarn-et-Garonne, and Vaucluse.

13. There are six different weighting schemes in all because we use two different population weights—the population of the arrondissement, and the population of the chef-lieu, the administrative center of the arrondissement.

Chapter 9

1. For Law's attempted reforms, see Hoffman, Postel-Vinay, and Rosenthal (2000, 69–95) and Neal (1990, 2012).

2. Our recent financial crisis is only one example. For others, from French and American history, see Hoffman, Postel-Vinay, Rosenthal (2001, 326; 2007, 42–43).

3. Carter et al. (2006, table CJ212–224). A broader measure used by Raymond Goldsmith suggests that in 1900 commercial banks held 5 percent of farm mortgages and 7 percent of non-farm mortgages. By 1952, the numbers had crept up to 15 and 18 percent (Goldsmith 1958). Goldsmith's banks include state chartered banks that had fewer restrictions on the assets they could hold.

4. The same is true for banking crises in general, as Calomiris and Haber (2014) demonstrate.

5. For Upstart, see http://www.investopedia.com/articles/investing/092315/7-best-peertopeer-lending-websites.asp (consulted December 16, 2016).

6. One might worry that in the past, lack of competition would make our notaries monopolists. Referrals and the fact that there were always multiple notaries nearby kept that from happening. For a discussion, see Hoffman, Postel-Vinay, and Rosenthal (2000).

7. La Porta et al. (1997, 1998) use cross-country regressions to show that French civil law had a negative effect on financial development in countries

that borrowed it from France. By contrast, Acemoglu, Cantoni, et al. (2009) find that the French Revolution had a positive effect on long-run economic growth, at least in the countries adjacent to France.

8. It is worth noting here that notaries existed outside of continental Europe too. The Spanish brought them to their colonies, and the same was true of some areas settled by the French (including Quebec, West Africa, and Indochina) and Portugal (e.g. Brazil, Angola).

9. Sabean (1990, 66–74); Gelderblom, Jonker, and Kool (2016). An interesting question is whether the alternatives arose from efforts to keep track of property rights or to tax wealth and income (borrowers could conceivably deduct their debts and lenders could be taxed on their income from loans). See Herlihy and Klaplish (1985); Scherman (2013); and Touzery (2013). There were sporadic efforts in this direction in France.

10. Marglin (2016); Kuran and Rubin (forthcoming).

11. Snowden (1995); Hoffman, Postel-Vinay, Rosenthal (2015, 41). See also Eichengreen (1984, 1987); Snowden (1987), Hoffman, Postel-Vinay, Rosenthal (2007, 42–44).

12. See, for instance, Allen (1992, 102–104); Offer (1981); Bogue (1955); Eichengreen (1984, 1987); Snowden (1987, 1995).

13. Feldstein, "A 'New Economy" in the United States,' The Trilateral Commission, 2000 Tokyo Meeting," Bernanke, interview on CNBC's Squawk box, July 1, 2005.

Appendices

1. These numbers would have to be revised down if some lenders were more active than average and revised up if we eliminated households unlikely to borrow or lend (those households without any wealth).

2. The reason is that for a market of population *n* we expect that the total number of borrowers and lenders who arrive in time *t* will be *npt*. If *npt* is odd, there must be a queue, because the number of borrowers cannot equal the number of lenders. If *npt* is even, the probability that the number of borrowers is exactly equal to the number of lenders approaches $\sqrt{2 / npt\pi}$ and so can be made arbitrarily close to zero by extending *t* or letting market size *n* grow.

3. If we ignore the outside option, the expected wait time is the sample average from drawing $N=npt$ independent random variables that take on the value –1 with probability 0.5 and 1 with probability 0.5. By the law of large numbers, this sample average without the outside option will converge to 0 in probability as the population n and hence N increase. Adding the outside option will decrease the absolute value of the resulting sample average, so it too will converge to 0 in probability.

4. If there are queue lengths k_Y, k_X such that the borrower is indifferent between *X* and *Y* then he or she may mix, but we can refine these mixed strategies out by simply assuming that the borrower travels from *X* to *Y* only if there is a strict positive gain to doing so.

Bibliography

Commercial directories and annual statistical journals

Almanach du commerce de la ville de Paris. Paris, 1800–1805.

Almanach du commerce de Paris, des départements de la France et des principales villes de l'Europe. Paris, 1805–1806.

Almanach du commerce de Paris, des départements de l'Empire français et des principales villes du monde. Paris, 1807–1813.

Almanach du commerce de Paris, des départements de la France et des principales villes de l'Europe. Paris, 1814–28.

Almanach du commerce de Paris, des départements de la France et des principales villes du monde by Jean de la Tynna continué et mis à jour par S. Bottin. Paris, 1829–45.

Almanach royal. Ed. Laurent-Charles d'Houry. Paris: D'Houry. 1780.

Annuaire général du commerce, de l'industrie, de la magistrature et de l'administration ou almanach des 500,000 adresses de Paris, des départements et des pays étrangers. Paris, 1838–56.

Annuaire-Almanach du commerce et de l'industrie ou almanach des 500,000 adresses. Paris, 1862–98.

Annuaire statistique de la ville de Paris. Vols. 1–21. Paris, Masson et cie. 1880–1900.

Annuaire statistique de la France. INED Paris. 1966.

Critchett & Woods, Great Britain. Post Office: *The Post-Office annual directory . . . : being a list of upwards of 16,000 merchants, traders, &c. of London, and parts adjacent*. 1830–34.

Critchett & Woods, Great Britain. Post Office: *The Post-Office London directory for 1830: being a list of l22,000 merchants, traders, &c. of London and parts adjacent*. 1830.

J. Pigot & Co. *The Commercial Directory for 1818-19-20 Contains the Names, Trades and Situations of the Merchants, Manufacturers, Tradesmen . . .* 1818–20.

J. Pigot & Co. *Pigot and Co.'s national commercial directory for 1828–9 comprising a directory and classification of the merchants, bankers, professional gentlemen, manufacturers and traders . . .* 1829.

J. Pigot & Co. *Pigot and Co.'s national commercial directory of the whole of Scotland, and of the Isle of Man: with a general alphabetical list of the nobility, gentry and Clergy of Scotland . . .* 1837.

I. Slater (late Pigot & Co.). *I. Slater's national commercial directory of the whole of Ireland: including in addition to the trades' lists Alphabetical directories of Dublin Belfast Cork and Limerick . . .* 1846.

I. Slater (late Pigot & Co.). *Royal National Commercial Directory and Topography of Scotland: With a General Alphabetical and Referential List of the Nobility, Gentry and Clergy*. 1852.

E. Thom. *Thom's Irish Almanac and Official Directory for the United Kingdom for the year . . .* Dublin: Exander Thom & Sons. 1856.

Online Digitized Sources

Population by municipality for France: http://cassini.ehess.fr/cassini/fr/html/6_index.htm.

Population by subdistrict for the British Isles: http://www.histpop.org/ohpr/servlet/.

Military conscript data: http://federation.ens.fr/wheberg/dataweb/conscription/yndex/.

Other references

Acemoglu, Daron, Davide Cantoni, Simon Johnson, and James A. Robinson. 2009. "The Consequences of Radical Reform: The French Revolution." Paper w14831. National Bureau of Economic Research.

Acemoglu, Daron, Simon Johnson, and James A. Robinson. 2002. "Reversal of Fortune: Geography and Institutions in the Making of the Modern World Income Distribution." *The Quarterly Journal of Economics* 117 (4): 1231–94.

Acemoglu, Daron, and James A. Robinson. 2012. *Why Nations Fail: The Origins of Power, Prosperity, and Poverty*. New York: Crown.

Akerlof, George A. 1970. "The Market for 'Lemons': Quality Uncertainty and the Market Mechanism." *The Quarterly Journal of Economics* 84 (3): 488–500.

Allen, Robert C. 1992. *Enclosure and the Yeoman: The Agricultural Development of the South Midlands, 1450–1850*. Oxford: Oxford University Press.

________. 2009. *The British Industrial Revolution in Global Perspective*. Cambridge: Cambridge University Press.

Allen, Robert C., Jean-Pierre Bassino, Debin Ma, Christine Moll-Murata, and Jan Leuten Van Zanden. 2005. "Wages, Prices, and Living Standards in China, Japan, and Europe, 1738–1925." Global Price and Income History working paper, no. 1. At http://gpih.ucdavis.edu.

Allinne, Jean-Pierre. 1983. *Banquiers et bâtisseurs, un siècle de Crédit Foncier (1852–1940)*. Paris: CNRS.

Anderson, B. L. 1969a. "The Attorney and the Early Capital Market in Lancashire." In *Liverpool and Merseyside: Essays in the Economic and Social History of the Port and its Hinterland*, ed. R. R. Harris, 50–77. London: Routledge.

________. 1969b. "Provincial Aspects of the Financial Revolution of the Eighteenth Century." *Business History* 11 (1): 11–22.

Andrews, D., A. Caldera Sánchez, and Å. Johansson. 2011. "Housing Markets and Structural Policies in OECD Countries," *OECD Economics Department Working Papers*, no. 836, OECD Publishing. At http://dx.doi.org/10.1787/5kgk8t2k9vf3-en.

Arnold, Lutz G., and John G. Riley. 2009. "On the Possibility of Credit Rationing in the Stiglitz-Weiss Model." *The American Economic Review* 99 (5): 2012–21.

Arnoux, Mathieu. 1996. " Essor et déclin d'une forme diplomatique : les actes coram parrochia (Normandie, XIIe-XIIIe siècle)." In *Bibliothèque de l'École des Chartes* 15 (2): 325–57.

Arnoux, Mathieu, and Olivier Guyotjeannin, eds. *Tabellions et tabellionages de la France médiévale et moderne*. Paris: Ecole des Chartes.

Baehrel, René. 1961. *Une croissance: la Basse-Provence rurale (fin XVIe siècle-1789)*. 2 vols. Paris: SEVPEN.

Bairoch, Paul, Jean Batou, and Pierre Chèvre. 1988. "The Population of European Cities. Data Bank and Short Summary of Results: 800–1850." Genève: Droz.

Balzac, Honoré de. 1990. *Illusions perdues*. Ed. Philippe Berthier. Paris: Flammarion.

Banerjee, Abhijit V., Timothy Besley, and Timothy W. Guinnane. 1994. "Thy Neighbor's Keeper: The Design of a Credit Cooperative with Theory and a Test." *Quarterly Journal of Economics* 109: 491–515.

Baubeau, Patrice, Eric Monnet, Angelo Riva, and Stefano Ungaro. 2018. "A New History of French Banks during the Interwar." Working paper, Paris School of Economics.

Bazot, Guillaume. 2014. "Local Liquidity Constraints: What Place for Central Bank Regional Policy? The French Experience during the Belle Époque (1880–1913)." *Explorations in Economic History* 52: 44–62.

Béaur, Gérard. 1994. *L'immobilier et la Révolution. Marché de la pierre et mutations urbaines 1770–1810*. Cahiers des Annales. Paris: Armand Colin.

Bergeron, Louis. 1978a. *Banquiers, négociants et manufacturiers parisiens du Directoire à l'Empire*. Paris-La Haye: Mouton.

________. 1978b. "Les capitalistes en France. (1780–1914)." *Collection Archives*, no. 70. Paris: Gallimard.

Bernanke, Ben S. 1983. "Nonmonetary Effects of the Financial Crisis in the Propagation of the Great Depression." *The American Economic Review* 73: 257–76.

Bogue, Alan. 1955. *Money at Interest: The Farm Mortgage on the Middle Border*. Ithaca: Cornell University Press.

Bordo, Michael D., Angela Redish, and Hugh Rockoff. 2011. "Why Didn't Canada Have a Banking Crisis in 2008 (or in 1930, or 1907, or . . .)?" Working paper, National Bureau of Economic Research.

Botticini, Maristella. 2000. "A Tale of 'Benevolent' Governments: Private Credit Markets, Public Finance, and the Role of Jewish Lenders in Medieval and Renaissance Italy." *The Journal of Economic History* 60 (4): 164–89.

Bouvier, Jean. 1961. *Le Crédit lyonnais de 1863 à 1882. Les années de formation d'une banque de dépôt*. 2 vols. Paris: SEVPEN.

Burgess, Robin, and Rohini Pande. 2005. "Do Rural Banks Matter? Evidence from the Indian Social Banking Experiment." *The American Economic Review* 95 (3): 780–95.

Brennan, Thomas Edward. 1997. *Burgundy to Champagne: The Wine Trade in Early Modern France*. Baltimore: Johns Hopkins University Press.

________. 2006. "Peasants and Debt in Eighteenth-Century Champagne." *Journal of Interdisciplinary History* 37 (2): 175–200.

Calomiris, Charles W. 1995. "The Costs of Rejecting Universal Banking: American Finance in the German Mirror, 1870–1914." In *Coordination and Information: Historical Perspectives on the Organization of Enterprise*, eds. Naomi R. Lamoreaux and Daniel M. G. Raff. Chicago: University of Chicago Press.

Calomiris, Charles W. and Stephen H. Haber. 2014. *Fragile by Design: The Political Origins of Banking Crises and Scarce Credit*. Princeton: Princeton University Press.

Cameron, Rondo. 1967. *Banking in the Early Stages of Industrialization*. Oxford: Oxford University Press.

________. 1961. *France and the Economic Development of Europe, 1800–1914: Conquests of Peace and Seeds of War*. Princeton: Princeton University Press.

Carlson, M., and K. Michener. 2006. "Branch Banking, Bank Competition, and Financial Stability." *Journal of Money, Credit, and Banking* 38 (5): 1293–1328.

———. 2009. "Branch Banking as a Device for Discipline: Competition and Bank Survivorship during the Great Depression." *Journal of Political Economy* 117 (April): 165–210.

Carrière, Charles. 1973. *Négociants marseillais au XVIIIe siècle. Contribution à l'étude des économies maritimes*. 2 vols. Marseille: A. Robert.

Carter, Suzan B., ed. 2006. *Historical Statistics of the United States*. Electronic edition. Cambridge: Cambridge University Press.

Chassagne, Serge. 2012. *Veuve Guerin et fils; banque et soie; une affaire de famille; Saint-Chamond-Lyon, 1716–1932*. Lyon: BGA Permezel.

Claustre, Julie. 2013. "*Vivre à crédit dans une ville sans banque Paris (XIVe-XVe siècle)*." *Le Moyen Age* 119 (3): 567–96.

Cramer, Marc. 1946. "Les trente demoiselles de Genève et les billets solidaires." *Revue suisse d'économie politique et de statistique* 82 (2): 109-38.

Crouzet, François. 1993. *La grande inflation: La monnaie française de Louis XVI à Napoléon*. Paris: Fayard.

Darnton, Robert. 1994. *The Forbidden Best-Sellers of Pre-Revolutionary France*. New York: Norton.

________. 1979. *The Business of Enlightenment: A Publishing History of the Encylopédie 1775–1800*. Cambridge: Harvard University Press.

D' Angeville, Adolphe. 1836. *Essai sur la statistique de la population française: considérée sous quelques-uns de ses rapports physiques et moraux*. Bourg: Fred Dufour.

Daumard, Adeline. 1973. *Les fortunes françaises au 19e siècle*. Paris: Mouton.

D'Auvilliers, eds. 1850. *Journal du Palais. Recueil le plus ancien et le plus complet de la jurisprudence française*. Paris: Répertoire Général de Jurisprudence.

Davis, Lance. E. 1963. "Capital Immobilities and Finance Capitalism: A Study of Economic Evolution in the United States, 1820–1920." *Explorations in Economic History* 1 (1): 88.

________. 1972. "Banks and their Economic Effects." In *American Economic Growth: An Economist's History of the United States*, eds. L. Davis, R. Easterlin, and W. Parker, 304–65. New York: Harper & Row.

Davis, Lance E., and Robert E. Gallman. 1978. "Capital Formation in the United States During the Nineteenth Century." In *The Cambridge Economic History of Europe*, eds. P. Mathias and M. M. Postan, vol. 7., pt. 2. 1–69, 496–503, 557–61. Cambridge: Cambridge University Press.

de Maddalena, Aldo. 1988. *Dalle cita all borgo. Avio di una metamorfosi economica e sociale nella Lombardia Spaniola*. Milan: Franco Angeli.

Dell, Melissa. 2010. "The Persistent Effects of Peru's Mining Mita." *Econometrica* 78 (6): 1863–1903.

Demetriades, Panikos O., and Kul B. Luintel. 1996. "Financial Development, Economic Growth, and Banker Sector Controls: Evidence from India." *Economic Journal* 106: 359–74.

Demirguc-Kunt, Asli, and Ross Levine, eds. 2004. *Financial Structure and Economic Growth: A Cross-Country Comparison of Banks, Markets, and Development*. Cambridge: Cambridge University Press.

Descimon, Robert. 2004. "Les notaires de Paris du XVI au XVIIIe siècle; office, profession archives." In *Offices et officiers "moyens" en France à l'époque moderne: Profession, culture*, ed. Michel Cassan. Limoges: PULIM.

Diderot, Denis and Jean le Rond d'Alembert, eds. 2016 [1751–72]. *Encyclopédie, ou dictionnaire raisonné des sciences, des arts et des métiers, etc.* 17 vols. Eds. Robert Morrissey and Glenn Roe. University of Chicago: ARTFL Encyclopédie Project (Spring 2016 edition). At http://encyclopedie.uchicago.edu. Consulted August 15, 2016.

Dormard, Serge. 2005. "Le marché du crédit à Douai aux XVIIe et XVIIIe siècles." *Revue du Nord* 87 (362): 803–33.

Dupont-Ferrier, Pierre. 1925. *Le marché financier de Paris sous le Second Empire*. Paris: Alcan.

Durand, Yves. 1971. *Les fermiers généraux au XVIIIe siècle*. Paris: Presses universitaires de France.

Eichengreen, Barry, 1984. "Mortgage Interest Rates in the Populist Era." *The American Economic Review* 74 (5): 995–1015.

_________. 1987. "Agricultural Mortgages in the Populist Era: Reply to Snowden." *The Journal of Economic History* 47 (3): 757–60.

The Encyclopaedia Britannica. 1910–11. 29 vols. Ed. H. Chisolm. Cambridge: Cambridge University Press.

Engerman, Stanley L., and Kenneth L. Sokoloff. 1997. "Factor Endowments, Institutions, and Differential Paths of Growth among New World Economies." In *How Latin America Fell Behind*, ed. Stephen Haber, 260–304. Stanford: Stanford University Press.

Engerman, Stanley L., Kenneth L. Sokoloff, with Stephen Haber, Elisa Mariscal, and Eric Zolt. 2012. *Economic Development in the Americas since 1500: Endowments and Institutions*. Cambridge: Cambridge University Press.

Etienne, Geneviève, and Marie-Françoise Limon-Bonnet, eds. 2013. *Les archives notariales: Manuel pratique et juridique*. Paris: La documentation française.

Flandreau, Marc, Christophe Galimard, Clemens Jobst, Pilar Nogues-Marco. 2009. "Monetary Geography before the Industrial Revolution." *Cambridge Journal of Regions, Economy and Society* 2 (2): 149–71.

Fohlin, Caroline. 2007. *Finance Capitalism and Germany's Rise to Industrial Power*. Cambridge: Cambridge University Press.

Forster, Robert. 1971. *The House of Saulx-Tavanes: Versailles and Burgundy, 1700–1830*. Baltimore: Johns Hopkins University Press.

Fujita, Masahisa, Paul Krugman, and Anthony J. Venables. 1999. *The Spatial Economy: Cities, Regions, and International Trade*. Cambridge, MA: MIT Press.

Furet, François, and Jacques Ozouf. 1977. *Lire et écrire: l'alphabétisation des Français de Calvin à Jules Ferry*. 2 vols. Paris: Minuit.

Garnier, Josette. 1982. *Bourgeoisie et propriété immobilière dans le Forez aux XVIIe et XVIIIe siècles*. Saint-Etienne: Centre d'Etudes Foréziennes.

Gaston, Jean. 1991. *La communauté des notaires de Bordeaux 1520–1791*. Toulouse: Presses universitaires du Mirail.

Gelderblom, Oscar, Joost Jonker, and Clemens J. M. Kool. 2016. "Direct Finance in the Golden Age." *The Economic History Review* 69: 1178–98.

Gerschenkron, Alexander. 1962. *Economic Backwardness in Historical Perspective: A Book of Essays*. Cambridge, MA: Belknap Press/Harvard University Press.

Ghatak, Maitreesh, and Timothy W. Guinnane. 1999. "The Economics of Lending with Joint Liability: Theory and Practice." *Journal of Development Economics* 60: 195–228.

Gille, Bertrand. 1959. *La banque et le crédit en France de 1815 à 1848*. Paris: Presses universitaires de France.

___________. 1979. *La banque en France au XIXe siècle*. Geneva: Droz.

Georges, Colette, and Alain Droguet. 1993. *Contrôle des actes des notaires et sous seing privé: insinuation, centième denier et droits joints: 1693–1791: répertoire numérique de la sous-série 2 C / Archives départementales des Côtes d'Armor*. Saint-Brieuc: Archives départementales des Côtes d'Armor.

Gjerstad, Steven D., and Vernon L. Smith. 2014. *Rethinking Housing Bubbles: The Role of Household and Bank Balance Sheets in Modeling Economic Cycles*. Cambridge: Cambridge University Press.

Glaeser, Edward L., and Matthew G. Resseger. 2010. "The Complementarity between Cities and Skills." *Journal of Regional Science* 50 (1): 221–44.

Goldberg, J. 2012. *Trade and Institutions in the Medieval Mediterranean: The Geniza Merchants and Their Business World*. Cambridge: Cambridge University Press.

Goldsmith, Raymond William. 1958. *Financial Intermediaries in the American Economy Since 1900*. Princeton: Princeton University Press.

_________. 1969. *A Study of Saving in the United States*. 4 vols. Princeton: Princeton University Press.

Goni, Marc. 2017. "Assortative Matching and Persistent Inequality: Evidence from the World's Most Exclusive Marriage Market." Unpublished paper, University of Vienna.

Greif, Avner. 1989. "Reputation and Coalitions in Medieval Trade: Evidence on the Maghribi Traders." *Journal of Economic History* 49: 857–82.

_________. 1993. "Contract Enforceability and Economic Institutions in Early Trade: The Maghribi Traders' Coalition." *American Economic Review* 83: 525–48.

_________. 2006. *Institutions and the Path to the Modern Economy: Lessons from Medieval Trade*. Cambridge: Cambridge University Press.

Grenier, Jean. 1824. *Traité des hypothèques.* 2 vols. Clermont-Ferrand: Thibaud-Landriot.

Griollet, G. and C. Verge, eds. 1910–26. *Répertoire pratique de législation, de doctrine et de jurisprudence.* 12 vols. Paris: Dalloz.

Grossman, Sanford J. 1981. "The Informational Role of Warranties and Private Disclosure about Product Quality." *Journal of Law and Economics* 24: 461–89.

Guide de la comptabilité notariale: Etude de Maître Delorme. 1890. Paris: Imprimerie Chaix.

Guinnane, Timothy W. 2001. "Cooperatives as Information Machines: German Rural Credit Cooperatives 1883–1914." *Journal of Economic History* 61: 366–89.

________. 2002. "Delegated Monitors, Large and Small: Germany's Banking System, 1800–1914." *Journal of Economic Literature* 40: 73–124.

Guinnane, Timothy W., Ron Harris, Naomi Lamoreaux, and Jean-Laurent Rosenthal. 2007. "Putting the Corporation in its Place." *Enterprise and Society* 8 (September): 687–729.

Guyot, Joseph-Nicolas. 1765–83. *Répertoire universel et raisonné de jurisprudence civile, criminelle, canonique et bénéficiale.* 64 vols. Paris: J. Dorez-Panckoucke.

________. 1784–85. *Répertoire universel et raisonné de jurisprudence civile, criminelle, canonique et bénéficiale.* 17 vols., new edition. Paris: Visse.

Habakkuk, John. 1994. *Marriage, Debt, and the Estates System: English Ownership. 1650–1950.* Oxford: Oxford University Press.

Haber, Stephen H. 1991. "Industrial Concentration and the Capital Markets: A Comparative Study of Brazil, Mexico, and the United States, 1830–1930." *Journal of Economic History* 51: 559–80.

Herlihy, David, and Christiane Klapisch-Zuber. 1985. *Tuscans and their Families: A Study of the Florentine Catasto of 1427.* New Haven: Yale University Press.

Hoffman, Philip T., Gilles Postel-Vinay, and Jean-Laurent Rosenthal. 2000. *Priceless Markets: The Political Economy of Credit in Paris, 1662–1869.* Chicago: University of Chicago Press.

________. 2001. *Des marchés sans prix: Une économie politique du crédit à Paris, 1660–1870.* Paris: Ecole des hautes études en sciences sociales.

________. 2003. "No Exit: Notarial Bankruptcies the Evolution of Financial Intermediation in Nineteenth-Century Paris." In *Finance, Intermediaries, and Economic Development*, eds. Stanley L. Engerman, Philip T. Hoffman, Jean-Laurent Rosenthal, and Kenneth L. Sokoloff, 75–110. Cambridge: Cambridge University Press.

________. 2007. *Surviving Large Losses: Financial Crises, the Middle Class, and the Development of Capital Markets.* Cambridge, MA: Harvard University Press.

________. 2009. "The Role of Trust in the Long Run Development of French Financial Markets." In *Whom Can We Trust? How Groups, Networks, and Institutions Make Trust Possible*, eds. Karen S. Cook, Margaret Levi, and Russell Hardin, 249–85. New York: Russell Sage Foundation.

________. 2010. "French Lessons: Mortgage Markets 1740–1899." Manuscript, California Institute of Technology.

________. 2011. "History, Geography, and the Markets for Mortgage Loans in Nineteenth-Century France." In *Understanding Long-Run Economic Growth: Geography, Institutions, and the Knowledge Economy*, eds. Dora Costa and Naomi Lamoreaux, 155–76. Chicago: University of Chicago Press.

________. 2011. "Contracts and Revolution: The View from the Gard's Notaries, 1779–1808." Unpublished paper, California Institute of Technology.

________. 2014. "Capitalism and Financial Development: The Case of Mortgage Markets in France, 1807–1899." *Social Science History* 38 (1–2): 13–41.

________. 2015. "Entry, Information, and Financial Development: A Century of Competition between French Banks and Notaries." *Explorations in Economic History* 55: 39–57.

Hoffmann, Walther G. 1965. *Das Wachstum der deutschen Wirtschaft seit der Mitte des 19 Jahrhunderts*. Berlin: Springer.

Homer, Sidney, and Richard Sylla. 1991. *A History of Interest Rates*. 3rd edition. New Brunswick: Rutgers University Press.

Isambert, François-André et al. 1822–33. *Recueil général des anciennes lois français depuis l'an 420 jusqu'à la Révolution de 1789*. Paris: Belin-Leprieur.

Jackson, Matthew O. 2010. *Social and Economic Networks*. Princeton: Princeton University Press.

Jobert, Philippe. 1975. "Naissance et faillite d'une banque d'affaires: la maison Bouault, Dijon, 1816–1843." *Revue d'histoire économique et sociale* 53 (2–3): 329–59.

________. 1999. "Naissance et faillite d'une banque d'affaires dijonnaise: la maison Bouault, Dijon, 1816–1843." In *Banques locales et banques régionales en France au XIXe siècle*, eds. M. Lescure and A. Plessis, 21–54. Paris: Albin Michel.

Johnson, Noel D. 2006. "Banking on the King: The Evolution of the Royal Revenue Farms in Old Regime France." *The Journal of Economic History* 66 (4): 963–91.

Jovanovic, Boyan. 1982. "Selection and the Evolution of Industry." *Econometrica: Journal of the Econometric Society* 50 (3): 649–70.

Kelly, Morgan, Joel Mokyr, and Cormac Ó. Gráda. 2014. "Precocious Albion: a new interpretation of the British industrial revolution." *Annual Review of Economics* 6 (1): 363–89.

Kindleberger, Charles P. 2015. *A Financial History of Western Europe*. New York: Routledge.

King, Robert G., and Ross Levine. 1993. "Finance and Growth: Schumpeter Might Be Right." *Quarterly Journal of Economics* 108: 717–37.

Kleibergen, Frank, and Richard Paap. 2006. "Generalized Reduced Rank Tests Using the Singular Value Decomposition." *Journal of Econometrics* 133: 97–126.

Koch, R. ed. 1911. *Articles on German Banking and German Banking Laws*. Vol. 11. Washington, DC: Publications of the National Monetary Commission.

Kuran, Timur, and Jared Rubin. Forthcoming. "The Financial Power of the Powerless: Socio-Economic Status and Interest Rates under Partial Rule of Law." *Economic Journal.*

Lamoreaux, Naomi. 1994. *Insider Lending: Banks, Personal Connections, and Economic Development in Industrial New England*. Cambridge: Cambridge University Press.

Lamoreaux, Naomi, and Jean-Laurent Rosenthal. 2005. "Legal Regime and Contractual Flexibility: A Comparison of Business's Organizational Choices in France and the United States during the Era of Industrialization." *American Law and Economics Review* 7 (1): 28–61.

Lavoisier, Antoine-Laurent. 1893. *Oeuvres de Lavoisier*. 6 vols, vol. 6., eds. Jean-Baptiste Dumas, Edouard Grimaux, and Ferdinand Fouqué, 158. Paris: Imprimerie nationale.

Ledru-Rollin, Alexandre-Auguste, ed. 1842. *Journal du Palais. Recueil le plus ancien et le plus complet de la jurisprudence française* 27: 1835–36.

Lemercier, Claire. 2003. *Un si discret pouvoir: Aux origines de la Chambre de commerce de Paris*. Paris: La Découverte.

Lepetit, Bernard. 1984. *Chemins de terre et voies d'eau: réseaux de transport et organisation de l'espace en France, 1740–1840*. Paris: EHESS.

________. 1988. *Les Villes dans la France moderne 1740–1840*. Paris: Albin Michel.

Lescure, Michel, and Alain Plessis. 1999. *Banques locales et banques régionales en France au XIXe siècle*. Paris: Albin Michel.

Leslie, Philipp, and Ginger Zhin. 2003. "The Effects of Information on Product Quality: Evidence from Restaurant Hygiene Grade Cards." *Quarterly Journal of Economics* 118 (2): 409–51.

Levine, Ross. 1997. "Financial Development and Economic Growth: Views and Agenda." *Journal of Economic Literature* 35: 688–726.

________ 1998. "The Legal Environment, Banks, and Long-Run Economic Growth." *Journal of Money, Credit and Banking* 30 (3): 596–613.

________. 2005. "Finance and Growth: Theory and Evidence." *Handbook of Economic Growth* 1: 865–934.

Levratto, Nadine and Alessandro Stanziani, eds. 2011. *Le capitalisme au futur antérieur*. Bruxelles: Bruylant.

Lévy-Bruhl, Henri. 1933. *Histoire de la lettre de change en France aux XVIIe et XVIIIe siècle*. Paris: Sirey.

Levy, Juliette. 2004. "Yucatan's Arrested Development: Credit Markets and Social Networks in Mérida between 1850 and 1899." PhD dissertation, Economics, UCLA.

Lévy-Leboyer, Maurice. 1964. *Les banques Européennes et l'industrialisation internationale dans la première moitié du XIXe Siècle*. Paris: Publications de la Faculté des Lettres et Sciences Humaines de Paris.

________. 1976. "Le crédit et la monnaie." In *Histoire économique et sociale de la France*, vol. 2, eds. F. Braudel and E. Labrousse, 347–89. Paris: Presses universitaires de France.

________. 1977. "L'étude du capital et l'histoire des recensements fonciers en France aux XIXe siècle." In *Pour une histoire de la statistique*, vol. 1., ed. J. Mairesse, 393–416. Paris: INSEE.

Lévy-Leboyer, Maurice, and François Bourguignon. 1985. *L'Économie Française au XIXe siècle: analyse macroéconomique*. Paris: Economica.

Li, Bozhong, and Jan Luiten Van Zanden. 2012. "Before the Great Divergence? Comparing the Yangzi Delta and the Netherlands at the Beginning of the Nineteenth Century." *The Journal of Economic History* 72 (4): 956–89.

Limon, Marie-Françoise. 1992. *Les notaires au Châtelet de Paris sous le règne de Louis XIV: étude institutionnelle et sociale*. Toulouse: Presses Universitaires du Mirail.
Lindgren, Haken. 2002. "The Modernization of Swedish Credit Markets, 1840–1905: Evidence from Probate Records." *Journal of Economic History* 62: 810–32.
Loyseau, Charles. 1614. *Traité de la garantie des rentes*. Paris: n.p.
Lüthy, Herbert. 1959–61. *La banque protestante en France : De la Révocation de l'Édit de Nantes à la Révolution*. 2 vols. Paris: SEVPEN.
Maddison, Angus. 2007. *Contours of the World Economy, 1–2030 AD: Essays in Macro-Economic History*. Oxford: Oxford University Press.
Marglin, Jessica M. 2016. *Across Legal Lines: Jews and Muslims in Modern Morocco*. New Haven: Yale University Press.
Marion, Marcel. 1968 [1914–31]. *Histoire financière de la France depuis 1715*. 6 vols. Paris: 1914–31; reprint, New York: Burt Franklin, 1968.
Massaloux, Jean-Paul. 1989. *La régie de l'enregistrement et des domaines aux XVIIIe et XIXe siècles: étude historique*. Geneva: Droz.
Massé, Antoine Jacques. 1827. *Le parfait notaire*. 2 vols., 6th edition. Paris: Garnery.
Matringe, Nadia. 2016. *La Banque en Renaissance: Les Salviati et la place de Lyon au milieu du XVI siècle*. Rennes: Presses universitaires de Rennes.
Merlin, Philippe-Antoine. 1812–25. *Répertoire universel et raisonné de jurisprudence*. 17 vols., 4th edition. Paris: Garnery.
________. 1825–28. *Répertoire universel et raisonné de jurisprudence*. 36 vols., 5th revised edition. Bruxelles: Tarlier.
Meyer. Jean. 1969. *L'armement nantais dans la deuxième moitié du XVIIIe siècle*. Paris: SEVPEN.
Michel, Edmond. 1908. *La propriété*. Paris and Nancy: Berger Levrault.
___________. 1934. "Dette hypothécaire." *Journal de la société de statistique de Paris* 75: 1–11.
Milhaud, Cyril. 2017. "Sacré Crédit! The Rise and Fall of Ecclesiastical Credit in Early Modern Spain." PhD dissertation, Paris School of Economics.
Miles, M. 1981. "The Money Market in the Early Industrial Revolution: The Evidence from West Riding Attorneys." *Business History* 23: 127–46.
Milgrom, Paul. 1981. "Good News and Bad News: Representation Theorems and Applications." *Bell Journal of Economics* 12: 380–91.
Mitchell, Brian R. 1981. *European Historical Statistics: 1750–1975*. 2nd revised edition. New York: Facts on File.
Mitchell, Brian R., and Phylis Deane. 1962. *Abstract of British Historical Statistics*. Cambridge: Cambridge University Press.
Morton, Joseph. 1956. *Urban Mortgage Lending: Comparative Markets and Experience*. Princeton: Princeton University Press.
Mueller, Reinhold C. 1997. *Money and Banking in Medieval and Renaissance Venice*. Baltimore: Johns Hopkins University Press.
Musset, Benoît. 2008. *Vignoble de Champagne et vins mousseux, 1650–1830*. Paris: Fayard.

Murphy, Antoin E. 2005. "Corporate Ownership in France: The Importance of History." In *A History of Corporate Governance around the World: Family Business Groups to Professional Managers*, ed. Randall K. Morck, 185–222. Chicago: University of Chicago Press.

Neal, Larry. 1993. *The Rise of Financial Capitalism*. Cambridge: Cambridge University Press.

_____ 1994. "The Finance of Business during the Industrial Revolution." In *The Economic History of Britain since 1700*, 2 vols., 2nd edition, eds. Roderick Floud and Donald [Deirdre] McCloskey, 1: 151–81. Cambridge: Cambridge University Press.

_____ 2000. "How it All Began: The Monetary and Financial Architecture of Europe during the First Global Capital Markets, 1648 1815." *Financial History Review* 7 (2): 117–40.

_____ 2010. "Conclusion: The Monetary, Fiscal, and Political Architecture of Europe, 1815–1914." In *Paying for the Liberal State: the Rise of Public Finance in Nineteenth Century Europe*, eds. José Luis Cardoso and Pedro Lains. Cambridge: Cambridge University Press.

Neal, Larry, and Stephen Quinn. 2001. "Networks of Information, Markets, and Institutions in the Rise of London as a Financial Centre, 1660–1720." *Financial History Review* 8 (1): 7–26.

________. 2003. "Markets and Institutions in the Rise of London as a Financial Center in the Seventeenth Century." In *Finance, Intermediaries, and Economic Development*, eds. Stanley Engerman et al.,11–33. Cambridge: Cambridge University Press.

Nogez-Marco, Pilar. 2013. "Competing Bimetallic Ratios: Amsterdam, London, and Bullion Arbitrage in Mid-Eighteenth Century." *The Journal of Economic History* 73 (2): 445–76.

Norberg, Kathryn. 1985. *Rich and Poor in Grenoble: 1600–1814*. Berkeley: University of California.

Nunn, Nathan. 2008. "The Long-term Effects of Africa's Slave Trades." *The Quarterly Journal of Economics* 123 (1): 139–76.

O'Brien, Patrick, and Caglar Keyder. 1978. *Economic Growth in Britain and France, 1780–1914: Two Paths to the Twentieth Century*. London and Boston: G. Allen & Unwin.

Offer, Avner. 1981. *Property and Politics, 1870–1914*. Cambridge: Cambridge University Press.

Paulson, Anna L., and Robert Townsend. 2004. "Entrepreneurship and Financial Constraints in Thailand." *Journal of Corporate Finance* 10 (March): 229–62.

Perrot, Jean-Claude. 1992. *Une histoire intellectuelle de l'économie politique, xviie-xviiie siècle*. Paris: École des Hautes Études en Sciences Sociales.

Pezzolo, L. and Tattara, G. 2008. "'Una fiera senza luogo': Was Bisenzone an International Capital Market in Sixteenth-Century Italy?" *The Journal of Economic History* 68 (4): 1098–1122.

Piketty, Thomas, Gilles Postel-Vinay, and Jean-Laurent Rosenthal. 2006. "Wealth Concentration in a Developing Economy: Paris and France, 1807–1994." *The American Economic Review* 96 (1): 236–56.

________. 2014. "Inherited vs. Self-made Wealth: Theory and Evidence from a Rentier Society (Paris 1872–1927)." *Explorations in Economic History* 51: 21–40.

Poisson, Jean-Paul. 1985–90. *Notaires et société: Travaux d'histoire et de sociologie notariales*. Paris: Economica.

La Porta, R., F. Lopez-de-Silanes, A. Shleifer, and R. W. Vishny. 1997. "Legal Determinants of External Finance." *Journal of Finance* 52 (3): 1131–50.

________. 1998. "Law and Finance." *Journal of Political Economy* 106 (6): 1113–55.

Postan, Michael Moissey. 1935. "Recent Trends in the Accumulation of Capital." *Economic History Review* 6 (1): 1–12.

Postel-Vinay, Gilles. 1998. *La terre et l'argent*. Paris: Albin Michel.

Preußisches statistisches Landesamt. 1905–1906. *Preussische Statistik*. "Die ländliche Verschuldung in Preußen. " Vols. 191 and 192.

Quinn, Stephen, 1997. "Goldsmith-Banking: Mutual Acceptance and Interbanker Clearing in Restoration London." *Explorations in Economic History* 34: 411–32.

________. 2004. "Money, Finance, and Capital markets." In *Cambridge Economic History of Modern Britain*, vol. 1., eds. Roderick Floud and Paul Johnson, 147–74. Cambridge: Cambridge University Press.

Rajan, Raghuram G., and Zingales, Luigi. 2003. *Saving Capitalism from the Capitalists: Unleashing the Power of Finance to Create Wealth and Spread Opportunity*. New York: Crown.

________. 2003b. "The Great Reversals: The Politics of Financial Development in the Twentieth Century." *Journal of Financial Economics* 69 (1): 5–50.

Roehl, Richard. 1976. "French Industrialization: A Reconsideration." *Explorations in Economic History* 13: 233–81.

Roover, Raymond de. 1953. *L'évolution de la lettre de change, XIVe-XVIIIe siècles*. Paris: A. Colin.

Rosenthal, Jean-Laurent, 1993. "Credit Markets and Economic Change in Southeastern France 1630–1788." *Explorations in Economic History* 30: 129–57.

________. 1994. "Rural Credit Markets and Aggregate Shocks: The Experience of Nuits St. Georges, 1756–1776." *Journal of Economic History* 54 (2): 288–306.

Rothschild, Emma. 1998. "An Alarming Commercial Crisis in Eighteenth-Century Angouleme: Sentiments in Economic History." *The Economic History Review* 51 (2): 268–93.

________. 2014. "Isolation and Economic Life in Eighteenth-Century France." *The American Historical Review* 119 (4): 1055–82.

Roulleau, Gaston. 1914. *Les règlements par effets de commerce en France et à l'étranger.* Paris: Dubreuil, Frèrebeau, et Cie.

Rousseau, Peter L. 1999. "Finance, Investment, and Growth in Meiji-era Japan." *Japan and the World Economy* 11: 185–98.

Rousseau, Peter L., and Richard Sylla. 2003. "Financial Systems, Economic Growth, and Globalization." In *Globalization in Historical Perspective*, eds. M. D. Bordo, A. M. Taylor, J. G. Williamson, 373–415. Chicago: University of Chicago Press.

________. 2005. "Emerging Financial Markets and Early U.S. growth." *Explorations in Economic History* 42: 1–26.

________. 2006. "Financial Revolutions and Economic Growth: Introducing This EEH Symposium." *Explorations in Economic History* 43: 1–12.

Ryan, Joseph. 2007. "Credit Where Credit Is Due: The Evolution of the Rio de Janeiro Credit Market, 1820–1900." PhD dissertation, University of California, Los Angeles.

Sabean, David W. 1990. *Property, Production, and Family in Neckarhausen, 1700–1870*. Cambridge: Cambridge University Press.

Saint-Marc, Michèle. 1983. *Histoire monétaire de la France, 1800–1980*. Paris: PUF.

Santarosa, Veronica Aoki. 2015. "Financing Long-Distance Trade: The Joint Liability Rule and Bills of Exchange in Eighteenth-Century France." *The Journal of Economic History* 75 (3): 690–719.

Sargent, Thomas J., and François R. Velde. 1995. "Macroeconomic Features of the French Revolution." *Journal of Political Economy* 103 (3): 474–518.

Scherman, Matthieu. 2013. *Familles et travail à Trévise à la fin du Moyen Âge, vers 1434-vers 1509*. Rome: École française de Rome.

Schnapper, Bernard. 1957. *Les rentes au XVIe siècle: Histoire d'un instrument de crédit*. Paris: SEVPEN.

Servais, Paul. 1982. *La rente constituée dans le Ban de Herve au XVIIIe siècle*. Bruxelles: Crédit Communal de Belgique, Collection Histoire, no. 62.

Sewell, William. 2014. "Connecting Capitalism to the French Revolution: The Parisian Promenade and the Origins of Civic Equality in Eighteenth-Century France." *Critical Historical Studies* 1 (1): 5–46.

Sheppard, David K. 1971. *The Growth and the Role of U.K. Financial Institutions, 1880–1962*. London: Methuen.

Snowden, Kenneth A. 1987. "Mortgage Rates and American Capital Market Development in the Late Nineteenth Century." *The Journal of Economic History* 47 (3): 671–91.

________. 1995. "The Evolution of Interregional Mortgage Lending Channels, 1870–1940: The Life Insurance-Mortgage Company Connection." In *Coordination and Information: Historical Perspectives on the Organization of Enterprises*, eds. Naomi Lamoureaux and Daniel Raff. Chicago: University of Chicago Press.

Stiglitz, Joseph E., and Andrew Weiss. 1981. "Credit Rationing in Markets with Imperfect Information." *The American Economic Review* 71 (3): 393–410.

Sylla, Richard. 1969. "Federal Policy, Banking Market Structure, and Capital Mobilization in the United States, 1863–1913." *The Journal of Economic History* 29 (4): 657–86.

________. 1999. "Emerging Markets in History: The United States, Japan, and Argentina." In *Global Competition and Integration*, eds. R. Sato, R. Ramachandran, and K. Mino. New York: Springer Science and Business Media.

Temin, Peter, and Hans-Joachim Voth. 2006. "Banking as an Emerging Technology: Hoare's Bank, 1702–1742." *Financial History Review* 13: 149–78.

________. 2013. *Prometheus Shackled: Goldsmith Banks and England's Financial Revolution After 1700*. Oxford: Oxford University Press.

Thuillier, Guy. 1966. *Aspects de l'économie nivernaise*. Paris: A. Colin.
Toutain, Jean-Claude. 1987. *Le produit intérieur brut de la France de 1789 à 1982*. Grenoble: PUG.
Touzery, Mireille. 2013. *L'invention de l'impôt sur le revenu: la taille tarifée 1715–1789*. Paris: La Documentation Française.
Trenard, Louis. 1992. *La Révolution française dans la région Rhône-Alpes*. Paris: Perrin.
Trivellato, Francesca. 2012. "Credit, Honor, and the Early Modern French Legend of the Jewish Invention of Bills of Exchange." *The Journal of Modern History* 84 (2): 289–334.
Trivellato, Francesca. 2014. *The Familiarity of Strangers: The Sephardic diaspora, Livorno, and Cross-Cultural Trade in the Early Modern Period*. New Haven: Yale University Press.
Van der Wee, Herman. 1963. *The Growth of the Antwerp Market and the European Economy (Fourteenth-Sixteenth Centuries)*. Lewen: Martinus Nijhoff.
________. 1977. "Monetary, Credit, and Banking Systems." In *The Cambridge Economic History of Europe*, vol. 5, ed. E. E. Rich and C. H. Wilson, 290–392. Cambridge: Cambridge University Press.
Velde, François R., and David R. Weir. 1992. "The Financial Market and Government Debt Policy in France, 1746–1793." *The Journal of Economic History* 52 (1): 1–39.
Vigne, Marcel. 1903. *La banque à Lyon du XVe au XVIIIe siècle*. Lyon: A. Rey.
Vlasic, Bill. 2009. "Choosing Its Own Path, Ford Stayed Independent." *New York Times*, April 8.
Vovelle, Michel. 1973. *Piété baroque et déchristianisation en Provence au XVIIIe siècle*. Paris: Plon.
Vries, Jan de. 1984. *European Urbanization, 1500–1800*. London: Methuen.
Wandschneider, Kirsten. 2013. "Lending to Lemons: Landschafts-credit in Eighteenth-Century Prussia." Working paper, National Bureau of Economic Research.
Weingast, Barry R. 1995. "The Economic Role of Political Institutions: Market-Preserving Federalism and Economic Development." *Journal of Law, Economics, & Organization* 11 (1): 1–31.
Weir, David R. 1991. "Les crises économiques et les origines de la Révolution française." *Annales* 46 (4): 917–47.
White, Eugene N. 2001. "California Banking in the Nineteenth Century: The Art and Method of the Bank of A. Levy." *The Business History Review* 75 (2): 297–324.
Wigmore, Barrie A. 2010. "A Comparison of Federal Financial Remediation in the Great Depression and 2008–2009." *Research in Economic History* 27: 255–303.
Woloch, Isser. 1994. *The New Regime: Creation of the French Civic Order, 1789–1820s*. New York: Norton.
Wrigley, Anthony E. 1967. "A Simple Model of London's Importance in Changing English Society and Economy 1650–1750." *Past & Present* 37: 44–70.
Zegarra, Luis F. 2015. "Political Instability, Institutions and Mortgage Credit in Peru, 1830–65." Working paper, CENTRUM Católica, Lima.

Index

THE PRINCETON ECONOMIC HISTORY
OF THE WESTERN WORLD

Joel Mokyr, Series Editor

Growth in a Traditional Society: The French Countryside, 1450–1815 by Philip T. Hoffman
The Vanishing Irish: Households, Migration, and the Rural Economy in Ireland, 1850–1914 by Timothy W. Guinnane
Black '47 and Beyond: The Great Irish Famine in History, Economy, and Memory by Cormac Ó Gráda
The Great Divergence: China, Europe, and the Making of the Modern World Economy by Kenneth Pomeranz
The Big Problem of Small Change by Thomas J. Sargent and François R. Velde
Farm to Factory: A Reinterpretation of the Soviet Industrial Revolution by Robert C. Allen
Quarter Notes and Bank Notes: The Economics of Music Composition in the Eighteenth and Nineteenth Centuries by F. M. Scherer
The Strictures of Inheritance: The Dutch Economy in the Nineteenth Century by Jan Luiten van Zanden and Arthur van Riel
Understanding the Process of Economic Change by Douglass C. North
Feeding the World: An Economic History of Agriculture, 1800–2000 by Giovanni Federico
Cultures Merging: A Historical and Economic Critique of Culture by Eric L. Jones
The European Economy since 1945: Coordinated Capitalism and Beyond by Barry Eichengreen
War, Wine, and Taxes: The Political Economy of Anglo-French Trade, 1689–1900 by John V. C. Nye
A Farewell to Alms: A Brief Economic History of the World by Gregory Clark
Power and Plenty: Trade, War, and the World Economy in the Second Millennium by Ronald Findlay and Kevin O'Rourke
Power over Peoples: Technology, Environments, and Western Imperialism, 1400 to the Present by Daniel R. Headrick
Unsettled Account: The Evolution of Banking in the Industrialized World since 1800 by Richard S. Grossman
States of Credit: Size, Power, and the Development of European Polities by David Stasavage
Creating Wine: The Emergence of a World Industry, 1840–1914 by James Simpson
The Evolution of a Nation: How Geography and Law Shaped the American States by Daniel Berkowitz and Karen B. Clay
Distant Tyranny: Markets, Power, and Backwardness in Spain, 1650–1800 by Regina Grafe
The Chosen Few: How Education Shaped Jewish History, 70–1492 by Maristella Botticini and Zvi Eckstein

Why Australia Prospered: The Shifting Sources of Economic Growth by Ian W. McLean

Cities of Commerce: The Institutional Foundations of International Trade in the Low Countries, 1250–1650 by Oscar Gelderblom

Lending to the Borrower from Hell: Debt, Taxes, and Default in the Age of Philip II by Mauricio Drelichman and Hans-Joachim Voth

Power to the People: Energy in Europe over the Last Five Centuries by Astrid Kander, Paolo Malanima, and Paul Warde

Fragile by Design: The Political Origins of Banking Crises and Scarce Credit by Charles W. Calomiris and Stephen H. Haber

The Son Also Rises: Surnames and the History of Social Mobility by Gregory Clark

Why Did Europe Conquer the World? by Philip T. Hoffman

The Rise and Fall of American Growth: The U.S. Standard of Living since the Civil War by Robert J. Gordon

Unequal Gains: American Growth and Inequality since 1700 by Peter H. Lindert and Jeffrey G. Williamson

Brazil in Transition: Beliefs, Leadership, and Institutional Change by Lee J. Alston, Marcus André Melo, Bernardo Mueller, and Carlos Pereira

The Great Leveler: Violence and the History of Inequality from the Stone Age to the Twenty-First Century by Walter Scheidel

The Mystery of the Kibbutz: Egalitarian Principles in a Capitalist World by Ran Abramitzky

The European Guilds: An Economic Assessment by Sheilagh Ogilvie

Dark Matter Credit: The Development of Peer-to-Peer Lending and Banking in France by Philip T. Hoffman, Gilles Postel-Vinay, and Jean-Laurent Rosenthal